A
CONSUMER'S
GUIDE
TO HOME
IMPROVEMENT,
RENOVATION,
AND REPAIR

A CONSUMER'S GUIDE TO HOME IMPROVEMENT, RENOVATION, AND REPAIR

The Enterprise Foundation
Robert M. Santucci
Brooke C. Stoddard
Peter Werwath

Foreword by James W. Rouse

JOHN WILEY & SONS, INC.
New York • Chichester • Brisbane • Toronto • Singapore

PUBLISHER: Therese A. Zak
EDITOR: Steve Ross
MANAGING EDITOR: Frank Grazioli
DESIGNED AND TYPESET by Stanley S. Drate/Folio Graphics Co., Inc.

Library of Congress Cataloging-in-Publication Data

Santucci, Robert M.
    A consumer's guide to home improvement, renovation, and repair /
the Enterprise Foundation ; Robert M. Santucci, Brooke C. Stoddard,
Peter Werwath ; foreword by James W. Rouse.
        p.   cm.
    Includes bibliographical references (p.   ).
    ISBN 0-471-51922-7.—ISBN 0-471-51923-5 (pbk.)
        1. Dwellings—Remodeling. 2. Dwellings—Maintenance and repair.
3. Consumer education. I. Stoddard, Brooke C. II. Werwath, Peter.
III. Enterprise Foundation. IV. Title.
TH4816.S26   1990
643'.7—dc20   90-12207
                                                                   CIP

Printed in the United States of America

90 91 10 9 8 7 6 5 4 3 2 1

Contents

Methods and Materials

5 WINDOWS

72

6 DOORS

84

7 CABINETS AND STORAGE

96

8 MASONRY

107

⑨ **CARPENTRY** **115**

⑩ **ELECTRICAL WORK** **131**

⑪ **PLUMBING** **145**

12   HEATING AND COOLING SYSTEMS   162

13   ROOFING   177

PART TWO | Money-Saving Strategies

Foreword

The facts and advice in this book are powerful tools for cutting the costs of maintaining or renovating your house.

We at The Enterprise Foundation know this firsthand. We have sought out new ideas (and many tried-and-true ideas) from professionals in the housing industry. For example:

- The researchers at The National Association of Home Builders provided invaluable, tested data on cost-saving techniques for framing, roofing, foundations, and other major construction work.
- In a national competition, we awarded $25,000 in prizes to renovators who shared with us their tricks of the trade for reducing renovation costs.
- In the 30 cities and several rural areas where we have both learned and applied this cost-cutting information, it has resulted in savings of 10, 20, or even 50 percent of the cost of home renovations versus using more conventional remodeling practices.

A number of the ideas in this book were published by The Enterprise Foundation in *The Cost Cuts Manual*. This technical manual, written for professionals in the building industry, was the brainchild of Bob Santucci, who did most of the research for this book and for *The Cost Cuts Manual*. It was favorably reviewed by *The Wall Street Journal, Custom Builder, Journal of Light Construction,* and 27 other publications.

This book is even more rigorous and thorough. The research is more comprehensive than any we have done to date on home improvements. It is full of good ideas from award-winning professionals and our country's best construction-industry researchers. It has been written for homeowners, in nontechnical language, so that you will have all the information you need to make the best decision for renovations, improvements, or repairs in your home.

Reading this book, and applying its advice, can save you a hundred, or even a thousand, times the purchase price of the book. Our research has shown that once the average home is 10 to 20 years old, the owner will spend about $800 a year on repairs and improvements, and at least that much again on energy costs. *The Consumer's Guide to Home Improvement, Renovation and Repair* shows how both these costs can be reduced by $200, $500, or more each year.

The Enterprise Foundation is a national, nonprofit organization that my wife, Patty, and I founded in 1982. The Foundation's mission is to help ensure that all very low-income Americans have access to fit and affordable housing within a generation to help themselves up and out of poverty and into the mainstream of American life. To this end, The Foundation works with local nonprofit housing organizations to find low-rate financing, increase their housing production and preservation activities, and reduce construction costs. This has involved the renovation of over 7,000 homes and apartments. In the process of meeting these challenges, one of our goals has been to help develop new nationally accepted, lower cost systems to renovate housing in the United States.

The Enterprise Foundation also works with local nonprofit developers and for-profit contractors to carry out demonstration projects that show ways to reduce housing costs. In Baltimore, for example, we helped create City Homes Inc., which has brought and renovated more than 200 substandard row houses for total average costs of $23,000 and rents of $150 to $350 a month. City Homes uses many of the techniques in this book, and even helped invent some of them.

In addition to providing money-saving, state-of-the-art home improvement advice to you, the consumer, the publication of this book rewards The Enterprise Foundation in four ways:

- The proceeds will help us advance our work with local nonprofit housing groups.
- The additional research supported by this project has already made our work more effective and will continue to do so.

- For the first time, our work will allow not just businesses and nonprofit organizations, but individual homeowners, to share the knowledge base we helped to develop. This furthers our mission in a new way—helping people to help themselves in making their homes more affordable to own and maintain.
- Finally, we believe that more widespread use of these techniques will lead to gradual change in the whole business of housing repairs and renovation—making ownership of older housing more affordable for average families, as well as ones with low incomes.

High housing costs are an increasing and knotty problem for our nation—one that must be unravelled if every American is to have a decent home. The housing industry is responding by getting outmoded and unreasonable codes changed and by identifying how to cut costs without sacrificing quality.

Our existing housing stock is an irreplaceable resource. Today, the average price of a new home is $130,000—out of reach for the majority of our citizens. Americans with the lowest incomes, and even much of the middle class, must rely on our aging, existing housing stock.

Fortunately, much of our older housing is more solid and comfortable than new homes, and much more affordable. Today's home builders are not negligent. They simply can't re-create a time when land, construction, and mortgage money were much less costly. This book is intended to help you preserve those resources at an affordable cost.

This book was possible only because of the resourceful work and strong backing of Peter Werwath, Director of the Foundation's Rehabilitation Work Group. He and his team have done the work in the field and learned and taught the lessons the book provides.

JAMES W. ROUSE
Chairman
The Enterprise Foundation

Introduction

If you are shopping for a car or stereo, you can get advice from books and magazines on what models are available and their prices, features, and performance. Now, for the first time, this new *Consumer's Guide* offers the same kind of information on over 300 different home repair and improvement options.

This book is equally useful to experienced do-it-yourselfers and to homeowners who never plan to set foot on a ladder or pick up a hammer. It features extensive how-to information throughout—specifically on cost-saving techniques—but its main purpose is to help you make intelligent *buying* decisions.

The *Consumer's Guide* tells you:

- What are the most common home repair and improvement options used by homeowners.
- What are the acceptable methods and materials (including those that are either new or often overlooked) that have moderate to low costs.
- What's involved in doing the work yourself, versus hiring one or more contractors.
- What *kinds* of contractors or tradespeople are likely to do a particular job for you at the lowest cost.
- How you can make sure there are adequate plans and contracts for the work, to avoid disputes and cost overruns.
- For larger remodeling projects, how you can reduce the costs of planning and managing the job—which can account for as much as 40 percent of your bill.

Using this advice can add up to big savings. For example, in Chapter 16, Planning and Design, we apply our recommended techniques to a sample renovation project involving kitchen and bath remodeling, window replacement, energy improvements, a new closet, and repairs to floors and walls—all done by contractors.

First, we estimated a total project cost of nearly $14,400, assuming typical choices of materials. Then, we estimated the project assuming more cost-conscious methods and materials, and the total came to just over $7,700—a saving of 46 percent.

We did similar comparisons with a 640-sq-ft, two-story addition. In this case, the conventional costs were nearly $30,800, while a cost–conscious approach saved almost $7,800, or 25 percent.

In the construction industry, this method is called *value engineering.* This means breaking a job down into smaller components and choosing the highest value, lowest cost methods and materials for each component. And since "value" is subjective, we give you equally detailed cost and other information about each option, but don't try to make decisions for you.

A FEW WORDS ABOUT SAFETY

Although we emphasize saving money on home improvements, we recognize, and so should you, that protecting yourself and others from harm comes first. Making repairs, even walking about a worksite inspecting the work of others, can be dangerous, and you must keep safety foremost in your mind.

Wear protective clothing and equipment. Wear goggles when working around debris that might fly into your eyes. Wear a respirator to protect your lungs from dust; wear a respirator with a charcoal activated filter when toxic fumes are present. Read manufacturers' labels when working with paints, stains, or any other chemicals, carefully, and heed warnings about proper ventilation. Wear long sleeves and gloves when needed to protect arms and hands.

When working outdoors, keep ladders well away from overhead electrical lines. When performing electrical tasks, make sure that you have turned off live circuits and use a circuit tester to ensure that they are off before beginning work.

Use tools with care and only for their intended purpose; even a simple screwdriver can gouge a finger if used incorrectly. Be especially cautious with power tools, and check to make sure that their safety features, such as the blade guard on a power saw, are working as they should.

If you are stuck and cannot figure out a problem, stop. Consult an expert. It is better to get the job done right than to risk a mistake and possible harm to yourself. And when you get tired, stop. Injuries often stem from fatigue.

Always work with a first-aid kit nearby, in case of a real accident, and always know the location of the nearest telephone.

Getting the job done correctly also means being responsible for the safety of others. If your work creates toxic fumes, see that those around you also have respirators; if you are working with falling debris, see that they have hardhats and goggles. Tell others around you when you move electrical extension cords or ladders in their vicinity. Be a "safety officer" all around your work, and everyone will be better off.

Lastly, be sure to read carefully any discussions on safety included in this guide. Look for cautions and warnings throughout the book in **bold type.**

A BOOM IN REMODELING

Today, the typical homeowner spends about four times more on home repairs and improvements than he or she did ten years ago. Some of the increase is price inflation, but most of it is simply the result of more renovation activity. Americans, it seems, have suddenly fallen in love with buying older homes and fixing them up. The national home-improvement industry grew from less than $30 billion in 1980 to an estimated $120 billion in 1990.

This love affair is now almost legendary, but is not without some negative connotations. Books, movies, articles, and even comedy routines characterize home improvements as a "black hole" or "money pit."

We believe that we know the source of this fear and trepidation: *The average person does not have sufficient information to make informed decisions on repairs and remodeling.* Even the most experienced do-it-yourselfer, faced with even a simple need (let's say, fixing drafty windows), has no readily available data on what the available options are and what they typically cost.

"Fix the windows" can mean anything from reglazing, painting, and weatherstripping (about $60 per window), to new fit-in sashes (about $150 per window), to a quality generic replacement window (about $300), to name-brand designer windows ($600 and up).

Lacking information like this, homeowners must rely on the advice of remodeling salespeople, often noncommunicative repair persons, or conventional wisdom. We think much of the mythology about remodeling is simply wrong. Let's look at some common misconceptions.

Conventional Wisdom About Home Improvements

Rule 1: You never know what a remodeling job will cost until you get started and tear into things.

Rule 2: It's best to go with "all new"—such as total replacement of windows—repairs will cost you more over the long haul.

Rule 3: You are at the mercy of the contractor regarding what you have to pay—they all overcharge and never stick to their prices.

Collectively, the authors of this book have helped to remodel thousands of houses and apartments and have conducted extensive research into the industry. Early on, we made our share of mistakes and, yes, saw costs run out of control. We have worked mostly for those with average or lower incomes, so we had to learn to pinch pennies and make the costs predictable. Now, our typical renovation project is more likely underbudget than overbudget.

Our experience has boiled down to a few simple principles that are contrary to conventional wisdom. Here they are, in a nutshell.

New Wisdom About Home Improvements

Rule 1: *Carefully assess your house and your needs, weigh options and their costs, write down clear plans, and then stick to them.* By doing this, you can usually predict the cost of a remodeling project with 95 percent accuracy.

Rule 2: *If it isn't broken, don't fix it.* Tearing out functional cabinets and fixtures, gutting out plaster, and moving walls around may be nice if you can afford it, but steady, careful maintenance and strategic replacements are *always* cheaper than trying to modernize everything all at once.

Rule 3: *Don't settle for vague estimates from contractors.* Draw up your own list of the tasks you want done and the materials you want used, or pay somebody to do it, and make sure your contractor does the work carefully. Shop contractors as you would new car dealers. Check references as you would a surgeon's. For bigger jobs, get a tight contract.

USING THIS BOOK

The Enterprise Foundation wants to share with you not only our own experience in applying these rules, but also the knowledge we have gained from the best low-cost renovators in the country. Acquiring this knowledge will take some work. We don't expect you will read the *Consumer's Guide* in a few sittings—it's not intended for that.

Part One, Methods and Materials, is essentially a reference manual or buyer's guide. Each chapter focuses on a type of work you may be considering—for example, *floor treatments* or *windows.* We expect that you will read each chapter only as the need arises.

We advise you to read Part Two, Money-Saving Strategies, more thoroughly. We know that you are likely to spend money on some improvements during the next year, and this part of the book shows you the general approaches that save money: *good planning, ways to cut energy consumption, how to hire and manage contractors, money-saving tools,* and *shopping materials.*

THE COST GUIDE TABLES

Extensive research went into the cost guide tables, conveniently included at the end of each chapter. They are similar to other product comparisons in consumer publications, except that we rarely mention name brands.

The cost guides cover the home repair and improvement projects that you are most likely to encounter, such as replacing a furnace or the siding on your house. They also cover more modest repairs: caulking, fixing doors, or replastering, for example. Several cost guides show the costs associated with new additions. For over four dozen different projects, the cost guides will help you to:

- *Learn about the most common methods and materials and their average costs* across the United States. For instance, we show pine clapboards, vinyl, aluminum, and nine other re-siding options, along with their costs, for an average two-story house.
- *Assess some "least cost" options.* For example, we show that a new stainless-steel kitchen sink costs almost 70 percent *less* than a designer enamel sink. These "cost cutters" are indicated by a CC. We

consider these the lowest cost, acceptable options in terms of safety and performance.

- *Know when the cheapest approach simply isn't a good investment.* For example, we list low-cost ABS plastic pipe as the cheapest option for replacing waste line, but don't recommend it above ground because of its danger in the event of a fire.
- *Identify exceptional values.* For instance, insulated metal exterior replacement doors cost only a few dollars more than the cheapest wooden doors, yet they last longer, are more secure, and save more on heating and cooling bills. These "value buys" are indicated by a VB. Sometimes, they also happen to be the same option as the cost cutter.
- *Decide whether to "do it yourself" (DIY) or hire a contractor.* For each task, we tell you the skills involved, time-saving tools you may want to rent, the relative costs of materials for each option, and other key information.

For example, this is a simplified version of one cost guide:

Kitchen Faucets	Contracted Price	DIY Price
Plastic	$130	$20
Cast Metal	$140 CC	$30 CC
Cast Brass	$147 VB	$37 VB
Epoxy Finish	$235	$125

In this case, cast metal faucets were considered an acceptable option (a cost cutter), but cast brass, at only $7 more, is the value buy. Plastic faucets, cheaper than the cost cutter, were not considered durable enough. The actual cost guide table above explains the pros and cons in more detail.

In all cost guide tables, the options are arranged in order from the cheapest to the most expensive. DIY costs are shown side by side with the contracted costs, but because DIY costs do not include the expense of labor or project management, these don't follow the same neat progression from cheapest to most expensive.

Merely because an option is included in the cost guide does not mean that we recommend it. However, we did feel obligated to show all the widely available options, whether we like them or not.

The comparison between contracted and DIY cost is useful in several ways. It can help you determine if the savings gained from doing the work yourself are worth your time and headaches. In addition, you can see why a low-cost, do-it-yourself project is sometimes not worth contracting out. For example, if you like tinkering, you can save lots of money by making extensive repairs to old windows yourself. But we do not recommend having a contractor reputty and paint windows if the work is extensive, because of the labor cost. Contractors can put in replacement sashes almost as cheaply, and they'll last a lot longer.

Obviously, repair and remodeling costs vary significantly from one part of the country to another. So do materials that are available and commonly in use. A $2,000 job in Des Moines may cost $6,000 in Manhattan. Stucco siding may be very affordable in Albuquerque, while in Anchorage it won't hold up as well, and it's hard to find someone to put it on properly.

So we offer this caveat:

Warning Regarding Prices

The estimated costs in this book are national averages derived from the authors' experience and nationally recognized estimating manuals. We believe that the estimated costs are accurate within plus or minus 20 percent in most parts of the country. However, in high-cost areas or for very small projects, actual costs may be as much as 200 percent higher.

Difficulty Levels

Each project task has been assigned a difficulty level ranging from 1 to 5. Level-one tasks are the easiest and safest, while level-five tasks are the most difficult and are potentially dangerous. The criteria used to define difficulty levels are personal safety, need for hand-eye skills, possibility of damaging expensive material or other house components, and need for experience handling tools.

Interior painting is a level-one task because heights are below 6 ft so the need for climbing ladders is diminished, the skills are easy to practice without much material loss, and the tools are uncomplicated.

Repairing plaster walls is a level-three task because plaster is caustic but not poisonous, the hand-eye movements to level the final coat can be learned easily, and the hand tools involved are common to a basic tool set.

Sanding wood floors with a belt sander is a level-five task because the materials used in finishing surfaces may be toxic, the wood dust is a respiratory irritant, the sander must be operated with a precise movement to avoid major damage to the floor, and the tools are heavy and rarely used by homeowners.

Before attempting any new task, read all the manufacturers' instructions, look for advice from someone who's tried it before, and have a good do-it-yourself manual on hand that covers the basic techniques, materials used, and tools involved.

COST VARIABLES

Even if typical costs are higher or lower where you live, the cost guides will be valuable, because we have found that the *relative costs* among options will remain close to the same. As you use this book, you will find your own "multiplier." For example, if the bids you get on replacement windows are half again as high as those shown in the cost guide, it's very likely that new siding will also cost you about one and a half times as much as the national average we show. Most of the geographic variance will occur with contracted jobs, since labor costs vary much more than do material costs.

If you find a big variance (over 40 percent or so) from our predictions, there may be other contributing factors besides high local construction costs. If you see a large variance, these are factors to look out for:

1. *Is your job big enough?* Contractors have a basic cost just mobilizing for a job: making a detailed estimate, assembling materials, getting to your house, and so on. For very small jobs, such as putting in a sink, you may pay twice the figure you see in the cost guide. But if you add in some other plumbing work, you are more likely to get prices like the ones we show.
2. *Are your plans firm and clear?* The less you have decided on when a contractor bids, the more you will pay. If you don't specify alternatives with moderate cost, most contractors will estimate higher cost options. If you leave things really open-ended ("We'll see how it looks"), you will pay dearly. Good contractors will cover these contingencies in the bid you get. Less professional contractors may bid low and then present you with change orders.
3. *Have you shopped enough?* A word-of-mouth refer-

ral to a *single* contractor is the most common way that a homeowner finds someone to do remodeling work. As we advise in Part Two, doing some more thorough research and getting multiple bids can lower costs dramatically. Make sure you look for the right *kind* of contractor—for example, a repair person is a better candidate for fussy door repairs than is a remodeling contractor. Throughout the book, we give advice on who to look for to perform different kinds of work.

Following these rules takes some work and discipline. But in using them, the authors get remodeling bids in many cities that are 30 to 50 percent lower than what the average homeowner pays.

Some of the ideas you will run across in this book may be new to you; others will strike you as just plain common sense. Others still you may have heard of, but did not know either how to carry them out or what their cost would be. We throw them all into the pot, and let you decide which ones you want.

The choices we have left out are (1) those that are a step above basic home improvements, such as installing hot tubs; (2) those in which the options are mainly brand comparisons, such as which manufacturer's garbage disposal to install; (3) those with limited or regional application, such as adobe or reinforced-concrete construction; and (4) price comparisons of expensive brand-name products, such as top-of-the-line windows or doors—we definitely believe in generic building materials.

What we do in this book is to propose typical alternatives that save money. Some save a great deal of money. With recommended options, such as plywood siding, concrete slab floors, and plastic water lines, we have tried to push the limits on saving money by indicating a "least cost" option for homeowners operating on a very tight budget. The choice of how to proceed is yours. Just as there is "more than one way to skin a cat," there is more than one way to make a particular improvement to your home.

Well-informed individuals can maintain and improve their homes without falling into the fabled money pit. Knowing that to be true, The Enterprise Foundation has created this book to show you how.

Methods and Materials

Walls and Ceilings

Because walls and ceilings are the most prominent part of home interiors, they deserve careful attention. Repairing or replacing them can require a great deal of time and money.

Expanse is what makes work on walls and ceilings costly. So if you can reduce the costs of treatment by even a few pennies a square foot, you can make significant savings overall. But first, you have to figure out what the different treatments cost.

We have done much of that work for you in Table 1.1 (page 22). In general, the least expensive and most desirable way to rejuvenate an old plaster wall, even if it is in bad shape, is to carefully patch and then paint or wallpaper it. Covering it with drywall or paneling is the next cheapest option. By far the most expensive approach is tearing out the old plaster and installing new drywall and trim.

Your decision about how much work to do on your old walls depends, of course, on how much you are willing to spend. It also depends on the condition of the walls and on the amount of demolition required to conceal new wiring, heating ducts, plumbing pipes and so on.

Usually, you can avoid complete demolition. Many general contractors, mechanical and electrical contractors, and even architects prefer this option because it gives them a new start. They have more freedom and less headache in running their pipes, ducts, and cables. But such demolition is worth the cost only when walls have to be relocated, the plaster or drywall is very badly damaged, or you simply cannot find a contractor who will repair rather than replace.

Throughout this book, we present a number of cost-saving techniques that show how selective repairs and replacements can take the place of expensive demolition and rebuilding. In most cases, the slightly higher costs of routing wires and pipes behind existing walls and ceilings are more than offset by the big savings made from not having to demolish and rebuild.

These days, it is possible, though difficult, to find general contractors, carpenters, plasterers, electricians, and other tradespeople who will take this more frugal approach. In addition, our save-and-repair techniques are easily adapted by do-it-yourselfers, even those with moderate skills.

Here is an example of how you can save money by demolishing as little as possible and repairing or covering over damage. If you were to remove the plaster on the walls of a typical 12 × 12-ft room and put up new drywall, we estimate the cost at about $1,300. If you were to cover the old plaster with new drywall, the cost would be about $700. And if you were merely to repair and patch up to a third of the old plaster and then repaint, you could complete the job for under $600.

Given clear tear-out directions and liability for their own patching, competent renovation contractors can do their work with amazingly little damage to walls. Plumbers can completely replace waste and supply piping by removing the ceilings under baths plus a section between studs in the wall below. Electricians can snake their cables through wall cavities, drilling only small holes here and there.

In keeping with Table 1.1 (page 22), we first discuss repairing plaster and using drywall. Then, we take up the options of paneling, wallpapering, painting, and other ways to make old walls look good again at a bargain price.

MAKING THE MOST OF OLD PLASTER

Old plaster should be cherished: It is stronger and more soundproof than drywall; it is more solid to the touch; it gives a handmade, slightly wavy textured surface that contributes to the character of an older home; and it can shape curves better than drywall. Moreover, when you save the original plaster, you can reuse the original base moldings, door trim, window trim, and other wood finish-work that runs over the walls. This saves the cost of removing the trim pieces, buying new ones if the originals were damaged in removal, and then reinstalling and refinishing the trim.

Repair Costs

The advantage of saving plaster walls that are only slightly damaged is fairly obvious. The decision is more difficult when much of the plaster wall is deteriorated, crumbling, missing, suffering from water damage, or loosened from its supporting *lath* (the wooden slats or metal mesh behind the plaster, to which the plaster attaches).

Our experience has shown that it is less expensive to replace 50 percent of walls and ceilings with sound plaster repairs than it is to remove all the plaster and lath and replace it with drywall over the entire surface. In addition, any time the old lath is solid, is fairly level, and has all loose bits of plaster removed, it is less expensive to leave it in place whether the repair method is replastering or patching with drywall. The reason is that very old studs often are uneven and need to be shimmed if the old lath is removed. Also, by leaving the old lath in place, you leave on the trimwork around the doors and windows that are nailed over it. That saves the trouble of taking the trim off and reinstalling it.

Repair Techniques

Plaster, which is applied when it is about the consistency of wet cement, stays in place by oozing between lath of wood strips or, in houses built after about 1930, perforated wallboard or metal mesh. After oozing through gaps in the lath, the plaster slithers partway down the backs of the lath to form what are called *keys,* really a grip like curled fingers on the lath's back side. Water damage, vibration, or settling of the house can cause the keys to break away from the face of the plaster. That leaves the plaster loose; it will eventually fall out and leave a hole.

Often, cracks do not include separation of the face plaster from the keys. Fixing these cracks is relatively simple, and we will discuss it first.

To ensure that cracks do not reappear after repair, identify their cause. If you suspect that the house is settling or the framework is spreading apart, you must solve that problem first; otherwise, the crack will reappear. Other movement that has caused cracks also must be remedied if a repair is to last.

Once the causes of cracks have been fixed, treat the cracks like seams in drywall rather than widening them by undercutting and then patching with plaster. Instead of buying the paper tape that drywall finishers normally use to cover seams, buy fiberglass mesh tape with a self-sticking back (see Figure 1.1).

Clean the crack of dirt and dust, and then press a length of the tape right over it. Although fiberglass mesh tape is slightly thicker than paper tape, it has two advantages. First, it allows a little more flex than paper tape, meaning that the walls can move a bit more before a crack reappears. Second, unlike ordinary drywall paper tape, fiberglass mesh tape does not

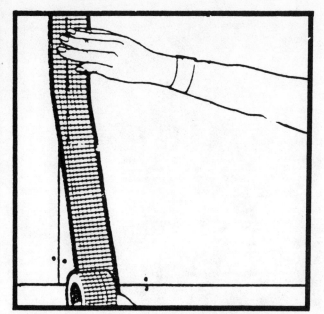

FIGURE 1.1 Fiberglass self-adhesive mesh tapes goes on without any initial coating of drywall joint compound. It is strong and saves time.

require an initial coat (sometimes called the *bedding coat*) of drywall joint compound to hold it in place.

Once the fiberglass mesh tape is in place, cover it with joint compound using a wide trowel. Even if you do not want to do this repair yourself—and with fiberglass rather than paper tape, the work is much easier for an amateur—the method makes a durable repair and is worth requesting from whomever is going to do the work.

To repair holes in plaster, first examine the extent of the damage. If the hole is less than 6 in. across and the lath behind is sound, use patching plaster followed, when dry, by a top coat of drywall joint compound.

An alternative method is filling in with drywall. First,

make the hole a regular shape, usually a rectangle. Then, cut the gypsum portion of a drywall board into a patching piece of slightly smaller dimensions than the hole you have cleared. Leave the paper portion of the patching piece larger than the hole, however, by about ¾ in. all around.

Cut this way, the gypsum portion of the patching piece fits neatly into the hole, and the paper portion laps onto the plaster. The paper is then covered with joint compound. This type of patching is also suitable for repairing a drywall-covered wall.

If the hole is larger than about 6 in. on a side, definitely repair it with drywall instead of plaster. Again, cut the hole to a regular shape, preferably to the studs on either side. If the plaster still feels loose around the hole, use drywall screws and plaster washers to hold the plaster fast against the lath (see Figure 1.2).

Cut the drywall to the same shape as the hole and about ¼ in. smaller all around the hole's edges—there is no need for a paper flare around the hole if the patching piece is going to be nailed to studs. If the drywall is significantly thinner than the plaster, glue or screw wooden shims onto the lath to make it flush with the surrounding plaster. Fasten the drywall to the studs with screws. Cover the joint between the drywall and the plaster with fiberglass tape, and then cover the tape with joint compound.

LAMINATING WALLS AND CEILINGS

Where more than half of a plaster wall needs repair, the least expensive, high-quality treatment is laminating with drywall. The board merely goes over the old plaster, and the joints are covered with joint tape and joint compound. For walls, ⅜-in.-thick drywall is sufficient; for ceilings, ⅜-in. drywall is easier to handle and

FIGURE 1.2 When patching large areas with drywall, enlarge the hole to a regular shape. Use plaster washers and drywall screws around the edges if needed to reinforce the connection of the edges of plaster to the lath.

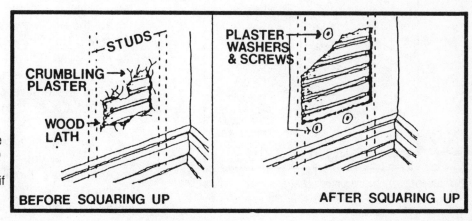

is acceptable if carefully fastened on joists or *strapping* (1 × 2-in. furring strips running across the joists) set no more than 16 in. apart. For wider spacings, ½-in. board is best, because it is less likely to sag in the areas between lines of nails or screws.

Before laminating ceilings, however, make sure that the framing can stand the extra weight of the drywall. Occasionally, ceilings with no floor above them were made with small joists. If the old ceiling moves upward slightly when you push on it hard, consider removing all the old plaster before you put up the drywall.

Clean away any crumbling plaster from walls and ceilings before you put up the drywall boards; otherwise, chunks may fall behind the boards and cause unsightly bulges. At major holes, glue or screw shims to the lath flush with the surface of the plaster (see Figure 1.3).

Next, apply adhesive to the plaster; use a caulking gun to spread ⅛-in. beads 12 in. apart. Press the boards onto the adhesive, holding the bottom of each board out into the room so that it is pushed against the adhesive last.

Then use screws, not nails, to complete the fastening job—hammering nails will loosen weak plaster. You can rent a screw gun (see Figure 1.4) from a tool-rental store for under $10 a day. We recommend them for large jobs. For smaller jobs, use a variable-speed drill and a screw-driving attachment that costs less than $8. Make certain that the screws you use are long enough to penetrate well into the studs, and screw them into the studs, not just the lath. That way, the lath, plaster, and drywall will all be fastened tight to the studs.

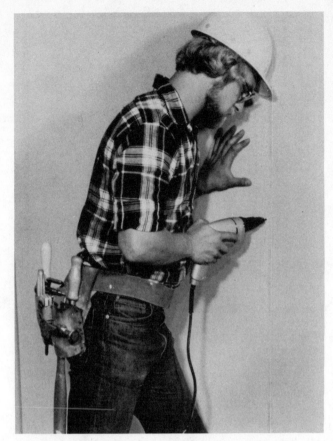

FIGURE 1.4 A screw gun quickly drives a screw through drywall and the support behind, making their rental cost worthwhile in time saved.

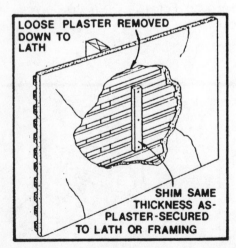

FIGURE 1.3 The section of damaged plaster wall has been prepared to accept a new layer of screw-attached drywall over the entire surface.

If you are working in a room where the plaster is particularly loose, you can screw the plaster to the studs—using metal or plaster washers—before you apply the drywall. By doing so, you make certain that the worst sections of plaster are firmly secured to the framing members.

For ceilings, use a second set of screws through the ½-in. drywall and into the floor joists above to firmly anchor the whole ceiling. Don't trust screws in the lath alone to support new drywall—nails holding the lath to the floor joists may pull loose with the added weight.

You may be able to save money by creating a *wainscot* (decorative paneling that covers the lower portion of a wall). Often, the most damaged portions of plaster walls are the lowest; say, below window level. The damage comes from furniture bangings, water from leaking windows, and so forth, while the upper portions of the plaster walls are relatively sound.

When you see this situation, we recommend covering only the lower 3 to 4 ft of the wall with drywall. This

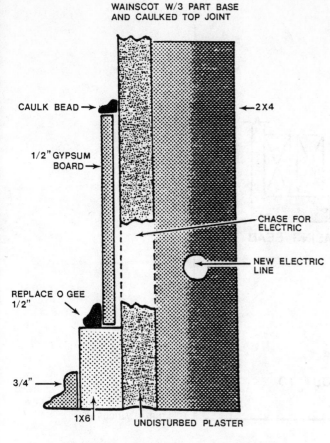

WAINSCOT W/3 PART BASE
AND CAULKED TOP JOINT

CAULK BEAD →

←2 X 4

1/2" GYPSUM
BOARD →

CHASE FOR
ELECTRIC

NEW ELECTRIC
LINE

REPLACE O GEE
1/2"

3/4"

1X6

UNDISTURBED PLASTER

OLD PLASTER
(PLASTER & PAINT
IN GOOD CONDITION
ABOVE NEW WAINSCOT
HEIGHT)

CASING BEAD

NEW BOARD
WAINSCOT

4'-0"
MIN

OLD BASE RESET
OR NEW WOOD
BASE (ATTACH
WITH TRIM HEAD
SCREWS OR
NAILS)

CASING BEAD

EXISTING BASE
NOT REMOVED

ALTERNATE "A"

ADHESIVE

SEE ALTERNATE "A"

EXISTING PLASTER
GROUND

ADD NAILER IF
REQUIRED

FIGURE 1.5 Drywall laminated over the lower portion of a wall can be made to blend in by using caulk, beading, molding, or a combination of the three.

may even lead to savings from mechanical contractors and electricians, who—before laminating begins—can remove parts of the damaged lower wall to make their runs and leave the upper portion intact.

To cover the top junction of the drywall and the old plaster, attach wood chair rail or other molding over the top edge of the drywall (the usual height of chair rail is 36 in. off the floor, or level with the lower trim on windows).

Two cheaper ways to disguise the joint between the drywall and plaster are shown in Figure 1.5. One technique is to run molding and a bead of caulking along the upper and lower edges of the drywall; the other is to use a drywall casing bead, available in drywall supply stores.

If your home has three-part base molding, you can remove the top strip, usually a piece called an *ogee*, and lay the drywall on the larger piece below. Then, install a thinner ogee strip. The old shoe molding remains in place. If you do not have three-part base

molding, you can remove what molding there is in place and run the drywall to the floor. Then, the old molding—or new, if you prefer—goes down in place at floor level. If you are installing an entirely new baseboard, vinyl cove molding fastened with adhesive is the cheapest method.

Entire rooms should receive the same treatment on all of their walls. In most cases, using 12-ft boards eliminates the need for vertical joints between boards, except at corners.

Covering plaster with drywall may cause troubles with wooden trim at doors and windows, as well as with base molding. You could, of course, remove all the trim, install shims on the jambs, and then set the trim back in place after the board has been installed. But you needn't. Instead, you can abut drywall to the wood trim and fill the slight gap between drywall and trim with latex caulk (not joint compound, which will crack over time in this application) (see Figure 1.6). To speed the work, smooth the latex caulk in the crack

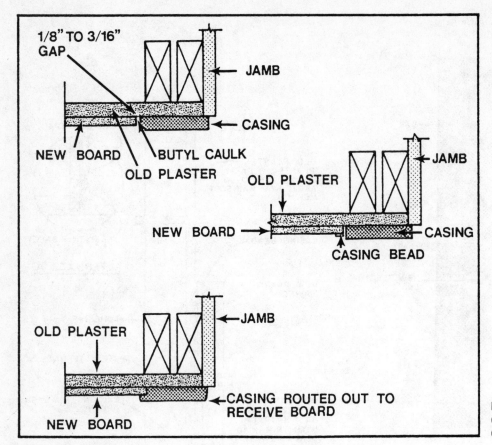

FIGURE 1.6 Drywall laminated over plaster can be made to fit the old trim in various ways.

with a wet sponge. You can paint over the joint with latex paint while the joint is still damp.

Paneling is also good as a wainscoting, rising from the baseboard 3 or 4 ft up a wall. Paneling takes the punishment of chair backs and children's toys, and dark paneling hides dirt. In kitchens and bathrooms, plastic-faced paneling has the greatest resistance to moisture and is the easiest to clean. A wainscot of tough paneling such as tempered hardboard is particularly suited to a stairway. The base-molding treatments discussed above work just as well on paneling as on drywall laminate.

Lamination costs considerably less than replacement. Covering a whole room of deteriorating plaster with new drywall saves the costs of demolition and of replacing trim. Obviously, the savings are greater if you can get away with laminating only the bottom 3 or 4 ft of each wall.

NEW DRYWALL WALLS AND CEILINGS

The invention of drywall had almost as large an impact on building construction as television had on social customs. TV replaced expensive entertainment; drywall replaced expensive gypsum walls. Drywall is cheaper than plaster because it can be installed quickly and requires less skilled labor.

Even so, professionals are continually devising ways to put up boards even more quickly and easily. Here are some of them:

1. *Place boards horizontally, not vertically.* Horizontal, or laid-down, drywall has 20 percent fewer joints than vertical, or stood-up, drywall (see Figure 1.7). A finished assembly of studs and laid-down board is more resistant to racking and movement. Horizontal seams are easier to work and are less noticeable than vertical ones.

2. *Use the largest boards you can.* Although more cumbersome, boards that are 12 or 14 ft long make stronger and better-looking walls. Unfortunately, they may be hard to carry into rooms that are up a stairway. Sometimes, for larger jobs, the supplier will deliver them through a second-story window with a cherry-picker type of lift.

But if they can be maneuvered into a room, they have definite advantages. A 10 × 12-ft room finished laid-down with 12-ft boards has no vertical seams except at the room corners and needs only 264 linear

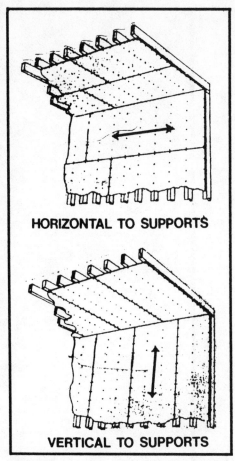

HORIZONTAL TO SUPPORTS

VERTICAL TO SUPPORTS

FIGURE 1.7 Fasten drywall boards horizontally; you make fewer joints and build a stronger wall.

feet of tape. The same room finished with 8-ft sheets stood-up has eight nontapered joints (ones not able to take advantage of the tapering along the factory-cut sides of drywall sheets) and needs 304 linear feet of tape. In addition, nontapered joints show a slight bulge of joint compound when finished, unlike tapered joints, which end up completely flush to the surrounding board.

The projected saving of horizontal installation with 12- or 14-ft boards is 15 to 24 percent of normal finishing costs.

3. *Use screws, not nails.* Screws hold better, draw tighter, are easier to use on ceilings, and result in lower finishing costs than do nails.

Because screws have greater holding power, ceiling boards can be held with screws 12 in. apart; nails should be 7 in. apart. On walls, screws can be 16 in. apart; nails should be 8 in. apart. A contractor saves the equivalent of about $2/board in labor costs using screws instead of nails.

The best way to install screws is with a screw gun, but a hand drill with an $8 screwdriving attachment makes a good substitute. A screw gun can be rented for about $6 a day. New, a gun costs about $100, but it pays for itself in reduced labor after about 50 boards.

Note: In either new work or on an old wall, if a screw or nail pops (that is, its head works loose to protrude into the room), the best way to fix it is to drive it in firmly. Drive it in far enough to recess the head in the drywall. If you think it is not firmly engaged in the stud behind, drive in another nail or screw an inch away that does get a solid grip. If the first nail or screw is loose, remove it, then spackle over the recess.

4. *At ceilings, use floating angles.* We do not recommend using nails or screws at the intersections of walls and ceilings. Instead, use the top edge of the board on the wall to support the edge of the board on the ceiling (see Figure 1.8). This system of *floating angles* saves time. It also makes a joint that can flex with slight movements of the building, which is particularly important in older houses that may settle slightly. Generally, using floating angles on walls saves about 75 cents for each 4 × 8-ft sheet when the work is contracted.

Attach drywall to the ceiling first. We recommend the *double-nailing* technique: place screws in pairs about 2 in. apart. This helps prevent screws from loosening and allows you to place the first screws about 16 in. away from the wall. If you put up screws singly, the first one should be placed about 12 in. from the wall.

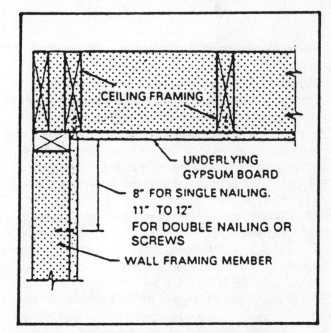

CEILING FRAMING

UNDERLYING
GYPSUM BOARD

8" FOR SINGLE NAILING.

11" TO 12"

FOR DOUBLE NAILING OR
SCREWS

WALL FRAMING MEMBER

FIGURE 1.8 The ceiling board of a floating angle is supported at the edge by the board on the wall below.

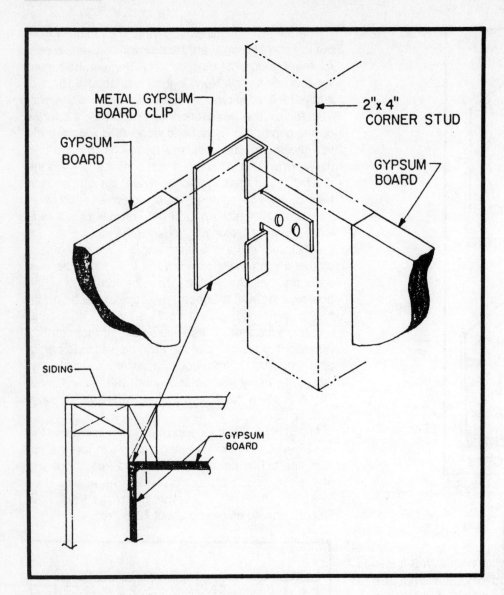

METAL GYPSUM
BOARD CLIP

GYPSUM
BOARD

2"x 4"
CORNER STUD

GYPSUM
BOARD

SIDING

GYPSUM
BOARD

FIGURE 1.9 Drywall clips are placed on boards at edges, thus eliminating the requirement for additional framing at wall intersections.

Install drywall on the walls so that the edges abut tightly against the boards overhead. Place screws 8 in. down from the ceiling for single screws, 12 in. down for pairs. If you are doing the job yourself, mark the location of studs or joists on the floor, baseboard, or ceiling edges before fastening a board. Then, mark a line on the new board to show where to drive your nails or screws.

5. *Use drywall clips.* Another money-saving trick in corners is to use clips (see Figure 1.9). These save the cost of an inside corner stud or other additional framing at partition intersections. Often, in older houses with lath and plaster, there was just one inside corner stud—and perhaps a thin board to catch the lath on one wall. Clips replace this board. Using clips also makes a more crack-resistant joint.

6. *Use fiberglass tape and special compound.* Fi-

berglass tape comes in two types, self-adhesive and staple-on. We recommend the self-adhesive type (Figure 1.1). Both kinds cost more than paper tape, but save labor.

The main reason for labor savings is that no bedding coat is needed for fiberglass tape. Paper tape needs a bedding coat to adhere to the wall in the first place. Furthermore, using fiberglass tape is simple. An unskilled worker or an amateur can apply it, working just ahead of professionals who are spreading on the joint compound.

In addition, using just two coats of special joint compound such as Durabond low consistency with fiberglass tape creates a stronger joint than does using three coats of ordinary compound with paper tape. The saving in labor costs is about 6 to 12 percent.

7. *In corners, caulk, don't tape.* Taping tight-fitting

wall-corner and wall-ceiling joints is troublesome and time-consuming. Instead, fill the joints with acrylic latex caulk. Tape and joint compound require at least two or three coats, with drying time between. Caulking is completed in a single swift operation—a damp sponge to smooth the caulk speeds the work further—and is much easier if you are doing the work yourself.

To be sure, along the tapered edges of boards (a narrowing of the board to accommodate tape and compound), the appearance will be better if the joint is taped. But where the tapered edge has been cut away, or where appearance is not quite so important—as in garages, closets, and basements—caulking is a low-cost and presentable technique. Moreover, with caulk, the joint is free to expand and contract slightly.

The saving from using caulk instead of tape and compound at corners is about 15 percent of the normal finishing costs of an entire room.

PANELING

Using paneling is a good, long-lasting way to renew a wall surface. A variety of paneling types is available, from expensive solid wood boards to veneer panels and simulated patterns on particleboard. They go up quickly, nail easily, and change a room dramatically. They can be nailed directly over plaster or wallboard into the studs beneath. Use panel adhesive on the back surface for an even surer grip. Use threaded nails—they don't pop back out.

Paneling is good for laminating the lower 3 to 4 ft of a damaged plaster wall (see discussion on page 12). It is also useful for boxing around pipes and heating ducts.

The different types of paneling vary in price. Generally, photographic prints on hardboard are the least expensive, about $4 to $8/sheet, but must be used over drywall, plaster, or other rigid backing. Wood veneer over ⅜-in. plywood—a good-quality paneling—costs about $16/sheet and does not need rigid backing. Paneling is a cost-efficient solution to overhauling a room until the cost per sheet rises above $16.

Unfortunately, normal paneling has a drawback: Unlike plaster, it is flammable. Consequently, many building codes forbid its use in multifamily dwellings. It is never acceptable as a fire separation, which is often required between duplex units or townhouses.

For these applications, fire-rated gypsum walls must be in place between dwelling units. However, paneling usually may be laminated over a fire-rated wall in single-family construction, although holes in the drywall or plaster first must be patched. For a higher price ($20 to $30/sheet), fire-rated paneling can be bought, but it is never cost-effective compared to drywall.

Code officials in most localities accept non-fire-rated paneling in single-family homes. However, it is prudent to avoid its use near kitchen stoves, wood stoves, and other areas with a high fire risk.

WALLPAPERING

Wallpaper hides blemishes on walls and dramatically transforms the appearance of a room in hours. After paint, it is the cheapest new finish for a wall.

Wallpaper varies in price, generally from around $2 to $20/roll. Putting up the paper yourself is not as difficult as it used to be: Some papers come with the adhesive already applied; they are merely moistened and applied to the wall. There is time to straighten the paper if it does not go up exactly as planned. Pre-pasted papers, however, are not as effective as un-pasted types in disguising blemishes.

Preparation of the walls is important. Smooth old plaster or drywall, fill any holes or cracks with joint compound, and sand the repair flush with the surrounding surface. If the surface looks porous, treat it first with a wallpaper glue called *size*. Another smoothing technique is to put up a backing layer of paper horizontally; this layer is covered with the top layer vertically.

If you don't want to put up the wallpaper yourself, consider just preparing the walls, which is a big part of a wallpaper hanger's expense when loose paper has to be removed or plaster patched. There's no need to strip a wall bare when repapering; use joint compound and a 10-in. joint-compound trowel to smooth old paper seams and areas where loose paper was removed.

FABRIC AND FIBER COVERINGS

Remember that wall-covering stores offer more than rolls of paper. They can show you rolls of canvas, hemp, burlap, grass cloth, cork, or felt. Cork is generally laminated on top of paper or burlap, and felt is laminated on top of paper.

These heavier wall coverings cover irregularities much better than does a single layer of wallpaper (although a double layer of wallpaper is effective and generally less expensive). Their thickness and rough texture smooth over pebbly or poorly patched plaster, hairline cracks, and thick layers of old paint.

Canvas, in particular, has a long and honored history as a wall covering—for centuries, it has been applied over plaster to prevent hairline cracks. Although heavier wall coverings cannot disguise holes, large dents, or grossly uneven patches, they require far less wall preparation than do wallpaper or paint, and thereby keep costs down.

These coverings attach to walls like wallpaper, but with less fuss. Generally, there are no patterns to line up, although many people reverse every other strip to prevent abrupt changes in shading.

Canvas and similar materials comes in rolls of varying widths. The wider ones are for experienced hangers, the narrower ones for novices. Ask for them at any wallpaper store.

PAINTING

Homeowners take on painting as their major do-it-yourself project more often than they take on any other task, and with good reason: With a little instruction, almost anyone can paint, even a whole house interior. You can save a lot by doing your own painting, and knowing how to paint and what paint to use can save you even more.

The least expensive way to paint a whole house interior is to spray on an off-white latex paint, coating even the woodwork trim. Latex paint is the least expensive you can buy. Spraying is fast, and thus saves labor. Covering the woodwork trim along with the walls saves the time and cost of applying a second color. If you do not like a flat paint on wood trim, you can spray the whole room with an eggshell finish instead. (Eggshell is a finish that falls between flat and semigloss.) However, flat paint hides more imperfections than does a semigloss and is preferred by most professional drywallers.

Table 1.2 (page 24) is a guide to the cost of painting equipment and the relative time it takes using the various equipment types. If you don't have special skills, and if you'll be painting while living in the house, we recommend manual rollers.

Color

Off-white is inexpensive and also helps save energy. Its light-reflecting power reduces the need for electric lighting and increases the efficiency of lights by 20 to 40 percent. Pure white reflects from 70 to 90 percent of available light; ivories and creams, 55 to 70 percent. White also makes a room appear larger and allows easier room decoration. Moreover, it does not fade over time.

That said, if you are on a budget, you'll do far better to add color to rooms with paint rather than with plumbing fixtures, floor stains, kitchen appliances, and the like—you pay dearly for color in these items, but paint tinting is usually free.

If you are concerned about fading and color change—mainly a result of the chemical breakdown of pigments—choose stable colors, the most prominent of which are white, red oxide, and black. Blue and green are susceptible to fading.

White can also have good *hiding power,* meaning that the paint covers well what is below it. Hiding power is a product of the pigment used, the percentage of total solids in the paint, and the particle size of the solids.

For tips on painting different surfaces and the prices of different kinds of paints, consult Table 1.3 (page 26).

TUB SURROUNDS

Unless bathtubs do not have showers attached, the walls above them need water protection (see Table 1.4, page 27). The cheapest option is a free-standing tub-shower combination; a wraparound rod and shower curtain provide the waterproofing.

Ceramic Tile

The traditional tub surround is made of individual ceramic tiles adhered, for the longest life, to ½-in. portland cement board. Grout is spread into the joints.

Now you can buy the same 4 × 4-in. ceramic tiles in pregrouted sheets. The silicone grout already applied between tiles on these sheets all but eliminates manual grouting once the tiles are mounted. This kind of grout also resists mildew and increases the life of the tub surround. Pregrouted sheets are more expensive than their equivalent in individual tiles, but even when a contractor puts them in, the labor savings make them a slightly better buy. These tiles also create a more waterproof wall surface.

Epoxy Paint

A two-part polyamide-epoxy paint is a relatively quick, low-maintenance, low-cost way to seal leaky tub enclosures. It can be used over finished ½-in. water-resistant drywall or even over old, damaged ceramic tile. In both cases, use two coats and finish seams with silicone caulking. Painting over new drywall offers an estimated two-year life before repainting is necessary. Painting over ceramic tile should effect a waterproof seal for four years.

Panels of Fiberglass, Acrylic, or Polyvinyl Chloride (PVC)

Three- and five-piece shaped panels of these synthetic materials can be installed quickly (see Figure 1.10). A variety of colors and styles is available.

The drawbacks are that these panels must be carefully caulked during installation and require care with special cleaners. Fiberglass panels are more expensive than acrylic or PVC panels.

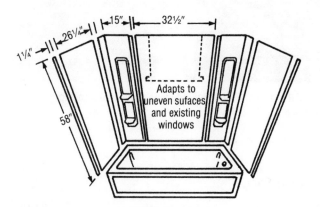

This five-piece surround, made by Burawall, has a center panel that adapts to uneven surfaces and permits a cut-out for existing windows.

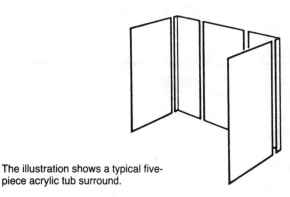

The illustration shows a typical five-piece acrylic tub surround.

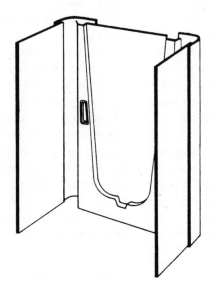

This is a fancier five-piece surround made by Pronto.

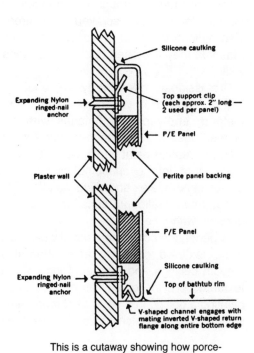

This is a cutaway showing how porcelain-on-steel panels are installed.

FIGURE 1.10 Fiberglass and plastic panels are less expensive than ceramic tile for the area around a bathtub and are installed relatively easily.

Panels of Melamine

These are the cheapest of the tub surrounds and also the shortest-lived. Unlike the panels above, they come as flat, not shaped, 5 × 8-ft sheets that are cut with a saw. Essentially, they are a Masonite paneling coated with waterproof Melamine. When they are installed, they are sealed at the joints with silicone caulk and special plastic moldings. The sheets are available in smooth or tile-embossed surfaces.

Application of the panels directly over studs is not recommended. Instead, they should be installed over furring strips.

TEXTURED FINISHES

A quick, inexpensive way to rejuvenate walls and ceilings that have only minor blemishes is to apply a textured finish. Their rough surfaces of swirled plaster, grainy paint, and the like adequately cover old patches, chipped paint, and other irregularities.

The drawbacks of textured surfaces are that they are difficult to apply by brush (but can be sprayed or rolled on), they are rough to the touch, and they are hard to clean. Heavy, sprayed-on textured finishes are also difficult to repair or cover over later. For these reasons, they are often applied to ceilings, but not to walls.

Professionals often spray on rough finishes (see Figure 1.11). But you don't need their equipment. Instead, apply plaster finishes with a trowel and painted ones with a sponge-rubber applicator, special roller, or regular paint brush. Some people like to swirl the texture into overlapping circles. Textured paint comes in both latex and alkyd varieties. The latex type is good over wallboard because it covers seams and goes on without a primer.

Experienced contractors usually can save money by using textured coatings rather than first preparing smooth ceilings and then applying paint. Here's how textured spraying compares in price to patching and painting a ceiling in a 10 × 12-ft room that would need several hours of patching work if it were to be painted:

Patch and Paint

Scrape ceiling	$21.00
Patch cracks and feather edges	$55.00
Apply two coats of flat latex paint	$38.40
TOTAL	$114.40

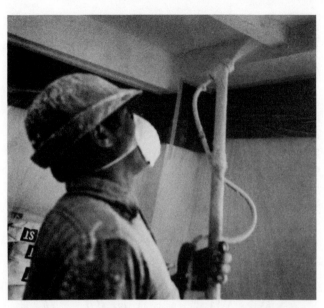

FIGURE 1.11   Spraying a textured finish on a ceiling covers a multitude of irregularities.

Textured Spray

Scrape ceiling of loose material	$21.00
Spray ceiling with a perlite-containing coating	$68.40
TOTAL	$89.40

Prices, of course, may be different in your area, but they probably will stay in the same relationship.

The example shows that because plaster-patching and painting are avoided with a textured, spray-on coating, using a textured surface is 22 percent cheaper than using a smooth one. In addition, textured coatings can have a sound-deadening effect in a room, much like acoustical tile.

Note, however, that the example also shows that if little patching is needed, or you are doing all the work yourself, a spray-on ceiling will be more expensive. And keep in mind that if the job is limited to a single room rather than a whole floor or whole house, the contractor-sprayer is likely to charge more because the fixed costs of setup and cleanup will be the same for one room or ten.

SUSPENDED CEILINGS

We flatly don't recommend suspended ceilings. Often, they are used as a bandage over major problems (namely, crumbling ceilings) that will lead to continual dust and potential fire hazards until they are fixed. In addition, many suspended-ceiling products on the market are highly flammable and even highly toxic in a fire. Foam panels are the worst, especially if a poorly or illegally wired light fixture is loosely dropped through them from above.

One important, but often overlooked, function of walls and ceilings is blocking the spread of fire. Fires contained in one room—even for half an hour while fire fighters are getting to work—do far less damage to life and property than do ones that spread quickly. Everyone who does renovations should be conscious of fire-stopping; that is, making sure that fire cannot travel quickly from room to room and floor to floor.

When old plaster or drywall has fallen from a ceiling over which you will install a suspended ceiling, it ought to be replaced, even with a crude patch, to prevent the *chimney effect,* the creation of drafts that can carry flame to the floor above when a fire starts. In addition, something flammable (such as paperboard panels) should not be hung under a ceiling.

Therefore, in our opinion, the most acceptable method of installing a suspended ceiling is to cover over ceiling holes with drywall patches, install the grid of channels that holds the panels, and then install at least minimally fire-rated panels.

Where codes require a fire-rated ceiling (as in multi-family buildings), a rated steel grid and panels with the correct rating should be installed. Hold-down clips are also required. In addition, ceiling lights should be installed according to their instructions and the fire code. This normally means covering the old fixture box with a plate and running a cable down in what is called a *fixture stud,* which is fireproof, to a new, enclosed fixture box. Improperly installed recessed lighting is a major cause of house fires.

We estimated the cost of a suspended ceiling against that of demolishing the old ceiling, furring, and redrywalling a 12 × 12-ft ceiling; the drywall method was over $100 cheaper. Also, from a house appraiser's point of view, a drywall ceiling adds more value. For example:

	Contractor	DIY
12 × 12-ft Suspended Ceiling Fire-patch old ceiling; install steel grid; install light fixtures; install 2 × 4-ft panels at $5/panel	$511	$268
Redrywall 12 × 12-ft Ceiling Demolish and remove old ceiling; furr ceiling with 1 × 3's; install, tape, and finish ½-in. drywall; apply two coats of paint	$396	$182

The only good reasons for a suspended ceiling are the need to lower a very high ceiling so that heat in the room is held down to the living level, or to obscure a tin ceiling that cannot be repaired or demolished. Even in these cases, we estimated that, for $650 you could hire a contractor to frame a new, dropped 12 × 12-ft ceiling, drywall it, and paint it.

THE NO-FINISH FINISH

The last finish we'll consider for walls and ceilings is the least costly, and it is almost no finish at all: Ceilings can be left with their beams exposed and brick walls can be left bare.

These options usually become apparent after some demolition. Stripped of their normal coverings, the ceilings and walls can be left that way, with minor attention. Modern tastes and styles do not in the least take offense to unfinished surfaces.

Exposed ceiling beams can be left as they are. If wires, pipes, or ducts run through or alongside them, some people prefer to spray-paint the whole area, blending in all the utilities plus the beams.

You can save about $1,200 on a typical 700-sq-ft floor by leaving ceilings exposed instead of covering them with drywall. You will, however, lose a good deal of soundproofing if the area above is occupied. Also, if you cannot install adequate insulation on the roof side of the uppermost ceiling, leaving it exposed is a poor choice.

Exposed brick walls require slightly more preparation. If the brick was formerly covered with plaster, it may be necessary to rerun electrical wires in the baseboard or in conduit. Alternatively, and usually less expensively, you can rerun the wires to other locations, as long as code requirements for sufficient switches and outlets are met.

The old mortar, sometimes concocted with horsehair, may have to be shorn of loose chunks and then patched. In addition, if the plaster has left unsightly lime stains on the brick, you can scrub them away with a stiff brush and water.

Finally, to prevent the brick and mortar from powdering, which leaves dust on nearby furniture and flooring, coat them with a sealer. A good one is varnish cut to half strength with solvent; use two coats.

If you do want to expose brick, do not choose an exterior wall that has to be insulated, or you will soon feel the chill. Limit exposed brick to interior walls or ones that separate two apartments or townhouses.

TABLE 1.1	THE PROJECT
Wall and Ceiling Treatments	Repair and replace the wall and ceiling surface in a 12′ × 12′ × 8′ bedroom with 1 door and 2 windows.

Options	Cost/sq ft Contracted	Cost/sq ft DIY	Project Contracted	Project DIY	Difficulty Level DIY Advice	Comments and Recommendations
Patch and Wallpaper Remove loose plaster, patch, and feather up to 30%. Apply vinyl wallpaper. At $5/roll At $10/roll	$1.03 $1.34	$0.34 $0.49	$473 $616 CC	$156 $225	**3** Choosing a nonrepetitive pattern without a match-up requirement makes it easiest.	Where wallpaper is preferred, it is the lowest cost new finish. If you do the prep and buy the paper, a pro will hang for $200/ room and you'll save $120/ room.
Repair Plaster and Paint Remove loose plaster and/ or apply 2 coats perlite plaster (replace 35% of plaster). Spot, prime, and topcoat.	$1.27	$0.34	$584	$156 CC	**3**	Least expensive option if at least 65% of wall is OK.
Paneling Over Plaster Prep wall. Hang ¼″ prefinished panels with adhesive and trim. At $8/sheet At $16/sheet	$1.20 $1.55	$0.39 $0.69	$550 $713	$230 $361	**4** Precise cutting required.	Cleanest and quickest way to cover problems. Plastic-faced panels are great for kitchens and baths.
Drywall Over Plaster, Paint Prep wall. Laminate ⅜″drywall. Prime and topcoat.	$1.47	$0.45	$677	$207 VB	**3** Messy job, but wet sanding minimizes dust.* Rent a drywall lift for ceilings. Screw directly to studs.	Best option for ceilings. Lamination is less expensive than options that require furring and retriming doors and windows. Prep the wall, hang the board. Have a pro do the finishing at $150/ room. You'll still save $320/room.

Options	Cost/sq ft Contracted	Cost/sq ft DIY	Project Contracted	Project DIY	Difficulty Level DIY Advice		Comments and Recommendations
Patch and Canvas, Paint Remove loose plaster. Patch with gypsum. Apply canvas, prime, and topcoat.	$1.70	$0.74	$785	$340	**2**	Easiest system for painted walls.	Best for rooms with lots of paint chipping where a painted finished product is preferred. Expensive for paintable surface.
Demo, Drywall, Paint, and Trim Complete demolition of room. Remove trash, furr, and hang ½″ drywall, new trim. Prime and topcoat.	$2.45	$0.78	$1,295	$410	**3**		Starting all over again is expensive. Consider a room-by-room approach.

*Wet sanding is a technique used instead of sandpaper sanding. A damp sponge is drawn across the joints, smoothing the compound into the board surface without creating dust. A drywall lift is a mechanical hoist for lifting and holding in place a sheet of drywall to the ceiling until it can be fastened in place.

TABLE 1.2
Painting Equipment for Do-It-Yourselfers

Method	Cost	Time Considerations	DIY Comments	Recommended Equipment Choices
Brush	$2–$20	Painstakingly long.	Easy to control. Longer bristles provide more paint and more coverage per stroke. Buy good brushes.	Trim: 2½″ angle-cut sash at $7–9 Floors: 4″ wide with at least 5″ of bristle at $9–$11 Cutting in:* 3″ wide at $7–$11 Latex: Nylon/polyester blend with flayed bristle tips Oil: Natural bristle at $9–$14
Roller Setup Pan, extension pole, roller frame, and covers.	$18–$26	50% faster than brush work.	Double-roll in crisscross pattern for best coverage. Buy good rollers.	Pan: 4″–5″ deep, metal at $6 Panliners: Plastic at $1 Extension Pole: Adjustable metal or PVC at $10–$14 Frame: Full wire cage at $6–$8 Rollers: Expensive, $3–$4 each on phenolic core • ⅜″ nap for smooth surfaces • ½″ nap for semismooth and rough surfaces
Power Roller Electric pump and specialized roller frame and covers.	$110–$140 purchase	Applies paint faster than normal rolling, but lots of cleanup time needed.	Not recommended.	

Method	Cost	Time Considerations	DIY Comments	Recommended Equipment Choices
Small Airless Sprayer Hand-held unit.	$100–$240 purchase $22–$45 daily rental	80% faster than brush.	Good option for intricate work such as balustrades. Use multiple light coats. Provides very smooth finish.	Whatever setup can be rented.
Large Airless Sprayer	$200–$3,000 + purchase; $50–$70 daily rental	Very fast; up to 10 times faster than rolling.	Good option for entire vacant houses. Start in a practice area like the garage or basement, then move to other areas. Must mask floors, windows, etc.	Whatever setup can be rented over weekend. Least expensive and quickest option for large areas and vacant houses, despite initial investment in rental equipment and masking rooms.

*Cutting-in is the application of paint in corners before the job of rolling. Phenolic cores are the hard round cores to which the nap of rollers is attached. Power rollers force-feed paint from a small pump through the roller nap.

TABLE 1.3
Interior Paints—Their Uses and Costs

Surface	Preparation	Primer	Top Coat	Comments	Price Range
Gypsum Board	Wash off grease and oil with ammonia or TSP solutions.	Unpainted: vinyl primer. Painted: acrylic latex primer.	Flat acrylic latex.	Flat paint hides well.	$8–$14/gal.
Plaster	Spot-prime with white shellac.	"Low-perm" alkyd oil primer.	Flat acrylic latex.	"Low-perm" primers can be effective vapor barriers in older homes.	$8–$14/gal.
Wood Trim	Wash off grease and oil with TSP solution.	Bare wood only: oil-based primer.	Semigloss acrylic latex.		$12–$17/gal.
Wood Floors	Wash with TSP solution and rough sand with sanding stick.	Pigmented polyurethane floor finish.	Pigmented polyurethane floor finish.	Epoxies also work well, but cost more.	$6–$21/gal.
Concrete Floors	Wash with TSP solution.	Specialized primer or clear sealer.	Chlorinated rubber top coat (pool paint).		$27–$39/gal.
Concrete Walls	Wire brush.	Diluted vinyl latex masonry paint.	Vinyl latex masonry paint or waterproofing powder mixes or expoxies.	For waterproofing stick with 2-part epoxies or UGLs powder products mixed with water.	Powders: $12–$22/gal. Epoxy: $30–$48/gal. Vinyl Latex: $4–$8/gal.

TABLE 1.4
Tub Surrounds

THE PROJECT
Replace a tub surround in a 5′ tub including any required tear-out to 5′ above tub edge.

Options	Cost Per Surround	Project Cost Contracted	Project Cost DIY	Difficulty Level DIY Advice		Comments and Recommendations
Melamine Paneling Install a 4-piece tub surround without shelves using manufacturer's edge and corner molding.	$47	$200	$52 CC	**1**		The lowest cost option, but the shortest life. If well cared for, can last 10–15 years. But if you're calling a contractor, step up to acrylic panels.
Acrylic and PVC Panels Install a 5-piece tub surround with 3 shelves	$130	$275 CC	$139	**2**		A less expensive option than fiberglass. Requires special cleaners. Leak-free if caulked well.
Fiberglass Panels Install a 5-piece tub surround with 3 shelves, choice of 8 colors.	$220	$400	$229	**2**		Most expensive of the synthetic materials. Needs special cleaners. Can be leak-free if caulked well.
Ceramic Tile Pieces Install 4″ × 4″ ceramic tile glued over portland cement board. Use latex-modified grout in joints.	$150	$500	$150	**3**	Rent a tile cutter.	More work for DIYers, but there are thousands of colors and patterns available.
Ceramic Tile Sheets Hang pregrouted 4″ × 4″ ceramic tile in 2′ × 4′ sheets over portland cement board. Grout joints with siliconized material.	$175	$500 VB	$190 VB	**3**		Quick, no-leak way for DIYers to install real ceramic tile. Use fiberglass-reinforced cement board for a backing.

2 | Floor Treatments

If you are considering floor improvements, you have two broad choices: Work with the flooring that is already there or replace it with a new surface. Let's look at the wood renovation options first.

REUSING OLD WOOD FLOORS

Sanding

Wood grain is attractive, and many U.S. homeowners like to show it off. The grain of pine or oak, either in its natural color or stained, is beautiful, but showing it off after years of neglect can be troublesome.

Most often, you begin refurbishment of an existing wood floor by sanding away the old finish and the top surface of the grain (see Table 2.1, page 39). Sanding works better on hardwoods like oak. Since softwood floors gouge more easily, painting may be the better choice.

For sanding, professionals use a belt sander. They sand with a coarse (36-grit) paper first and progress in three stages to a finer paper (100 grit)—the lower the grit number, the rougher the paper. In addition to a belt sander, professionals use edgers (small disk sanders) on stairs and close to baseboards.

Both belt sanders and edgers can be rented. However, they are a bit tricky to use. Belt sanders take some strength and precise timing to control, and a beginner can end up gouging the floor. In any case, a novice should not begin with 36-grit paper, which can gouge a floor quickly. Use 80-grit paper if you're not an experienced sander.

Pretreatment for sanding includes a number of chores. First, replace worn or damaged floorboards and fill any holes with wood cut to size (a job for professionals or very skilled do-it-yourselfers). Second, look for and remove (or set below the surface) nail heads protruding out of the wood—these can rip the sandpaper to shreds. Last, remove any heating registers and cover the duct holes with plastic.

For do-it-yourselfers, a more controllable way to sand is to use a circular floor buffer with a fabric sanding mesh (a mesh covered with gritty aluminum oxide) (see Figure 2.1). The buffer follows the existing contours of the floor more closely than does a belt sander and removes substantially less wood. In addition, buffers are cheaper to rent. Use a reciprocating sander as an edger and a sharp scraper to treat damaged areas.

Repairing Wood Floors

A wood floor may require repairs far beyond the nail-setting and sanding just described. The main problems are deep stains, bad gouges, broken wood, cupped or warped boards, and big bulges. The last three problems are usually the result of water leaks.

The most common repair technique is to cut out the bad flooring using a circular saw and carbide-tipped blade. Clean cuts can be made more easily by nailing down a board temporarily as a straight-edge. A carbide

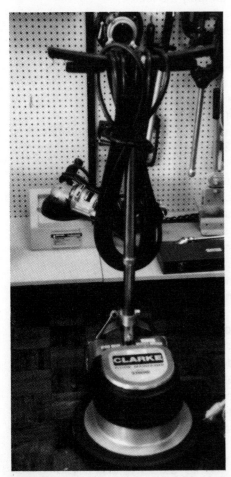

FIGURE 2.1   A rental floor buffer and a grit-coated sanding mesh can allow inexperienced workers to sand floors without fear of gouging soft pine.

tip can cut through nails, but do not use an expensive one—the teeth may be chipped no matter how careful you are. **CAUTION: Use safety glasses.**

Next, pry up the bad section; repair the subfloor, if necessary; and lay down new flooring. (See the section on new flooring surfaces, page 30, for installation techniques.) If you are replacing tongue-and-groove flooring, there will be one joint that does not have all the nailing concealed and does not have the lower lip of one groove (unless the repair is next to a wall). This board must be *face-nailed* (drive the nails through the top surface of the board, recess them, and then cover with putty).

For bulging floor areas, there is another, simpler technique that is appropriate only if the floor is being painted or covered. In this case, the carbide-tipped blade cuts *relief joints,* grooves that take away enough of the expanded wood that it can be nailed or screwed flat again; use drywall screws for this work. If you are painting, make sure that the screws are recessed enough to allow the putty a good grip.

Finishing

Once the sanding is done, a protective finish must be reapplied. Spread on a tough urethane and leave the natural wood color the way it is, or apply any of a number of colored stains.

Once the stain (if used) is dry and the floor both vacuumed and dry-mopped, apply the urethane. Because urethane bubbles, it is best to spread it with a lamb's-wool pad or varnish brush. Refer to Table 2.2 (page 40) for additional kinds and costs of clear finishes.

The floors in some older houses may have been patched previously with different kinds of wood, each staining differently. In this case, making all the woods appear the same is practically impossible. If a consistent appearance is desired, consider painting or using a floor covering.

In a lightly trafficked room, a urethane finish can last for decades without refinishing, but in a kitchen, bath, or entry area, refinishing may be necessary after five years or even sooner.

Painting

Of course, you do not have to go to all this trouble to show off the wood grain—you can paint over it. Displaying grain was not nearly as popular in the 18th and

19th centuries as it is today. Most early floors were left bare, but many were painted to add color to a room.

Colonial floors were usually painted solid colors; gray, dark green, yellow, brown, and terra-cotta red predominated. Between the Revolution and the 1840s, stenciled floors were popular. Splatter painting—flicking specks of lighter colors onto a background of brown, black, blue, or gray—was used widely in the 19th century and had the advantage of camouflaging dirt.

Wood is an ideal surface for paint, but don't overlook the fact that paint also can be used on concrete (such as in a basement or heavily trafficked area of the house). But, painting cannot be used on any form of vinyl or asphalt tile. Also, tile should not be sanded or scraped to remove dirt or rejuvenate the surface.

As with any painting job, preparation is important. First, drive any protruding nails in a wood floor below the surface with a nail set. If the floors are exceptionally dirty and greasy, mop them with TSP (trisodium phosphate) cleaner. (Using TSP is illegal in some parts of the country because of phosphate pollution. Ask a hardware store for an acceptable substitute.) Then, sand the boards lightly with 100-grit paper. A hand orbital sander or a floor buffer with a sanding mesh will do the job.

See Table 2.3 (page 41) to help you select the proper paint. Use only a floor paint, or cover a nonfloor paint with a clear floor finish. If you do it yourself, use a roller and apply two coats. Let the top coats dry for 48 hours before replacing heavy furniture.

If you want to color a concrete floor, you can use a stain covered with two coats of clear polyurethane sealer. This makes an attractive, nonslip, cleanable surface. If there are any moisture problems at all, as in a basement, use chlorinated rubber paint, sometimes called *pool paint*.

NEW FLOORING SURFACES

If the old surface is just not going to do, you have three replacement options: wood, resilient materials, or carpet (see Table 2.4, page 42). (We will discuss a fourth, ceramic tile, in the later section on kitchens and baths, page 36.) Let's first consider wood as a new flooring material.

Wood

Although new wood flooring will last a long time, it is expensive. Saving an old wood floor rather than covering it with new wood is more cost-effective, even if it means patching up to 20 percent of the old surface. If more than that has to be repaired, it is much more cost-effective to cover the old wood with tile or carpeting than it is to cover it with new wood.

But if wood is what you want, go right ahead. For wood-floor choices, consult Table 2.5 (page 43). Keep in mind that the wider the board, the less expensive the finished floor. For example, 2-1/4-in. tongue-and-groove pine costs $4.40/sq ft, thus, for an average sized room of 9 × 12 ft, the savings would amount to over $175; but 5-3/8-in. pine costs only $3.75/sq ft. (However, narrow boards do expand and contract less, producing narrower cracks during winter, when humidity is low.)

A "prefinish" increases material costs even further. Wood purchased with a stain and clear finish already applied costs $1.50 to $2.00/sq ft more than unfinished stock. With that kind of surcharge, you can save money by finishing the floor yourself. It may even be cheaper to hire a painter to apply the finish.

New wood for flooring falls into two categories: (1) solid—also called dimensional—lumber, and (2) laminated lumber.

DIMENSIONAL LUMBER Dimensional lumber is the traditional flooring. It comes in strips nominally 1-in. thick (really about 3/4-in. thick). Figure 2.2 shows dimensional strip flooring dimensions and fastening methods. Parquet flooring comes in square panels and individual strips. Figure 2.3 shows parquet flooring patterns and dimensions.

Dimensional-lumber flooring is usually oak or pine. (Maple, cherry, and walnut are also available, but cost two to four times more than oak.) Oak is either red or white and comes in two grades, common and select. Pine, which is softer and wider grained than oak, can be bought in grades C (showing imperfections, but structurally sound), B (showing very small imperfections), and A (no imperfections other than possible heavy graining).

Common-grade oak, which might show small knots and other imperfections, is about 20 percent cheaper than select-grade oak, which is cut from the heartwood and shows no large blemishes. For most purposes, the slightly marred common grade is suitable and, depending on your taste, actually makes a floor more attractive. Oak, no matter what the grade, costs more than pine.

All hardwood flooring is cut tongue-and-groove style so that the edge of one piece fits into the edge of another. Strip flooring is nailed to the *subfloor* (a plywood or other composite material) and finished.

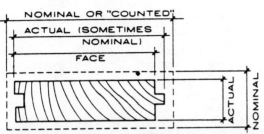

CROSS SECTIONAL DIMENSIONING SYSTEMS VARY AMONG SPECIES, PATTERNS, MANUFACTURERS. TRADE ORGANIZATIONS PROVIDE PERCENTAGE MULTIPLIERS FOR COMPUTING COVERAGE

CROSS SECTIONAL DIMENSIONS

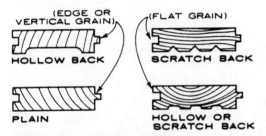

THE UNDERSIDE OF FLOORING BOARDS MAY BE PATTERNED AND OFTEN WILL CONTAIN MORE DEFECTS THAN ARE ALLOWED IN THE TOP FACE. GRAIN IS OFTEN MIXED IN ANY GIVEN RUN OF BOARDS

BOARD CHARACTERISTICS

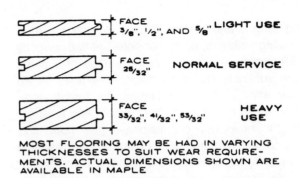

MOST FLOORING MAY BE HAD IN VARYING THICKNESSES TO SUIT WEAR REQUIREMENTS. ACTUAL DIMENSIONS SHOWN ARE AVAILABLE IN MAPLE

VARIOUS THICKNESSES

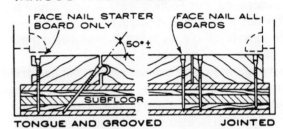

JOINTED FLOORING MUST BE FACE NAILED, USUALLY WITH FULLY BARBED FLOORING BRADS
TONGUE AND GROOVED BOARDS ARE BLIND NAILED WITH SPIRAL FLOOR SCREWS, CEMENT COATED NAILS, CUT NAILS, MACHINE DRIVEN FASTENERS, USE MANUFACTURER'S RECOMMENDATIONS

FASTENING

FIGURE 2.2 Dimensional strip flooring.

PARQUET FLOORING—SQUARE PANELS

THICKNESS	FACE DIMENSIONS
5/16″ (most common) 9/16″, 11/16″, 3/4″	6″ x 6″, 6¼″ x 6½″, 12″ x 12″, 19″ x 19″ Other sizes are available from certain manufacturers

PARQUET FLOORING—INDIVIDUAL STRIPS

THICKNESS	FACE DIMENSIONS
5/16″	2″ x 12″ typical strips can be cut, mitered, etc., to obtain pieces required for special patterns

FIGURE 2.3 Parquet flooring patterns.

Nailing tongue-and-groove flooring is easier with a floor-nailing machine, which positions the nail correctly at a 50-degree angle through the tongue of a piece into the subfloor. This machine can be used by an amateur after a demonstration at the rental store. Parquet blocks are glued to the subfloor and finished. Figure 2.4 shows how dimensional-lumber flooring is applied to the subfloor, and Figure 2.5 shows how base molding conceals the crack (needed for expansion of the flooring in hot, humid weather) between the wall and the nearest piece of flooring.

Dimensional-lumber flooring lasts a long time—at least 75 years if cared for—and can be resanded when it wears unevenly. It is easy to install, but takes a great deal of effort to sand and finish.

Sometimes, wide pine boards without tongues and grooves are used as flooring. They are nailed or screwed down through the face (top), and the recessed nail or screw heads later are covered with putty or stubby pegs. This is the easiest flooring method, because pine is easy to work with, and wide boards cover a floor quickly. However, pine scratches more easily than hardwood, and wide boards can expand and contract, leaving wide gaps between them. We do not recommend pine for high-traffic areas.

Unless you want a strictly colonial look and can put up with the cracks, we recommend that you buy only kiln-dried 1 × 6-in. pine and then condition it in a very dry interior space for four to six weeks before beginning installation. The proper conditioning method is to stack the boards with spacers and run a fan to circulate the air. Even pine that has been kiln-dried to 8 percent moisture content will absorb enough moisture in an open lumberyard to reach a 15 percent moisture content. During dry, northern winters, the installed boards could shrink by ⅛ in. or more in the heating season if you do not condition the wood first.

When it comes to finishing, remember that it is never cost-effective to skimp on the quality of the finish or the number of coats. Use alkyd urethane on a new floor. Three coats of high gloss last the longest of any finish and add only slightly to your initial cost.

A pleasing but inexpensive finish for pine is called *pickling*. You apply paint, then wipe it off. After the residue is dry, you coat it with a clear finish. Using a gray paint results in boards that resemble aged cypress. Other attractive results can be obtained with pastel green, pink, blue, or white.

LAMINATED LUMBER About ⅜-in. thick, laminated lumber is usually a veneer of oak glued to a plywood subbase. The regular strips are 3 in. wide, but you can

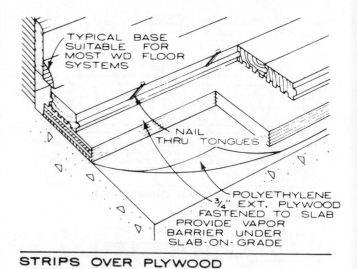

STRIPS OVER PLYWOOD UNDERLAYMENT A NOFMA STANDARD

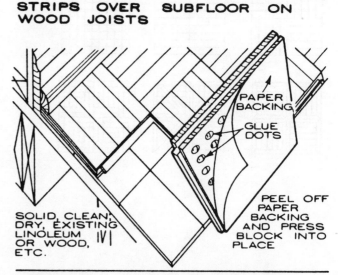

STRIPS OVER SUBFLOOR ON WOOD JOISTS

PRESSURE-SENSITIVE "DO-IT-YOURSELF" PANELS (PRE-FINISHED)

FIGURE 2.4 Dimensional-lumber flooring fastened to subfloors.

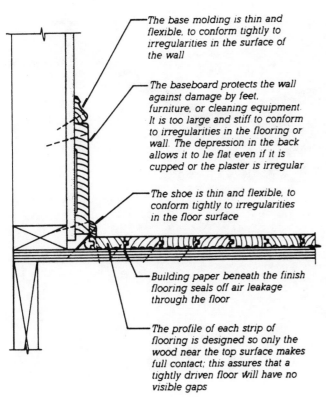

The base molding is thin and flexible, to conform tightly to irregularities in the surface of the wall

The baseboard protects the wall against damage by feet, furniture, or cleaning equipment. It is too large and stiff to conform to irregularities in the flooring or wall. The depression in the back allows it to lie flat even if it is cupped or the plaster is irregular

The shoe is thin and flexible, to conform tightly to irregularities in the floor surface

Building paper beneath the finish flooring seals off air leakage through the floor

The profile of each strip of flooring is designed so only the wood near the top surface makes full contact; this assures that a tightly driven floor will have no visible gaps

A one-piece baseboard is economical, but cannot fit as closely as a three-piece baseboard

Wood sleepers are fastened to the concrete block wall and concrete slab with concrete nails or powder-driven fasteners. Wood paneling and wood flooring are then nailed to the sleepers

If the concrete slab lies directly on grade, a sheet of polyethylene is laid beneath the sleepers to prevent moisture from entering the building

FIGURE 2.5   Strip flooring is nailed at an angle into the subfloor; the gap (needed for expansion in warm, humid weather) between the wall and the nearest piece of flooring is concealed by base molding.

also buy strips in widths that range from 2 to 8 in. Parquet blocks come in 9- and 12-in. squares. Both strip and parquet laminated lumber come tongue-and-groove, unfinished or prefinished, waxed or unwaxed.

To install some types of strip laminated flooring, first put down a paper or foam liner on the subfloor. Then, secure the flooring by gluing the edges together—the assembly "floats" over the liner. Both strip and parquet are glued to the subfloor with either a self-sticking or troweled adhesive, like installing vinyl tile.

Unfortunately, laminated lumber has a relatively thin wearing surface and cannot stand up to sanding. Therefore, its useful life is shorter than that of dimensional lumber. But it is quick and easy to install and, if prefinished, requires no messy finishing, as dimensional lumber does. In addition, laminated lumber does not expand and contract with the seasons and is less likely to buckle.

We recommend buying the prefinished, unwaxed version; deglossing the surface; and applying an additional coat or two of polyurethane. If you are going to have someone else do the work, compare bids for

dimensional and laminated wood—you may find a low contractor's price for the more durable solid wood flooring.

Resilient Flooring

Resilient flooring is a term used for sheets or squares of synthetic floor-covering materials. Linoleum was the first resilient flooring, followed by asphalt tiles and then vinyl flooring. Figure 2.6 shows vinyl-composition tile and vinyl-sheet flooring. Resilient flooring can be laid over either concrete or wood.

All resilient flooring, whether in the form of tiles or large sheets, is thin. Consequently, any irregularities in the subfloor show through. Where the subfloor is rough, it is cheaper to cover it with carpeting. But where the subfloor is smooth, resilient flooring offers low cost, abundant colors and patterns, resistance to moisture and stains, and easy cleaning.

Nowadays, most resilient flooring is either vinyl- or asphalt-based. Vinyl-based flooring types include solid

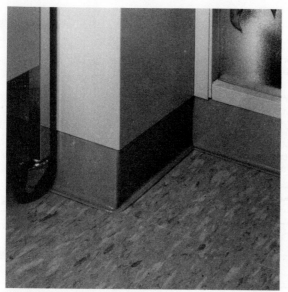

(Photo by the makers of Armstrong vinyl flooring.)

FIGURE 2.6 Resilient flooring can come in tile (left) or sheet (right). Tiles take a separate base molding; sheet flooring can be turned up the wall to create an integral base.

vinyls and vinyl-composition materials. Refer to Table 2.6 (page 44) for resilient-floor options.

SOLID VINYLS This material is considered the highest quality, but it is also the most expensive. It is washable and easiest to clean; it resists oils, bleach, acid, and grease. It has good acoustical properties, wears well, and is comfortable underfoot. Moreover, solid vinyls come in a great variety of patterns and colors.

However, solid vinyls have the disadvantages of high initial cost, low resistance to solvent-based cleaning materials, and a tendency to dull under heavy foot traffic. This last problem is remedied by rubbing with steel wool or an acrylic-based compound.

VINYL-COMPOSITION TILES These are the most popular flooring materials used today. Since they resist oil, grease, acids, and alkalis, strong cleaning agents can be used on them.

Vinyl-composition tile, also referred to as VCT, resists cracking and denting. It is relatively cheap, is a good insulator, is very durable, and is suitable for use over concrete.

The decoration on vinyl-composition tiles is applied by embossing. In addition, *indexed embossed* designs are available, meaning that separate tiles can be matched edge to edge to give the tiles the look of a much larger piece. The decoration, however, may or may not go all the way through the materials—if it does not, of course, the decoration is more likely to wear away.

ASPHALT TILES Asphalt tiles largely have been replaced by VCTs, because asphalt does not resist grease well and comes only in a limited number of colors and styles. Nevertheless, asphalt tiles are the toughest of the resilient flooring materials. They also are the least expensive to both purchase and maintain.

Asphalt tiles are preferred in basements because of their moisture resistance. They are also fire resistant and skidproof. However, they tend to crack and show dents over time.

SHEET FLOORING Sheet flooring is laid down as a single unit, rather than as individual units like tiles; so, at least in small- to medium-size rooms, there are no seams. Sheet flooring falls into two types: linoleum and vinyl.

Linoleum is a smooth-surfaced flooring made of linseed oil and wood fillers applied to a felt or burlap backing sheet. In wet areas (for example, kitchens and baths), it has been replaced by vinyls, which have greater resistance to moisture and chemicals.

Still, linoleum has its place. It is inexpensive, especially if laid down like a rug over a floor area. You don't necessarily need to fit it to the exact dimensions of the floor, as you do with wall-to-wall carpeting, nor must you use a base molding to join it to the wall. Generally, linoleum is sold in room-size "rugs" of 6 × 8 ft, 8 × 10 ft, and so on. Laid down as a rug, without further trouble, it costs only about 35 to 55 cents/sq ft. Where it does not meet the wall, you can paint the subfloor with a complementary color or pattern.

Vinyl-sheet goods are all made with a vinyl base and fall into two categories: inlaid and rotovinyl.

Inlaid vinyl is the stronger, more durable, and better value of the two. It consists of thousands of vinyl granules built up layer by layer and then fused under heat and pressure. The process yields a rich look with a noticeable depth of color.

Inlaid vinyl is particularly durable and resistant to gouges and chips. Even if it does chip, the blemish is not likely to show because the pattern extends all the way through the material.

Inlaid vinyls are heavy and, thus, difficult to handle. Generally, a prudent homeowner has them installed by professionals.

Rotovinyls are decorated by a rotogravure process, which combines photography and printing. Rotogravure allows great variety and clarity of designs, which are protected by a topping of clear vinyl or polyurethane. This top coating is called the *wear layer* and should have a minimum thickness of 10 mils; 25 mils is best.

All rotovinyls are made with an inner core of foamed or expanded vinyl that provides cushioning. Generally, the more cushioning there is, the higher the price.

Below the cushion is a mineral-fiber layer that prevents stretching. It also resists moisture and alkaline elements that might seep up from below.

Carpeting

Good value from carpets is a function of how long they stand up to wear. Their wear resistance depends mainly on four factors: fiber, pile, texture, and backing.

FIBER The bulk, luster, and soil-hiding characteristics of various synthetics are determined by the shape of the fiber as it is spun from a heated liquid. Synthetics such as nylon, polyester, and olefin are often combined or blended with natural fibers to achieve the best characteristics of both natural and synthetic fibers.

Table 2.7 (page 45) summarizes the qualities of the most popular fibers. Figure 2.7 shows some types of carpet construction.

PILE The wear resistance of a carpet is also determined by its construction, or pile. There are three main types: woven, needle punch, and tufted. Woven pile is the most expensive and needle punch the least.

The old style of making rugs was to weave fibers in and out of a jute and cotton backing, producing a woven pile. The process is expensive and the quality high.

Needle-punch fabric is formed by binding loose fibers to a backing material using the random action of a barbed sewing needle. Needle-punch carpeting is useful outdoors and in heavily trafficked areas. It has a dense pile, which allows it to stand up to heavy use, but it does tend to attract lint.

Tufted construction is now by far the most common type. Tufted carpet is made by machine-stitching the pile onto a premade backing. The good wearability of tufted carpet, as exemplified by high-quality commercial carpeting, results from low pile height and high density.

TEXTURE The texture of carpet is a function of the shearing that takes place after the fiber is attached to the backing. Three basic types are made: loop pile, cut pile, and selectively sheared pile.

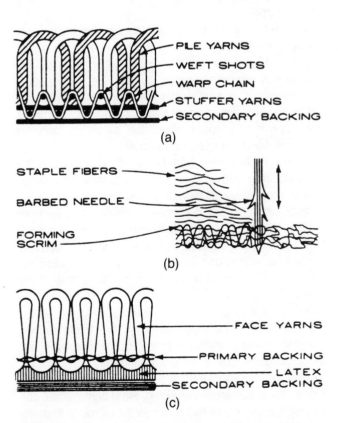

FIGURE 2.7 Three carpet constructions: (a) woven, (b) needle-punch, (c) tufted.

Level loop (also called round wire) means that the fibers stitched to the backing have not been cut off at the top. This pile has excellent crush resistance, is easy to maintain, and wears well. Low-level loop is excellent for a kitchen or family room, especially with a rubber backing.

Cut pile means that the tops of the loops have been sheared off. *Selectively sheared* styles combine level loop and cut pile, making different levels of pile that form patterns.

In the cut-pile group, the luxury texture is smooth-cut pile, also called *plush.* The yarn is sheared at a single level so that it appears smooth. Its high density makes it desirable for formal areas, such as living rooms. But, since it does show footprints and furniture marks, it is not recommended for high-traffic areas.

Shag and *minishag* piles are very long and are usually preferred in low-traffic areas. They collect dirt easily, and small items can be lost in them.

Saxony, which is similar to plush, uses a heavier yarn. Each tuft is individually distinguishable in a saxony.

BACKING A primary backing of synthetic olefin or natural jute is fixed to tufted carpeting as it is produced. A second backing is attached later and adds stability to the carpet.

Synthetic backings, which can be woven or nonwoven, are immune to rot and mildew and are nonallergenic. Unwoven synthetic backings are superior because they cannot unravel.

Jute, which is sometimes available only erratically, offers greater dimensional stability than do synthetics. Because it is a rough fiber, the carpeting adheres better to jute than to other materials.

Foam rubber also can be used as a secondary backing that provides a built-in cushion. Cheaper, lower quality carpets have foam backing.

PADDING Although it increases initial costs, padding is desirable because it adds immensely to the durability of a carpet. Padding also increases resilience, comfort, insulation, and sound absorption. If padding is too soft or thick, however, it is easier to punch a hole in the carpet by accident.

Padding can be separate from or bonded to the carpet. Commonly used paddings are foam rubber, sponge rubber, urethane foam, polyesters, and felt. Sponge rubber offers the most softness.

TIPS ON BUYING CARPETING Watch out for advertisements for commercial carpeting. Real commercial carpeting usually costs two or three times more than the residential kind.

Get at least a 12 × 12-in. sample of your carpet

purchase so you can check on delivery day that you have been sent the proper goods.

Don't use a foam pad or backing in a room heated with electric baseboard heat, because the rubber will dry out.

Have your purchase agreement state:

1. The kind of fiber by weight
2. The kind of weave
3. The color, with code number
4. The exact yardage and price
5. The installation fee, if any
6. The total price

In addition, make sure your contract states that the carpet meets flammability standards and guarantees such qualities as colorfastness, durability, and shrinkage resistance. If you are exceptionally concerned about color, look at the rolls in stock and take down a lot number—actual colors can vary lot to lot.

If your carpet buckles in high humidity, wait and see if it flattens again in low humidity. If buckles are serious, have the installer restretch the carpet—restretching is common following an installation and should not add to the price.

FLOORING FOR KITCHENS AND BATHS

Kitchen and bathroom floors have special requirements because of the water that usually lands on them. The traditional high-grade method of dealing with the water threat in bathrooms was to pour 2 in. of concrete and lay in ceramic tile. Today, that method is inordinately expensive.

More and more, protection for bathroom and kitchen floors is provided by applying synthetic sheets or tiles to a plywood underlayment with adhesive. The underlayment is laid over plywood or other paneling nailed to the floor joists. Although no synthetic has the 50-year life of ceramic tile in cement, putting tile or sheet flooring in kitchens and baths is a lower cost alternative. Only when inexpensive ceramic tiles are purchased at a discount and glued over underlayment does the cost come into line with that of synthetic materials.

Subflooring and Underlayment

Where resilient flooring is to be used, the support below should consist of two layers: (1) the subfloor,

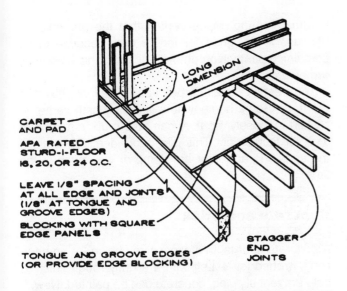

APA RATED STURD-I-FLOOR

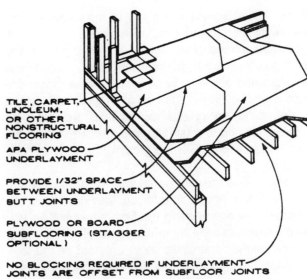

PLYWOOD UNDERLAYMENT

FIGURE 2.8 Subfloors and underlayment for wet areas need to be rot resistant. For baths and kitchens, use two layers—a bottom subfloor and then an underlayment—on which the finish floor will be laid.

which is plywood or other board nailed to the floor joists, and (2) a smoother layer of panels making up the underlayment.

Of the three layers—subfloor, underlayment, and finish flooring—the underlayment is the most likely to fail when exposed to moisture. Non-water-resistant paneling, untempered hardboard, and uncoated particleboard are poor choices for underlayment. Exterior-grade plywood is best, tempered hardboard is second best, and particleboard specially treated for wet application is third best (see Figure 2.8).

Resilient Flooring

For the finish flooring, the new no-wax, vinyl-composition tiles and sheet flooring have very little resilience and cost more than 1/8-in. asphalt tiles, even though they are only half as thick.

No-wax tiles have other problems as well. They usually bear a design that is merely printed on the surface and, thus, is susceptible to wearing away. In addition, their shine can wear off under heavy use, and you will discover that the no-wax tiles really do need care, after all.

Here is our recommendation: For the most cost-effective flooring in kitchens and bathrooms, choose asphalt tiles. Asphalt is an older material and the colors are more limited, but these tiles last a long time and cost half as much as vinyl-composition tiles.

Ceramics

Ceramic tiles are made of clays that are glazed and fired in a kiln. Quarry tiles, a variation, are unglazed, are larger than standard ceramic tiles, and are usually 1/2-in. thick—a quality that makes them exceptionally long-lasting.

Most ceramic tile is removed by a homeowner not because it is failing, but because its color and pattern look out of fashion. For the longest tile service life, select conservative colors and patterns and add style to the room with other materials like paint, shower curtains, accessories, or window treatments.

If you use ceramic tile, the entire floor support below must be very sturdy and inflexible or the tiles will pop off. Nail down the subfloor and underlayment materials with 7-penny, tempered, screw-shank flooring nails set at an angle. Use floor-patching filler to smooth out depressions.

Choose smooth-faced tiles for floors, to make cleaning easier. Reserve quarry tiles for kitchens; they absorb water and receive less of it in kitchens. Bear in mind that larger tiles have fewer joints—thus, there is less grout to become dirty—but they also require the sturdiest subfloor and underlayment. Conversely, mosaic tiles have more grout, but don't require such a sturdy subfloor and underlayment. The 1-in.-square tiles come already adhered to a 1-ft-square backing sheet. These sheets are glued to the underlayment and the tiles on top are grouted in place.

One advantage of ceramic tiles is their easy maintenance—they are highly resistant to oil, grease, and moisture and are easy to clean. But some grouts are porous and retain dirt. New kinds of grout now on the market, either epoxy- or silicone-based, are said to be less porous and to retain dirt less easily. Even so, we recommend wiping over the grout with a liquid silicone sealant.

Ceramic tiles are considered a classy accessory and add value to a house. In addition, they can be laid by an amateur—even cutting the tiles is easier than you would think with a tile cutter and a pair of nipper pliers. Unfortunately, ceramic-tile floors are hard on the feet, are painful to children's knees, and are the nemesis of dropped glasses.

Carpeting

Bath carpet is a good choice for the bathroom. To compare carpet with ceramics in a bathroom, consult Table 2.8 (page 46). Bath carpet is the least expensive flooring for a bath, but it also is the least durable. If you treat the underlayment with preservative and replace the carpet every few years, however, the long-run cost of carpet is still less than that of both vinyl and ceramic flooring. Make certain that the preservative you use is designed for indoor use, because those containing pentachlorophenol and inorganic arsenates are highly toxic.

You needn't install carpet wall to wall or affixed to the floor. Some homeowners like their bath carpet to be laid in loosely, so they can take it up from time to time for laundering. This is a good idea, especially if the carpeting and floor are damp or wet much of the time.

Concrete and Brick

A concrete floor is an inexpensive choice for an addition's ground level. Left with a slightly rough finish to help prevent slipping, concrete can be painted. New, it can be stained, sealed, and polished for only about 40 cents/sq ft. Painted or stained, concrete makes an attractive, nonslip, energy-efficient, cleanable floor. Concrete can be made even more decorative if, when wet, it is pressed with molds of patterns.

If poured as a slab in new construction, a concrete floor is inexpensive, but it is always ready for a more upscale topping of area rugs, tile, wood, or carpeting when the pocketbook allows. Still, keep in mind that walking on the unforgiving surface of concrete, as on ceramic tile, can be tiring to the feet and legs.

TABLE 2.1
Wood Floor Improvements

THE PROJECT
Refinish 60-year-old oak strip flooring in a 12′ × 12′ living room, 10′ × 10′ dining room, and adjoining hall.

Options	Cost/sq ft Contracted	Cost/sq ft DIY	Project Contracted	Project DIY	Difficulty Level DIY Advice		Comments and Recommendations
Paint and Stencil Clean and prep. Apply 2 coats of pigmented polyurethane. Make stenciled border.	$1.14	$0.48	$185 w/o stencil $435 with stencil	$107 w/o stencil CC $160 with stencil	**2**	Totally changes the feel of a room in one day.	Good option for bedrooms and dark rooms where pastel colors can reflect light.
Circular-Sand and Refinish Spot-scrape damage. Circular-sand with a buffer. Edge and apply 2 coats of a polyurethane finish.	$1.15	$0.46	$385 VB	$154 VB	**2**	A perfect DIY task. Low skill requirement and high quality. Rent buffer and reciprocating sander at $35–$48/ day.	Best all-around option. Also excellent for parquet.
Strip and Refinish Apply paint remover. Wash surface. Apply 2 coats of penetrating oil.	$1.63	$0.56	$546	$188	**3**	Potentially dangerous job. Methyl chloride vapors are harmful for extended periods. Change filters in canaster frequently.	Recommended *only* for historic buildings. Most floor finishes are difficult to apply after paint remover.
Belt-Sand and Refinish Sand and edge, 3 passes. Apply 2 coats of polyurethane finish.	$2.10	$0.85	$704	$285	**5**	Don't ever use 36 grit. It gouges too easily. Rent sander and edger at $60–$75 a day.	Best for heavily damaged and extensively patched floors.
Add-ons: Floor Staining	$0.45	$0.11	$150	$37	**1**		For heavily stained floors and somber atmospheres.
3rd Coat of Finish	$0.27	$0.11	$94	$37 VB	**1**		*Always* use 3 coats. The additional cost is minimal but protection is significant.

TABLE 2.2
Clear Floor Finishes for Wood

Options	Base	Cost/Gal.	Difficulty Level DIY Advice		Comments and Recommendations
Shellac	Alcohol	$14–$22	**2**	Dries fast. Least durable. OK as primer.	Avoid as top coat. Extremely flammable.
Varnish	Oil-based alkyd resin	$18–$36 CC	**2**		Can be touched up very easily.
Penetrating Oil	Oil	$20–$25	**2**	Easy, but no surface film to protect wood.	Not recommended unless bimonthly recoating is desired.
Urethane Resins Alkyd	Oil	$20–$36	**2**	Easy to apply. Very durable.	Best buy. Use 3 coats. Can't be touched up without sanding off gloss.
Moisture-cured	Oil	$32–$38	**3**	Hard to apply.	
Water-based	Water	$35–$60	**3**	Can be hard to apply.	Safer to apply than oil-based resins.
Acrylic Finish	Water	$28–$32	**2**	Easy to apply.	Option where solvent-based finish is outlawed or undesirable.
Epoxy	Oil-based with epoxy esters	$32–$36 VB	**3**		Very hard finish. Best life-cycle costs. Will last longer than the furniture.

TABLE 2.3
Floor Paints

Options	Cost/gal.	Difficulty Level DIY Advice		Comments and Recommendations
Acrylic Latex Floor Enamel	$12–$18 CC	**1**	Easiest to use.	Least expensive and safest.
Alkyd-Oil Floor Enamel	$15–$19	**1**		
Pigmented Polyurethane	$16–$21 VB	**1**		Best balance of durability and price.
Chlorinated Rubber	$27–$39	**2**		This pool paint is the only way to go below grade on concrete.
2-Part Epoxy	$30–$48	**3**	Must mix and use right away.	Longest lasting, most expensive option.

TABLE 2.4	THE PROJECT
New Flooring Options	Replace the flooring in a carpeted 10′ × 14′ den with existing rough plywood subfloor.

Options	Cost/sq ft Contracted	Cost/sq ft DIY	Project Contracted	Project DIY		Difficulty Level DIY Advice	Comments and Recommendations
Carpet and Pad Install 25- to 35-oz. nylon over ½″ rebond pad with tack strips and hot-melt tape at seams.	$18/yd	$14.85/yd	$280 CC	$230 CC	**3**	Rent a carpet stretcher. Pull carpet onto tack strips.	Quick-change option. Absorbs sound. Let the pros install it.
Vinyl Composition Tile Install ⅜″ plywood underlayment and 12″ × 12″ self-adhering tiles (0.080 gauge).	$2.51	$1.83	$352	$257	**1**	Easiest DIY floor.	Good DIY option for dens, kitchens, and play areas.
Vinyl Sheet Flooring Install ⅜″ plywood underlayment and 0.065 no-wax vinyl sheet 12′ wide.	$3.23	$2.26	$452	$316	**3**	Buy an installation kit.	Bath floors benefit most from seamless flooring.
Prefinished Oak Parquet Install 5⁄16″ thick, 12″ × 12″ oak squares set in adhesive.	$4.50	$3.65	$630	$512	**2**	Easiest DIY wood option.	Wear surface only ⅛″ thick. Add additional layers of finish to extend life.
3″ Prefinished Oak Strip Install ⅜″ × 3″ × 48″ oak set in adhesive.	$5.33	$4.58	$746	$641	**2**	Quick.	For a longer lasting floor, don't buy prewaxed, and add 2 coats of floor finish. Wear surface only ⅛″ thick.
2¼″ Oak Strip Flooring Install clear red or white oak, sand, and apply 3 coats of urethane finish.	$6.14	$2.93	$860	$410 VB	**5**	Takes lots of carpentry and sanding skills. Rent a power nailer at $15/day and buy nails at $8/100 sq ft.	High quality and long lasting, but expensive.

TABLE 2.5
Wood Floor Choices

THE PROJECT
Install a new wood floor in a 12′ × 14′ living room with a plywood subfloor and worn carpet.

Options	Cost/sq ft Contracted	Cost/sq ft DIY	Project Contracted	Project DIY		Difficulty Level DIY Advice	Comments and Recommendations
Unfinished Pine Strip Install ¾″ × 3½″ grade C or better solid pine. Sand, stain, and apply 3 coats of finish.	$4.37	$2.27	$735 CC	$385 CC	5	Rent a power nailer.	Use a stain or pickled finish for elegant results.
Prefinished Oak Parquet Install ⁵⁄₁₆″-thick, 12″ × 12″ laminated oak squares in mastic.	$4.50	$3.65	$857	$713	2	A table saw makes cutting much easier.	Quick; no sanding mess, but wear surface is only ⅛″ thick.
3″ Prefinished Oak Strip Install ⅜″ × 3″ × 48″ laminated oak over foam, edge glued only.	$5.33	$4.58	$895	$770	2		No sanding mess, but wearing surface is only ⅛″ thick. A pro might underbid your DIY costs. Quick one-day job.
2½″ Oak Strip Install clear, red or white solid oak. Sand and apply 3 coats of finish.	$6.14	$2.93	$1,030 VB	$490 VB	5	Rent a power nailer. Sanding well is a very difficult task.	A good value no matter who installs, because of long life and resale value.
Unfinished Oak Parquet Install ¾″ thick solid white oak 6″ × 6″ woodblocks. Sand and apply 3 coats of finish.	$7.31	$2.95	$1,230	$495	5		A high-quality option over concrete subfloors.
Prefinished Random-Width Planks Install 3″–8″ wide, 4′–16′ long, ⁵⁄₁₆″ thick laminated oak in mastic and nail.	$8.25	$5.15	$1,385	$865	2		Expensive.

TABLE 2.6
Resilient Floor Choices

THE PROJECT
Install a resilient floor in a 6'-wide × 15'-long kitchen with cabinets at each side.

Options	Cost/sq ft Contracted	Cost/sq ft DIY	Project Contracted	Project DIY	Difficulty Level DIY Comments		Comments and Recommendations
Linoleum Install precut, rollout sheet not glued down.	$0.85	$0.45	$75 CC	$40	**1**		Great for bedrooms and dens. Will rot in contact with water, so stick with vinyl in baths and kitchens.
Asphalt Tile Install ⅛"-thick asphalt tile, 9" × 9"-square C/D color group with trowel-applied adhesive.	$1.36	$0.45	$122	$40 CC	**1**		Best below-grade option. Wears very well if not in contact with solvents.
Vinyl-Composition Tile Self-Stick, No-Wax					**1**		
0.080" thick	$1.74	$1.00	$135 VB	$90			The cheapest grades are not bargains
0.050" thick	$1.25	$0.60	$114	$54			Thicker grades are good kitchen choices.
Vinyl-Composition Tile Install ³⁄₃₂"-thick vinyl-composition tile 12" × 12" square with trowel-applied adhesive.	$1.56	$0.84	$140	$75	**1**		
Sheet Vinyl, No-Wax					**3**	Buy an installation kit.	Inexpensive sheet goods are fine choices for low-wear areas like baths.
0.065" thick at $8/yd	$2.55	$1.20	$230	$110 VB			
0.090" thick at $22/yd	$3.80	$2.40	$345	$216 VB			
Solid Vinyl Tile Install ¹⁄₁₆"-thick solid vinyl tile 12" × 12" square with trowel-applied adhesive.	$2.85	$1.20	$256	$108	**1**		Expensive, but lasts a long time.

TABLE 2.7

Comparison of Carpet Materials

Fiber	Trademark	Characteristics
Wool	Woolmark	Wool feels and looks good. Its rough surface hides dirt, and it is an easy material to clean with solvent. Wool also is resilient and withstands high traffic. Disadvantages: Wool is expensive. It holds static electricity. Moths like it, and some people are allergic to it.
Nylon	Anso, Antron, Cadon, Caprolan, Cumuloft, Enkalure, Enkaioft	Developed in 1938 by DuPont. It is strong, colorfast, and resistant to matting. It withstands heavy traffic and resists abrasions and dirt. It is not allergenic. It is easy to clean and is resistant to mildew. Nylon is shiny, hard, and slick. If you rub your hand back and forth on it, it can make your skin raw. Disadvantages: Sunlight can fade the color, and nylon can attract static electricity unless treated with an antistatic substance.
Polyester	Avlin, Dacron, Fortel, Encron, Kodel, Trevira	Polyester looks like a combination of nylon and acrylic. The fiber has an internal cross section that hides dirt well. It comes in a variety of colors, resists abrasion, and cleans well. It also is low cost. Polyester usually is soft and slick and has a waxy, almost silky feel. Disadvantages: Because of its high bulk, some manufacturers put in less than acceptable pile, which can be crushed and looks bad.
Polypropylene	Vectra, Herculon, Harvees, Polycrest	This is a petrochemical fiber derived from petroleum oil. It is nonallergenic and has good bulk. It is abrasion-resistant and most forms are also resistant to stains, mildew, and moths. It is best in a flat weave. It is sometimes difficult to tell the new polypropylene from nylon. Disadvantages: It has low resilience and only fair color clarity. It has a low melting point, so can be damaged easily by a dropped cigarette. It also is not very resistant to cleaning solvents.

Acrylic	Acrilan, Creslan, Orlon, Sayelle, Zefram, Zefkrome	Acrylics were developed in 1957 by Monsanto. They usually are used in luxurious textured rugs. Acrylics have good wear qualities, but are less durable than nylon. They resemble wool more than any other synthetic fiber and provide an excellent cover and bulk. They come in a wide range of colors and retain their color well. They also have good resilience to high traffic, are easy to clean, and are not susceptible to moth damage. You can tell acrylics by their nonglossy, clear colors.
		Disadvantages: They have low resistance to abrasion, and they tend to "fuzz."
		Carpet Notes:
		
		There is no such thing as stain-proof carpet—they all stain, some very badly. The two best fibers are
		  1. Anso V by Allied Chemical
		  2. Stainmaster by DuPont

TABLE 2.8
Options for Flooring Wet Areas

THE PROJECT
Replace the flooring in a 7′ × 6′ bath.

Options	Cost/sq ft Contracted	Cost/sq ft DIY	Project Contracted	Project DIY	Difficulty Level	DIY Advice	Comments and Recommendations
Vinyl-Composition Tile Install 3/32″-thick vinyl-composition tile 12″ × 12″ square with trowel-applied adhesive.	$1.56	$0.84	$110	$35	**1**	Quick.	The excess moisture in baths often seeps through the seams in a tile floor.
Carpet Install acrylic plush with a nonskid back over preservative-treated plywood.	$2.85	$0.84	$120	$35 CC	**1**	Carpet by the roll cuts with scissors.	Use a preservative-treated deck to head off decay. Toss carpet out with the shower curtains.
Sheet Vinyl, No-Wax Install 0.065″ thick at $8/yd.	$2.55	$1.20	$145	$56	**3**	Buy an installation kit.	Inexpensive sheet goods are fine choices for low-wear, high-moisture areas like baths.
Quarry Tile Install 6″ × 6″ latex grout, thin set.	$6.45	$3.08	$270	$150	**4**	Rent a heavy-duty tile cutter ($12) or tile saw ($40) to handle these ½″-thick tiles.	Quarry tiles are great for large areas that require maximum durability.
Ceramic Tile Install 1″ × 1″ latex grout, thin set.	$9.20	$4.10	$390	$172 VB	**3**	Good job for DIY. Rent a tile cutter for $6/day.	Consider using at front door or in very heavy traffic areas.

3 Exterior Finishes

The face that your house shows to the world is its exterior finish. Even if that exterior finish is not out of sight, it usually is out of mind.

But one day, you may find that you need to pay attention to your house's exterior. You may need only to do repair and preventive maintenance, you may want to cover unattractive siding with something new, or you may have to put a whole new exterior on an addition or an outbuilding. Table 3.1 (page 54) lists the costs of using different siding materials on large areas of exterior walls.

PAINTING

Without question, the most frequent exterior maintenance task is periodic painting. During the late 1980s, painting the exterior of a house was one of the top ten remodeling values. Nothing makes a house look better to passersby—or potential home-buyers—than a fresh coat of paint. The economic return on a do-it-yourself exterior painting job, if you plan to sell your house, can run to more than ten times the investment. Even when the job is contracted out, the value added is generally higher than that of most other home improvements.

If you plan to stay where you are, however, painting is just a periodic (but necessary) expense. Paint protects the wood underneath from the effects of weather. At the same time, unless it is exceptionally thick, it allows moisture from inside the house to permeate to the outside air.

The problem with paint is that it must be renewed frequently, which makes painting one of the most expensive recurring maintenance jobs. This does not mean that you should automatically cover a house with a so-called no-paint siding such as aluminum or vinyl. There are other ways to reduce the cost and frequency of painting.

Preparation, Preparation, Preparation

Unfortunately, much of the work of painting is not in the painting itself, which at least shows the pleasing results of your labor, but in the preparation. Preparing the siding for painting, in fact, often makes the house look worse—temporarily—but is the single most important chore to make the new coat of paint last longer.

Dirty and continually wetted surfaces must be remedied before a new coat of paint can do its job. In addition, painting over loose paint is just an invitation for the loose base paint to fall away, negating your efforts.

Peeling or cracking paint generally is caused by moisture getting into the boards behind the paint and pushing it off from the inside. The moisture can come from rain, as when gutters do not channel water away from siding, when cracked caulking or eaves allow water behind boards, or when water stands against the house at ground level. Or the moisture can come from inside the house, as when steam or splashing from a shower wafts or seeps through the walls to the inside of the siding. These problems must be corrected at the source before paint is applied to the siding, or new moisture will simply push off the new paint, and you will have wasted your time and money.

If the source of water is a faulty gutter, eave, or caulking, fix it first. If the source is a leaking bathroom wall that allows moisture to pass through to the siding, repair the interior wall of the bathroom.

On the outside, there are additional methods to let the moisture escape. For lapped siding, you can drive thin wedges between the boards. For tongue-and-groove siding, you can drill small holes into the siding for ventilation. Both techniques allow moisture to escape easily so that it will not push against the paint from the inside. The problem of moisture-popped paint is especially prevalent in older houses, where layer after layer of paint has formed an impervious barrier to moisture flow; cracking and peeling result.

If these remedies have been tried or ruled out, and you still have moist wood, ask a home inspector for an opinion. Sometimes, peeling is the result of a poor painting job. Rarely, it may be caused by the wood itself—some resinous pines simply will not hold paint, and it might be best to cover these woods with a new siding.

After correcting leakage problems, the next step is to remove peeling or cracked paint. Use a wire brush, paint scraper, or disk sander. **CAUTION: Wear goggles and a dust mask.**

If you suspect that the old paint contains lead, and 80 percent of pre-1950 homes do, call your local health department. They will tell you how to test for lead paint. Ask them about local laws on lead-paint removal and if they can recommend local contractors certified in removing lead paint.

If there are no laws about lead-paint removal, take these precautions as a minimum: (1) seal off the area with a wind screen from the building to the ground and use a drop cloth on the ground itself; and (2) use removal methods that make as large a particle as possible—large particles are more easily cleaned up and do not so easily become airborne dust, which is poisonous.

Wet scraping is one method used by contractors, and water blasting is an option if the runoff can be contained and carried away. For your health and that of those around you, burning and sanding are the worst methods—the fine particles created become absorbed into the bloodstream and can cause irreversible brain damage, to which young children are particulary susceptible. If your house was built after 1975, it is unlikely to have lead-based paint on the exterior.

A fast way to remove loose paint is to use a 3,000-lb/sq-in. pressure washer. One rents for about $45 to $60/day and attaches to your outdoor faucet and electrical receptacle. It not only blasts away loose paint, but also washes the house, doing the job in about half the time for a fifth of your effort, although some hand scraping may still be needed. Incidentally, sometimes a dingy appearance may signify only that your house is in need of a wash, not a new coat of paint; the neighbors will be just as impressed with your home's new look at considerably less trouble and cost to you.

If your house has a condition called *chalking,* which is the presence of dusty pigment that has separated out from the surface, you eliminate that at the same time as you wash away regular dirt. If you have mildew, you can get rid of that, too, by mixing a bleach solution in with the water—washers usually come with tanks into which such mixing solutions can be placed.

After removing loose paint and allowing the siding time to dry, prime the bare wood as soon as possible. Use an acrylic latex primer that is compatible with the finish coat you will use, preferably one that is made by the same manufacturer.

Preparation for painting can be a time-consuming nuisance. But done well, it makes the paint last twice as long as when done poorly.

Selecting Paints

Choosing the right paint is important. The difference in price per square foot between cheap and expensive paint is minor compared with the total labor that goes into repainting. A good paint also will last longer, so you don't save much by buying cheap paint.

Read the labels. Paint is composed of three ingredients: pigment, binder (or resin), and solvent. Generally, you want a high percentage of binder and of pigment.

If you have a chalking condition, use an oil-based primer. Otherwise, a good-quality acrylic latex exterior primer-and-paint combination gives a longer service life than does oil primer and paint and is cheaper. Latex also "breathes" better than do oil paints and lets more moisture pass from the siding to the atmosphere.

Exterior stains, which are increasingly popular, soak into the wood and leave little or no surface film. They are available in a range of colors: Some are opaque (only the texture of the grain shows through); others are semitransparent (allowing variations in the natural tones of the wood's grain to show through).

The big advantage of stain is that it is easier to apply than paint. Labor is saved at restaining time, too— without paint buildup on the surface, there is little scraping required. Unfortunately, restaining has to be done more frequently than repainting—about every three years instead of every seven—although some of the newer and more expensive brands claim a life of six to seven years. The U.S. Forest Products Laboratory suggests that stains be reapplied when the surface no longer sheds water.

Opaque stains last the longest and protect the best. Some, however, do not soak into the wood as well as the semitransparent ones do, and merely coat the wood. This makes opaque stains more vulnerable to chipping and peeling, like regular paint. Still, they can be applied over paint.

Semitransparent stains should contain wood preservatives; other desirable ingredients are water-repellents and mildewcides. At least one testing group, the Practical Homeowner Institute, has concluded that the oil-based stains protect better and last longer than the latex-based ones. Semitransparent stains should have dark pigmentation, which gives better protection against ultraviolet light.

Durable woods such as cedar, cyprus, and redwood, do not require stain. Still, some homeowners prefer staining and restaining to the natural weathered look.

TYPES OF SIDING

Wood

Lapped wood siding is popular not just because of its architectural allusions to early America, but also because it is economical, handsome, and tough. With the proper insulation, it is a good protection against the elements. Figure 3.1 shows various types of lapped wood siding and how they are attached to the house.

The cost of replacing wood clapboard, which is the most common form of lapped siding, is about $2.90/sq ft installed. Practically speaking, there is hardly ever a reason to totally replace old pine clapboards with new ones. Sometimes, on the sides of a house facing prevailing storms, clapboards crack and curl, particularly if they haven't been painted. Replace these, but if clapboards look all right, leave them. Total replacement should be only a last-resort method used to remove lead-based paint or many layers of built-up paint that no longer let moisture permeate from the inside of the house out.

However, if 20 to 30 percent of the clapboards need replacing, or if you don't like painting, consider other options. Vinyl siding will cost less over its 25-year (or more) life than will repairing a lot of wood siding and doing the two or three required paint jobs. Untreated cedar shingles with natural preservatives are the next least expensive and are very long-lived.

Low maintenance is the main reason to choose a vinyl or aluminum covering. New pine siding or cedar shingles will last longer, if well maintained, and are easier to repair. In historic areas, they may fit in better, too. Unpainted cedar shingles require little or no maintenance; other types of wood siding require periodic caulking (discussed later) and painting.

Aluminum

The two main claims of aluminum siding are that it hides poor-looking or damaged siding underneath and that it requires practically no maintenance. It lives up well to the first claim, less well to the second.

Aluminum siding costs about $3.20/sq ft installed. It is difficult to install yourself because of the expensive tools required for cutting the siding and forming coverings for trim.

True to its advertising, aluminum siding does not rot, rust, or decay. The factory finish will last a long time, but will lose its luster after 10 to 15 years; eventually, it will peel or just wear away.

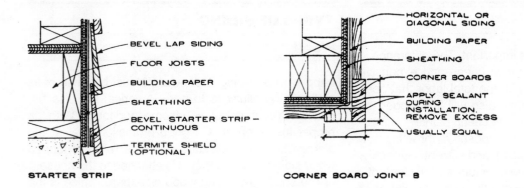

BEVEL LAP SIDING
FLOOR JOISTS
BUILDING PAPER
SHEATHING
BEVEL STARTER STRIP — CONTINUOUS
TERMITE SHIELD (OPTIONAL)

STARTER STRIP

HORIZONTAL OR DIAGONAL SIDING
BUILDING PAPER
SHEATHING
CORNER BOARDS
APPLY SEALANT DURING INSTALLATION. REMOVE EXCESS
USUALLY EQUAL

CORNER BOARD JOINT B

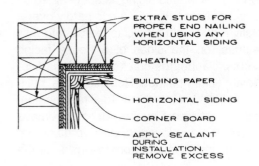

EXTRA STUDS FOR PROPER END NAILING WHEN USING ANY HORIZONTAL SIDING
SHEATHING
BUILDING PAPER
HORIZONTAL SIDING
CORNER BOARD
APPLY SEALANT DURING INSTALLATION. REMOVE EXCESS

CORNER BOARD JOINT D

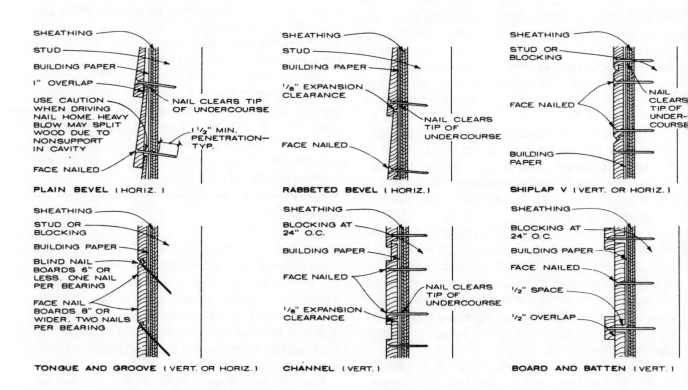

SHEATHING
STUD
BUILDING PAPER
1" OVERLAP
USE CAUTION WHEN DRIVING NAIL HOME. HEAVY BLOW MAY SPLIT WOOD DUE TO NONSUPPORT IN CAVITY
FACE NAILED
NAIL CLEARS TIP OF UNDERCOURSE
1 1/2" MIN. PENETRATION — TYP.

PLAIN BEVEL (HORIZ.)

SHEATHING
STUD
BUILDING PAPER
1/8" EXPANSION CLEARANCE
FACE NAILED
NAIL CLEARS TIP OF UNDERCOURSE

RABBETED BEVEL (HORIZ.)

SHEATHING
STUD OR BLOCKING
FACE NAILED
BUILDING PAPER
NAIL CLEARS TIP OF UNDER- COURSE

SHIPLAP V (VERT. OR HORIZ.)

SHEATHING
STUD OR BLOCKING
BUILDING PAPER
BLIND NAIL BOARDS 6" OR LESS. ONE NAIL PER BEARING
FACE NAIL BOARDS 8" OR WIDER. TWO NAILS PER BEARING

TONGUE AND GROOVE (VERT. OR HORIZ.)

SHEATHING
BLOCKING AT 24" O.C.
BUILDING PAPER
FACE NAILED
1/8" EXPANSION CLEARANCE
NAIL CLEARS TIP OF UNDERCOURSE

CHANNEL (VERT.)

SHEATHING
BLOCKING AT 24" O.C.
BUILDING PAPER
FACE NAILED
1/2" SPACE
1/2" OVERLAP

BOARD AND BATTEN (VERT.)

FIGURE 3.1 Wood-siding fastening techniques. Repairing damaged areas and applying a new coat of paint is often most cost-effective.

When it does peel, it must be painted. After that, it must be painted about every two to three years, because aluminum is not porous and paint does not adhere to it as well as it does to wood. Premium acrylic latex paints can be used, but most aluminum-siding manufacturers provide a special paint for their product. Our recommendation is to replace the siding rather than begin a cycle of periodic painting.

Another drawback to aluminum is that it dents easily. In addition, it offers no insulation, but normally the sheathing below does stop drafts. Insulated aluminum siding is available, but for the extra money, you probably will not save enough energy to make the purchase worthwhile. Foam backing sheets are a cheaper form of insulation than the built-in kind, but have a very poor payback unless the present wall is totally lacking any form of insulation. In that case, you may want to blow in insulation.

Vinyl

Vinyl siding has all the virtues of aluminum siding and is also less expensive. (Figure 3.2 shows how aluminum and vinyl siding are attached to a house.) It can be installed with fewer specialized tools, but does require allowance for expansion and contraction—something that many amateurs do incorrectly.

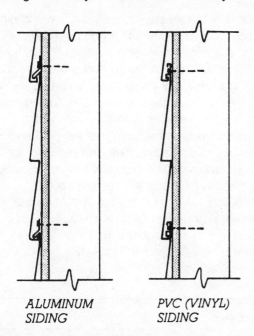

ALUMINUM SIDING   *PVC (VINYL) SIDING*

FIGURE 3.2 Vinyl and aluminum sidings both imitate wood horizontal lapped siding. Their chief advantage is low maintenance. Vinyl is a little cheaper and may last longer. Aluminum must be grounded electrically and can cause interference with radio and television reception.

Vinyl has attained high acceptance by builders and homeowners in recent years, overcoming a mixed reputation when it was first introduced. In those days, the vinyl formulas used by the manufacturers led to siding that sagged and cracked. Most of these problems have been solved.

A common prejudice against vinyl and aluminum siding is that they cause moisture problems. This isn't true, unless they are so poorly installed that water leaks around the edge trim. Both vinyl and aluminum products are designed to promote adequate ventilation behind the sheets.

Vinyl never needs refinishing, because the color runs throughout the piece, front to back. In addition, factory molding can give it patterns that imitate wood siding. Vinyl siding, however, can fade in the sun. It can also crack in very cold weather, or from the force of a well-hit baseball, and strong winds have been known to break if loose. Still, vinyl siding is usually rated for a life of 25 years; the product has been improving and may last 30 to 50 years—no one really knows yet. And it requires exceptionally low maintenance.

Shingles

Shakes and shingles for siding (see Figure 3.3) have been popular for centuries. Cedar shingles are traditional; redwood shingles are also popular.

Finish is mostly an aesthetic consideration. There is, of course, a tradition behind weathered cedar—many people consider it attractive even though it grays and cracks. If you prefer less graying, you can apply a clear preservative, which slows the growth of microorganisms that cause graying and also helps make the shingles last almost indefinitely if applied every 5 to 10 years; even without preservatives, they have been known to last 50 to 75 years. Redwood does not enjoy cedar's weathered-look tradition; it is usually painted or stained.

Shakes are rough and irregular; shingles are milled and appear more orderly when fastened to the house. We recommend unpainted cedar shingles as a good value (either contracted out or done by you) in any climate where they don't turn mossy and if shingles are not an expensive, special-order item. In most places, they can be installed more inexpensively than can pine clapboards.

Both shakes and shingles can be applied over wood surfaces. They can go up even over lapped wood siding without preparation, by nailing them over the

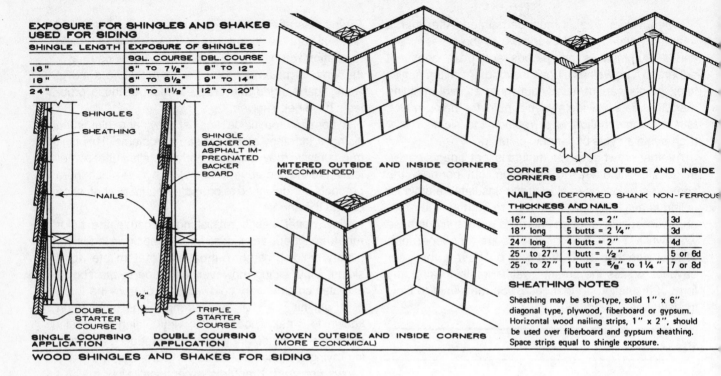

EXPOSURE FOR SHINGLES AND SHAKES USED FOR SIDING

SHINGLE LENGTH	EXPOSURE OF SHINGLES	
	SGL. COURSE	DBL. COURSE
16"	6" TO 7½"	8" TO 12"
18"	6" TO 8½"	9" TO 14"
24"	8" TO 11½"	12" TO 20"

SINGLE COURSING APPLICATION — DOUBLE COURSING APPLICATION

WOOD SHINGLES AND SHAKES FOR SIDING

MITERED OUTSIDE AND INSIDE CORNERS (RECOMMENDED)

WOVEN OUTSIDE AND INSIDE CORNERS (MORE ECONOMICAL)

CORNER BOARDS OUTSIDE AND INSIDE CORNERS

NAILING (DEFORMED SHANK NON-FERROUS) **THICKNESS AND NAILS**

16" long	5 butts = 2"	3d
18" long	5 butts = 2 ¼"	3d
24" long	4 butts = 2"	4d
25" to 27"	1 butt = ½"	5 or 6d
25" to 27"	1 butt = ⅝" to 1¼"	7 or 8d

SHEATHING NOTES

Sheathing may be strip-type, solid 1" x 6" diagonal type, plywood, fiberboard or gypsum. Horizontal wood nailing strips, 1" x 2", should be used over fiberboard and gypsum sheathing. Space strips equal to shingle exposure.

FIGURE 3.3 Shingles and shakes are easy DIY sidings; at corners, they can abut in one of two ways or meet corner boards.

lower edges of the siding. The job of nailing up shakes or shingles goes much faster with a power nailing machine.

Roofing Shingles

Roofing shingles are by far the least expensive total-replacement option for wall siding; installing them is even cheaper than repairing and painting damaged clapboard. Although they invoke images of tarpaper shacks, roofing shingles are often used tastefully on outbuildings. Even on very valuable, antique New England houses, roofing shingles are sometimes found on the north face or back side of the house. They are installed easily, do not need painting, and are fire resistant. In addition, maintenance is practically nil over their 30-year life.

Brick

As a new siding, brick is expensive. A contractor charges between $9 and $11/sq ft to build a veneer of brick around a house. There are only two reasons to sheathe an existing house in brick: your fire code requires it or you love brick. Brick's lower maintenance

costs do not usually offset the extremely high initial costs.

Brick is relatively easy to maintain; even cleaning is optional. Until recently, experts thought that dirt and pollutants ate into brick, deteriorating it. Now, however, they think that such coatings add protection and that abrading them away exposes the softer insides of the brick. If cleaning is done, it should be done gently.

A garden hose often works fine, or you can rent a pressure washer. Its scouring spray, plus any added cleansing agents, blasts away grime. Only as a last resort should brick be sandblasted—it can damage the brick, requiring a sealer to keep out water.

Bricks that have been painted should be periodically repainted. Where the mortar is crumbling, it should be scraped out and reapplied fresh, a process called *repointing* (see Chapter 8, Masonry). This is a tedious but necessary job.

Stucco

Stucco has been popular since before recorded history, and for good reason: It is tough, fireproof, and offers no seams into which water can seep. However, it can develop pits and cracks over time, and those must be patched to prevent water penetration into the house. The rate of deterioration depends on the climate and the quality of the original work.

At half the price of brick, stucco is commonly used in hot climates and even in hot, wet climates. It resists both the sun and organisms that cause rot. Stucco holds up less well in the freeze-thaw cycles of colder regions, and very severe salt air erodes it unless it is painted.

Stucco is difficult for an amateur to apply over large areas, but it is relatively easy to patch. When repairing stucco, it is best to work out of direct sunlight and at a temperature between 40°F and 80°F. Low humidity also causes the stucco to dry too rapidly, which makes for poor adhesion to the subsurface.

Some stucco is colored as it is mixed and does not require paint; some is painted after being applied; and some is left its natural light gray. In the long run, leaving the stucco untreated is the least expensive option, even considering the cost of greater maintenance and the shorter life. However, untreated stucco does streak and stain.

Traditionally, stucco is applied over masonry such as cinder blocks or bricks, or, for wood-sided houses, over wire mesh. In applications over wire mesh, portland cement is used. Some new stucco is applied over styrofoam, using acrylic cement. Styrofoam adds insulation value, but is expensive; we recommend it only when other kinds of insulation, such as blow-in insulation, are not feasible. In addition, stucco over styrofoam is more susceptible to dents and gouges because stucco is thin and styrofoam is soft. And the durability of the installation is highly dependent on the skill of the installer in fastening the material, applying the stucco in the proper thickness and number of coats, and sealing joints so they don't crack or leak.

Hardboard and Plywood Panels

Faced with a major overhaul of a home's exterior, remember hardboard and plywood panels. They go up quickly and, unlike vinyl or aluminum siding, provide strength as well as a covering. However, they are not quite as durable as some of the other kinds of siding.

In modern construction, builders often divide the function of strengthening the frame of a house from that of keeping weather out. First, they apply strong panels to studs, then they fasten the structually weak vinyl or aluminum siding on top. A hardboard or plywood panel made to withstand weather as well as give strength does both jobs with only one installation effort

and saves money, too. If you are building a new addition or rebuilding walls from the studs out, there are important savings in one-step wall coverings. For instance, let's compare a dual-siding system with single-paneling:

- ½-in. asphalt-impregnated sheathing plus vinyl siding: $3.50/sq ft
- Hardboard panel plus a factory-applied finish: $2.36/sq ft

The saving is $1.52/sq ft.

The plywood panels used for exterior siding are usually called T1-11, a term based on federal standards for plywood production. They are grooved parallel to the 8-ft edges and look like board-and-batten siding when put into place vertically (see Figure 3.4). They can also be nailed on horizontally.

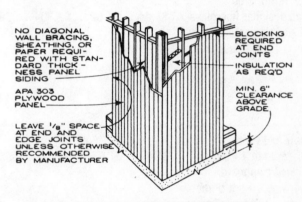

NO DIAGONAL WALL BRACING, SHEATHING, OR PAPER REQUIRED WITH STANDARD THICKNESS PANEL SIDING

APA 303 PLYWOOD PANEL

LEAVE ⅛" SPACE AT END AND EDGE JOINTS UNLESS OTHERWISE RECOMMENDED BY MANUFACTURER

BLOCKING REQUIRED AT END JOINTS

INSULATION AS REQ'D

MIN. 6" CLEARANCE ABOVE GRADE

PANEL SIDING VERTICAL APPLICATION

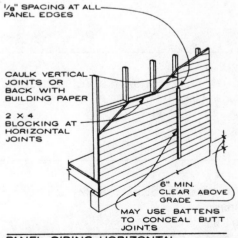

⅛" SPACING AT ALL PANEL EDGES

CAULK VERTICAL JOINTS OR BACK WITH BUILDING PAPER

2 X 4 BLOCKING AT HORIZONTAL JOINTS

6" MIN. CLEAR ABOVE GRADE

MAY USE BATTENS TO CONCEAL BUTT JOINTS

PANEL SIDING HORIZONTAL

FIGURE 3.4 Plywood panels go up quickly and act as both the structural sheathing and the exterior siding. Prestained, preservative-treated panels minimize maintenance and finishing costs.

Such panels are often seen on vacation houses in the mountains or along the seashore. Order them factory-stained. Stained surfaces need periodic recoatings, but these go on two to three times faster than installing unfinished panels and then painting them.

Lower grade panels have the reputation of coming apart over time. Ask for "agency certified" brands rather than "mill certified" ones. The former is manufactured to higher specifications.

TABLE 3.1
Siding Repair and Replacement Options

THE PROJECT
Renew the exterior finish of a clapboarded, 24' × 32', 2-story frame house requiring 15% new siding and a paint job.

Options	Cost/sq ft Contracted	Cost/sq ft DIY	Project Contracted	Project DIY	Difficulty Level DIY Advice		Comments and Recommendations
Asphalt Shingles Install designer fiberglass-asphalt shingles over Dupont Tyvar housewrap.	$1.44	$0.62	$2,304 CC	$980	**2**	Easy.	Heavy asphalt fiberglass shingles are a 30-year, maintenance-free, class-A, fire-resistant siding. Consider them at the gable ends of houses and for second stories.
Repair and Paint Replace up to 15% of damaged clapboard; power wash. Spot prime; topcoat with acrylic latex paint.	$1.70	$0.36	$2,728	$580 CC	**3**		Highest payback option if you plan to sell your house. Acrylic latex paints last about 7 years between coats. Old clapboard will last forever if you touch it up once a year.
Plywood Siding Install 5/8"-thick T-111 siding with 1" × 4" pine trim, all stained.	$1.97	$0.76	$3,152	$1,216	**3**		Can serve as both sheathing and siding. Get a good grade and keep it painted or stained, or it will delaminate.
Hardboard Panels Install 4' × 9' sheets or 7/16"-thick preprimed hardboard with battens. Apply one coat of paint.	$2.02	$0.72	$3,520	$1,150	**3**		Not recommended. Needs paint frequently and is subject to moisture damage. For a little more, buy vinyl or cedar shingles.

Options	Cost/sq ft Contracted	Cost/sq ft DIY	Project Contracted	Project DIY	Difficulty Level DIY Advice		Comments and Recommendations
Hardboard Lap Siding Install 8"-wide, 7/16"-thick prefinished strips with 1" × 4" pine trim.	$2.36	$0.95	$3,770	$1,520	**3**		Not recommended, although this is a very prevalent siding in new construction. You have to repaint every 7 years or so. Lots of patterns available.
Cedar Shingles Install 18"-long #1 grade shingles with 8" exposure.	$2.60	$0.65	$4,160	$1,040 VB	**2**	Most time-consuming method.	Especially good as DIY project, or contracted if you are set on natural wood siding. Treat siding with a preservative for longer life. Its natural perservatives will protect it 40–50 years in colder climates.
Vinyl Siding Install over ½"-thick insulated board. Clapboard appearance with 4" laps, wrap trim.	$2.60	$0.88	$4,160 VB	$1,408	**3**	Can be difficult to hang correctly.	Very low maintenance. Lasts 25 years or more. Best long-term investment. Pick your color carefully—it's not changeable. Won't dent and hides scratches. In very hot or cold climates, use 0.04"-thick material.
Pine Siding Install boards 6"-wide stained, with 1" × 4"-wide pine trim.	$2.86	$0.92	$4,576	$1,472	**3**	Easy replacement option, but time-consuming.	Must be restained every 3–4 years to protect wood. Staining is easier than painting over the long haul, since it requires no scraping. Oil-based opaque stain protects best.
Aluminum Siding Install on insulation board backing. Clapboard appearance with 4" laps, wrap trim.	$3.20	$1.25	$5,120	$2,000	**4**	Requires specialized metal tools.	Fairly low maintenance. Finish stays attractive for 15–20 years. Dents.
Stucco Over Mesh Apply 2 coats stucco over expanded wire mesh.	$3.85	$0.96	$6,160	$1,535	**4**		Requires trowling skills and a strong arm.

(Continued on next page)

TABLE 3.1 Continued

Options	Cost/sq ft Contracted	Cost/sq ft DIY	Project Contracted	Project DIY	Difficulty Level DIY Advice	Comments and Recommendations
Stucco Over Styrofoam Apply 2 coats latex-based stucco over 1″ styrofoam.	$5.20	$1.90	$8,320	$3,040	4	If you want stucco, this is expensive insulation. Blown-in insulation is more cost-effective.
Brick Install 4″ veneer brick including window and door extensions.	$9.39	$2.46	$21,000	$4,000	5	Refacing a frame house with brick is a low-maintenance measure, but this doesn't offset high initial cost.

Caulking, Weatherstripping, and Insulating

Chosen intelligently, improvements around the house that keep the inside air comfortable can end up saving you far more money than you spent to do the improvements. When your energy bill goes down, there's newfound money in your pocket.

The three basic ways to keep inside air comfortable are (1) plug leaks through which outside air enters and inside air escapes; (2) install insulation, which makes heat transfer through walls far more difficult; and (3) make the heating source more efficient. The first two methods are the subject of this chapter and should be part of any strategy for making a home more comfortable at low cost. The third method is discussed in Chapter 12, Heating and Cooling Systems, and in Chapter 17, Energy-Saving Ideas.

In Chapters 12 and 17, we'll take a closer look at energy-saving strategies and how to decide which large-ticket energy-saving investments to make. For now, we'll look at the smaller improvements that bring down energy costs almost immediately.

PLUGGING LEAKS

Energy experts estimate that between 15 and 50 percent of the heating and cooling costs in older houses can be blamed on air leaks in the building shell. A small amount of air exchange is desirable to rid the house of stale (even unhealthy) air, so something like a 15-percent heat loss from infiltration is inevitable without a heat exchanger, a device that will let inside air escape outdoors while retaining indoor heat. But 50 percent is far too much. Fortunately for homeowners, fixing these leaks with caulk and weatherstripping can reap bigger savings than can any other measure, and at relatively low costs.

Studies have found where leaks tend to occur and to what extent (see Figure 4.1). Some research has shown that in an average house, the lengths and widths of leaking cracks add up to the equivalent of one or two open windows. Indeed, engineers measure heat loss from air infiltration in square inches or square feet.

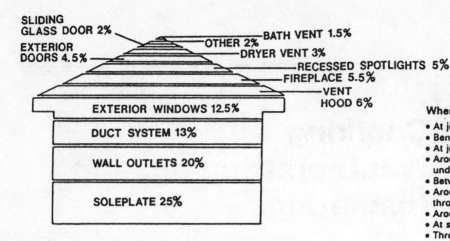

Where air infiltration occurs

- At joints between basement walls and floor slab
- Beneath soleplate of frame walls
- At joints between eave sheathing and fascia
- Around door bottom and threshold,
  under threshold
- Between chimneys, vents and ducts
- Around pipes and electrical feeds that pass
  through exterior walls
- Around electrical outlets and switches
- At siding seams and corners
- Through loose siding

FIGURE 4.1   Pressurize a tract house with a device called a *blower door* (a fan powerful enough to blow air through the cracks of a door frame) and you will probably find that it leaks heat in several easy-to-address areas, especially the soleplate, the electrical outlets, the duct seams, and the windows. The illustration shows the average percentage of infiltration from the common sources. Eliminate those leaks and you reduce infiltration as much as 70 percent.

Where to Find Leaks

FOUNDATION The worst leakage of outside air in most wood-frame buildings occurs where the lower wooden wall rests on the masonry foundation (see Figure 4.2). The lowest piece of wood, the horizontal one, is called the *soleplate;* normally, it is laid on the foundation of concrete or cinder block without any kind of seal underneath. (In very old houses, this may be a sill beam.) Since this area is above ground, wind can push through unless the crack is plugged. A good solution is to stuff the crack with fiberglass insulation and either rope caulk or acrylic caulk.

WINDOWS AND DOORS Windows and doors are obvious places to look for leaks, and many materials on the market are made specifically to stop infiltration there. But air gets through walls in other places as well.

BASEBOARD AND TRIM Wind blowing against windows, doors, and siding can enter through a wall and escape where the baseboard and the trim around windows and doors fit imperfectly against the plaster or wallboard. The remedy is a clear or paintable caulk applied on the inside of the house.

OUTLETS, WALL SWITCHES, AND FIXTURES Electrical outlets and switches are housed in metal or plastic boxes that are several inches deep. When these out-

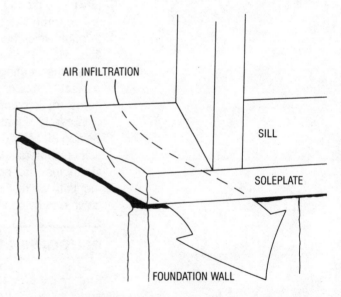

FIGURE 4.2   Air leaks are worst where a framed wall meets the top of the foundation. The crack should be filled with fiberglass insulation, rope caulk, or acrylic caulk.

lets and switches are set into an exterior wall, small gaps between them and the wall surfaces occur. Air also can enter the house through the holes in the box and attached cover plate. Leaks around and through wall outlets and switches and fixtures, in fact, can account for as much as 10 percent of a home's heating or air-conditioning costs.

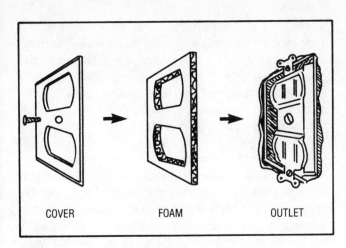

COVER   FOAM   OUTLET

FIGURE 4.3   Outlets and switches are a major source of air infiltration. A foam gasket between the cover and the wall effectively stops air from getting into the room.

To prevent heat exchange and air filtration, try to remove the box or tilt it out so that you can stuff fiberglass insulation behind it. In addition, install inexpensive foam gaskets (Figure 4.3). Then, when you reattach the cover plate, check for cracks between it and the wall; seal any you find with caulk.

Some of worst sources of heat loss are lighting fixtures in the uppermost ceilings, including recessed lighting fixtures. Warm air escaping around them draws cold air in from windows. Caulk any cracks around ceiling light fixtures. If you replace light fixtures, make certain that they are installed according to code; with insulation just above them, they are a serious fire hazard. Make certain that any recessed light fixture is in a nonflammable box that allows for a code-approved air gap between the fixture and any insulation.

FIREPLACES A fireplace can be the focal point of a room, but it is also a constant funnel for heat loss. When not in use, warm air forms a natural draft up the chimney in winter; when in use, much stronger drafts from the fire draw heated interior air up with the smoke.

If you use the fireplace, buy glass doors to save heat both when in use and when not. If the fireplace is now a mere decoration, block the flue as best you can. One method is to bolt a painted board to the brick with L brackets; you can remove it if you ever want to reuse the chimney. Closing off the air that escapes up a fireplace when it is not in use cuts down on a house's total air leakage by about 5 percent.

An alternative is to fit the fireplace with a wood stove made just for this purpose. You get some heat out of the fireplace, but not as much warmed room air is drawn up through the chimney.

DUCTS Another source of leaks is a home's duct

work. Air, warmed by the furnace or cooled by the air conditioner's condenser, leaks out of the ducts into nonlivable space, such as an unfinished basement or attic.

There's no reason to heat or cool these regions, and by stopping those sources of leaks, you deliver more heated or cooled air where you want it—your living rooms, bedrooms, and other habitable areas. If uninsulated ducts are helping to keep pipes from freezing in an otherwise unheated area, this can be done more cost-effectively. Insulate the pipes heavily, or reroute them in or next to heated space. One trick is to run them between floor joists in a crawl space or basement and hang insulation below them. The best way to stop leaks in ducts is to tape duct-work seams with a high-grade aluminum-faced duct tape (see Figure 4.4).

In addition, check where exposed chimneys penetrate an insulated ceiling or exterior wall and caulk the cracks.

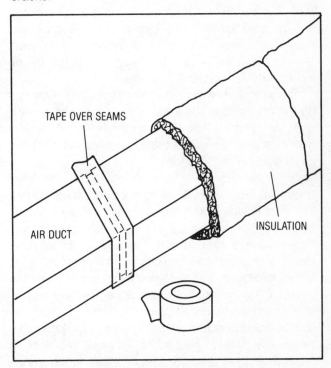

TAPE OVER SEAMS

AIR DUCT

INSULATION

FIGURE 4.4   Fiberglass insulation made especially for air ducts helps to stop leaks from the ducts and prevent heat transfer through the thin duct walls. Use a high-grade aluminum-faced duct tape over seams.

Ventilation

Don't worry about making the average older house too tight; it's almost impossible without extraordinary measures. A tighter house, though, means that you should be more conscious of moisture and toxic fumes building up. You will need good kitchen and bath ventilation. Vent cooking smoke and shop for cleansers that are advertised as containing no toxic chemicals such as petroleum distillates. In addition, if you have a wood stove or fireplace, make sure these aren't adding smoke to the room air because of a dirty chimney, a chimney of insufficient height, or a leaky stove.

If you don't take these precautions, a tighter home may indeed cause health problems, like respiratory irritation and allergic reactions. And if you are unfortunate enough to have urea-formaldehyde insulation in your walls, or radon in your water or basement, *don't* tighten up without remedying these problems first.

Caulk

Caulks available in stores can change rapidly. In the last six months of 1984, for example, siliconized acrylic, water-cleanup 100 percent silicone, and butyl rope caulks were introduced and widely distributed. Prior to that, silicone, latex, and butyl caulks had begun to replace interior oil-based caulks.

Just as there is a dazzling array of caulking materials on the market, there is a wide range of prices, quality, and appropriate uses. Knowing these variations and how to take advantage of them is the best way to keep costs down in caulking jobs.

With one exception, we can offer little advice on controlling labor costs if you contract out caulking work. Our best advice is to make sure the contractor's crew takes its time and does a careful job. Labor costs almost always exceed material costs and vary only slightly if one-part caulking compounds are used.

The exception is this: Have caulkers work from the inside of the house, not the outside. The old way to caulk and weatherstrip focused on filling holes and cracks from the outside. New studies have shown that better energy savings can be achieved by blocking holes from the inside. This should lead to labor savings, because there are no ladders to set up and no cold and rain to slow down the work. The only reason for caulking outside is to prevent water penetration behind the siding or trim. Inside, clean and fill cracks at the baseboard and around door and window trim; using a wet sponge to smooth the latex caulk makes the work go faster.

After you've applied these labor-saving techniques, you must look to the compounds themselves for savings, both in a low purchase price and in that price divided by the number of years of useful life. An analysis of purchase prices and the life spans of a wide range of materials showed that the caulk with the lowest purchase price was not the least expensive over the long run. Yet, even among similar types of long-lasting materials, an astounding range of purchase prices was found, showing that a wise shopper can come up with some real bargains.

For example, Elmer's Tub and Tile silicone caulk was 40 percent cheaper than Dow silicone caulk, according to a *Consumer Reports* study. Store brands of high-performance materials were considerably cheaper than their brand-name counterparts. Further savings, from 10 to 40 percent, were available to buyers of case lots (30 to 36 cartridges or 750 linear feet).

Table 4.1 (page 69) gives costs and characteristics of the major kinds of caulking materials, plus recommendations on the jobs to which they are best suited.

Overall, the following four materials are the most cost-effective for specific, but common, uses:

- Siliconized acrylic: Use for interior and exterior cracks that do not change width because of humidity or the seasons.
- Silicone: Use for interior and exterior cracks that do move with humidity or the seasons. Generally, these are cracks between unlike materials, such as brick and wood, or where wood trim shrinks and swells.
- Silicone with fungicide: Use in bathroom and kitchen applications.
- Copolymer: Use for exteriors when application is possible only in temperatures below 40°F.

Weatherstripping

New Shelter magazine, now known as *Practical Homeowner,* conducted a wide-ranging survey on weatherstripping to identify the most effective materials and methods among the many products available. The magazine discovered that there were 476 possible combinations of materials and applications, not considering brand, and thousands of combinations if brand were included.

The magazine selected 28 kinds of materials and 17 applications, then polled 13 energy experts representing all climatic regions. The experts were asked, "What weatherstripping do you recommend based on your own personal opinions for this particular application?" Of the 28 types of weatherstripping materials offered, 14 did not receive a single vote for any application.

The following list shows common weatherstripping

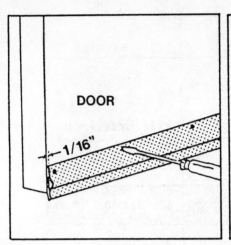
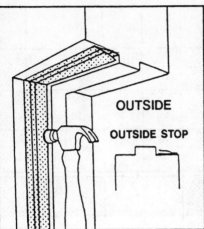

FIGURE 4.5 Thin spring-metal weatherstripping is recommended for doors and goes up with only a hammer and nails. A door sweep (left) needs only a screwdriver, but closes the large gap beneath a door and cuts down significantly on infiltration.

jobs and the materials that the experts recommended for each.

- Standard doors: Spring-metal tension strips (see Figure 4.5) and door sweeps
- Sliding glass doors: Factory-installed weatherstripping, especially those with the bristles held in a plastic retainer
- Exterior basement doors: Foam strips
- Wood double-hung windows: Metal or plastic tension strips
- Wood casement windows: Closed-cell foam strips (air bubbles in the foam are not connected, preventing water penetration and providing greater insulating protection)
- Metal casement windows: Metal tension strips
- Horizontal sliding windows: Metal tension strips

INSULATION

Diminishing Returns and Paybacks

Like putting more and more people to work on a single and limited job, putting more and more insulation in your house eventually brings you up against the law of diminishing returns. The more insulation you have, the more heat it holds in, but at a diminishing rate.

The first inch of insulation in an uninsulated house does more for you than the second, the second more than the third, and so on. The tenth inch of insulation,

in fact, is only 1/76th as effective as the first inch. Somewhere between one and ten inches, there is a point at which the cost of extra insulation is greater than the savings it will generate in reduced fuel consumption (see Figure 4.6).

Therefore, it is important to pay attention to the payback period of insulation. We define this as the number of years it takes for the dollar savings realized by reduced fuel consumption to equal the cost of the improvement, including all the labor and repair required. Sometimes, you will find that the payback period of the insulation improvement is so long that the improvement is not worth the cost and effort.

For example, in mild climates, the cost of blowing in wall insulation, adding a vapor barrier, and repairing damage to the walls caused by the insulation work can take 20 to 30 years to recover—an annual return on the investment of only 3 to 5 percent and not worth the trouble.

When an insulation payback period stretches to ten years or more, you should first spend your resources looking for more effective energy-saving measures. These might include reducing air infiltration, installing storm windows on north-facing walls, or improving the efficiency of your furnace.

For more on payback periods, rates of return, and effective energy-saving techniques, see Chapter 17, Energy-Saving Ideas.

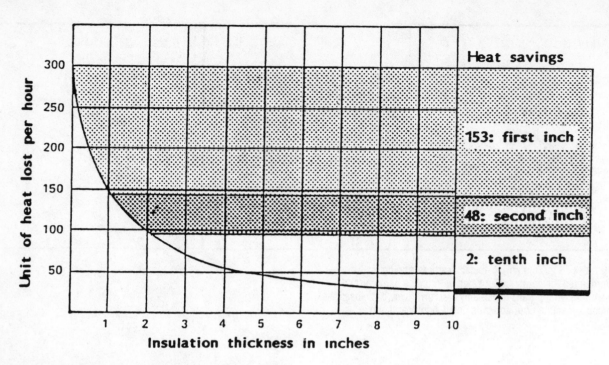

FIGURE 4.6 The first inch of fiberglass insulation is 76 times more effective than the tenth inch. The graph shows that you can save money on insulation by knowing when to stop. You always reach a point when another inch costs more than it saves over time. When adding small amounts of insulation is costly or difficult, don't do it. Look elsewhere for energy savings.

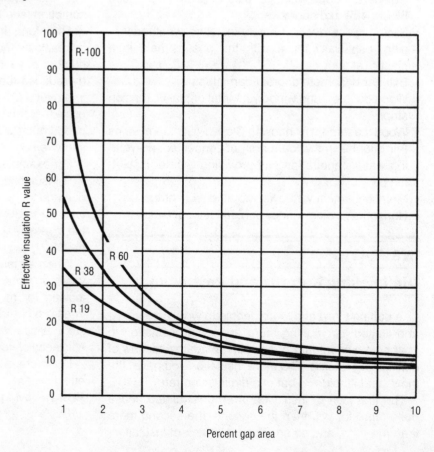

FIGURE 4.7 The graph shows that the difference can be enormous between the R-value of insulation that totally fills the cavity and that of insulation that leaves tiny gaps. If 6-in. fiberglass is installed with just a ⅔-in. gap along the side, its potential R-value of 19 is immediately reduced to 11. Attention to detail is imperative if fuel savings are to be achieved.

How Much Is Needed?

How much insulation should you have? This is a common question, and the answer is, it depends. The U.S. Department of Housing and Urban Development (HUD) recommends that in most parts of the United States, in new homes, the uppermost layer of insulation—that is, the ceiling beneath a roof or unheated attic—should have an R-value (a measure of a material's resistance to heat flow) of 26 to 38, and the walls should have an R-value of 11 to 17 (see Figure 4.7). The R-values required vary depending on the climate and the kind of heating used. For the R-values of different insulations, their costs, and their characteristics, see Table 4.2 (page 70).

The HUD-recommended levels are based on costs of insulation in new construction compared to average fuel savings. They assume about a seven- to ten-year payback, or a 10 to 15 percent annual return on the insulation's initial cost. In a new addition, we strongly recommend walls of 2 × 6's spaced 24 in. apart, with 6-in. fiberglass insulation (R19), in climates where heating or air-conditioning costs exceed $800 a year for an average-size house. (See Table 9.1 [page 127] in Chapter 9, Carpentry.)

But these rules do not hold true for remodeling, where installation cost can run much higher, thus lowering the payback of the improvements for older homes. If you have less than 2-½ in. of fiberglass (R11) in the ceiling, we recommend that you add 6 in. of fiberglass or blow-in cellulose to bring the R-value up to at least 19. Fiberglass insulation comes in 16- or 24-in.-wide rolls, called *blankets,* and 4- and 8-ft blanket sections called *batts.*

If you have more than 2-½ in. of existing insulation in the ceiling and would use a contractor to do the work, the payback period for the new insulation might be 9 to 14 years in a non-air-conditioned, moderate climate—an improvement that should not be a high priority. Obviously, the payback periods differ by climate, fuel type, air-conditioning load, and whether you do the work yourself or pay to have it done.

Fortunately, insulating an attic is relatively easy, and the payback period is greatly shortened if you do it yourself. In that case, and if you have less than 6 in. of insulation in the attic, we recommend that you bring it to 10 in., or even more in very cold climates.

Our recommendations are summarized as follows.

Insulation Recommendations

EXISTING HOUSES
Attics:

If there is less than 2-½ in. of insulation, add 6-in. (R19) batts, or 9-½-in. (R30) batts in very cold climates.

If there is R8 now, add 6-in. (R19) batts.

If there is more than R8 now, take other energy-saving steps first.

Walls:

In a mild climate, never add insulation, unless you are opening the walls for another reason.

In cold climates or air-conditioned houses, blow cellulose into wall cavities to get R13.

NEWLY BUILT HOMES OR ADDITIONS
For walls, use 6-in. (R19) batts set between 2 × 6 studs placed 24 in. apart.

For ceilings, use 9-½-in. (R30) batts or about 10 in. of loose fill insulation.

If you do not know the R-value of the insulation you have in your walls and ceilings, you can often call the local electric or gas company and ask them to make a free or low-cost energy audit for you. Many of them will include an evaluation of your home's construction and the R-values of walls, ceilings, windows, doors, and sometimes floors. Make sure the evaluators check all the walls to see that they are insulated, because some walls might be, while others are not. Generalizations can lead to gross mistakes that make the audit worthless.

When installing insulation, remember that a very small installation error can lead to a very great loss in heat-retaining efficiency (see Figure 4.7). The graph shows that even a small gap created by an ill-fitting batt causes a dramatic loss in R-value and cost-effectiveness, despite the thickness of the insulation. For example, a 10 percent gap in a superinsulated R60 ceiling, which would be exceptionally good, reduces the effectiveness of the insulation to R10, which is mediocre.

Consequently, if you are having a contractor do the work for you, watch carefully when the crew is fitting the batts to the studs, rafters, and joists. If you see insulation poorly cut, fit, or stuffed, make the workers correct the problems or stop work. Otherwise, you'll never stop paying (in fuel consumption) for the mistakes.

A method for ensuring low leakage is to install unfaced friction-fit batts so that you can see and correct any gaps, and then cover the whole with a polyethylene sheeting or other vapor barrier. (Vapor barriers are discussed on page 67.)

Where and How to Install Insulation

The most important place to have good insulation is in the uppermost ceiling of the house. This may be the flat ceiling beneath an unheated attic or, if the attic is heated for a living space, the pitched ceiling that attaches to the roof rafters (see Figure 4.8). In addition, proper insulation and venting at the uppermost parts of the house prevent snow from melting and then refreezing into ice dams that can cause major leaks (see Figure 4.9).

Good insulation is especially important in flat ceilings, because horizontal surfaces lose heat more rapidly than do angled ones. Fortunately, flat ceilings are often the easiest to insulate in older homes, because you can lay the insulation into the ceiling from the attic above.

The most common insulations for open-attic ceilings are fiberglass and cellulose. Both can be poured between ceiling joists from above, or fiberglass blankets or batts can be fitted into place. Ideally, a layer of insulation should cover the joists themselves, not just fill the cavities between. The wood in the joists is not as good an insulator as the insulation around it and, unless the joists are covered at the top, you do not really get the full R-value of the purchased insulation.

Walls are insulated in a number of ways. Existing walls can be insulated with blown materials—fiberglass, mineral wool, or cellulose—from the exterior or interior. For this method, 2- or 3-in.-diameter holes are drilled in the walls and insulation is forced in through a tube from a machine on the ground. Often, blow-in insulating is less expensive if you work from the inside, because it is cheaper to patch drywall than exterior siding, especially if some of the holes are 20 feet off the ground. But if you are covering old siding with new, working through the exterior and then covering with the new siding probably will be the cheaper method. Of the three types of blown material, cellulose is the cheapest, has a high R-value, and recycles paper.

Where a frame wall is new or where either its inside or outside surface has been removed in a repair, the most cost-effective way to add insulation is to staple in fiberglass R13 blankets or batts. Figure 4.10 shows proper fiberglass insulation installation techniques.

Masonry walls are trickier. The most effective, yet expensive, way to insulate is to build an interior wall of 2 × 3 or 2 × 4 studs 24 in. apart directly in front of, but not touching, the masonry. Then 6-in.-thick fiberglass batts are placed between the studs and lapped over the studs' outside edges. In this way, the R-value of the whole wall is increased because less heat is transferred through the studs themselves.

A lower-cost alternative along the interior of most masonry walls is to install rigid fiberglass panels due to their low cost and absence of toxic hazards. Other possibilities are panels that are molded from foamed plastics like polystyrene; these panels contain thousands of air pockets, just as fiberglass and mineral

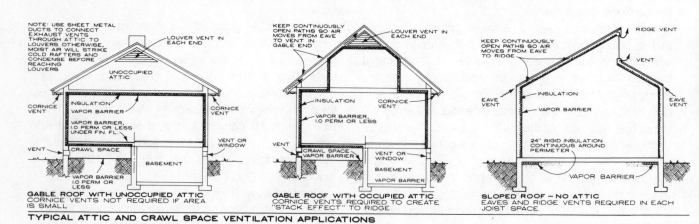

TYPICAL ATTIC AND CRAWL SPACE VENTILATION APPLICATIONS

FIGURE 4.8 The most important insulation for winter is the uppermost insulation, whether above a flat ceiling or among slanted rafters. For summer air conditioning, crawl spaces are the biggest insulation problem.

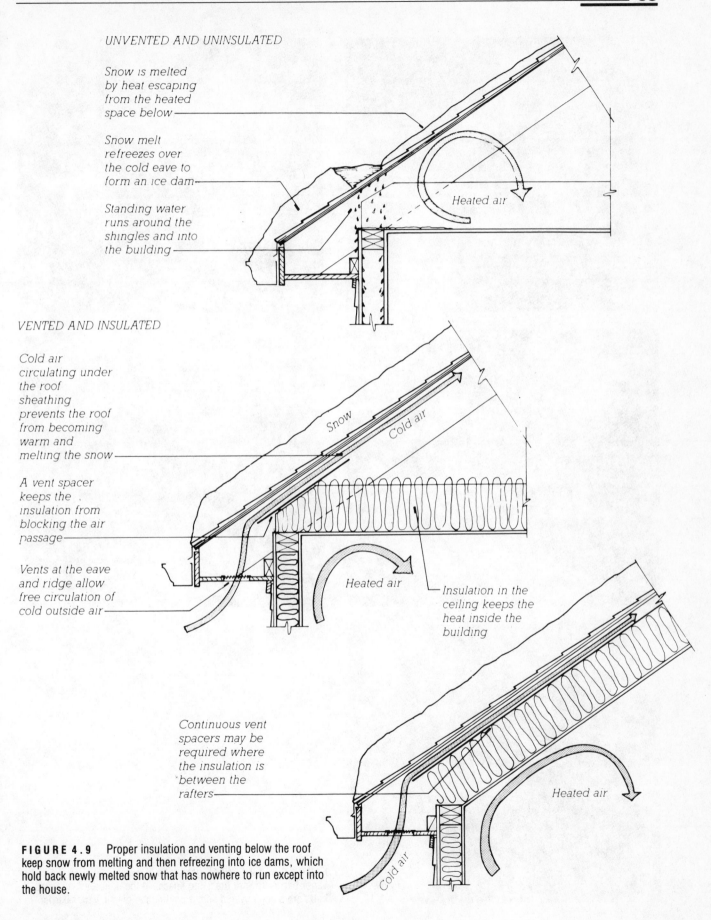

UNVENTED AND UNINSULATED

Snow is melted
by heat escaping
from the heated
space below

Snow melt
refreezes over
the cold eave to
form an ice dam

Standing water
runs around the
shingles and into
the building

Heated air

VENTED AND INSULATED

Cold air
circulating under
the roof
sheathing
prevents the roof
from becoming
warm and
melting the snow

A vent spacer
keeps the
insulation from
blocking the air
passage

Vents at the eave
and ridge allow
free circulation of
cold outside air

Snow

Cold air

Heated air

Insulation in the
ceiling keeps the
heat inside the
building

Continuous vent
spacers may be
required where
the insulation is
between the
rafters

Cold air

Heated air

FIGURE 4.9 Proper insulation and venting below the roof
keep snow from melting and then refreezing into ice dams, which
hold back newly melted snow that has nowhere to run except into
the house.

FIGURE 4.10 When installing fiberglass insulation, keep the vapor barrier toward the living space. In the upper left, unfaced batts are being covered with a continuous plastic vapor barrier.

wool do, that act as barriers to heat transfer. Adhesive holds the panels to brick, cinder block, or stucco. However, uncovered polystyrene burns rapidly, produces toxic smoke, and must be covered with gypsum wallboard for interior use.

Covering over the exterior of a masonry wall with stucco-covered styrofoam is another possibility, but an expensive one. Its virtue is that the masonry remains on the living-space side of the insulation barrier. The homeowner then can take advantage of such cheap heat as the warmth from solar gain and wood burning: The masonry's thermal mass stores heat when room air is warmer than it is and releases it again slowly when the room air is cooler.

Vapor Barriers

Anytime you add insulation, you must consider the vapor barrier. Without it, moisture in heated indoor air condenses as it passes into insulation and cools. The same is true of hot, moist exterior air passing through insulation into air-conditioned homes. To prevent such condensation in the insulation, which would lower the insulation's R-value and also lead to water damage, a vapor barrier of plastic film behind the wall covering should ideally be placed along the living-space side of the insulation. However, unless the walls or ceilings are being torn out, it is impossible to achieve a high-grade vapor barrier for blown-in wall insulation or new attic insulation.

Although some experts do not agree with us, we believe insulation can be blown in most walls with little potential for structural damage. We do think a vapor barrier should be used, however, for blown-in insulation in rooms where the interior humidity is expected to be very high, as in kitchens and bathrooms.

Where installing a plastic vapor barrier would be difficult, a reasonable facsimile can be created by complete caulking followed by painting with a paint rated at less than 1 perm (a measure of permeability to moisture). Vapor-barrier paints or a Sears oil-based primer minimize water transmission.

If you think you are at high risk of vapor problems, keep in mind that in cold weather, cold, dry air enters on the windward side (usually the north), picks up moisture as it warms, and moves out the south side. In hot weather in air conditioned homes, moist air enters the windward wall and then loses moisture as it is cooled. Thus, in cold climates, the downwind side of the house is where the best vapor barrier needs to be; in hot climates, the reverse.

Fiberglass blankets and batts may have vapor barriers of foil or kraft paper attached to one side. This side should face the living space. Unfortunately, these vapor barriers are imperfect since it is nearly impossible to seal the many joints between the batts, and the foil rips easily. Where insulation is poured in or does not have a vapor barrier attached, a 4-mil-thick plastic sheet or other impervious material should be laid in to take its place. In attic floors, the vapor barrier is placed beneath the insulation; along walls, it is stapled over new insulation on the interior side.

For most installations, we recommend that you buy fiberglass rolls or batts that are *unfaced*—that is, without a vapor barrier attached—and, for a vapor barrier, use a plastic sheet. Plastic sheeting is a better vapor barrier because stapled foil or paper makes, at best, an imperfect barrier. No matter what the vapor barrier, though, be very careful to tightly seal edges and seams, even at electrical boxes. For the ultimate in vapor protection, look for new sheeting specifically designed for interior vapor barriers. These can take the place of 4-mil-thick polyethylene plastic sheeting— some builders worry that polyethylene breaks down over time, even in a wall.

If insulation is being added to existing insulation, do not allow a double vapor barrier. That is, if you are laying in fiberglass over old insulation in an attic floor, buy unfaced batts. If you install fiberglass with a vapor barrier, this second barrier will trap any moisture that has passed the first. That will lead to condensation, water damage, and a lower R-value. You want any moisture that has gotten past the first vapor barrier to meet no hindrance to its moving right through the exterior wall to the outdoors.

Insulating Water Heaters

Our recommendations here are brief. If the water heater sits in a heated space, and it is a gas water heater, it needs only R4; if it is an electric water heater,

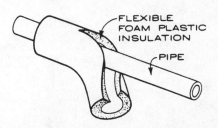

FIGURE 4.11 Foam insulation for pipe comes preslit and ready to slide onto pipes. Four feet of the cold-water pipe leading into the water heater and all the exposed hot-water pipe can be easily insulated by most homeowners for a 1-year payback.

it needs R7. Some models come already insulated to these values. If they are labeled "energy efficient" or show an R-value of 4 or 7, do nothing extra. If they are not so labeled, the chances are that they are insulated only to R2 and could use the added insulation of a water-heater insulation kit.

In an unheated space, a gas water heater needs R7 and an electric heater needs R11. You should buy and install a water-heater insulation kit to bring the heaters up to these R-values. Water-heater insulation kits are usually rated at R6 and normally require only a pair of scissors to install.

In addition, if the water heater is in an unheated space, buy lengths of foam slip-on pipe insulation and place them on all exposed hot-water pipes and the first 6 ft of cold-water pipe that comes out of the water heater (see Figure 4.11).

TABLE 4.1
Caulking Options

Caulk Type	Cost/ 11-oz. Cartridge	Expected Life (years)	Cost/ Year of Service	Max. Joint Width (approx.)	Initial Shrinkage (%)	Degree of Flexibility	Adhesion Quality	Ease of Application	Time to Tack-free/ Final Cure	Recommendations
Oil-Based	$0.55–$1.15	3–5	$0.15–$0.76	¼"–½"	5–10	Inflexible	Fair to good	Easy	1–2 days/ up to 1 yr	None.
Latex (Polyvinyl acetate and other vinyl latexes)	$1.00–$1.60	3–5+	$0.23–$0.66	⅜"	5–10	Low	Fair to good	Very easy	15–30 min/ 5 days	None.
Acrylic Latex	$1.10–$1.75	3–8	$0.16–$0.75	⅜"	5–10	Low	Fair to good	Very easy	15–30 min/ 5 days	None.
Siliconized Acrylic Latex	$1.25–$2.00 CC	15–20	$0.10–$0.30	½"	5	Medium to high	Good	Very easy	20–30 min/ 3 days	Good interior use, but silicone is better for wet areas.
Butyl	$2.00–$3.00	4–10	$0.20–$0.75	½"	10–35	Low	Good	Easy	2–72 hr/ 120 days	Messy.
Butyl Blend 3M	$4.00–$5.50	10–15	$0.26–$0.55	1–2"	None	Very high	Good	Very easy	Remains pliable.	Good window glazing for do-it-yourself.
Ethylene Copolymer (Geocel)	$3.00–$6.00	15–20	$0.15–$0.40	1"	None	Very high	Excellent	Easy	2 hr/ 14 days	Exterior cracks when temperature drops below 40°F.
Polyurethane	$3.50–$4.50	20–30	$0.11–0.22	¾"	None	High	Good to excellent	Difficult	Remains slightly tacky until weathered.	Not a do-it-yourself caulk.
Silicone	$3.20–$6.60 VB	20–30+	$0.10–$0.33	1"	None	High to very high	Good to excellent	Easy	1 hr/ 2–5 days	Good for all wet-area cracks.
DAP Plus (Water-based silicone rubber)	$5.00–$6.00	20–30	$0.16–$0.30	1"	None	High to very high	Good to excellent	Very easy	1 hr/ 2–5 days	Good for do-it-yourself bath applications.
Urethane Foam	$5.00–$8.00	10–20	$0.25–$0.80	1"–2"	None	Inflexible	Good	Easy to difficult	2–24 min/ ½–1 day	For wide cracks and openings: will expand with great force and twist or bow lumber if overfilled.

TABLE 4.2
Insulation Choices

Material	R-Value/in.	Material Cost/ Board ft*	Material Cost/sq ft of "R"	Contractor Cost for R19/sq ft	Difficulty Level	Comments and Recommendations
Blown-in Walls					2	Blow in walls from the inside when you're repainting interior. Blow in from outside when you're repainting exterior. Also good for attics. Machines are rented out. Wear a mask.
Cellulose	3.7	$0.045	$0.029	$0.68 CC		Best buy, and it uses recycled material.
Fiberglass	2.2	$0.045	$0.045	$1.04		
Mineral wool	2.8	$0.05	$0.065	$1.08		
Poured-in Attics					1	Easiest way to insulate an exposed attic.
Cellulose fiber	3.2	$0.034	$0.036	$0.68		
Fiberglass	4	$0.022	$0.031	$0.59		Pouring fiberglass is more dense, so its R-value is better.
Rigid 1″ Board					1	Good for basement walls, cathedral ceilings, and to boost R-value in solar homes or homes heated exclusively by electric resistance.
Unfaced fiberglass board 1.5 lb/ cu ft	4.1	$0.22	$0.053	$0.52 CC		Won't burn, sheds water. An underused option that balances cost and performance.
Molded polystyrene	3.85	$0.17	$0.044	$0.53		Flammable, must be covered with ½″-thick drywall.
Isocyanorate foil-faced	7.2	$0.36	$0.05	$0.74		Highest R-value and excellent vapor barrier in foil facing.
Extruded polystyrene	5.35	$0.58	$0.108	$0.79		Flammable, must be covered with ½″-thick drywall.

Material	R-Value/in.	Material Cost/ Board ft*	Material Cost/sq ft of "R"	Contractor Cost for R19/sq ft	Difficulty Level	Comments and Recommendations
Blankets and Batts, 3½" thick					**1**	Use for open walls.
Fiberglass R11 blanket, kraft paper faced	3.1	$0.062	$0.02	$0.33		More widely available than rock wood.
Rock wool R13 blanket, kraft paper faced	3.2	$0.08	$0.025	$0.39		A good value if you can find it.
Fiberglass unfaced R11 batt with 4-mil polyethylene vapor barrier	3.1	$0.064	$0.62	$0.34		Polyethylene makes a much more air-tight vapor barrier. Unfaced batts are easier to position correctly between studs or joists. Costs slightly more, but is worth it. If contracted, labor savings offset most of extra material costs.

*1 sq ft, 1" thick

5 | Windows

If windows were perfect, they would always keep out water, bugs, and noise. In summer, they would let in a breeze and keep out the radiant heat of the sun; in winter, they would keep out breezes and let in sunshine.

But panes of glass enclosed in a frame just don't meet these ideal standards. So until the perfect window is created, we must repair or replace what we have and then work to keep it in good condition.

Intelligent choices about windows can yield big savings. Much money (and sometimes good architecture) is wasted because of premature replacements and inflated claims of energy savings.

It is less expensive to repair and save a basically sound window than it is to replace it. If you are concerned about energy costs, there are many repairs that are more cost-effective than new windows. Keep in mind that replacement has costs over and above the price of the new window: the cost of removing the old window; the possible cost of reworking some of the wall framing so that the new window will fit; and the possible added costs of new interior trim and new exterior flashing. All these costs can be avoided if the old windows are repaired instead. Saving the old window is almost always cost-effective, especially if you are doing the work yourself.

That said, there are times when partial replacement makes sense: (1) When you have old, single-glazed windows that need a lot of puttying and paint, (2) when you don't have storm windows and could use an extra layer of glass plus tighter windows to help reduce energy costs, and (3) when you don't want to do any of the work yourself.

In these situations, we strongly recommend *replacement-sash kits,* vinyl or vinyl-coated sashes that come with new tracks in which the sashes move. They are not a complete window replacement—they leave the old frame and trim in place. But, properly installed, they require little maintenance and cut down on both air infiltration and heat loss.

When thinking about window repair or replacement, keep in mind that windows have multiple functions: allowing in light, allowing ventilation, and keeping out winter cold and summer heat. They can also act as fire escapes: In every room of the house, one window should open wide enough to serve as an escape and as a possible passage for a fire fighter on a ladder. This is just as important on the third floor as the first; often, it is the law.

Now, a few window definitions: *Double-hung* means two sashes, both of which move vertically. *Single-hung* means two sashes, only one of which moves. *Sliding* means that the sashes are mounted beside one another and slide horizontally. A *casement* window is one whose sash is hinged on the side and swings to the outside. *Glazing* is a term for panes of glass. *Double-glazing* means a window made with an insulating air gap between two panes of glass. *Fixed-glazing* means a window of one or two large panes that do not open in any way. Finally, *lite* is the manufacturer's term for a pane of glass and crops up in such terms as *a four-lite sash* or *a six-lite sash.* Figure 5.1 shows some of the window types.

Two relatively new terms are *low-E glass* and *gas-filled* glazing. Low-E stands for low-emissivity, meaning that the glass has a coating that allows certain wavelengths of light through and reflects others—it tends to block summer heat and trap winter sunlight. Gas-filled glazing is double-glazing with an inert gas such as argon between the panes—the inert gas is a better insulator than ordinary air. Incidentally, a vacuum between panes would be the best insulator yet, but manufacturers have not been able to come up with a cost-effective way to maintain the exceptional seal needed to retain the vacuum over many years.

Windows have been improved and improved, but what matters is the relationship among (1) the long-term energy savings, (2) the initial cost, and (3) the long-term maintenance and replacement costs. We'll discuss this later.

WOOD WINDOW RENOVATION

Wooden double-hung windows have been the residential windows of choice for over 200 years. They are attractive, open and close readily, and do a fairly good job of keeping out the weather. Recently, steel, aluminum, vinyl, and fiberglass have been used as alternative materials for double-hung windows. Wood remains the leader, but solid vinyl and vinyl-clad wood, which do not need periodic painting, are overtaking wood in some sections of the country.

To save the most money in window repair, it is better to consider windows individually than to do the same thing to all the windows of a house. Each window may require a different level of work, and to do more than

is needed on some of them will just add to the labor time and expense.

Table 5.1 (page 80) contains different approaches to individual window repair. Table 5.2 (page 82) looks at a project of replacing 16 windows at once. Use both to help you decide which window renovation option is best for you.

Permanent Closure

The least expensive way to take care of a sound but troublesome window is to caulk it shut. If a window is working poorly, is leaking air, or poses a security problem, closure may be the best solution, especially if the window is not needed for ventilation or emergency escape. But take note: In most areas, fire codes require one operating window in each bedroom and most other living areas.

Screw the sash to the frame, caulk the exterior perimeter, and paint over the repairs. If the window has sash-weight pockets behind the channels, fill these with pour-in insulation. The result is an efficient, low-maintenance window; it no longer lets in breezes, but still excludes prowlers and reduces air infiltration.

To further improve a window's insulation and to extend its life, add a storm window to it. (Storm windows are discussed on page 76.) The storm window also provides added protection against burglary.

Repair and Weatherstrip

If you have double-hung wood windows, and you are doing the work yourself, it is much cheaper to repair, weatherstrip, and add a storm-screen sash than it is to install new double-hung, double-glazed windows and sashes. In addition, repairing rather than replacing can save even more energy: The average R-value of a new ½-in.-thick double-glazed window is 1.7 to 1.9 (a ⅝-in. thickness is slightly better), but a repaired, weatherstripped window with a storm sash is rated at 2.0 to 2.3.

Different kinds of weatherstripping are available. All work fairly well, but for a window that is opened ten or more times a year, the best value is probably spring-metal strips. For windows that are rarely opened, the least expensive and also the best value are vinyl *V-strips.*

Window locks also help prevent air infiltration. When functioning properly, the locks pull the upper and lower sashes together, making an airtight seal.

There are various ways to deal with balky sashes.

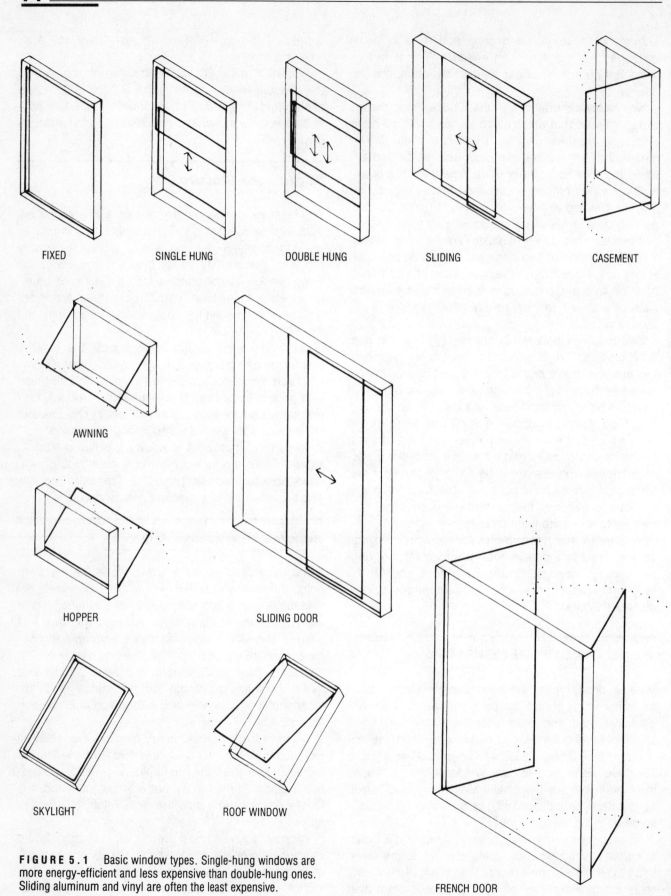

FIXED   SINGLE HUNG   DOUBLE HUNG   SLIDING   CASEMENT

AWNING

HOPPER   SLIDING DOOR

SKYLIGHT   ROOF WINDOW

FIGURE 5.1 Basic window types. Single-hung windows are more energy-efficient and less expensive than double-hung ones. Sliding aluminum and vinyl are often the least expensive.

FRENCH DOOR

The channels in which the sashes slide may have been painted so many times that the sashes stick in the channels. You can pare away excess paint with the beveled side of a chisel. Clean the jambs first and then the insides of the stops on the interior and exterior sides of the sash. Then, sand and repaint. If the channels are made of plastic or aluminum, or if weatherstripping runs in them, use steel wool for cleaning. Figure 5.2 shows the parts of a window.

Sashes may bind because of slight shiftings of the building's frame or because of swelling wood in wet climates. In this case, remove the sash from its frame and plane it down until it slides smoothly in the channel. At the same time, you can adjust the position of the interior stop (the piece of molding that holds the sash in from the interior) or plane the parting strip (the piece that runs between the sashes of a double-hung window).

Once the frame or sash has been repaired, you can make the sashes operate more smoothly by running a block of paraffin up and down them. For metal windows, use a spray lubricant instead of paraffin.

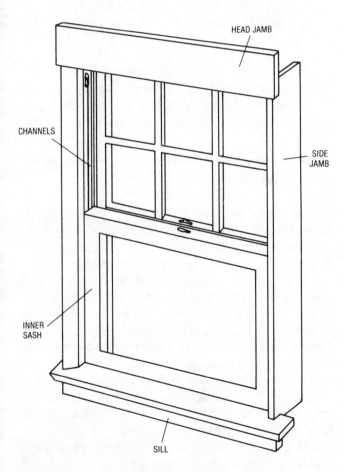

FIGURE 5.2 The parts of a double-hung window.

Water and outside air can penetrate into your house around window glass where the putty—also called *glazing compound*—has cracked or fallen out in chunks. Eventually, all putty has to be replaced. But keep in mind that a poor reglazing job is almost worthless. Where putty has fallen out, there's a good chance that the wood the glass fits into has dried excessively. Remove all loose putty and apply a coat of linseed oil to the wood before the new putty goes on.

Many contractors consider these kinds of repairs too fussy and unprofitable compared to installing new windows, which is a job with a good profit margin. Writing down what you want done to each window will keep the contractor from applying unnecessarily expensive solutions and, consequently, will hold your costs down. If a contractor's bid for repair is more than an average of about $50/window, look for a repair person who is used to doing this type of work—some contractors bid high simply because they don't like repairing windows.

The glass itself should be bedded in a thin coat of the new putty. Then the glazing points, small pieces of metal that hold the glass in place, should be pushed into the wood about every 4 in. (see Figure 5.3). These, in turn, are covered with putty. To complete the work of reglazing a window, apply at least one coat of paint, and preferably two, over the putty, the wood alongside, and a fingernail's-width of the new glass. The paint will help seal the joint between the putty and the glass, keeping out moisture and extending the life of the repair.

Ask your contractor in advance how he or she reglazes, and say that you want very careful work. Most professionals know what to do, but some cut corners. A good glazing job takes much longer than a poor one. Consequently, don't pay someone to fix your old windows when the windows need a lot of work and weatherstripping and when you don't have good storm windows. In this case, our cost estimates indicate that your best buy for contracted work is double-glazed replacement-sash kits. They come with vinyl-covered or solid vinyl sashes and two jamb liners that the windows glide in.

Replacement-Sash Kits

Replacement-sash kits are a good buy from contractors in certain situations and also make a good do-it-yourself choice. Some window sashes and channels must be replaced because they are damaged or rotted beyond repair. Often, the trouble starts at the sill, which can be subjected to standing water. A sill can be replaced, but the effort involves some strength and carpentry.

Once a sill is replaced (if needed), replacing sashes and the channels they move in is comparatively simple. A kit contains two new, double-glazed, weather-stripped sashes and metal or vinyl jamb liners. The parts must be ordered and built especially to fit the opening you have. They can be installed with little experience in carpentry and no disruption of the trim.

Generally, the sash kits don't require the weights and pulleys that helped operate old wood double-hung windows. Before installing the new sash, fill the old sash-weight channels with insulation and tape the opening shut (see Figure 5.4).

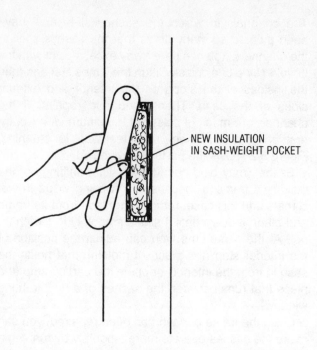

NEW INSULATION
IN SASH-WEIGHT POCKET

FIGURE 5.4   Before installing metal or vinyl sash guides, fill an empty sash-weight pocket with insulation and tape over the old pulley hole.

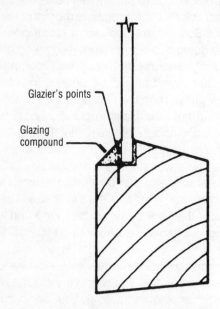

Glazier's points

Glazing compound

FIGURE 5.3   To keep air and water out, glazing must be done properly. That includes setting the glass in a thin bedding of putty before the glazier's points are pushed into the wood of the window.

Replacement Channels

Sometimes, it is not the sash that is the problem but the channel it slides in. Replacement channels, called *inserts, glides,* or *jamb liners,* fit over the old frame and are made of aluminum or vinyl. Installed correctly, they make a window more airtight. They eliminate the need for pulleys and sash weights, because they hold the sash in a snug friction fit—when the sash is raised, the window stays in place by friction, and yet it is easily moved because the aluminum or vinyl is smooth.

Vinyl is generally the more energy-efficient channel material; aluminum allows more heat transfer.

When buying replacement channels, avoid the cheapest—they don't work as well or last as long. Buy ones that are of higher quality, since the added cost will more than pay for itself over a life of 20 or more years.

Storm Windows

Adding storm windows to single-glazed windows is usually worth the cost and trouble, unless the main windows are in bad shape and you have to use high-cost labor. For that situation, we recommend sash kits.

Storm windows not only thwart air infiltration, but also create a pocket of insulating air between their single sashes and the ones of the regular window. Storm windows also provide some protection against burglars, who may be less inclined to pry away or break two layers of glass.

Storm windows protect the sashes behind from rain and snow. This can allow you to preserve a home's original windows and retain an old look that is particularly valued in a historic building or district.

Still, it is important to repair the main window first—replacing cracked glass, mending damaged wood, and painting—before putting up storm windows.

REPLACING WINDOWS

In some instances, repair or even replacement-sash kits are not the answer. Perhaps the window frame is rotted, or the window is simply not wanted or needed. There are three other options: (1) eliminate the window altogether and fill the opening with wall material; (2) remove the sashes and replace them with a fixed-glass pane; or (3) remove all the old window, including the frame, so that a whole new window can be substituted.

Contractors, particularly window-replacement specialists, often advise that the same treatment be given to all windows. This is for their own convenience and can lead to unneeded work. You can save hundreds of dollars by replacing only what you have to.

Replacing Windows with Solid Wall

Consider eliminating unnecessary windows. Most older homes were designed to let in far more light and air than we really need. The average detached house built from 1920 to 1940 has about 20 windows, but only about seven major rooms. Since the average room needs only one window for a fire exit and perhaps a second for proper light and ventilation, at least seven windows potentially could be replaced with wall material.

Windows are notorious sources of air infiltration and heat loss. Even a double-glazed window has an R-value of only 1.7. If it were taken out and wall framing plus insulation put in its place, the R-value of the area would jump to 14 or 15 (see Figure 5.5). The long-run energy savings would more than make up for the conversion costs. Moreover, there is no maintenance to do once the window is gone.

If you consider eliminating windows, two kinds are good candidates: north-facing windows, which lose more heat than ones facing in any other direction; and windows splashed by a shower, which are a continual maintenance problem. The best time to eliminate windows is when you are repainting or re-siding; otherwise, the cost of matching the new siding attractively can be prohibitive.

On the other hand, bear in mind that *fenestration*—the size and placement of windows—as seen from the outside of the house is an important design feature that can add to or detract from a house's character. Symmetry and grouping are important factors. If you are thinking of removing windows and don't have a designer's eye, ask the advice of an architect or someone else who does. In addition, try to avoid making dark corners in rooms. And be sure to consult the building and fire codes—they may require a minimum amount of window space in each room, as well as emergency exits of a certain size.

Fixed Glazing Instead of Operable Windows

Replacing an operable window with fixed glazing may be less expensive than either repairing the window or eliminating it altogether. There are drawbacks, however. A fixed-glazed pane cannot be opened for ventilation. Also, a fixed-glazed pane may disrupt the harmony of the original fenestration. For example, a single, fixed-glazed window on the front of a colonial house with six-lite over six-lite double-hung windows

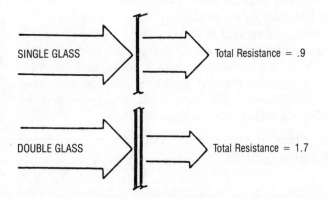

SINGLE GLASS   Total Resistance = .9

DOUBLE GLASS   Total Resistance = 1.7

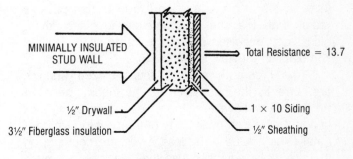

MINIMALLY INSULATED STUD WALL   Total Resistance = 13.7

½″ Drywall
3½″ Fiberglass insulation
1 × 10 Siding
½″ Sheathing

FIGURE 5.5 Glass, even two layers, cannot come close to the insulating value of a wall. Where windows are not needed, make walls and not windows—your energy bills will be lower.

would look awful. In addition, most fire codes require one operable window in each room.

Even with these drawbacks, fixed glazing can be a good repair option in some situations. A fixed-glazed window lets in as much light as any window. The factory-sealed double-glazing makes the window a fairly good insulator and, because there are no movable sashes, there is no air infiltration and little maintenance required.

Fixed-glazed windows are good options in kitchens and baths that have some mechanical form of ventilation. Where fans or vents exhaust bad air or bring in good, windows aren't needed for ventilation. Other good locations for fixed-glazed windows are in rooms where other windows can provide ventilation and along stairways.

Installing New Windows

Replacing old windows with new ones—frames as well as sashes and channels—is expensive. Replacement is often promoted by contractors, sometimes by inflating predictions of energy savings, because the work is both relatively easy and highly profitable. But sometimes, it is the only thing to do. Where your window frames are so old and rotten that replacement sashes won't work (highly unusual), your windows are too large or small for your liking, or you have deteriorated metal windows with no wood frame to which a replacement sash could attach, you need total-replacement windows.

Standard replacement windows are available in wood, aluminum, solid vinyl, solid fiberglass, and vinyl- and aluminum-clad wood in single and double glazing. They come as sliders, as casements, and single-and double-hung.

You can buy replacement windows with energy-saving features. These include triple glazing—that is, three layers of glass, forming two insulation pockets rather than the one of double-glazed glass; low-E glass; and gas-filled glazing, which is useful only in combination with low-E glass.

Of the three options, low-E double-glazed windows are currently the best value for the money, because the enhanced R-value of the window gives a payback in about a year in most parts of the country. Unfortunately, their value is far less if you are counting on them for solar gain, because they block out so much sun. Consequently, in cold climates, low-E glass is best put on the north side; on the south side, regular double-glazed windows will let in more solar warmth, which you can retain with closed drapes at night.

Triple glazing usually has a very long payback period—except in arctic climates—and usually is not worth the extra cost unless the price difference over comparable double glazing is only about $20 a window.

Gas-filled glazing, usually using argon, is now more common and therefore cheaper than when it first came on the market. Some manufacturers sell these windows for only $5 more than nongas windows, and one manufacturer plans to put argon in all its low-E, double-glazed windows. The improvement in R-value is substantial, at least until all the argon leaks out, and no one knows how long that will take.

Keep in mind that replacement-sash kits come with some or all of these features.

As shown in Table 5.2 (page 82), replacement windows run from about $220 to almost $550. Since there are about 20 windows in an average house, replacing all of them would cost between $4,000 and $11,000. You will pay more if you buy the extras like low-E glass (which we generally recommend), triple glazing (which we recommend only for the very coldest climates), or gas-filled glazing.

COPING WITH STEEL CASEMENTS

Occasionally, a new product comes out that seems like a good idea, but does not live up to expectations and should be dropped. Steel casement windows are such a product.

Steel casements were introduced in the 1930s, and it is now apparent that they do many things a window should not do. They leak air and water, transmit heat and cold, and are too susceptible to damage and breaking. They can, of course, be repaired or replaced (at very high cost), but there are two more cost-effective ways to deal with them: Replace them with a different kind of window, or seal them tight with caulking.

We recommend that you or your contractors *not* repair them with weatherstripping, paint them, or install new crank mechanisms, because the cost is generally very high and the end product is still a single-glazed window. If they are in good shape, you can, with some difficulty, install storm sashes over them.

Replacement

The least expensive replacement method is to take out the steel casement window and insert into the wall opening in its place a new, double-insulated aluminum slider. This should cost about 10 to 20 percent less than making major repairs to the original window. Alternatively, a single-hung aluminum window could be put in place of the steel casement window. When you buy an aluminum window, get one that meets Aluminum Manufacturers Association standards for infiltration and insulation.

If you feel that taking the entire old casement window out is too tough a job, try removing the old sash—a cutting torch or power saw will be needed—and leaving the casement frame in place. Then, you can butt a new window against the old casement.

Sealing

The least expensive way to deal with a deteriorating or nonworking steel casement window is to seal it shut permanently, if it is not required as a fire exit. Remove the cranking mechanism and use sheet-metal screws to fasten the sash to the frame. Save the cranking mechanisms in case you need them as replacement parts later for windows you choose to remain openable. Seal cracks with a high-grade flexible caulk like silicone. If insulation is a goal, install a storm window on either the inside or outside.

TABLE 5.1
Window Renovation Options

THE PROJECT
Repair 16 wood double-hung windows in a 2-story, vinyl-sided house.

Options	Cost/ Window Contracted	Cost/ Window DIY	Project Cost Contracted	Project Cost DIY		Difficulty Level DIY Advice	Comments and Recomendations
Paint Only Scrape, reglaze, and apply 2 coats paint.	$62	$6	$900	$105	1	Short-term solution. Paint unused windows shut.	If contracted, highest life-cycle costs due to short life and high energy costs.
Weatherstrip and Paint Install spring bronze weatherstripping and a sash lock; 2 coats paint.	$109	$14	$1,700	$225	1	This is the minimum for DIY treatment.	An expensive half-step for contractor-completed jobs.
Replace Sash and Liner Remove old window. Install vinyl-clad wood, double-glazed replacement sash and jamb liners.	$154	$90	$2,465 CC	$1,450 VB	2	Measure carefully.	Double-glazed, vinyl or vinyl-coated replacement sash and channels minimize maintenance and energy loss while remaining inexpensive. Reuses inside and outside trim. To minimize maintenance, don't use sash that requires painting.
Double-Glaze Opening Remove window. Install nonmovable double glazing.	$165	$90	$2,640	$1,450	2	Special order factory-sealed glazing with low-E coating.	Lowest energy-use window. An excellent option for up to 50% of openings. A low-cost way to add beneficial glazing to solar-effective southern exposures.
Wall-up Opening Replace window with 2″ × 4″ wall, insulation, ½″-thick gypsum, and exterior siding. Paint to match.	$170	$52	$2,700	$830	3		Lowest life-cycle and energy costs. Eliminate all excess windows during major rehabilitation. North-facing windows are the biggest energy wasters. Watch out that street view remains balanced.

Options	Cost/ Window Contracted	Cost/ Window DIY	Project Cost Contracted	Project Cost DIY	Difficulty Level DIY Advice	Comments and Recomendations
Storm Sash and Paint Weatherstrip; install exterior aluminum storm window and apply 2 coats paint.	$174	$46	$2,785	$735 CC	**2**	Storm windows extend life of the paint job and window while lowering energy costs. Recommended DIY option for windows in moderate to good condition.
Replace Windows Moderate-quality, solid vinyl or vinyl-clad double-glazed windows. Replace interior and exterior trim.	$295	$156	$4,100	$2,500	**3**	High initial cost, but a good long-term investment if windows are really worn out. Very expensive if windows are still in repairable condition.

TABLE 5.2
Replacement Window Options

THE PROJECT
Remove and replace 16 wood windows with double-glazed windows and wrap trim in vinyl. Paint windows if required.

Options	Cost/ Window Contracted	Cost/ Window DIY	Project Contracted	Project Cost DIY	Difficulty Level DIY Advice		Comments and Recommendations
Aluminum Sliders Install ½"-thick double-glazed, thermal-break window with white anodized finish.	$222	$78	$3,550	$1,250	**3**		Inexpensive, maintenance-free option for horizontal openings. Frame is poor insulator even with thermal-break frames.
Aluminum Single-Hung Install ½"-thick double-glazed, thermal-break window with white anodized finish.	$230	$80	$3,680	$1,290 CC	**3**		Least expensive, maintenance-free option for double-hung frame. Poor insulator even with thermal-break frames.
Wood and Storm Window Install single-glazed, double-hung replacement sash with an aluminium storm sash. Apply 1 coat paint on both sides.	$240	$104	$3,840	$1,665	**2**	Measure carefully.	Easiest DIY method. Reuses all trim. Measure twice and order sash and liners custom-milled to window jamb size. Excellent way to maintain historic characteristics.
Aluminum Double-Hung Install ½"-thick double-glazed, thermal-break window with white anodized finish.	$245	$156	$3,900	$2,500	**3**		In mild climates, this can be the window of choice because the top sash allows better circulation of warm air than do single-hung aluminum windows.
Solid PVC Install ½"-thick double-glazed window with white finish interior and exterior.	$270	$180	$4,320 VB	$2,880	**3**		No maintenance, good insulator, can't rot. Inexpensive and very versatile. Heat-welded joints are best. In hot or very cold climates, buy high quality to eliminate warping.

Options	Cost/ Window Contracted	Cost/ Window DIY	Project Contracted	Project Cost DIY	Difficulty Level DIY Advice	Comments and Recommendations
Wood Double-Hung Install ½"-thick double-glazed, factory-primed window with 1 coat paint on both sides.	$280	$145	$4,480	$2,320	**3**	High maintenance, but proven life span of 100 years. Can be easily painted (exterior storm window on single glazing provides the longest life at least initial cost).
Aluminum- or PVC-Clad Wood Install ½"-thick double-glazed window with 1 coat interior paint.	$366	$185	$5,860	$2,950 VB	**3**	Low maintenance. Can't paint exterior. Combines strength of wood with durability of aluminum or vinyl. Inside is painted to match decor.
Fiberglass Double-Hung Install ½"-thick double-glazed, thermal-break window.	$542	$275	$8,672	$4,320	**3**	This is the highest quality window, but costs twice as much as other options.

	Additional Cost/ Opening	Additional Job Cost Contractor	Additional Project Cost DIY			
Add-ons Triple Glazing	$45–$60	$1,000	$800			Save this option for Alaska.
Low-E Glass	$20–$30	$500	$400			Provides a 50% increase in R-value with a payback period of about a year in most parts of the country.
Gas-Filled Glazing	$15–$65	$560	$480			In time, this option may become cost effective as different gases are used and price drops.

Doors

Doors look simple enough, but they can present some of the toughest repair problems. Hanging a door correctly from scratch is an advanced carpentry skill. Today, however, both interior and exterior doors and their frames come as assemblies and can be installed without the painstaking and exacting work required to fit jambs and install hardware. There are many varieties of doors and door assemblies from which to choose, over a broad price range.

But let's begin with door parts—there are more than you might think. There is the door itself, of course, and the *hinges,* either two or three to a door. Three hinges are generally used for heavy exterior doors.

Surrounding the door on the sides and top are the *side jambs* and *head jamb* (see Figure 6.1). Jamb comes from the Latin word *gamba* meaning *leg;* jambs are the legs straddling the opening. They are held in the correct position within the framed opening by *shims,* usually cedar shingles, also called *wedges* or *blocks.* The jambs must be cut very accurately to make a ¹⁄₁₆-in. gap between them and the door at the top and sides, and a ¹⁄₄- to 2-in. gap at the bottom—depending on the height of rugs and the need for ventilation with some forced-air heating systems.

Then there is the *lockset* or *passage set* (the latter being doorknobs without locks) and the *strike plate* (also called the *striker*) where the latch fits. Both require drilling holes precisely, and the strike plate needs a *mortise.*

Mortise comes from an old French word meaning *groove.* It is the recess into which the hinge or strike plate is set, then screwed. It must be precisely marked and chiseled. The recess must be the exact width and depth of the hardware or the door will end up either rubbing the jamb or not latching properly.

Exterior doors, and sometimes interior ones, also need wooden or metal *thresholds,* again precisely fit. The word derives from old English times when a raised piece of wood at the cottage door was meant to hold back the thresh (that is, threshed grain) that might blow into the house from the threshing area nearby.

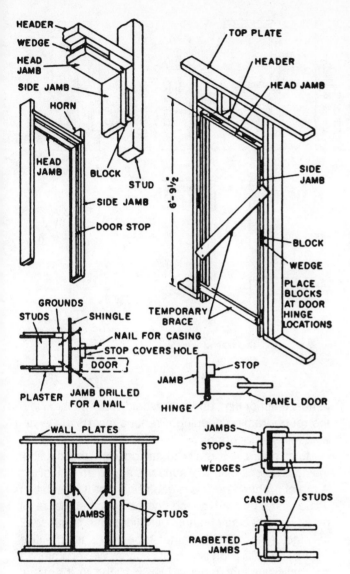

FIGURE 6.1 The head and side jambs of a door fit into the rough framing of 2-by-3 or 2-by-4 studs; use shims to make jambs perfectly square.

Understanding all these varieties of doors and their parts is important in choosing the most cost-effective door improvements. To make intelligent choices, answer the following questions, more or less in order.

1. *Is the jamb beyond repair and the door all right?* If so, we generally recommend putting in a new jamb only, a solution that requires mortising. But if you are working on an interior doorway and do not want to mortise, you can stick to a budget and still buy a prehung hardboard or lauan (Philippine mahogany) door. You will be left with the good original door, but you can sell it or use it somewhere else.

2. *Is the door beyond repair and the jamb all right?* If so, replace just the door. For interior openings, lauan plywood doors are an attractive, very low-cost option (about $25 plus installation); but shop carefully, because the discount store variety may be very flimsy. For exterior openings, install a metal insulated door in the opening if you can find a stock size that fits (the tolerances are only $1/16$ in.) Otherwise, buy a wood door that can be cut or planed.

3. *Are the door, jamb, or hardware damaged but repairable?* If so, consider repairs. Up to a point, repairing is cheaper than replacement. Read the section on repairs later in this chapter (page 88) to help you decide whether to fix or not to fix.

4. *Are the door and jamb both damaged beyond repair?* If so, in the most cost-effective option is to buy a prehung door.

Remember, there are two main factors in a good installation. The first is shimming to make sure the frame is plumb and perfectly square. Fit the shims carefully between the side jambs and the rough frame at two or three locations on each side, one always at the location of the strike plate. The second factor is proper nailing to keep the unit stable.

EXTERIOR DOORS

If you are considering a new exterior door, you have a number of options. You can buy a metal door, a solid wooden door, or a door that has a wood veneer over a particleboard fill. All can be obtained prehung. A number of styles are shown in Figures 6.2 and 6.3. Figure 6.4 shows an elaborate exterior doorway and cross sections through the door and jambs and through the door and threshold. Table 6.1 (page 93) lists exterior door options.

Most prehung exterior doors come with top and side

Trim, also called *casing,* includes the wood moldings that go around the top and sides of the head and side jambs where they meet the wall finish. Trim contributes to the stability of the whole assembly.

A prehung door is an assembly of door and jambs. Some come with top and side trim; exterior prehung doors have thresholds. Split-jamb doors are interior prehung doors with all the trim—two sides of the jamb lock together. Prehung insert doors have jambs that fit inside the existing jambs so that the old ones do not have to be removed. A prehung door may come with or without a lockset or passage set, but a hole will have been drilled for it in either case.

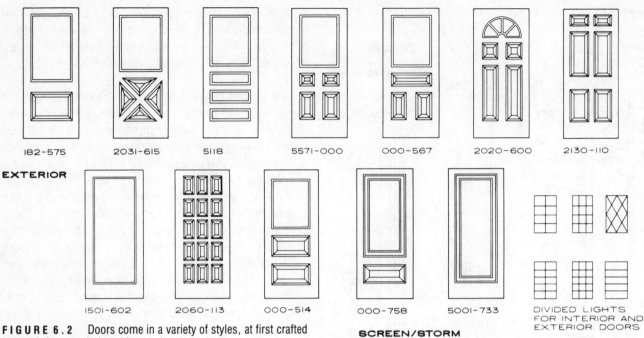

182-575   2031-615   5118   5571-000   000-567   2020-600   2130-110

EXTERIOR

1501-602   2060-113   000-514   000-758   5001-733

DIVIDED LIGHTS
FOR INTERIOR AND
EXTERIOR DOORS

SCREEN/STORM

FIGURE 6.2 Doors come in a variety of styles, at first crafted in wood, but now imitated in metal.

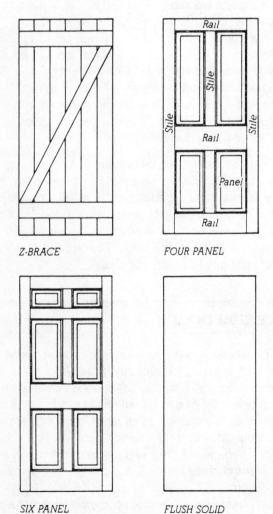

Z-BRACE

FOUR PANEL

SIX PANEL

FLUSH SOLID CORE

jambs, exterior trim, and a threshold. You slip them into the rough framing opening. Prehung inserts are available for exterior doors.

Metal doors are really metal only on the outside. Inside is a honeycomb of supports and foam insulation. A metal prehung door is a good bargain. Its insulation value is relatively high compared to other doors; it gives good security against intrusion; and, because of the factory-installed weatherstripping, it is effective against air infiltration around its edges. We recommend magnetic weatherstripping, which clings to the metal door. It is worth the additional few dollars.

Metal doors come in many decorative patterns, some imitating traditional wood door textures and designs. If you have alternating wet and dry weather, a metal door will not swell and stick. About the only drawback of metal doors is that if the door is ever badly bent on the edges—an attempted break-in is about the only way this can happen—repair is almost impossible. Dents in the front or back can be filled with auto-body filler or covered with sheet metal attached with adhesive.

You can buy nonprehung metal doors, but usually none of the stock sizes offered will fit the jambs and threshold of your doorway. Metal doors, of course, cannot be planed or otherwise cut to fit.

FIGURE 6.3 Panel and solid core flush doors are the most popular types of exterior doors.

When you install a prehung exterior door, you can often reuse the old interior trim around the door, but use the new jamb. Unlike the trim, which may be decorative and worth saving, jambs are featureless wooden slabs.

A pine panel door is stylish and made of solid wood. Many people find them attractive, especially when stained on one or both sides. They come in various designs, but not all designs are prehung. A fir panel door is usually a little cheaper, but not quite as strong as pine—it splits more easily. Both types are poorer insulators than are metal doors, and the panels are all too easily kicked out with a determined blow.

Flush doors, ones that have no panels, have a smooth surface on both sides and are made of composites. The outer wood is usually a birch or lauan veneer, and the inside is particleboard or gypsum filler.

Because flush doors have no panels that vary the contour of the door, they are plainer and less expensive. They come by themselves or prehung.

If the existing jambs and threshold are in good condition, you will save a significant amount of money if you buy a wooden or a flush door alone and use the existing jambs, hinges, thresholds, lockset, and weatherstripping. But the door will have to be mortised and fit carefully by sawing or planing.

INTERIOR DOORS

Interior doors are of two types: doors that are designed for closets, and *passage doors* that are suitable for bedrooms, baths, and other living areas. Table 6.2 (page 94) lists the different types and options.

Passage doors can be used for closets, but most closet doors are inappropriate for rooms. For some closets, you may want a *bifold* door, which does not require so much floor space to fully open, or a *louver* door, which allows air to circulate in and out of the closet (see Figure 6.5).

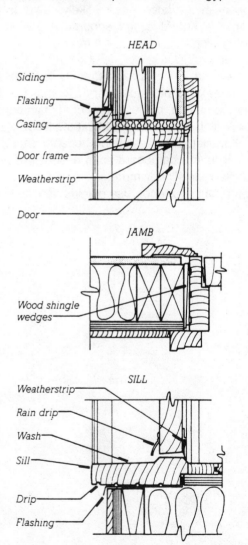

FIGURE 6.4 Doors must be precisely fit to work properly and keep out the weather. The carpentry around them is complex.

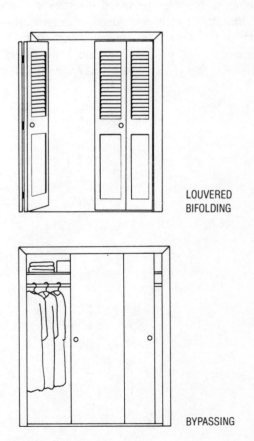

LOUVERED
BIFOLDING

BYPASSING

FIGURE 6.5 Closet doors.

Other kinds of closet doors are the *folding accordion* type, which takes up even less floor space than a bifold door (in fact, only inches), which makes it good in narrow spaces; and *bypassing* doors, which are akin to sliding patio doors and, in fact, are often called sliding doors. Bypassing doors do not arc out into a room at all. A 6-ft-wide pair of these doors can expose as little as a few inches of the inside of the closet or up to 3 feet of it, depending on how you slide the panels.

Accordion doors are made of wood or vinyl slats woven together with strands of cord or vinyl. They are relatively inexpensive. Generally, all that is needed to install them is to attach a track to the head jamb. The accordion door compresses into folds when it is closed and lengthens into a solid divider as it is pulled along the track to close off the space behind. You attach a small piece of hardware to one wall so that the door latches and holds fast when closed.

Passage doors come by themselves or prehung; some styles are shown in Figure 6.6. Prehung doors can be made of hardboard (difficult to distinguish from pine and significantly less expensive), solid pine, and lauan plywood. A number of different types, both hollow-core and solid-core, are shown in Figure 6.7.

Lauan is a Philippine wood resembling mahogany, of moderate strength and durability. A lauan flush door is the least expensive privacy door—and, in most cases, closet door—you can buy. They are attractive and serviceable and can be stained, urethaned, or painted. On average, lauan is easier to damage than pine or hardboard, but is cheaper to replace.

DOOR REPAIRS

Most often, you do not have to replace a door, only repair it. If a door is binding, the cause may be a loose hinge or strike plate. If you see loose screws, tighten them. If they no longer grip the wood, insert one or two glue-covered wooden matchsticks or toothpicks and try again; or fill the old hole with plastic wood, wait for it to dry, and try the screw again.

If the screws are tight and the door still binds, adjust the hinges before trying to plane the door. If a door binds on the top of the latch side and shows a gap at the bottom of the latch side, a likely cause is a top hinge that is not recessed enough. If the hinge is protruding slightly, remove it, cut more wood out of the mortise, and reinstall it.

You can make similar adjustments to recess any hinge or make it protrude more. To make a hinge protrude, remove it, place a cardboard shim behind it, and reinstall it. You can also adjust the location of the striker. If the latch bolt fails to protrude far enough into the striker, use a cardboard shim under the striker to make it protrude slightly more.

When repairing a door, use planing as a last resort.

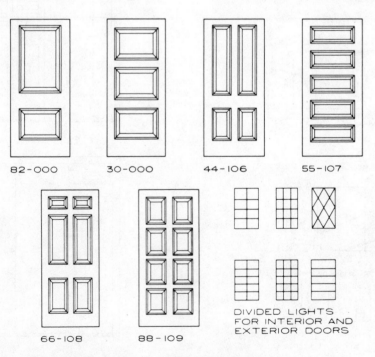

82-000   30-000   44-106   55-107

66-108   88-109   DIVIDED LIGHTS FOR INTERIOR AND EXTERIOR DOORS

FIGURE 6.6   Interior panel door styles.

TYPES OF HOLLOW CORE DOORS

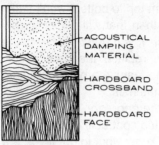

ACOUSTICAL DOOR

Uses gasketed stops and neoprene bottom seals to cut sound transmission.

HONEYCOMB FIBER

INSTITUTIONAL:

With cross rail.

INTERIOR:

Without cross rail. Uniform core of honeycomb fiber to form 1/2" air cells.

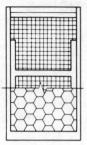

IMPLANTED BLANKS

Spirals or other forms separated or joined, implanted between & supporting outer faces of door.

MESH

Interlocked, horizontal & vertical strips, equally spaced, notched into stiles, or expandable cellular or honey-comb core.

TYPES OF SOLID CORES

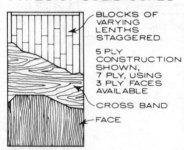

CONTINUOUS BLOCK STAVED CORE

Bonded staggered blocks bonded to face panels. Most widely used & economical solid core.

FRAMED BLOCK STAVED CORE

Non-bonded staggered blocks laid up within stile rail frame, bonded to face panels.

STILE AND RAIL

Horizontal blocks when cross banding is not used. Vertical panel blocks when cross banding is used.

PARTICLE BOARD

Extremely heavy, more soundproof, economical door, available in hardwood face veneer or high pressure laminate face.

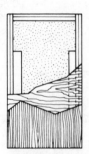

MINERAL COMPOSITION

Lightest weight of all cores. Details, as cut-outs, difficult. Low screw holding strength.

FIGURE 6.7 Construction of doors can vary widely; some are made to be low in price, others to keep out sound or fire. Think of your needs and shop around before you buy.

It is all too easy to remove too much wood, leaving a gap that is impossible to correct. If you do plane, try to plane from the hinge side; remove the door from its hinges and set it down on its latch edge. If you plane on the latch side, you have the problem of what to do around the latch. If you do not plane in the latch area, it bulges out slightly relative to the planed section; if you do plane there, you have to remove the hardware on the door side and, when you reinstall it, you may find that the latch does not work well.

This work is all relatively easy for do-it-yourselfers. If you don't want to do it, however, a contractor may resist these kinds of tedious repairs in favor of new doors. Make a list of all the problems you have, door by door, or prescribe the exact work you want—this may lower the contractor's resistance, because a lot of the work is just diagnosing the problems. If the contractor still balks, find a good repair person.

Unless a door is really banged up or split, it is cheaper to repair it than to replace it.

INSTALLING DOORS

Measuring Up

If you have decided to replace a door—or a door and jambs—whether you are going to do the work yourself or call on a contractor, you will save time and money by first making some careful assessments. Here are the steps:

1. *Is the old door plumb?* It is important whether the edge of the door and face of the door are straight up and down. Take an 18-in. or longer level and find out. If the old door is out of plumb in any direction, your house has probably settled, and the replacement job is going to be harder.

2. *Decide if you care whether the door is plumb.* Half an inch out of plumb from top to bottom won't make much difference. More than that will cause gravity to open or shut the door. If you don't care, and the jamb looks acceptable, replace the door if it is beyond repair. Fixing the leaning problem will take a lot of time and more materials.

3. *If you're replacing just the door, don't count on the opening being square.* If a contracting firm is doing the work, its people will know what to do. If you are doing the work, pop the door off the hinges and check all dimensions and angles with a tape measure and square. If it's anything but a perfect rectangle, make a diagram (see Figure 6.8).

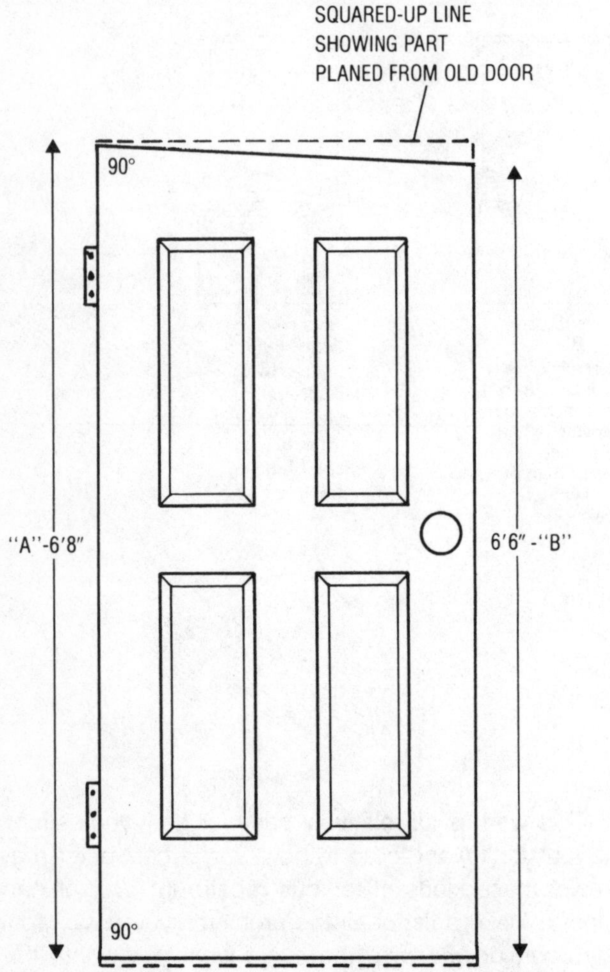

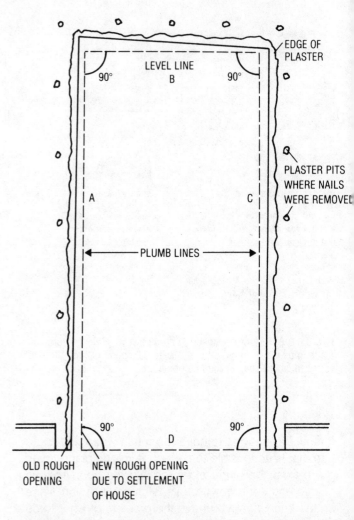

FIGURE 6.8 Measuring only the latch side of this door (B) would lead to ordering a replacement door of the wrong size. In very old houses, doors were often planed or cut as the house settled. Check doors like this with a square to make sure you order a new one large enough (A) to cut to the old jamb.

FIGURE 6.9 If you have removed the old door and jamb, and the opening is not level and plumb, it usually is not necessary to reframe the opening. Make a diagram on paper showing dimensions A–D, using a level and a tape measure to do the measuring. Then order a slightly smaller door and jambs and shim the jambs to the old opening.

4. *If you're replacing the door and jamb, don't count on the rough opening being square and plumb.* To do a good job, you or your contractor will have to tear things down to the frame. Every dimension of opening, the thickness of the frame, and the plumbness of the floor and frame will have to be checked. An out-of-plumb case is shown in Figure 6.9.

5. *If you are doing the work yourself, take your diagram to your supplier, unless you already know the stock size that will fit.* Come to an agreement with the supplier about the dimensions of the door or prehung door assembly, based on your measurements. If the measurements are wrong or the ordering faulty, the door is not going to work in the opening as planned.

Split-Jamb Doors

A split-jamb, prehung door can be used in an interior opening in a finished wall, where the old casing is not being preserved. A two-part jamb with trim on both sides interlocks when the door is installed. Otherwise, the installation is much like that of any prehung door, and manufacturers include instructions. Figure 6.10 shows a cross section of a split-jamb, prehung door.

Again, the key is shimming with shingles so that the jambs are tight and the gap between the jambs and the door, all around the door, is consistent. Nail the casing on one side to the wall beneath, then shim this first half of the jamb to the frame and nail through the jamb and shims into the frame. Finally, move into the other room and fit the other half of the jamb, with its casing, into the jamb already secured.

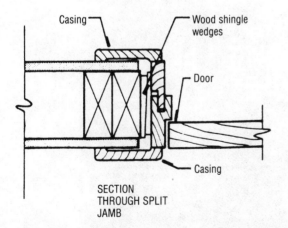

SECTION
THROUGH SPLIT
JAMB

FIGURE 6.10   A split-jamb, prehung door is a kit that is assembled from both sides of the wall. The assembly is relatively easy. The jamb and attached casing molding slide apart for quick and relatively easy installation.

You will be lucky to find a split-jamb door with trim that matches the other trim in your room. But the trim on a split-jamb door is easily removed, even after installation, and can be replaced with the kind you want.

Bifold Doors

Bifold and bypassing doors have no jambs and are installed in finished openings either trimmed or untrimmed. Installation to plaster or drywall is acceptable. Make certain that the top and sides of the opening are reasonably level and plumb. A bifold door can work in a slightly irregular opening, but will look funny. If anything is allowed to remain irregular, it should be the space at the floor—a trapezoidal gap is less noticeable there, and an adjustable pivot at the door bottom allows you to widen or narrow the clearance between the door and the floor.

After the track at the top is in place, use a plumb line to locate the pivot bracket that will hold the bottom pivot of the pivoting door. If you have carpeting, you can set the pivot bracket on a piece of wood to raise the bracket to the height of the carpet.

Once you get the top and bottom pivots into their respective brackets, the key to smooth operation is adjustment. Even professionals have to adjust the doors once they have them up.

Bypassing Doors

Order bypassing doors about 2 in. shorter than the finished opening, depending on the brand you buy and the salesperson's recommendation. This allows for a clearance of 1-½ in. at the top, where the door fits into its track, and ½ in. at the bottom, where it rides freely above the floor or carpet. Buy good-quality hardware; it lasts much longer than the cheap kind.

If the doors have an aligner that attaches to the floor at a point midway between the opening's sides, make sure that you position it when the doors are hanging freely and are plumb.

Again, as with bifold doors, the job is not quite done; alignment is called for. Generally, this is done by loosening and tightening screws that hold the door to the overhead track.

Locks

Installing locks requires as much or more precision as installing doors. A slight mismeasurement or a cut that is slightly off the mark is likely to make for a lock that does not latch. Lock installation, like door installation, is unforgiving. Figure 6.11 shows a typical lockset.

Knowing the trouble of installing locks properly, manufacturers make some doors with holes already drilled for standard locksets and passage sets. These are good buys and save time; they also save contractors' time and expense, because they would have to put a highly skilled carpenter to work installing locks.

Having a door with a predrilled hole for a lockset or passage set will save you lots of trouble. Even so, take care when handling lock parts, because they have to be separated before installation. If you lose a piece, you are out of luck—manufacturers do not include spares. Keep close at hand the box that the lock came in so that you can store the parts and screws in it; otherwise, round pieces are likely to roll under some piece of furniture and not be found for months.

Pushing the two main pieces of a lock together from opposite sides of a door usually takes a bit of jiggling. A helper is often useful, to hold one half while you maneuver the other. Setting the screws can take some patience, too, but yields to persistence and a steady hand.

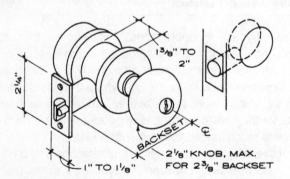

NOTES

1. Installation requires 2⅛ in. hole in door face. Door edge requires ⅞ in. or ¹⁵⁄₁₆ in. hole for standard lock, 1 in. hole for heavy duty lock.
2. Backsets: standard lock—2⅜ in. (regular), 2 in., 2¾ in., 3¾ in., 5 in., 7 in., 8 in., 10 in., 18 in. Heavy duty lock 2¾ in. (regular), 3¾ in., 5 in., 6 in., 7 in., 8 in., 18 in., 19 in. (42 in. special).

FIGURE 6.11 Many doors come with holes already drilled (right) for standard size locksets (left) and passage sets. Locksets like these divide into three pieces for assembly in the hole in the door.

No-Mortise Hinges

If you choose to hang a door the old-fashioned way, just remember that you must be as precise as a furniture-maker, but on a larger scale. You must mortise exactly or suffer a sticking door.

A good alternative to the ordinary hinges that require precise mortises are no-mortise hinges (see Figure 6.12). They are quick and easy to install and, if you value your time more than you do a traditional look, you should choose them wherever new hinges are called for.

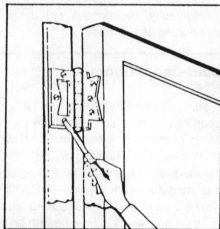

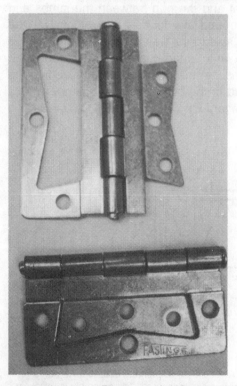

FIGURE 6.12 The no-mortise hinge saves work and money. It is installed on top of the jamb and door without the need for the precise chiseling of a mortise.

These surface-mounted butterfly hinges are self-aligning and reversible. They are available from the larger supply houses along the East Coast or directly from the New York manufacturer (Edward Leeds and Company, 139 East Merrick Road, Freeport, NY 11520).

With a no-mortise hinge, all you need to hang a properly fitting door is a pencil and a screwdriver. In addition, no-mortise hinges last as long as regular hinges for most doors; that is, ones that weigh less than 80 pounds and are less than 3 ft. wide. If a door is larger than this, the screws of a no-mortise hinge may work themselves loose.

TABLE 6.1
Exterior Door Options

THE PROJECT
Replace a 36″-wide front door. Reinstall the original lockset and make everything ready for painting or staining.

Options	Cost/Door Contracted	Cost/Door DIY	Difficulty Level	Comments and Recommendations
Flush Birch Prehung Install a solid-core door with spring bronze weatherstripping.	$360 CC	$190	2	Flush doors are good second-door options.
Metal Prehung Install a foam-core metal-skinned door with magnetic weatherstripping.	$365 VB	$195 VB	2	Metal-skinned doors have high R-values and low infiltration, and offer increased security. Buy ones that are galvanized.
Flush Birch Install a solid-core wood door in the existing jamb. Weatherstrip with spring bronze.	$375	$165 CC	3	Use separate parts only when the interior and exterior molding are unique and will remain.
Pine 6-Panel Prehung Install a colonial-style, solid wood door with spring bronze weatherstripping.	$480	$260	3	Over 35% more expensive than flush birch, but pick the door you want when aesthetics are important.

TABLE 6.2
Interior Door Options

THE PROJECT
Replace a 36"-wide door, including all hardware and finish.

Options	Cost/Door Contracted	Cost/Door DIY	Difficulty Level	Comments and Recommendations
CLOSET OPTIONS				
Folding Accordion Hang a woven wood and vinyl door from top track.	$90 CC	$36 CC	1	Can be an expensive, quick option for closets. Doesn't require construction skills or finishing.
Bifold Metal Install a prefinished set of doors on track and pivot.	$110 VB	$80	2	Prefinishing saves time and money. Can't be cut to match opening.
Bifold Flush Wood Install a set of primed doors on track and pivot. Topcoat to match room.	$154	$56	2	Bifold doors require minimal hardware, but must be high quality to last. Least expensive DIY option for a matching closet door.
Louvered Prehung Install a 1⅜"-thick full-louvered door on 2 hinges.	$186	$53 VB	2	An overlooked option for closets that adds visual interest while remaining one of the least expensive doors available, as long as you finish it yourself.
Bifold Louvered Pine Install a set of full-louvered doors on track and pivot. Topcoat with clear finish.	$189	$84	2	Full louvers are inexpensive to buy, but expensive to paint.
Bypassing Flush Install a set of hollow-core, hardboard, 6'-wide doors. Prime and topcoat to match room.	$240	$90 CC	2	Least expensive door for large openings (5' or more). Use the most expensive hardware offered to get the longest life.

Options	Cost/Door Contracted	Cost/Door DIY	Difficulty Level	Comments and Recommendations
BED & BATH OPTIONS				
Lauan Flush Install a hollow-core, prehung door and apply 1 coat of clear finish.	$145 CC	$49 CC	**2**	This door provides the basics of privacy and security at the minimum expense for both bedroom and bath.
Pressed Hardboard Install a 6-panel, primed, prehung door. Topcoat to match room.	$152 VB	$74 VB	**2**	This is the most widely used door in moderate-cost new construction. It looks like solid pine, but costs 50% less. It's a good bedroom door.
Solid Wood Install a 6-panel pine door stained. Apply 1 coat of clear finish.	$290	$126	**3**	Top of the line, recommended for historic applications and to match existing conditions.

7 | **Cabinets and Storage**

Have you ever heard of anyone with too much storage space? Neither have we. Everybody could use more space for the materials that are crammed into closets, stacked on shelves, stuffed into the basement, or wedged into the attic.

This chapter discusses ways to create more storage space around the house, including creating new closets, kitchens, cabinets, and shelves, or improving existing ones.

KITCHENS

When homeowners begin to consider making over a kitchen, they usually think about all-new cabinets and countertops. They rip out the old and bring in the new. This is the most expensive way to remodel a kitchen.

As you can see in Table 7.1 (page 103), buying and installing new, wooden, top-of-the-line kitchen cabinets is the most expensive of the six remodeling options listed. Moreover, this option traditionally reaps the least payback when the house is sold. Some homeowners put thousands, even tens of thousands, of dollars into cabinetwork and countertops, but do not recoup that money at sale time. The kitchen looks better, but a buyer does not see the money—he or she sees only nice cabinets.

Some far more cost-effective ways to spruce up a kitchen follow.

Install only a new countertop. Because there are so many colors and types to choose from, you can make a very bold interior design statement and give the kitchen a brand new feeling merely by installing a new countertop.

Install only new doors and handles. Because much of the visible cabinetry in the kitchen is doors, it makes sense to replace only doors and handles, rather than entire cabinets. The sides, backing, and shelves are mostly out of sight, and cabinets were often constructed better in the past than they are today.

Paint the cabinets. Painting the cabinets is another way to give a whole new feeling to the kitchen at minimal expense.

If you are thinking of taking out all the old cabinets, and if you don't mind a strictly functional look, consider replacing them with metal ones, which are relatively cheap and stand up well to heavy use. Another way to save money is to buy particleboard cabinets, but particleboard does not hold up well to heavy use or continual wetting. A good compromise is to buy cabinets that have particleboard sides and shelves, but real wood doors and frames.

You will save money if you buy the largest cabinet for the space. The larger the cabinet, the less the cost per linear foot. Two inexpensive 24-in.-wide cabinets will cost a total of about $225, but a single 48-in.-wide cabinet will cost only about $180.

Kitchen Shelving

Homeowners often overlook one of the lowest cost storage designs: open shelving. Open shelving also results in a more efficient kitchen space; less effort is required to reach pots, pans, spices, and other paraphernalia.

In 1869, Harriet Becker and Catherine Stowe published *The American Woman's Home.* They thought that a kitchen should be like the galley of a steamship, with every article and utensil arranged so that a cook could reach whatever was needed in a single step.

In their model kitchen, open shelving was used extensively. The shelving was also shallow, so that only one row of items could be stored on each shelf. Their color scheme called for sunny yellow walls and a gray floor.

Working along the same lines is Sam Clark, a modern designer and builder. In his book, *The Motion Minded Kitchen* (Houghton Mifflin, 1985), Clark reinvestigates the time-and-motion studies of 30 and 50 years ago that led to modern triangular kitchen layouts. Clark discovered that many of the early researchers' recommendations were misinterpreted or ignored. Instead of the triangular layout, he recommends three work centers, one each for mixing, serving, and cleaning. A Clark kitchen has utensils and ingredients stored on hooks and open shelves within easy reach of the stove. Bowls and saucepans are in open shelves near the sink (see Figure 7.1).

Hooks and open shelving are efficient—there is no cabinet door to open and close (see Figure 7.2). You can see at a glance where a utensil is, rather than having to open several cabinet doors.

We estimate that if you substitute open shelving for cabinets wherever possible, you save about $50/running foot of kitchen cabinets. So reduce the number of cabinets and store in them only seldom-used items.

We have seen exterior iron fencing recycled as an overhead pot rack, melon crates varnished and hung up to serve as open cabinets, and PVC pipe supporting open shelves. The possibilities are endless for low-cost kitchen improvements.

Cabinet Repairs

If you want to replace your old cabinets with new ones, is it because you no longer like the way they look, or because you no longer like the way they work? If the layout and style no longer suit you, then go ahead and replace old cabinets. But if you are considering a wholesale change because the shelves are sagging, the countertops are scorched, or the drawers would be

FIGURE 7.1 In Sam Clark's kitchen, pots and pans, utensils, and ingredients are stored on hooks and open shelves within easy reach of the three basic task areas—mixing, cooking, and cleaning.

FIGURE 7.2 In this kitchen, strips of pine lattice tacked to the wall hold a variety of frequently used utensils.

better off as shelves, relax—all these irritations can be corrected. Repairing kitchen cabinets instead of replacing them is one of the biggest opportunities for cost savings in home improvements.

Sagging shelves. The simple remedy is to take out the shelf, turn it over, and put it back where it was. Or put in a brace or a thicker shelf. If you cannot remove the shelf, glue and screw a 1 × 3 to the bottom edge or fasten an aluminum angle to the outside corner; that should stop further sagging.

Racked cabinet. If a cabinet is no longer square,

remove it from the wall. Tap open the joints that are not already open and force in glue. Then, close the joints with bar clamps that extend from one end of the cabinet to the other. Check the corners with a carpenter's square and make adjustments as needed; then wait for the glue to dry, remove the clamps, and rehang the cabinet.

Warped door. Cut a piece of oak strip shorter than the door and screw it to the door back. If that does not take out the warp, remove the oak strip, plane it so that it has a curvature opposite to that of the door's inside, and screw it in place again. Another alternative is to buy and install another door.

Broken drawer bottoms. Do not try to repair the drawer bottom—throw it away. But a new piece of plywood or tempered hardboard the same size as the discarded piece and slip it into the grooves along the drawer sides.

Broken drawer guides. Take the guides out and replace them with identical new wooden pieces. Installing a metal glide may be less trouble, however, and results in a fix that will last longer. Metal glides are made to fit most cabinet drawers and are installed with a drill and screwdriver.

Damaged countertop. If a countertop is scorched or otherwise damaged, it need not be replaced wholesale. Instead, cut out the damaged area of laminate and replace it with a ceramic-glass or butcher-block cutting area. Support the butcher block or ceramic glass with a metal rim similar to the rim that supports some sinks; these are available in kitchen supply stores. An alternative is to use a router to cut down into the countertop, making a shallow area into which decorative tile can be set. Set a thin piece of plywood into the hollowed area before laying the tile—it provides a better surface for the adhesive.

Damage to metal cabinets. If you have metal cabinets, especially base cabinets, they may be dented, nicked, or scraped. Fix such damage just as if the cabinet were a car body. Fill dents with auto-body filler, then sand and repaint. Hammer out bad dents from the inside first, or, if they are inaccessible that way, pull them out by inserting sheet-metal screws halfway and pulling on them with pliers until the dent pops. Fill holes with the auto-body filler.

Coverting shelves to drawers. Where shelves are not meeting your storage needs, you can take them out and replace them with drawers. Saw out the shelves and their supports, and then install new supports in the places you want the drawers to go. You can use wicker-wire drawer kits that have side-, top-, or bottom-mounted glides. Alternatively, have a cabinetmaker construct the drawers of wood, attach metal drawer glides to the drawers and the supports, and slide the drawers into place.

SHELVES AND CLOSETS

Inside or outside the kitchen, most of your storage needs will be met by shelves or closets. Here are some ideas for erecting shelves and closets cost-effectively.

Brackets

There are many ways to hang shelves on a wall. We'll discuss some of the most common.

Twelve-inch metal brackets that attach to studs behind wallboard or plaster are about $1.40 each. They are sturdy but somewhat ugly and are not adjustable.

Metal channels that accept brackets cost about $2.50 for a 3-ft length and $1.60 for each bracket. They have the virtue of being adjustable.

If you happen to be working on cabinet interiors, bookcases, or other spaces that can be bracketed on two sides by wood, consider small, L-shaped shelf clips (see Figure 7.3). They fit into ¼-in. holes drilled in the wood. Putting two lines of holes up and down the wood support gives you adjustable shelves.

For jobs where aesthetics are not too important, as in a closet, basement, or attic, consider metal shelf corner clips. These are sheet-metal Ts, Ls, and crosses that you can use to fasten ⅝-in. or ¾-in. cabinet sides and shelving boards. They forgive imperfect joints, add strength, and give a clean, finished look to wood shelving.

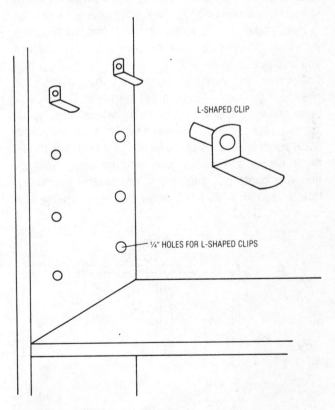

FIGURE 7.3 Metal L-shaped clips fit into holes drilled in wood supports and hold up shelves. The rows of holes make the shelves adjustable.

Shelves

Using open shelving rather than cabinetwork in the kitchen saves money. Common shelving materials are solid pine, laminated pine, ¾-in. plywood, and particleboard (see Table 7.2, page 105). Laminated pine is a good choice because it combines low cost, high strength, good appearance, and versatility.

Plywood is also a good shelving material, but its edges show the built-up layers of wood. To cover the edges, buy thin strips of ¾-in.-wide wood veneer with adhesive on one side; lay the veneer on the plywood edge and use a hot iron to soften the adhesive enough to stick to the plywood. Alternatively, you can buy or make a ¾-in. edge-molding strip that you glue and tack onto the edge.

There are yet other shelving materials. Veneer on particleboard, even vinyl-coated particleboard, is a little more expensive, but saves you the job of painting. Vinyl-coated wire racks are lightweight, easy to install, and easy to clean. Glass is especially good for lightweight plants in front of windows.

If an existing wall has been slightly damaged in renovation, there is no need to make it over for the sake of open shelving. Instead, if the plaster or drywall is intact, cover it with ¼-in. pressed hardboard paneling. This makes a sufficient backing for the shelves you add later.

Along a 6-ft wall, we compared the cost of the cheapest available hanging cabinets and the cost of open shelving. Using vinyl-coated particleboard hanging cabinets, we came up with a total of $329, including $156 for the cabinet and $92 for labor. Using three-tiered plywood shelving, quarter-round edge molding, and two coats of paint or a polyurethane finish, the total was only $125, including labor. The saving was more than $200.

Closets

No one seems to have enough closets. They can be added after the house is built, but this requires a bit of finagling. However, you do not have to build a full walk-in closet with a door to enjoy the benefit of added storage space.

A closet built by a contractor is the most expensive option, costing about $770 for one that is 2-½ ft deep, 3 ft wide, and 8 ft high (see Table 7.3, page 106). You can make one yourself for considerably less, about $190. Most building codes do not require a permit for a new closet, but many local electrical codes require a light in one. A new door in a room can also affect the calculation for the required number of wall outlets in a room. Both requirements can increase the cost of the work if your job is in strict compliance with codes.

If you need a lot of closet space, look for a narrow, rectangular room in the house where one partition near the end of the room can not only serve as the backing for a bed, but also set off a walk-in closet space (see Figure 7.4).

Another technique for adjoining rooms is to build a new partition wall about 3 ft away from the old one that divides the rooms (see Figure 7.5). The new partition is built with a doorway in it; the old one needs a doorway cut. The space created is divided in half by a short partition wall, resulting in two new closets, one for each room. The closet space also serves as a sound barrier between the two rooms.

Keep a sharp eye out for potential storage space. In some families, a child sleeps on an elevated bed, while below there is a closet full of toys or clothes and perhaps a desk. The space beneath a stairway can often be converted to storage space. The wall spaces above toilets or sinks are notorious for serving no use

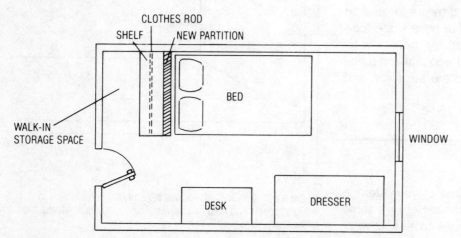

FIGURE 7.4 Long rooms can be inexpensively converted to a sleeping area with a large walk-in closet behind.

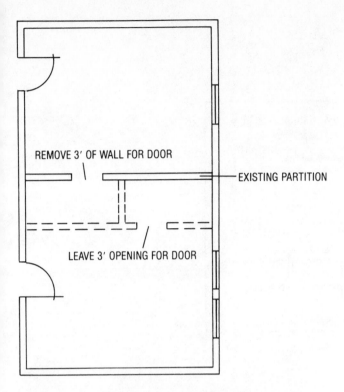

FIGURE 7.5 Back-to-back closets are efficient for adjoining rooms and can be created by building a new partition wall, dividing the space, and creating two doorways.

FIGURE 7.6 Open shelving is one-fourth the cost of cabinets and can fill almost any available space.

at all, but can easily accommodate towels and other supplies (see Figure 7.6).

In the old days, homes did not have closets. In 1910, homeowners considered it a luxury to find one 12-in.-deep, 2-ft-wide closet built into their new home. Clothing then was relatively more expensive than it is now—a $2 pair of work boots would be the equivalent today of a pair costing $144—and people stored what they had in furniture bureaus and chests.

You can still buy a wardrobe if you want more closed-off storage space. A wardrobe has all the virtues of furniture: It is movable, and you can take it with you to a new home. Many wardrobes are less expensive than closets built by contractors.

Of course, all you may want in a closet is a place to hang clothes, place shoes, and lay hats. These needs can be met by other constructions that are not full closets.

If you simply need a clothes-hanging rod in an attic or large storage space, you can hang a ¾-in. iron pipe or a wooden pole with wire from eyebolts fastened to ceiling beams. If you use a wooden pole and are putting a great deal of weight on it, support it in the middle with a 2 × 4.

Going a step further, you can put up a wall rack, such as the one shown in Figure 7.7. This makes two shelves plus a long clothes-hanging rod. The metal bracket that forms the support for both the wooden shelf above and the clothes-hanging rod is available in hardware stores.

You can make such rod-and-shelf arrangements that stand out in the room or are shielded from sight in varying degrees. Any rod and shelf can project from one wall and be supported out in the room by a rising piece of plywood (see Figure 7.8).

Alternatively, two pieces of plywood perpendicular to a wall can rise off the floor and support both shelving and rod. A curtain can be used to cover the assembly, or a bifold door can be added.

We estimate that constructing a standard closet is more than three times more expensive than constructing a simple, built-in wardrobe without a door. With a bifold door, the wardrobe is still less than half the cost of the closet. Having a contractor build a 3-ft closet using 2 × 4 framing, drywall, and a fairly inexpensive bifold door costs about $770. Making an open closet with ⅝-in. plywood sides and the same shelving and rod as the first costs only about $225. A bifold door adds about $80.

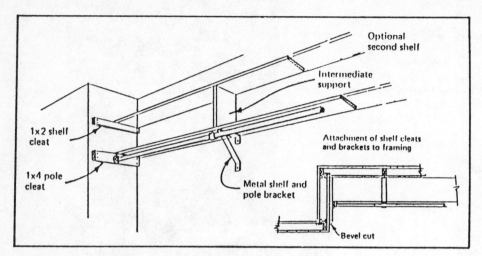

FIGURE 7.7 Readily purchased hardware can be used to make a space near a jog in the wall to store clothes, boxes, and a miscellany of other goods.

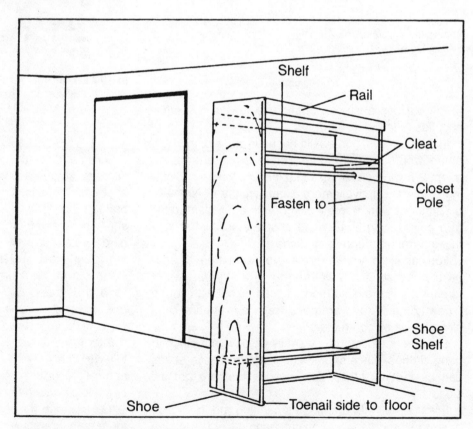

FIGURE 7.8 Constructing closets as furniture instead of permanent partitions creates storage quickly without the need for additional electrical outlets.

TABLE 7.1 Kitchen Facelift Options	THE PROJECT Update a 10′ × 14′, 2-wall kitchen with 14′ of older wood cabinets and a pink plastic countertop.

Scope of Work	Cost/lin ft Contracted	Cost/lin ft DIY	Project Cost Contracted	Project Cost DIY	Difficulty Level DIY Advice		Comments and Recommendations
Paint Cabinets Prepare and paint cabinets with one coat of gloss enamel. Install new handles.	$2.40/sq ft	$0.60/sq ft	$240 CC	$60 CC	**1**		Restaining, pickling, or repainting and adding new knobs has the highest payback. Striping and restaining can be completed at half the cost of new door fronts.
New Countertop Remove countertop. Install a postformed plastic laminate countertop.	$25	$10	$350	$140	**2**	Plan on replacing water supply tubes.	Changes the feel of a kitchen in one day. Measure accurately and have the shop cut the sink hole.
New Doors Install matching wood doors and drawers. Veneer all exposed stiles.	$60	$30	$900 VB	$425 VB	**2**	Buy a cabinet hinge drill template.	Saves 50% and has a very high rate of return for kitchens with good basic layouts. Lots of patterns to select.
New Laminated Cabinets Install laminated particleboard cabinets and countertop.	$125	$60	$1,750	$875	**3**		Least expensive new cabinet. Easy to clean. Will deteriorate if particleboard stays wet. Hardware pulls loose more easily than with plywood or solid wood.
New Metal Cabinets Install white enameled, steel cabinets and a postformed countertop.	$145	$85	$2,030	$1,190	**3**		Best option for heavy-duty use.

(Continued on next page)

TABLE 7.1 Continued

Scope of Work	Cost/lin ft Contracted	Cost/lin ft DIY	Project Cost Contracted	Project Cost DIY	Difficulty Level DIY Advice	Comments and Recommendations
New Stained Cabinets Install plywood and solid wood cabinets of stock size, average grade. Install countertop.	$185	$103	$2,620–$6,000	$1,450	**3**	Expensive kitchen cabinet replacements have very low rates of payback on resale. Solidly built low-end products are a good investment if the existing ones are truly unserviceable.
Custom Cabinets Install cabinets with solid wood doors, specialized hardware, and cabinet design. Install custom countertop.	$600	$240	$8,400	$3,640	**3**	A very poor value. Consider only if you're going to stay for at least 10 years. Upon resale, the average recapture rate is less than 50%.

TABLE 7.2
Shelving Material Options

THE PROJECT
Install a 4'-long shelf, 10" to 12" wide.

Options	Project Cost Contracted	Project Cost DIY	Difficulty Level	Comments and Recommendations
Select Pine Install 1" × 12" with 2 brackets.	$75	$15	1	Too high-quality for shelving unless it's to be stained or pickled.
Knotty Pine Install 1" × 12" with 2 brackets.	$75	$12	1	A quick option instead of sawing plywood.
Laminated Pine Install ¾" × 12" with 2 brackets.	$75	$15.50 VB	1	Use for wide and heavy loads like TVs. Much stronger than pine boards or plywood.
Particleboard Install ¾" × 12" with 3 brackets.	$75	$18	1	Least expensive option for well-supported shelving and light loads. Will sag if not supported every 18".
Vinyl-Coated Particleboard Install ¾" × 12" with 3 brackets.	$75	$27	1	Expensive way to avoid painting, but the job is complete in 30 min. Very cleanable.
Mahogany Veneer Install ¾" × 12" with 3 brackets.	$75	$21	1	Stain for real wood look but support it like particleboard.
Exterior Plywood Install ⅝" BCX with 2 brackets.	$75	$12	2	This is the best all-around material for strength, cost, durability, and appearance for DIYers with tools.
Glass Install ⅜" × 10" with 3 brackets.	$75	$22	1	Looks great in windows. For lightweight plants. Usually can't be cut because it's tempered glass.
Wire Rack Install vinyl-coated steel 12" wide with 2 brackets.	$75	$12 CC	1	This material will grow in availability. Best choice for wet-area shelves, baths, and inside kitchen base cabinets.

TABLE 7.3
Hanging Storage Options

THE PROJECT
Create 3'-wide × 8'-high × 30"-deep additional storage for hanging clothes.

Options	Project Cost Contracted	Project Cost DIY	Difficulty Level DIY Advice		Comments and Recommendations
Hang Rack Screw a 3'-wide wall-mounted metal rack and shelf to the wall.	$65	$6–$40 CC	**1**		A 3'-wide metal or wood rack is the least expensive, quickest way to handle storage problems.
Pole and Shelf Kit Add a metal pole and shelf kit to an existing closet.	$90 CC	$39	**1**		Kits can more than double the amount of accessible storage in an existing closet by adding poles and reorganizing space.
Buy Wardrobe Purchase a 48" walnut-patterned metal wardrobe.	N/A	$220	**1**		Least expensive way to create out-of-sight storage space without DIY energy.
Cost-Buster Closet Build a ⅝", BCX open plywood closet. Paint or stain, 2 coats.	$225 VB	$62	**2**	Excellent DIY project.	The back of this closet can double as backing for shelves in a bedroom or can be built under a bunk bed (see Figure 7.8).
Normal Closet Construct a closet using 2" × 4" studs, ½" drywall, metal shelf, and pole assembly.	$770	$190 VB	**3**	Be sure to extend any electrical outlets.	Permanent. Make it as big as possible.

8 | Masonry

Everyone hopes that the masonry in their home will never need repair. But eventually, it does. Even brick walls succumb to aging, and once they show their age, they need help.

STRUCTURAL PROBLEMS

Your ability to spot structural damage is important to the overall well-being of your house. Although cracking and bulging are far less common than slight deterioration of mortar joints, such major problems sometimes do appear on older buildings.

To assess the condition of brick walls, look along the walls to see if any sections are bulging outward. The most common locations are near the bottom of a wall and halfway up, near windows. Bulges in a structural brick wall usually result from failed mortar joints. In a veneer wall (which is a wood structural wall linked at intervals with metal ties to a covering layer of brick), bulges can usually be traced to ties that have come loose from either the wood or the brick.

Although bulges rarely threaten the integrity of a house—the trouble is usually confined to their immediate location—they will probably need work in time. The job of eliminating bulges is best left to the professional.

Cracking may be caused by settling of the soil below the wall. The wall may have been built on land that was not compact enough for it. Or, the soil may have shifted due to groundwater or other causes and carried one part of the wall with it. Other causes of cracks are a rotten ledger (horizontal beam) over a window, cycles of freezing and thawing, earthquakes, and impacts, as from a car. Masonry walls will tolerate a fair amount of movement without posing the danger of collapse or of sections falling out. It takes a lot of movement to cause these calamities, but if you are worried, call a masonry contractor or engineer for an inspection.

It's important to learn whether a crack has opened all it is going to—an indication that the source of the trouble has stopped—or is still widening (or even going through a cycle of widening and narrowing). Test to see if the crack is stable by filling it with plaster of paris. If there is any movement, the crack will reappear in the brittle plaster. Watch for several months, and check every few weeks; the crack may open and close.

If the crack continues to open—even a small fraction of an inch over many months—the structural problem must be solved before the wall suffers increased damage. Consult an engineer.

If you are sure that the crack is neither growing nor oscillating, fill it with grout, a thin mixture of nonshrinking mortar. Clean all loose mortar out of the crack. Use a small, specialized masonry chisel to undercut the surface of the crack so that the interior portion is wider than the portion at the surface—the grout will adhere better that way.

Next, wet the crack. Brace a 3-ft-long board against the lowest part of the crack and use a funnel to pour in grout. Work up the crack with additional boards, if necessary. Remove the boards once the grout has set, then scrape away excess mortar and repoint the whole length of the crack.

Cracks around windows and doors may not be caused by soil settling but by shrinking and expanding of the wooden framing of the door or window due to changes in moisture content. This shrinking and expanding may still be going on, so using mortar here may be a losing proposition. A better bet is to fill the cracks with a silicone caulk, which will flex with movement of the framing, eliminating the crack.

FIGURE 8.1   Water damage to old lime mortar is one of the most common problems of old brick buildings.

DETERIORATING MORTAR JOINTS

More common than bulges and cracks is deterioration of the mortar joints between bricks. The mortar weakens and crumbles out. The problem is especially prevalent in houses built before about 1930, when the mortar used was lime putty. Portland cement, which is a stronger binding agent, was not used. Water or acid leaches the lime out of the old mortar and, eventually, the mortar must be replaced (see Figure 8.1).

To test the integrity of your mortar joints, poke them with an ice pick. If the mortar seems sandy and falls out easily, the joints have deteriorated to the point where you have to do something. If you don't correct the problem, moisture will continue to work its way into the brick work, eventually causing more deterioration that requires even more work.

If the brick, the mortar, or both are deteriorating, you have three choices: Repoint the mortar joints, cover the entire brick face and joints with stucco, or touch up the worst of the damage and apply paint. The cheapest alternative is to repair and paint, the second cheapest is to apply stucco, and the most expensive is to repoint (see Table 8.1, page 114).

Repointing is often favored because it retains the original look of the wall; in some historic districts, this is mandatory. Moreover, if you decide to stucco or paint, you still probably will have to repoint the worst of the joints to maintain the integrity of the wall. So we'll take up repointing first.

Repointing

Repointing is highly labor-intensive. Although it involves small areas, the joints themselves, there may be thousands of joints over a huge expanse, requiring the erection of major scaffolding (see Figure 8.2).

If you are doing the repointing yourself, begin by chiseling out the damaged mortar. Remove any material that crumbles easily, using a specialized chisel

FIGURE 8.2 Repointing deteriorated brick is the most expensive kind of masonry repair, because it involves work on thousands of linear feet of small joints. But on historic buildings, like this 1810 one in Baltimore, it is the only choice.

available in masonry supply stores; don't hammer hard enough to crack the bricks. **CAUTION: Wear goggles for this or any work requiring the chipping or cutting of brick.**

Mix the mortar. If your old mortar was lime putty, use lime putty again or add only 20 percent portland cement. Using too much will make a mortar that is harder than the brick itself and will lead to harmful stress in the wall. If you are concerned about matching the color of the old mortar, test your new mortar mixture first in a small area. You can change the color by adding coloring or using colored sand in the mix (both available at masonry stores). Colored sand is especially helpful in matching some redder mortars, but matching any one mortar color can be very difficult.

Clean out the joints with a hose and pressure nozzle. Lay the mortar on a flat board. Use a *joint filler* (a long, thin trowel made especially for repointing) that is slightly narrower than the joint to push mortar from the board into the cleaned and wetted joint. Fill the vertical joints with a small trowel. Then, after the mortar has stiffened slightly, run the trowel or a shaping tool called a *jointer* (see Figure 8.3) along the new joints to make their profile match that of the old (see Figure 8.4).

You may have to replace a whole brick if it is very damaged. To do so, chisel out the mortar in the joints around the brick and then split the brick with a chisel and hammer. Clean out the hole. Cut off about ¾ in. of the back of a new brick so that it will fit easily into the hole. Put an ample amount of mortar into the hole

and then push in the new brick. Scrape away excess mortar that has oozed out and repoint any places the mortar has not oozed to the surface.

If you need to break bricks along exact lines, use a brick hammer and a tool called a *brick set,* which is a broad chisel. Use the brick set and hammer to tap along the line for the cut all around the brick. Set the brick on a resilient surface such as turf or a thin bed of sand and hold the brick set to the line again. Strike it hard, and the brick should split on the line you want (most of the time, that is—even pros mangle a few bricks using this method).

If you have a lot of bricks to cut, look into renting a brick cutter (a power saw) from a rental store; they rent for about $24/day. Alternatively, and for fewer cuts, use a masonry blade set in your circular saw. **CAUTION: The blade cuts slowly and makes lots of dust, so wear a mask and goggles,** but it costs less than renting a brick cutter and still makes a precise slice.

Covering with Stucco

The least expensive way to deal with a less-than-perfect brick wall is to repair the worst of the damage and then stucco or paint it. If you need to repoint more than 35 percent of a wall, consider these alternatives.

If you decide to stucco over the brick, you need only repoint the worst and deepest of the damaged joints.

FIGURE 8.3   A jointer shapes fresh mortar during a repointing job.

FIGURE 8.4   Masons make different joint profiles. Jointing tools of different shapes, available in masonry supply stores, make new joints match the old.

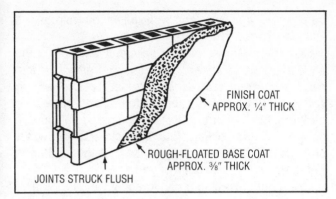

FINISH COAT
APPROX. ¼" THICK

ROUGH-FLOATED BASE COAT
APPROX. ⅜" THICK

JOINTS STRUCK FLUSH

FIGURE 8.5 The thicker, first coat of stucco should be left with a rough finish, even scratched, so that the finish coat adheres to it well.

The two layers of stucco that will cover the wall take care of minor joint faults.

Apply stucco over brick in two coats (see Figure 8.5). Wet the wall with a hose the night before the first coat is to be applied and again just before work begins. It is best to apply stucco on a humid, overcast day so that the water does not evaporate too quickly and weaken the bond.

About an hour after putting on the first coat, which should be about ⅜ in. thick, smooth it with a masonry tool called a *wooden float* (a piece of smooth wood with a handle). Then spray the stucco with a hose every 12 hours for 48 hours.

After five more days of drying, the stucco is ready for the top coat. This finishing layer, which is about ¼ in. thick, can be applied in a variety of textures. Some finishers scrape a piece of wood along the surface to give it a rough, scratched look, dab or sweep it with a whisk broom for a swirled or stippled texture, make it very smooth with a trowel, or splatter it by knocking a whisk broom full of mortar against a stick held close to the wall.

To repair stucco walls, see the Repairs to Stucco section at the end of this chapter (page 113).

Painting Over Brick

If you decide on paint rather than stucco, you still begin by repointing damaged mortar joints, but you take care to fix minor as well as major damage and finish the new mortar neatly. After the mortar has dried, paint over the wall with a highly penetrating sealer-primer; this will help to "reglue" old lime mortar and make a sound base for the top coats of paint. Good top coats of quality paint should solve any deterioration problems caused by water penetrating from the outside.

Parapets and Chimneys

Many urban townhouses have parapet walls, which act like dividing walls between roofs, and chimneys. Although they may be superficial to the structure, use, or appearance of the house, both parapets and chimneys can suffer exceptional damage. They are exposed to water and freezing from more than one side and are susceptible to blows from branches, workers, windstorms, and the like.

If damage to the masonry is extensive, consider removing the structure altogether. If a parapet or chimney provides no aesthetic, fire-code, heating, or structural function, it will be nothing but a source of repair demands in the future (see Figure 8.6). You will be better off to remove most of it from the body of the house. If you are removing a parapet that prevents rain water from streaming down a wall, leave enough of it intact to perform its retaining function.

If the damage to a parapet or chimney is confined to mortar joints and cosmetics, you can cover the structure with stucco as discussed in the previous section. Another covering for a parapet is Class A (not flammable) roofing material or *flashing* (sheet metal used for waterproofing).

Where parapets act as fire-separation walls, they must remain (they help keep fires from spreading from

FIGURE 8.6 This chimney on an old townhouse is still being used, but it had to be repointed to stop water infiltration. If it wasn't being used, the best solution would have been to remove it and avoid future repairs.

roof to roof). In this case, it is best to make sure that water does not penetrate the joints—deterioration will follow, more rapidly in freezing climates than in moderate ones. Make sure the capping on the parapet is sound. Repoint where necessary. Cover the whole parapet with stucco, roofing material, or flashing. If you are coating the brick with silicone, use only the new, semipermeable kind; the older silicone locks in moisture that may freeze and pull off the skin of the brick in cold weather.

CLEANING BRICK

Brick is meant to be a low-maintenance material, and no one minds if it is rubbed, bumped, scraped, dinged, or scratched. But occasionally, as both an interior and an exterior wall material, it may need cleaning. The job is a bit messy, but the results can be pleasing.

One thing to remember is that too much cleaning can be harmful. Years ago, sandblasting was popular, but it often removed the hardened, baked-on outer surface of the brick. The surface left behind was softer and more prone to deterioration from the elements. Consequently, sandblasting is out of favor; so, too, are other harsh cleaning methods. The slogan for cleaning brick is: Use the gentlest method that gives satisfactory results.

One way to remove grimy spots from brick is to take a similar brick, break it in half, and rub it against the spot. The brick in your hand acts as a kind of sandpaper to abrade away the soiled area. But you should use the softer, broken portion of the brick and not the hardened, baked-on surface.

You may be able to clean a brick wall with a garden hose and pressure nozzle. If a garden hose does not clean the wall to your satisfaction, you can rent a power sprayer from a tool-rental store. These attach to an outdoor spigot and run off either a gasoline engine or an electric motor powered by a cable you plug into an outdoor receptacle. The better models allow you to adjust the pressure up to about 4,500 lbs/sq in. and include small reservoirs for cleaning agents that feed into the water stream. Use the lowest pressure that gets the job done.

When using these pressure sprayers, it is best to cover any delicate shrubbery nearby, plus outdoor lights, with plastic sheeting. Begin at the top of a wall and let the water soak into the grime for half an hour before spraying over the same area a second time. Whether you're careful or not, you will probably be bombarded with spray, so wear full-length rain gear if you want to stay dry.

Stains caused by mortar or salts that leach out of the brick and form a whitish powder, called *efflorescence,* can be removed with a dilute muriatic acid. **Wearing safety goggles, heavy rubber gloves, and protective clothing,** mix ten parts of water with one part of muriatic acid in a plastic bucket. **Pour the acid into the water and not the other way around, so that the acid does not foam and splash back at you.**

Use a natural bristle brush to apply the mixture. The dilute acid will foam on the stains. Scrub them off. Then neutralize the acid on the wall by washing it down with a solution of two parts water to one part ammonia. Finally, flush the cleaned area with water.

CAUTION: If you use muriatic acid indoors, open all the windows, and wear a respirator along with the goggles. If your nose or eyes begin to sting from vapors, leave the room and splash your face with water. If you splash the acid on any parts of your body flush them immediately with water. If it has touched your eyes, get medical treatment immediately.

Removing Stains

Try the following methods to remove other kinds of stain on brick.

For moss, scrub on ammonium sulfamate, sold in garden-supply stores.

For oil and tar, use an emulsifying agent. For tough tar stains, add kerosene to the cleanser. Then flush the spot with water.

For rust, use a solution of one pound of oxalic acid to one gallon of water. Rinse with clean water.

For smoke, try a bathroom or kitchen cleanser and then flush with water.

For paint, use a paint remover. Be wary of the chemicals; read the cautions on the label and protect your skin and eyes. Brush on the paint remover with a paintbrush and let the chemicals soak into the stains. Then flush them away with a garden hose, aiming so that ricochets do not hit you.

CAUTION: Ammonium sulfamate, oxalic acid, and paint removers containing methylene chloride are toxic substances. Wear protective clothing and gloves; wear goggles. If any splash in your eyes, flush them with water immediately and get medical attention. If oxalic acid splashes on your skin, rinse it with water. If ammonium sulfamate or

methylene chloride splashes on your skin, wash it with soap and water. If you breathe too many fumes, go immediately to fresh air. If any of these are swallowed, call for immediate medical attention or a poison telephone hotline.

Sealing Brick

If the surface of brick has been so cleaned or damaged that its outer layer is allowing water to the interior, it is best to seal it. You can do this safely with new silicone sealers, which allow any trapped water vapor to escape. Another benefit of a sealer is that, on interior walls, it cuts down on the dust that emanates from the brick and often ends up on the floor and nearby furniture.

You can brush on the sealer. But for big expanses of wall, you can rent a tank-type garden sprayer that you sling over one shoulder. Fill the sprayer with the sealer and pump it onto the wall. If the sealer dribbles down the wall, smooth it with a brush.

Work on a day when the temperature is over 50°F, the wall has been dry for a week, and the 30-day forecast does not include freezing temperatures. Cover every square inch of wall, including joints, so that water cannot penetrate and get trapped behind the waterproofing solution.

REPAIRS TO STUCCO

If you have a stucco-covered wall to begin with, it may need maintenance. Some damage is obvious, such as where patches of stucco have fallen off the substrate—which can be brick, cinder block, or even wood covered with a wire mesh lath. To check for less visible damage, sight along the wall for bulges. If you see some, the problem is probably localized loosening of the stucco from the underlying brick, cinder block, or lath. Loose stucco should be removed and replaced with new.

However, bulges may be the result of poor structural members beneath. If the stucco appears tight, and there is no hollow sound when it is tapped, have a structural expert look at the wall. Some shoring up of the masonry or the wood frame behind the stucco may be needed.

To repair the stucco, clean out the damage as best you can. Clean down to solid backing, whether a lower layer of stucco or lath, brick, or cinder block. Apply one or two base coats of stucco to bring the level to within about ¼ in. of the surface. After the base coats are thoroughly dry, apply a top coat to match the surrounding stucco surface.

For more information about replacing stucco, including estimating costs, see Chapter 3.

TABLE 8.1	THE PROJECT
Masonry Repointing Options	Repair the deteriorating mortar on an 18'-wide, 3-story townhouse front and rear.

Options	Cost/sq ft Contracted	Cost/sq ft DIY	Project Cost Contracted	Project Cost DIY	Difficulty Level DIY Advice		Comments and Recommendations
Point and Paint Prepare wall with minor repointing (up to 20%). Apply an oil primer and a latex top coat.	$0.70	$0.16	$720 CC	$165 CC	**2**		Inexpensive, but must be repainted every 3–7 years. Hides minor imperfections and protects brick.
Stucco Trowel one coat of ⅜" exterior mortar over a latex bonding agent.	$2.07	$0.24	$2,130	$250	**3**	Long-lasting, low-skill job.	Good option for rear elevations. Best solution for parapets, basement walls. Long-lasting solution when applied correctly.
Scrub Coat Apply a sand grout coating over water-blasted walls.	$2.65	$0.24	$2,700	$290	**3**		Good option for badly deteriorated walls. May destroy historic resale value of attractive brick homes.
Scrape and Repoint Chisel out damaged mortar, repoint, and tool to match existing.	$2.95	$0.27	$3,040 VB	$280 VB	**4**	Rent scaffolding.	OK for small areas, but expensive contractor method for entire structure. Learning to point brick yourself results in a quick payback. The repointing will last 20 years.

Carpentry

Sooner or later, everyone who does home improvements needs to build a wall, a floor deck, or a roof. Whether you hire out the work or do it yourself, there are four general rules to save money in this kind of work, called framing:

1. Use high-quality lumber, but in dimensions that are slightly less than those traditionally used; in other words, don't buy framing lumber larger than you actually need.
2. Use structural particleboard sheathing or, if the appearance suits your taste, a structural siding such as textured plywood.
3. When appropriate, use adhesives and modern fasteners such as framing hardware, cement-coated nails, ring-shank nails, and so forth to ensure a stronger wall, floor, or roof. Saving pennies on these items is pound foolish.
4. Use prebuilt trusses instead of large (2 × 10 and 2 × 12) joists or rafters, if you are paying high labor costs for the work. Prebuilt trusses are generally simpler to install and contain openings for running wires and pipes.

BUILDING WALLS

Tradition holds that walls are made of 2 × 4 wooden studs spaced 16 in. apart. This method is so ingrained in building lore that any amendment to it is met with stubborn resistance.

But improved materials and an increased understanding of stresses have allowed carpenters to build strong walls in other ways. The traditional design for framing walls, 2 × 4's on 16-in. centers, was developed when lumber was roughly cut, ungraded, often undried, and attached with old-fashioned nails. Many carpenters frame walls (and floors and roofs) as if they were still using these old materials and refer to their method as the "right way" or "quality framing."

Recent testing, however, has shown that walls framed in the old way are nearly always stronger than they need to be. That also means that they're more expensive than they need to be.

As Tables 9.1 and 9.2 (pages 127 and 128) show, however, there are alternative ways to build walls—ones that use smaller dimension lumber, space the framing members farther apart, or both. Using such nontraditional methods costs less money initially or leads to savings over the long run.

We insert a caution here, however. Generally, the cost-saving methods we recommend have been promoted by national research and government agencies over the past decade or so. But they may not be appropriate in all applications, or even approved by the local building code. Where loads are heavy—because of, say, heavy equipment on floors or buildups of snow on roofs—these methods may not be sufficient. In addition, never build less substantially than the local building code requires. Ask an inspector if the method you choose is acceptable, either as a method specified in the code or as an equivalent. If the answer is no, do what the inspector says, or appeal the decision.

Next, we need an explanation of bearing and partition walls. *Bearing* means that the wall is holding up something above it—part of the roof, floor joists overhead, and so on. Such walls cannot be dismantled without temporarily supporting what they prop up and then putting something in their place—a new wall, a beam, or such—that does the work of supporting the weight above. Most exterior walls are bearing walls, although those that are under the ends of gables or shed roofs are technically not classified as such. Some interior walls are bearing walls. Construction involving removal or replacement of bearing walls requires a building permit almost everywhere in the United States.

A *partition* is a nonbearing wall. It merely divides one space from another and supports nothing. A partition wall can be removed and nothing is lost to the structure of the house; similarly, one can be erected anywhere in the house to divide space—so long as the resulting room sizes meet code.

Distinguishing an interior nonbearing wall from an interior bearing one is tricky and usually is best left to an expert—unless you are thoroughly familiar with the framing of your house, have and can interpret the blueprints, or know how loads are calculated.

Bearing Walls

The best long-term value in a new exterior wall is one made of 2 × 6's spaced 24 in. apart. The 2 × 6's cost more than 2 × 4's, but you buy fewer of them because you space them 24 in., not 16 in., apart.

In addition, with the 2 × 6's, you can use insulation batts that are 5-½ in. thick (actually, 6-¼ in. thick—they are compressed during construction), rather than 3-½ in. thick, as with 2 × 4's (see Figure 9.1). This results in a maximum R-value of 19, rather than 13, which leads to a reduction of heating bills. The one drawback of using 2 × 6's is that many stock door jambs and window frames have to be built out with pine strips to match the wider framing.

Using 2 × 4's spaced 24 in. apart is also acceptable. The strength achieved by spacing the studs 24 in. apart is more than sufficient to support a two-story house, because of the added strength of modern sheathing and because additional studs are placed around doors and windows. Using 2 × 4's spaced 24 in. apart is, in the short run, the cheapest do-it-yourself method of building a bearing wall.

Spacing the studs 24 in. apart saves money not only because there are fewer studs to buy, but also because there is less nailing to be done through sheathing and siding outside and drywall inside. In addition, 24-in. spacing is more energy-efficient. Studs conduct heat into and away from the interior far faster than do insulated wall cavities. The fewer the studs, the less the heat conduction.

There are other framing techniques that lead to buying fewer studs and doing less work. One is to use two studs, rather than the traditional three, at corners. Doing this saves 30 percent of the labor and materials at every corner. In addition, you can eliminate the short studs (called *cripple studs*) under windows that are less than 6 ft wide and use framing hardware (discussed on page 123) on the horizontal supports. You can also eliminate what are generally called *jack studs,* the shorter studs that support a header over a window or door.

There are two other ways to build bearing walls, but each has problems. Using 2 × 3's is sometimes possible, but stock window and door frames must be trimmed to fit. Although you save about 20 percent in the cost of studs, we don't recommend this method, because of the extra labor required to trim door and window frames and because the structural strength of 2 × 3 bearing walls is barely enough for the job.

Using metal studs is also possible (see Figure 9.2), but you need a crew that is familiar with them. In addition, when your wall studs are metal, you must use screws, not nails, when attaching drywall, sheathing, bookshelf brackets, or anything that is going to hold more weight than a picture frame. This can be a nuisance.

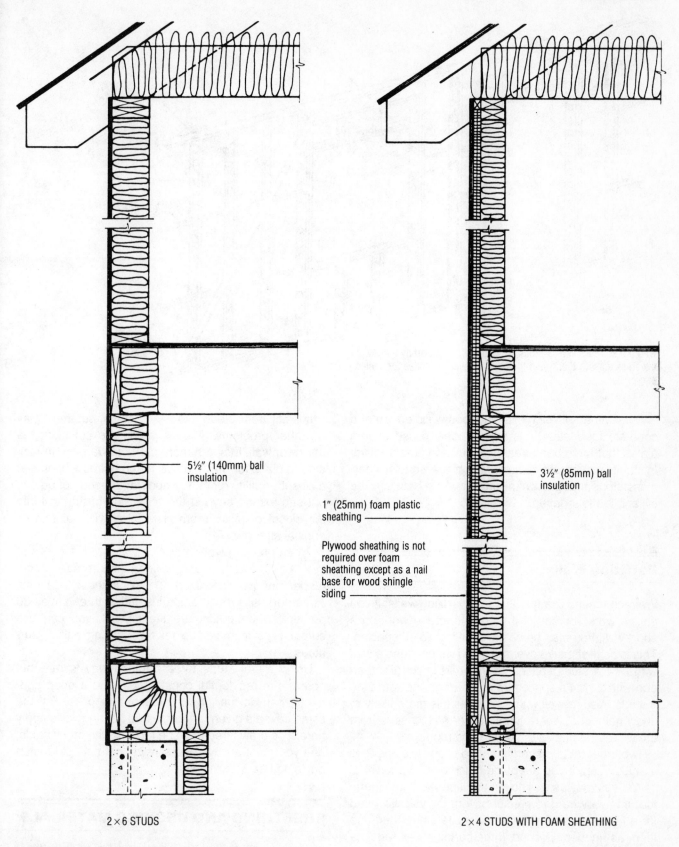

5½" (140mm) ball
insulation

3½" (85mm) ball
insulation

1" (25mm) foam plastic
sheathing

Plywood sheathing is not
required over foam
sheathing except as a nail
base for wood shingle
siding

2 × 6 STUDS

2 × 4 STUDS WITH FOAM SHEATHING

FIGURE 9.1 Framing with 2 × 6's spaced 24 in. apart
allows you to lay in thicker insulation, giving a value that can be
matched in a wall of 2 × 4's spaced 16 in. apart only when rigid
exterior insulation is added.

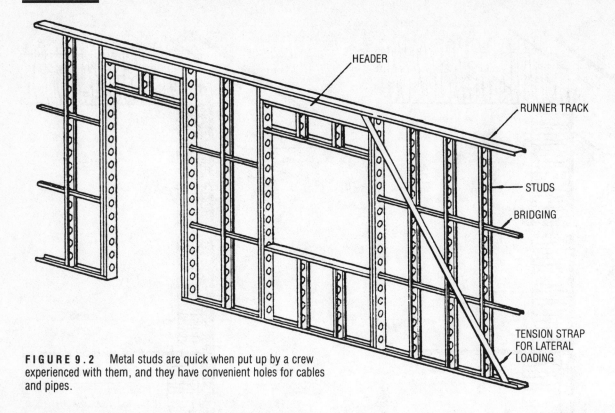

FIGURE 9.2 Metal studs are quick when put up by a crew experienced with them, and they have convenient holes for cables and pipes.

Note: When building exterior wood walls on top of a concrete foundation, it is a good idea to use bottom plates that have been treated with wood preservative. In addition, use *sill sealers,* which are special fiberglass strips that prevent air from leaking between the sill and the foundation.

Partition Walls

We recommend using 2 × 4's for partition walls. If you do the work yourself or if you contract the work on a short wall, you may be better off using 16-in. spacing. This is cost-effective over the long run, because a wall with 2 × 4 studs spaced 16 in. apart is sturdier than one with 2 × 4's spaced 24 in. apart or one with 2 × 3 studs. Also, a wall with 2 × 3 studs is more likely to show nail pops, where the screw or nail loosens from the wood and bulges out toward the room.

Two other factors strengthen the case for using 2 × 4 studs. First, if you are doing much other work with 2 × 4's, you may as well do the partition walls with them, too. It is very hard to predict how many you will need for a large job, and you can stockpile them, then use them as needed. Second, if the partition wall requires a good deal of drilling or notching for electrical cables and pipes, 2 × 4's will retain more of their strength than will 2 × 3's.

It is still possible to use 2 × 3 studs, but there may be other problems. If door jambs are cut to fit the narrower wall, they are more prone to warping. In fact, a good place for a 2 × 3 wall that requires a door is at a closet or utility room; the door jamb need not be cut, but can extend beyond the back side of the wall into the closet or utility room. The jamb will maintain its original strength.

When erecting wood partition walls, use 1 × 3's or 1 × 4's for the floor and ceiling plates to save about 45 percent over 2 × 3's or 2 × 4's in those locations. At corners, using two studs instead of three saves 30 percent; when putting up the drywall, you can use corner clips to make up for the missing nailing surfaces.

Using metal studs for a partition wall is rare but possible in residential construction, and a good contractor can do the job at a reasonable price. But the same caveats given for metal-stud bearing walls apply here: The crew hired must be familiar with metal studs, and you must always use screws, not nails, to fasten anything heavy to the wall.

SHEATHING AND DECKING MATERIALS

Modern sheathing and decking materials made of plywood and other manufactured composites are an advance over the old material, which was solid wood boards. They go down in larger pieces, saving labor, and lend greater binding strength to the wall or floor that they cover. Still, there are many different kinds, some of which should be used only in specific applications. You would do well to match the right board to the job so that the structure is sound and the price you pay is no higher than necessary.

Besides plywood, there are other major boards made of wood products: oriented-strand board, waferboard, and particleboard (see Figure 9.3). Each is made differently and has different characteristics (and hence, different uses).

Oriented-Strand Board

Oriented-strand board (OSB) is composed of elongated flakes, or strands, from 1 to 3 in. long, arranged in three or more layers perpendicular to one another. It is stronger and more stable than any manufactured sheathing board except plywood or waferboard, and it is less likely to warp than plywood.

FIGURE 9.3 Five types of wood sheathing products. From top to bottom: plywood, composite panel, waferboard, oriented-strand board, and particleboard.

Although OSB is not as widely available as waferboard, we consider it a high-quality, low-cost material for floor decks and wall sheathing. And where humidity and rainfall are low, we think it makes an adequate roof-decking material, as well.

For floor decks, except in kitchens and baths, we recommend ¾-in. tongue-and-groove OSB. Boards of this thickness adequately span joist spaces of up to 24 in. In kitchens and baths, we recommend a two-layer plywood floor.

For wall sheathing—the outside layer that stiffens the frame and backs up the siding—we recommend 5⁄16-inch. OSB, unless you are putting on shingle-type siding such as cedar. In that case, spend the extra money on ½-in. plywood—the nailing will be much more secure. Other types of siding can be nailed into the studs behind the sheathing.

For roofs in dry areas, we recommend 5⁄16-in. OSB when trusses or rafters are 16 in. apart and 7⁄16-in. OSB when they are 24 in. apart. But for most areas of the country, we advise using ⅜-in. or ½-in. plywood on roofs. The extra cost ensures a long-lasting deck.

Plywood

Made of three, five, or more layers of thin wood veneer, plywood is the most expensive sheathing and decking material (see Figure 9.4). It comes in a range of types for different uses; prices vary with type. When buying plywood, match the type to the job—a supplier can help.

Briefly, the plywood grades are as follows: N (natural finish grade, free of defects); A (smooth and paintable, also usable for a less exacting natural finish); B (circular repair plugs and tight knots allowed); C (knotholes and splits of limited size allowed); and D (similar imperfections, but somewhat larger than those for C, allowed).

Plywood is made with either exterior- or interior-rated glue. Grade labels state the best side first, then the other side, and sometimes the type of glue. Thus, CDX plywood is C-grade on one side and D-grade on the other and is made with an exterior-rated glue. We recommend that you buy plywood with exterior-rated glue for all uses, even if the interior-rated boards are cheaper. When interior glues become moist, they can release urea-formaldehyde gas which can cause serious allergic reaction.

As mentioned before, we recommend plywood for most roof-decking situations—CDX is the proper grade—and as floor decking in kitchens and baths. Especially in older homes, kitchens and baths may

FIGURE 9.4 Plywood comes in many different grades and surface finishes. Plywood for sheathing has a lower grade of surface but high strength.

require extensive replacement of the subfloor because of plumbing leaks and other water problems. Plywood expands a little with moisture, but is the least likely of all materials to delaminate and fall apart.

When you are laying decking as support for a finish floor in a kitchen or bath, use this two-step system. First, nail down ⅝-in. CDX plywood for the subfloor, or ¾-in. if any joists are farther apart than 20 in. Then, for the underlayment (or top) layer of decking, use special-grade ⁵⁄₁₆-in. underlayment-grade plywood nailed to the subfloor. With this system, the underlayment takes the brunt of water leaks and splashes. You can easily replace it, if needed, when you put on new tile, vinyl flooring, or carpet.

If you want a ceramic tile floor, you need a rock-solid base or the tiles will move and the grout joints will crack. Use ¾-in., not ⅝-in., plywood as the subfloor, and nail it down every 8 in., taking care that the nails go into the floor joists.

When installing this two-step decking, make sure that the joints of the underlayment do not match up with those of the subfloor. Otherwise, there will be small, but damaging, up-and-down movements at the joints. And if you want a floor to last 50 years or more, caulk all joints in and around the underlayment with silicone, as if the floor were the bottom of a boat. Such work is particularly needed in carpeted bathrooms, because water leaks can damage not only the subfloor, but the walls and ceilings below.

When applying underlayment plywood, use material rated as true underlayment. Never substitute wall paneling—it can't stand up to moisture.

Waferboard

Large flakes or wafers of wood, usually aspen, make up waferboard. The wafers are cut into random shapes, each roughly a square. Each has a tapered end and a controlled thickness.

Waferboard is low-cost material and is adequate for walls and decking. However, we think that oriented-strand board, sold at approximately the same price, is a better product. If you use waferboard, use the same thicknesses as recommended for OSB.

Waferboard has reasonably good ability to support is own weight and snowloads without bending and is reasonably stable; that is, it has little tendency to shrink and expand with changes in humidity. It does tend to swell in thickness when moist.

Waferboard roof sheathing can become slippery when wet. For roofs, specify boards with a commonly available nonslip pattern.

Particleboard

Typically, particleboard is made in heat- and pressure-cured mats from 4 to 8 ft wide and 16 or more ft long. Builders and manufacturers can order particleboard ranging in size from the standard 4 × 8-ft sheets to 8 × 28-ft sheets.

We do not recommend particleboard for any sheathing or decking applications, even though its cost is very low. It is not particularly strong; does not stand up well to moisture; and formaldehyde fumes, which cause allergic reactions in some individuals, may be a problem if gases from the material enter living space.

Type 1 particleboard generally uses urea-formaldehyde resin, is not water resistant, and gives off higher levels of formaldehyde fumes. If you must use particleboard for sheathing or decking, use Type 2. It generally uses phenol-formaldehyde resins, is water-resistant, and gives off lower levels of formaldehyde fumes.

Tables 9.3 and 9.4 (pages 129 and 130) give more details on our recommendations for sheathing floors and roofs. Figure 9.5 shows how sheathing is applied to an exterior wall.

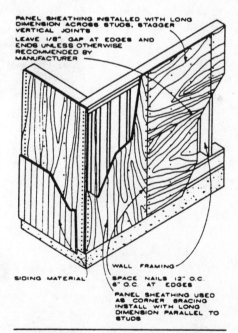

PANEL SHEATHING INSTALLED WITH LONG DIMENSION ACROSS STUDS, STAGGER VERTICAL JOINTS

LEAVE 1/8" GAP AT EDGES AND ENDS UNLESS OTHERWISE RECOMMENDED BY MANUFACTURER

SIDING MATERIAL

WALL FRAMING

SPACE NAILS 12" O.C. 6" O.C. AT EDGES

PANEL SHEATHING USED AS CORNER BRACING INSTALL WITH LONG DIMENSION PARALLEL TO STUDS

STRUCTURAL-USE PANEL WALL SHEATHING

PLYWOOD WALL SHEATHING

Common grade is same as used in roof sheathing. Refer to American Plywood Association recommendations for unsupported edges.

FIGURE 9.5 Panels of wall sheathing are nailed vertically at corners, horizontally elsewhere. Leave gaps at joints as recommended by manufacturer.

FIGURE 9.6 Adhesive binds subflooring to the joists, making for greater strength, fewer squeaks, and greater spacing between joists.

ADDING STRENGTH WITH GLUES AND HARDWARE

Adhesives

Modern adhesives attach wood parts so well that the composite can be thought of as a single piece. Glued and nailed together, the parts are significantly stronger than they would be if just nailed together. This means that smaller lumber and fewer fasteners can be used in place of larger pieces and yet do the same job. This in turn, leads to savings, as long as the cost of the adhesive and extra labor gluing is no more than the amount saved by purchasing smaller lumber.

Adhesives and plywood can be substituted for heavier assemblies of nailed-only wood made for floor decks, headers, and beams. For example, plywood that is only ⅝-in. thick, but that is glued and then nailed every 8 in. makes just as suitable a subfloor over joists spaced 24 in. apart as ¾-in. plywood not glued but nailed every 6 in. (see Figure 9.6). This saves approximately 10 percent in installation cost.

Glued and nailed beams made of ⅜-in. plywood sandwiched between 2 × 6's are structurally equivalent to three 2 × 8's nailed together. The saving is about 20 percent, including labor.

Fasteners

Traditional fasteners have been replaced by nails with greater gripping power, metal brackets, and clips that support plywood or drywall. In general, it is best to take full advantage of these new carpentry aids. They reduce the level of skill needed for framing and sheathing. They also allow the use of smaller dimension lumber and sheathing and make for stronger connections. Here are some examples.

Joist hangers and corner braces. Both joist hangers and corner braces make nailing easier, and generally, result in a stronger framing job because wood splitting or incomplete nailing is practically eliminated. In fact, quite a number of framing anchors are available to suit a variety of framing connections, and they are all meant to save labor while increasing the strength of the joint (see Figure 9.7).

Plywood clips. H-shaped clips slip onto one edge of a piece of plywood and receive the abuting edge of the adjoining piece (see Figure 9.8). With them, you can use ⅜-in. plywood sheets instead of ½-in. sheets for roof sheathing, except in areas that are exposed to very high winds or have heavy snow loads.

Drywall clips. These clips allow the drywall installer to forego extensive wooden backing at corners where walls meet walls or walls meet ceilings. They also come in handy for small drywall repairs.

Nails. Use 7-penny tempered screw-shank nails for sheathing and flooring—they don't bend and they hold tight. For flooring, they also have the advantage of small heads that do not protrude above the level of the decking and that otherwise would show through composition tile or sheet flooring.

Use hot-dipped galvanized nails on the exposed faces of exterior walls. They don't rust, and the extra cost now will save the cost of removing rust stains later.

When building walls, floor decks, roofs, and other framing constructions, use cement-coated nails, which have more holding power than ordinary nails. However, cement-coated nails are much harder to remove if you nail one in halfway and bend it, or if you want to remove one for other reasons.

Another tip: When you fear that a nail you are about to use will split open a piece of wood, turn the nail over on a hard surface and blunt the point with a hammer head. A dull point tears through fibers as it penetrates; a sharp point splits fibers apart as it traverses wood and is more likely to split the piece open.

Prebuilt Joists and Trusses

Although prebuilt or engineered trusses are mostly air, they actually provide more strength, dimensional stability, and predictable quality—dollar for dollar—than solid wood rafters or joists. Engineers have calculated the loads and stresses they can take, and these wood-and-metal-plate structures are beginning to replace ordinary solid joists in the professional building industry (see Figure 9.9).

Their advantages are as follows:

1. Because they are made of smaller pieces nailed together like the trusses of an old steel truss bridge, they have plenty of air spaces. The spaces serve as precut holes for wires, pipes, and air ducts, saving the time of drilling or cutting when electricians or plumbers run their lines.
2. They are stronger than solid wood joists and can span longer distances. This often eliminates the need for a column or bearing wall in midspan.
3. The cost is reasonable, at least for spans of 15 ft or more. For spans of 10 to 12 ft, prebuilt joist trusses

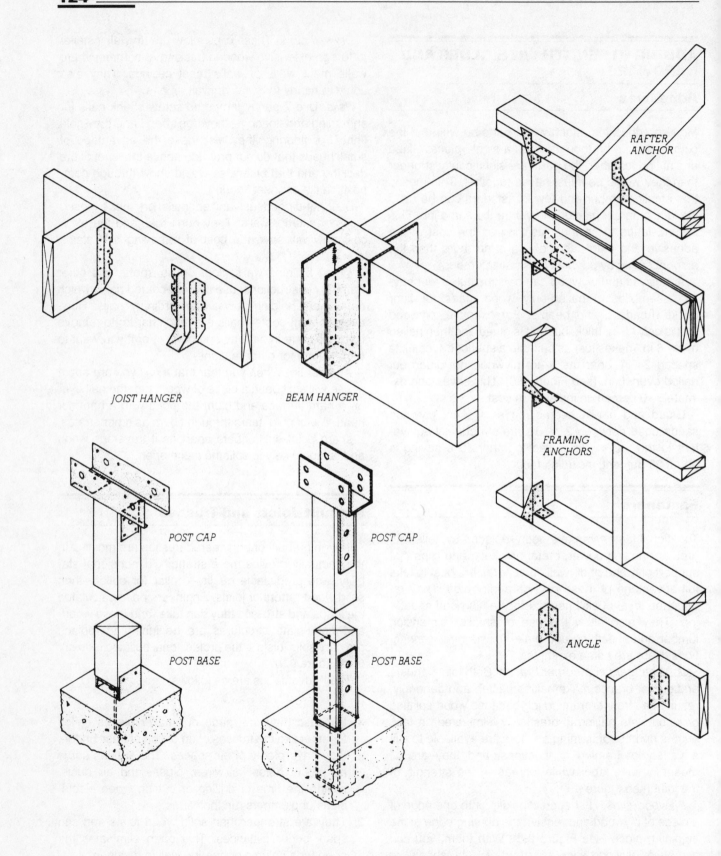

JOIST HANGER

BEAM HANGER

RAFTER ANCHOR

POST CAP

POST CAP

FRAMING ANCHORS

POST BASE

POST BASE

ANGLE

FIGURE 9.7 Commonly available framing connectors are made for various framing needs—their minor expense is worth the time saved and the strength given.

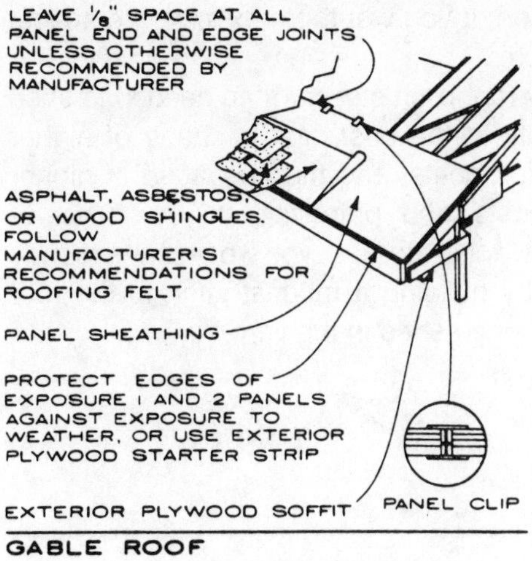

LEAVE ⅛" SPACE AT ALL
PANEL END AND EDGE JOINTS
UNLESS OTHERWISE
RECOMMENDED BY
MANUFACTURER

ASPHALT, ASBESTOS,
OR WOOD SHINGLES.
FOLLOW
MANUFACTURER'S
RECOMMENDATIONS FOR
ROOFING FELT

PANEL SHEATHING

PROTECT EDGES OF
EXPOSURE I AND 2 PANELS
AGAINST EXPOSURE TO
WEATHER, OR USE EXTERIOR
PLYWOOD STARTER STRIP

EXTERIOR PLYWOOD SOFFIT

PANEL CLIP

GABLE ROOF

FIGURE 9.8 Panel clips bind roof sheathing panels together, allowing for greater strength with thinner material.

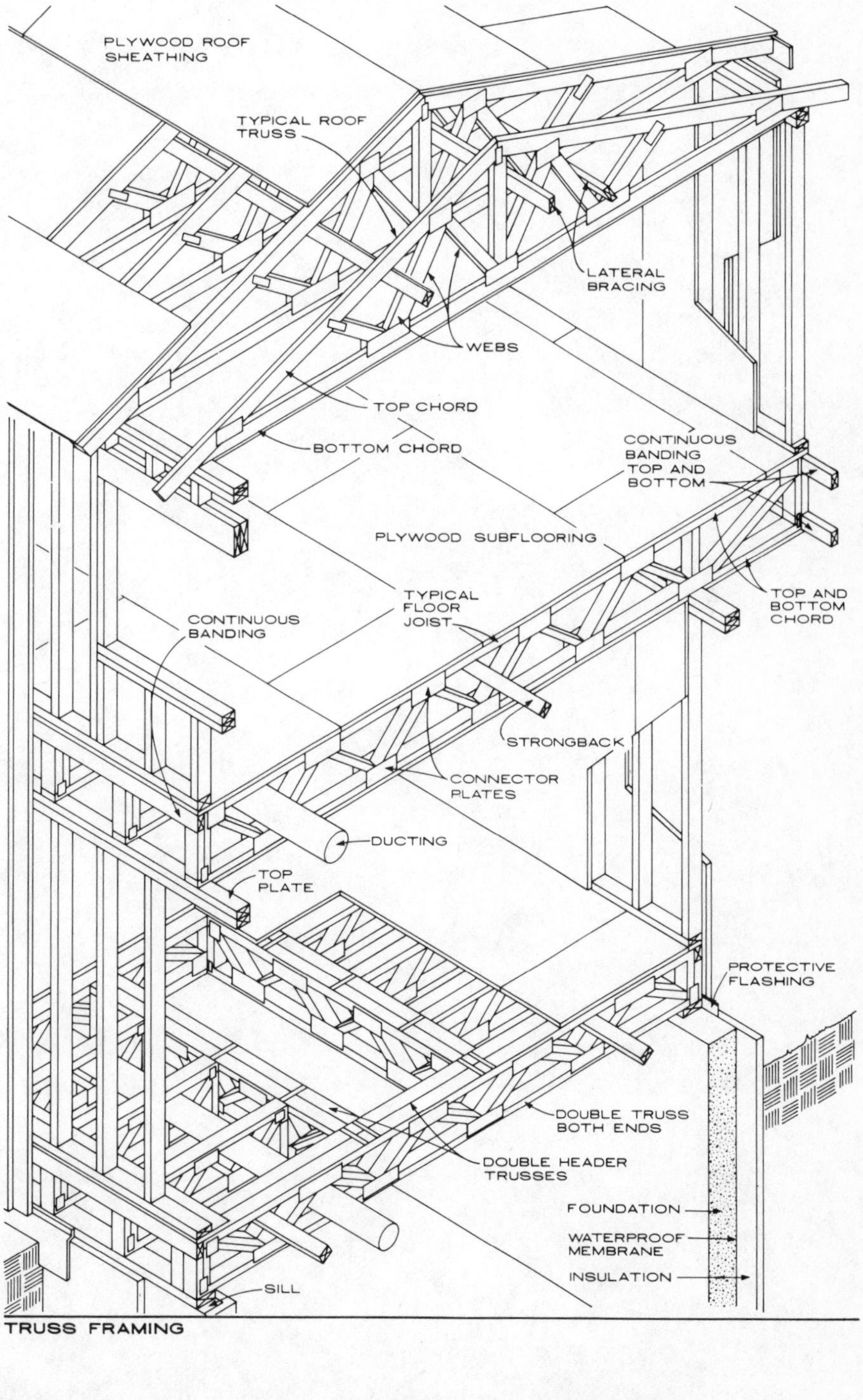

PLYWOOD ROOF
SHEATHING

TYPICAL ROOF
TRUSS

LATERAL
BRACING

WEBS

TOP CHORD

BOTTOM CHORD

CONTINUOUS
BANDING
TOP AND
BOTTOM

PLYWOOD SUBFLOORING

TOP AND
BOTTOM
CHORD

TYPICAL
FLOOR
JOIST

CONTINUOUS
BANDING

STRONGBACK

CONNECTOR
PLATES

DUCTING

TOP
PLATE

PROTECTIVE
FLASHING

DOUBLE TRUSS
BOTH ENDS

DOUBLE HEADER
TRUSSES

FOUNDATION

WATERPROOF
MEMBRANE

INSULATION

SILL

TRUSS FRAMING

FIGURE 9.9 Trusses used for joists are installed quickly and have ready-made holes for pipes, ducts, and wires. Both floor and roof trusses can span much farther than solid wood.

spaced 24 in. apart cost about the same as 2 × 12 joists spaced 18 in. apart.

When you are framing a roof yourself, you may find that using rafters is cheaper than using trusses, but you'll spend more time at the work, particularly when dealing with long spans. Definitely use rafters rather than trusses when you want the attic to be living or storage space, because the roof-truss crosspieces, called *webs* and *bottom chords,* protrude into that space. In addition, if you want to maximize the space, use a steep pitch.

However, any roof pitch steeper than needed to shed rain adds greatly to the cost, first because of higher initial construction costs, and then because of higher maintenance costs and potentially higher property taxes. If all you want is storage, you would save money in most cases by building a modest pitch to the roof and adding a storage shed in the yard.

TABLE 9.1	THE PROJECT
Framing Options for Bearing Walls	Provide framing for a 16′ × 20′, 2-story addition containing a full bath, 1 bedroom, and a 1st-floor den with a 16′ closet.

Options	Cost/lin ft Contracted	Cost/lin ft DIY	Project Cost Contracted	Project Cost DIY	Difficulty Level	DIY Advice	Comments and Recommendations
2 × 4—24″ On-Center	$7.10	$2.45	$740 CC	$255 CC	**2**		Additional studs required for off-center door and window openings will provide additional support.
2 × 3—16″ On-Center	$8.00	$2.20	$830	$230	**2**		Negligible savings and just enough structural strength, so stick with 2 × 4 for exterior walls.
2 × 4—16″ On-Center	$8.50	$2.70	$880	$280	**2**		Use on 1st story of 2- & 3-story frame houses.
3⅝″ Metal—24″ On-Center 18-gauge metal in metal tracks	$9.15	$2.40	$950	$250	**3**	Requires a screw gun for fastening drywall.	Not widely used, but carpentry crews accustomed to light commercial work may offer metal at considerable savings over wood. Otherwise, this is an expensive option.
2 × 6—24″ On-Center	$8.60	$3.60	$890 VB	$375 VB	**2**		This is the least expensive wall to insulate to R19 using 6″ batts, but window and door jambs must be wider.

TABLE 9.2
Framing Options for Partition Walls

THE PROJECT
Provide interior framing for a 16' × 20', 2-story addition containing a full bath, 1 bedroom, and a 1st-floor den with a 16' closet.

Options	Cost/lin ft Contracted	Cost/lin ft DIY	Project Cost Contracted	Project Cost DIY	Difficulty Level	Comments and Recommendations
2 × 3—24″ On-Center	$6.40	$2.07	$265	$85 CC	**2**	Least expensive wall. Recommended for closets and utility rooms. May require cutting down door jambs. Most prone to warping.
2½″ Metal 24″ On-Center	$6.40	$2.30	$265 CC	$95	**3**	Not widely used in homes, but commercial carpenters can quickly provide this wall. Remember, you'll have to screw things to the studs
2 × 4—24″ On-Center	$7.10	$2.30	$290 VB	$95	**2**	24″ spacing saves money while providing more than adequate strength. Uses the traditional size stock that accepts plumbing & electric devices.
2 × 3—16″ On-Center	$7.90	$2.34	$323	$96	**2**	Slight cost saving versus 2 × 4 isn't worth it. Has problems accepting stock-size door jambs and electric boxes.
2 × 4—16″ On-Center	$8.50	$2.60	$350	$106 VB	**2**	If you're doing the job yourself, 2 × 4's 16″ on center cost only slightly more and create a slightly more stable wall.

TABLE 9.3
Floor Sheathing Options

THE PROJECT
Provide structural floor sheathing for a 12 × 20 2-story addition

Options	Cost/sq ft Contracted	Cost/sq ft DIY	Project Cost Contracted	Project Cost DIY	Comments and Recommendations
Floor Deck					
Oriented-Strand Board Install ¾″ tongue and groove, glued and nailed.	$0.77	$0.31	$370 CC VB	$150 CC VB	¾″ oriented strand board will span up to 24″. Least expensive option. Less tendency to warp than plywood, but not recommended in kitchens and baths.
Plywood 1-Layer Install ²³⁄₃₂″ tongue and groove, glued and nailed.	$1.06	$0.55	$510	$265	Good selection for areas that are likely to stay dry. Glue-nailing also allows joists to be more widely spaced, thus reducing framing costs.
Pine Boards Install 1″ × 8″ laid diagonal.	$1.62	$0.88	$780	$420	Only for historic homes.
Plywood 2-Layer Install ⅝″ CDX subfloor and ⅜″ underlayment grade plywood, so that seams do not overlap.	$1.78	$1.02	$850	$460	Recommended for durability in bathrooms and kitchen. The 2-layer system allows a leak to deteriorate the underlayment while protecting the subfloor. This is also the most stable base for vinyl flooring because the seams in the subfloor will not move and damage the vinyl.

TABLE 9.4
Roof Sheathing Options

THE PROJECT
Provide structural roof sheathing for a 12′ × 20′ 2-story addition.

Options	Cost/sq ft Contracted	Cost/sq ft DIY	Project Cost Contracted	Project Cost DIY	Difficulty Level	Comments and Recommendations
Roof Sheathing						
⁷/₁₆″ Oriented-Strand Board 4′ × 8′	$0.58	$0.20	$155 CC	$53 CC	2	This inexpensive sheathing is most like plywood because it's built in layers, but is less expensive.
⁷/₁₆″ Waferboard 4′ × 8′	$0.58	$0.20	$155	$53	2	Use nonslip patterned board for roofing. Smooth board becomes dangerously slick in the rain. We prefer oriented strand board.
³/₈″ Plywood 4′ × 8′ CDX	$0.75	$0.35	$200	$85	2	Must use sheathing clips between rafters. May be too light for heavy snow or wind loads. An excellent option to sheath over very old decking of 1 × 4's spaced 4″–6″ apart, which was common on wood-shingled roofs.
½″ Plywood 4′ × 8′ CDX	$0.89	$0.44	$235 VB	$116 VB	2	All sheathing deteriorates with repeated exposure to moisture, but ½″ plywood will stand up longer. We recommend it for most roof decking, especially when rafter spacing is 24″. Also best as wall sheathing when shingles are the finish surface.
Pine Boards 1″ × 6″ laid horizontal	$1.64	$0.80	$450	$212	2	Use only to replace damaged boards. Too expensive as a new deck unless you live next to a sawmill.

10 | Electrical Work

Nothing is quite so satisfying in home improvement work as walking into a dark room that was once a mishmash of materials and clutter and then flicking on the light of a newly completed electrical circuit. Electrical work has its rewards, but getting it done cost-effectively takes some planning and savvy.

DESIGN

Using the Code That Costs You the Least

In the United States, most new electrical work is covered by the National Electrical Code (NEC), the publication of which is sponsored by the National Fire Protection Association and the American National Standards Institute. It is a purely advisory document, but has been adopted as law by thousands of jurisdictions.

The NEC specifies myriad wiring requirements, including how much electric power should be supplied to a house, the electrical rating of the circuit-breaker panel (or fuse box), the number and spacing of receptacles in a room, the locations of light fixtures, and so forth. It is exceptionally thorough.

Still, the NEC generally applies only to new construction or to newly installed electrical wires and equipment. Almost all older homes have electrical systems that do not meet NEC standards for new construction. Chances are, unless you are planning major renovation, you do not have to go to the expense of upgrading the system to NEC standards. Instead, you need only make certain that the electrical system meets the standards for existing housing, usually called housing code, for your city or county. If there are no such standards for existing housing, we recommend that you consult the *Basic National Existing Structure Code,* published by BOCA (Building Officials and Code Administrators International, Inc.). This document also has been adopted widely throughout the United States.

131

The differences between the NEC and BOCA codes are extensive. For example, the NEC code requires receptacles at least every 12 ft—which may mean that you need many receptacles in a large room—but the BOCA code requires only two receptacles in each room and one in a bathroom.

A special note, however: The *way* you install new materials and equipment is covered by the NEC. For example, when you wire light fixtures or install circuits, even if you are not putting in as many as the NEC calls for, you must do the work according to NEC standards—that is, grounding properly, using the proper equipment, and so forth.

The following chart compares the requirements of the NEC and BOCA codes and the costs of upgrading to those requirements, as the codes are applied to a real one-bath row house initially wired in 1932. It has a modern 60-amp electrical panel.

Items	National Electrical Code, 1988 Requirement and Cost	BOCA Existing Structures Code, 1988 Requirement and Cost
Service and panel	100-amp; 12 circuits; $460	4-circuit subpanel; no service change; $114
Outlets	Every 12 ft; $442	Two outlets per room; $26
Additional fixtures and switched outlets	Four; $208	None; $0
Ground-fault interrupted outlets	One in bathroom; $72	None; $0
TOTAL	$1,182	$140
SAVING		$1,042

Power Needs and Panels

You'll save money by buying the smallest panel that meets your needs. It is false economy to buy an oversized panel for future requirements. Some electric utility companies and contractors promote such purchases in case you will need more power later, but resist such logic.

The reason is that appliances are becoming more efficient and using significantly less electricity. Today's window air conditioners use about 65 percent less electricity than ones built 12 years ago. And soon, the Japanese will try to capture another American market with a refrigerator that uses half the electricity of current models. Therefore, don't buy a bigger panel than

you will need in the foreseeable future. Think of any appliances or heavy equipment (for example, a larger table saw) that you plan to buy someday, then ask your contractor to calculate their combined loads. This will determine the size of panel you need.

As a rule of thumb, an average home needs only 100-amp service. You can leave in place a 60-amp panel if it serves only two heavy-draw (240-volt) circuits; for example, one for an electric water heater and one for a dryer. Most codes allow existing 60-amp panels if they can carry the existing loads. But if you are replacing a 30-amp panel (yes, some exist), buy 100-amp service as a minimum. A 150-amp service would be justified only by many appliances, and a 200-amp service is suitable only for all-electric homes that use electric heat and a great number of electric appliances.

The difference in cost between a 100-amp panel and a 200-amp panel is much more than just the cost of the box and breakers. Almost all panel upgrades require a new weatherhead (where the power company line meets the house), an expensive heavy wire to the meter, a new meter box (usually at your expense), and more wire to the panel itself. The higher the amperage, the more expensive the parts and the more difficult it is to run the wire.

Laying Out the Work

To save the most money, do not do more than you have to, and plan in advance. For example, plan to put electrical boxes that will hold switches or receptacles for separate rooms back to back. This will save both the expense of extra wire and the trouble of routing wire a longer distance from box to box (See Figure 10.1).

Buy no more overhead fixtures than you really need. Overhead fixtures are required by code only in kitchens and baths, over stairs, and at exterior doors with two steps. If you are renovating, consider eliminating the expense of putting overhead fixtures in bedrooms, living rooms, and dens. You can control lighting with a lamp plugged into a receptacle that is operable from a wall switch. Save overhead fixtures for stairways, bathrooms, dining rooms, kitchens, and anywhere else that table lamps are inappropriate.

A note about lighting in kitchens: If you have dark cabinets in a kitchen, install more lighting than you would if the cabinets were light. If you're replacing dark cabinets, install light ones.

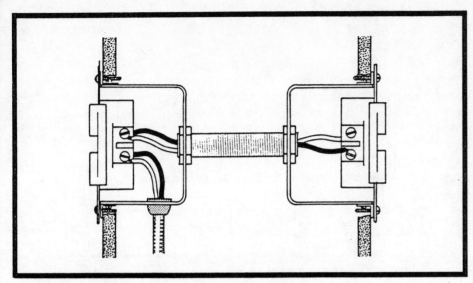

FIGURE 10.1 Two electrical boxes mounted for adjoining rooms are best placed back to back. This saves on the length of connecting cable and on the trouble of routing the cable a longer distance.

GETTING THE WORK DONE

Homeowners often think of electrical work as baffling and probably hazardous. They are quick to call an expensive electrician, and the electricians love it.

The truth is, electrical work is pretty straightforward, and much of it can be done before the electrician arrives and after he or she leaves. Indeed, a homeowner can also work alongside an electrician, doing the simple work while he or she makes the big decisions and connects the wire ends properly.

One thing that makes the work relatively straightforward is the fact that electrical equipment is standardized—parts made by one manufacturer will work with ones made by another. All the equipment generally available is listed by Underwriters Laboratories (UL) as safe.

If you do help an electrician, you will do well to learn as you go along; the best way to do so is to read a bit before you begin. Books can tell you how to strip cable ends and properly connect wires in the various junction boxes and outlets. Try to acquaint yourself with the National Electrical Code—whenever anything electrical is installed, the code must be followed to the letter. Inspectors, who examine the work allowed by each permit, enforce the law.

If you do undertake more than merely helping nail up boxes and pull cable for an electrician, that is, making connections yourself, be sure to take these precautions:

- Turn off the power to the circuit you are working on by switching off the circuit breaker or removing the fuse in the breaker panel or fuse box.
- Never work near live power. If you are drilling through a wall or fishing cable in walls, ceilings, or floors, turn off power in the vicinity.
- Never touch parts of the plumbing or gas piping systems when working with electricity, and never stand on a damp surface.
- If you are working on an appliance, unplug it first.
- Use a voltage tester, available from electrical supply stores, to make certain no electricity is coming in on any wire in the box you are working on.
- Always do your work according to prescribed code—never take shortcuts.
- After you turn on the power, use the voltage tester to make certain that the connections are correct and that any box you have worked on is properly grounded.
- After your work is complete, and if it is covered by an electrical permit, have an inspector approve the work before you turn the power back on.

Before you undertake any work without an electrician, call your local code-enforcement office and ask what an unlicensed owner is permitted to do and what permits are needed—this varies from jurisdiction to jurisdiction. Generally, as a homeowner, you can do your own electrical work—subject to normal electrical inspections—but you cannot hire out your services to others without a license.

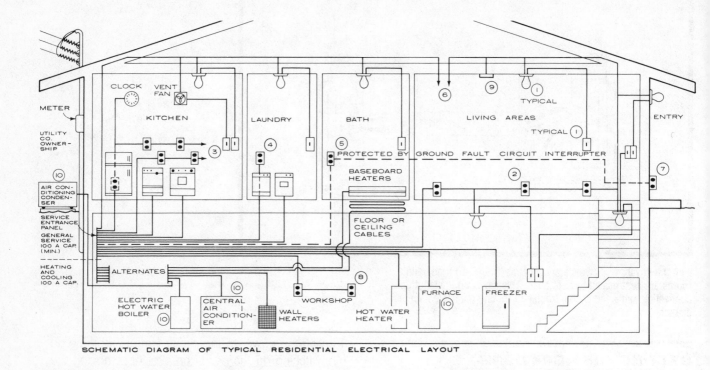

SCHEMATIC DIAGRAM OF TYPICAL RESIDENTIAL ELECTRICAL LAYOUT

FIGURE 10.2 This schematic shows typical National Electrical Code wiring for a house. Older homes need not upgrade to this level of circuits, fixtures, and outlets if the local code permits and the old system is safe.

Figure 10.2 illustrates typical routes for circuits in a house, Figure 10.3 shows standard locations for outlets and fixtures in rooms, and Figure 10.4 shows wiring diagrams for lights.

Sharing the Work

Even if you'd rather not turn off circuits and make wire connections yourself, there is a way to save enormous amounts of money in electrical work: Never let a $30/hour electrician do a $5/hour job. For example, have an electrician work with the wires and electricity while you hammer in the electrical boxes, pull the wires through the walls, feed the wires into the boxes, and patch the plaster or drywall.

To keep costs down, don't have electricians do demolition, plastering, carpentry, or cleanup. Make sure that the wire routes are exposed for the electricians and that there is easy access to panels and other places they will need to work. Patch any holes made in the walls for them. Doing these jobs yourself will save

you about 50 percent over the cost of having electricians do the entire job.

If you share the electrical work and set boxes, pull cable, strip wire ends, and hang all the lighting fixtures, the savings can run to 80 percent. The electrician still makes all the connections, installs the panel and devices, and checks the system with testing equipment. An electrician may not be able to give you a firm bid if you tell him or her that you will be doing a good part of the labor, because he or she cannot be too sure how much you really will get done. Instead, try to negotiate an hourly rate—the potential saving justifies the loose arrangement.

ROUTING WIRE

Generally, the biggest and most troublesome electrical task in existing homes is getting the wire from one place to another, from the source of electricity to where the electricity is needed. And generally, the most ex-

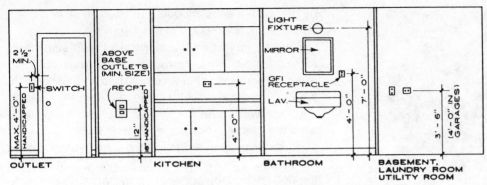

FIGURE 10.3 This schematic shows typical positions of switches, outlets, and fixtures in living areas, kitchens, baths, and utility rooms.

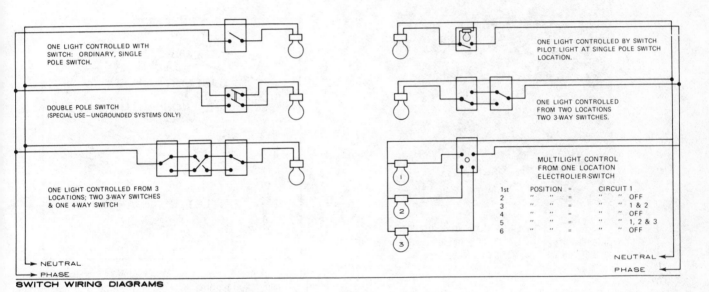

FIGURE 10.4 Wiring diagrams for lights and switches.

pensive way to do that is to run the wire behind existing walls so that it will not be seen, a process called *fishing* (see Figure 10.5). (Refer to Table 10.1, page 143, for a comparison of the various ways to run a new circuit.) Still, there are techniques to make even this job less expensive while minimizing the holes and channels that must be cut from walls. You save money when you pick the method that fits the construction of your house and the layout of your rooms.

You can save money by using as much 14-gauge cable as possible on large renovation jobs. This gauge is approved for lighting circuits—general-purpose circuits in living rooms, bedrooms, halls, and so forth. But if you are merely adding a circuit here and there, especially ones that might someday run appliances, think about using the heavier duty 12-gauge cable,

which is required for circuits that run such appliances as refrigerators, freezers, and washers. If you ever want to upgrade the circuit from 15 to 20 amps in order to run either more appliances or ones that require more current, then you have the required cable already in place.

Using a Fish Tape

In rooms where demolition is undesirable, the usual method of routing cable is to use one or two *fish tapes,* which can be rented from tool-rental stores. Fish tapes are long, stiff wires that are hooked at the end. They are pushed, hooked end first, into the hollows between studs or joists, toward an opening from which cable is

FIGURE 10.5 Fishing electrical cable from location to location is the least expensive way to upgrade the electrical service in houses with sound wall and ceiling surfaces.

by the local electrical code, but you will save a great deal of work on runs over long distances.

Similarly, if you want a new outlet, it is sometimes more convenient to tap power from a ceiling fixture that is just below the floor of an unfinished attic. Working in the attic, you can wire the cable into the ceiling fixture and then walk it over to the top of the wall in which you want the new receptacle (see Figure 10.6).

Where access to an unfinished basement or attic is not practical, you can use the fish tape to pull cable through the hollows between ceiling joists. This is more convenient, of course, when the ceiling joists are running in the same direction as you want to take the cable. Drilling through joists for a run perpendicular to them is troublesome, as is drilling through studs and turning corners in walls.

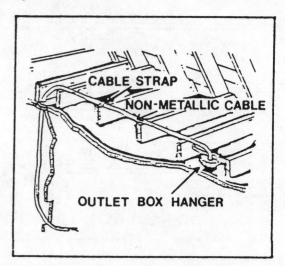

FIGURE 10.6 To tap power for a switch or receptacle, do not overlook ceiling light fixtures. Working in the attic, you can relatively easily feed a cable from a ceiling fixture to the wall where the new switch or receptacle is to be installed.

meant to be pulled. You can have a helper grasp the hooked end when it nears the opening, or, if it does not reach the opening, your helper can grasp it using the hooked end of a second fish tape that he or she pushes between the studs or joists toward the first fish tape. When your helper has pulled the hooked end out of the opening, by hand or by using the second fish tape, your helper attaches the end of a cable to it. The fish tape is then reeled in, pulling the cable between the studs or joists to its planned destination.

Whenever you have to route cable from one place to another in a finished room and the distance is more than half a wall, think about running the cable into an unfinished basement or attic. There, the cable is easily laid from the vicinity of one opening to the vicinity of the other without the need for much drilling of joists or studs. The cable must be stapled at intervals dictated

Channeling Out a Wall

An alternative method for running cable is to remove 4 to 8 in. of plaster or drywall at the height of the outlet. This exposes the studs, which then can be drilled or notched to accommodate the cable. If the studs are notched, rather than drilled, the cable must be protected with a metal plate before finish-wall material is replaced.

Once the cable is in place, plaster or drywall can go up again. The plaster or drywall can be patched-in level with the surrounding material, making a smooth repair. A quicker way to conceal the channeling is to cover the lower part of the wall with a wood-paneling wainscot or a layer of drywall that serves as a wainscot (see Walls, page 12).

Other Methods for Concealing Cable

UNDER A FLOORBOARD Renovation electricians use many tricks to conceal wire and minimize the need for demolition. One is to remove a floorboard, an especially useful tactic in a wallpapered room or above a tinned ceiling. This opens a cavity in the floor in which the cable can be run from one side of the room to another. The joists must be drilled for the run of cable; then, the floorboard is faced-nailed back into position. This technique is not without its troubles, however. Most floorboards are connected tongue to groove, so you have to saw off the removed board's tongue.

IN A FALSE WALL When you need to run cable up a wall, you can frame a false wall for the cable. This works best where there is a jog in a wall; say, next to a fireplace, closet, or flue. There, a few more inches of lost living space are hardly missed when the false wall is painted to match the rest of the room. The cable ascends in the new wall, which is then covered with drywall, plaster, or paneling. This is generally the best method for bringing many cables from a basement (where the panel might be) to second and third floors.

BEHIND TRIM When you need to run cable from low on one wall to low on the same or an adjoining wall, a possible method is to run a cable behind baseboard. You must remove the baseboard and fish the cable down to the level of the floor. In a plaster wall, you must remove a channel of plaster and lath. In a dry-walled room, you must remove the drywall. Then, drill holes in the studs or notch their fronts and run the cable through them.

If the cable passes the stud less than halfway to the stud's far side, the stud must have nailed to it a metal plate, available in electrical supply stores. The plate protects the wire from nails, not only yours when you put the trim back in place, but also those of a future owner of the home who will have no idea that wires are running where he or she is nailing. An additional precaution is to use metal-sheathed cable, also called *armored* or *BX cable,* to protect the wires from stray nails.

BEAMS, CINDER BLOCK, AND PLASTER Imagination is a useful asset when considering any wiring job. Look for places to run cable where it will not be damaged by moisture, structural movements, or future construction activities such as driving nails. In basements, look for boxed-in steel I beams. You can make a hole in the covering at one end, run cable along the lower lip of the I beam, and have it exit a hole at the far end.

You can run cable down the hollows of cinder block. If it is damp inside, however, you need to use cable that is rated for damp locations.

You can bury armored cable in the plaster that covers a brick wall. Chisel out a channel large enough for the cable and then patch over after the cable is in place.

One way to extend wiring from an electrical panel to a new outlet or fixture is to route the cable outdoors to metal conduit, channel it in the conduit along the exterior wall, and then route it back into the house again. This method is particularly suitable for running electricity to a window air conditioner. Naturally, the result of running conduit and cable on the outside of the house is most attractive when the conduit is mostly out of sight, as on a side or rear wall.

Surface Mounting

The quickest and cheapest way to run wire is to mount it on the wall surfaces themselves. Doing this eliminates the need for demolition, repair, and redecorating. The cable, however, must be protected along its whole length with a plastic or metal cover. These covers can be *raceways,* which are flattened coverings that fit well to flat surfaces, or *conduit,* which is made up of round pipes.

Indoors, a common method of surface mounting is to use metal raceway kits. A whole system of long, straight pieces; corners; plates that cover outlets from which wires egress into the raceway system and connecting switches; receptacles; and so forth are available from electrical supply stores (see Figure 10.7). For tips on buying such equipment from wholesale or trade outlets, see Chapter 19, Saving Money on Tools and Materials.

The raceway and cover outlets connect to the walls, ceilings, and floors; long strips are cut with a hacksaw. Raceway systems are especially useful in garages, basements, brick or plaster walls, or any areas where you want the wires covered for aesthetic or safety reasons. Most codes, however, do not require raceway or other concealment of cable in garages or other unfinished spaces.

Special raceway strips with outlets every 8 in. are handy just above kitchen countertops and basement worktables. Raceways are also useful in routing cable from one floor to another in an out-of-the-way place

FIGURE 10.7 Surface-mounted channels, also called raceway or wire mold, after the trade name of a popular brand, attach to walls and ceilings. They never entirely blend in with surroundings, but do save the trouble and expense of routing cable behind wall surfaces.

like a closet corner. Rather than concealing the cable in the wall, bring it out to the wall surface and run it in a raceway between floor and ceiling.

Outdoors, waterproof conduit must be used in some locations. Made of metal or PVC plastic, waterproof conduit connects piece to piece with screw-on fittings. The long runs can be bent using a rentable tool called a *conduit bender*. Conduit systems include right-angle elbows, connectors, access boxes, switches, and fixtures. Where waterproof cable alone is permitted, we still recommend conduit where a cable would be exposed to traffic, tools, lawn equipment, or other potential abuse.

DEVICES

Receptacles (also called *outlets* or *duplex receptacles*), switches, fuses, circuit breakers, and similar

components that do not use electricity from a motor or light are called *devices*. The most cost-effective device is one that is UL listed (the designation will be stamped on the device), that requires bare-wire grips, not screws, to make connections. The reason is that a device that requires bare-wire connections (i.e., connections made by stripping the end of the wire and pushing it into a gripping device) is less expensive—when you take into account the labor cost of installing—than one that requires you to strip the wire, bend it around a screw, and retighten the screw.

Electrical Boxes

Electrical boxes come in plastic, metal, and composition materials. Plastic and composition boxes cost about 25 percent less than metal ones. In addition, plastic and composition boxes already have nails attached; all you have to do is hold them against a stud and hit nails with a hammer. They are best used where the studs are exposed and there is no plaster or drywall up yet (see Figure 10.8). They also have wire connectors inside, one-way plastic tabs that hold the wires firmly in place, although not as firmly as the metal clamps in conventional metal boxes (see Figure 10.9).

For renovation work, where you have to deal with finished wall material, it is better to buy *renovation*, sometimes called *old work, boxes.* They are secured to a wall without having to be nailed to a stud. There are a couple of ways to do this (see Figure 10.10). One kind of box uses a steel flange that slides behind the wall surface and grips the box; another uses a screw and accordion cleat that presses on the back side of the wall once the box is in place.

Cover Plates

Cover plates that are mounted over switches and receptacles also come in plastic and metal. The plastic saves only a dime and is generally not worth its lower price, because the plastic cracks when the plate is overly tightened with the mounting screw. A metal plate, when tightened, not only doesn't crack, it also helps to support the box behind it.

Buying an oversized plate, which costs a mere 20 cents more than a standard-size one, is usually less trouble than making exact holes for new boxes or having to patch a hole that is too large. When you have an overly large hole on an exterior wall, remember to

FIGURE 10.8 Plastic-covered (NM) cable and plastic electrical boxes that come with nails preset in nailing holes are the least expensive option in a cable-and-box system. The boxes are nailed in place and the cable is routed to them. (Photograph: Edward Allen)

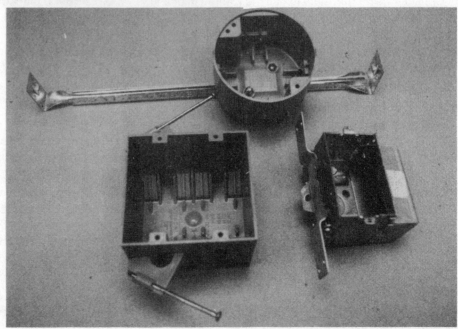

FIGURE 10.9 Plastic and composite-material boxes use preattached fasteners and one-way wire connectors, both of which reduce labor.

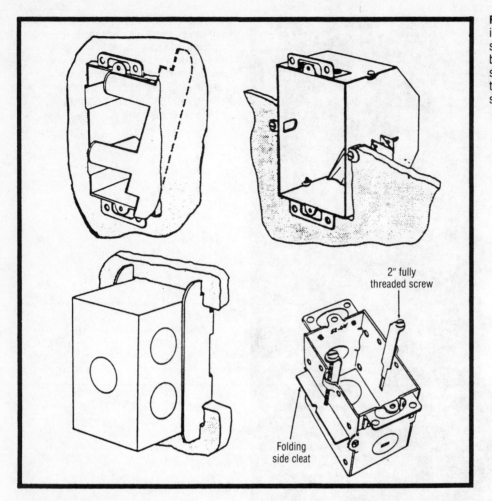

FIGURE 10.10 If you must install boxes in walls where the studs are not exposed, use *old work* boxes. They cost a bit more, but save demolition and patching. The two kinds shown here fit neatly into small holes cut into the wall.

2″ fully threaded screw

Folding side cleat

stuff it with insulation or at least tape over it so that air infiltration will be minimized.

Consider using rheostats to dim the fixtures in dining rooms and children's rooms. They cost about $23 installed or only about $5 to buy and put in yourself—not a difficult job—and they are exceptionally useful in these locations.

Ground Fault Interrupters

Ground fault interrupters (GFIs) are devices that trip a circuit in a fraction of a second if the smallest escape of electricity occurs outside the normal circuit path. This includes not only short circuits inside (say) a receptacle, but also ones that we call "shocks"—that is, ones that send electricity into the body. If a person in contact with water in a bathroom were to touch some part of a GFI-protected circuit that leaked electricity, the GFI would trip so quickly that the person would not be harmed. That is why the NEC now calls for GFIs in all new homes, all newly installed circuits that run to

bathrooms or near kitchen sinks, and all newly installed circuits that provide electricity outdoors.

GFIs can be placed in the main panel or mounted as a self-contained wall unit. Alternatively, one can be wired into a receptacle that serves a bath or kitchen or is located outdoors. In addition, for about $24, a type of GFI can be bought at general supply stores that merely plugs into a receptacle. This is a quick upgrade that does not require electrical work in either a panel or a receptacle.

Mini-Breakers™

Many older homes have fuses that seem to burn out in the middle of Thanksgiving dinner, forcing an emergency search for the one open store in town. For $7 per circuit, you can end blacked-out Thanksgiving dinners permanently and modernize your electric panel. Mini-Breakers are small circuit breakers shaped like fuses that screw into fuse sockets. If a circuit is overloaded, the Mini-Breaker trips, but it can be reset—there is no need to replace it.

LIGHT FIXTURES AND MOTORIZED COMPONENTS

Light Fixtures

Bear in mind that a $7 light fixture and a $300 one usually use the same bulb. The first gives light, the second gives light and satisfies an aesthetic taste.

An incandescent UL-listed fixture of low cost and reasonable quality is the best buy, unless the fluorescent equivalent costs only $25 more. Fluorescent fixtures provide the same amount of light as incandescent ones for about half the operating cost, so you can pay more for them and still come out ahead. Fluorescent tubes cost more than light bulbs, but a 40-watt tube gives the same amount of light as a 150-watt incandescent bulb. In addition, a fluorescent tube can last 25 times longer than a standard incandescent bulb. Still, you have to be able to tolerate fluorescent light—some people simply do not like it.

Vent Fans

Vent fans are often required by code in windowless bathrooms and are a good idea over a kitchen range. It is important for houses to keep in heated or air-conditioned air, but some air should be expelled. This includes air heavily laden with cooking fumes (some of them toxic) and high-humidity air whose moisture can lead to mildew and rot. Getting rid of this air also helps to change over the whole mass of air in the house, ridding the air you breathe of other pollutants—such as fumes from cleaning compounds and wood stoves—and bringing in fresher outside air.

It does little good to skimp on vent fans—an extra $35 to $60 will get you one that will be quieter and last longer. All vent fans are sound rated, and you'll be glad if you get one with a lower rating, meaning that the sound is less. In addition, good-quality vent fans have a damper that closes when the fan is not in use, thus saving the loss of heated air in winter and cooled air in summer.

A stainless-steel range hood is a good value. It costs about 20 percent more, but has a surface that really is cleanable, and it won't peel, chip, or go out of style. The best value in fans is the squirrel-cage type.

When installing any vent fan ducted to the outdoors, keep this tip in mind. If you live in the South, run the duct straight up to its exit hole. This will efficiently exhaust the hot range air or bath humidity; but in the winter months, which are relatively mild, there will not be much air leakage when the fan is not running. If you live in the North, run the duct down and then up. This "trap" configuration keeps warm air from continuously leaking during the winter months.

Never save money by venting a bathroom or kitchen into an attic; dumping the hot, moist air of the bath into this space invites mildew and rot on the wood rafters and sheathing.

Garbage Disposals

Garbage disposals are put to hard work, so avoid the bottom-of-the-line ones—they clog and break down too often. The best value in a disposal is one with a ½-horsepower motor, plus a stainless-steel grinding ring, hammer, and chamber. Do-it-yourselfers might take note that disposals are easier to install than they used to be—the recent models have half-turn connectors.

For a low-cost and environmentally friendly alternative in suburban and rural settings, consider a compost bin instead of a garbage disposal. There's no wiring to do and no electricity is needed to run it.

OTHER WIRING

Telephone Wiring

Telephone wiring is not what it used to be. Once, only a telephone company owned it, and only its people could install it for you, but now anybody can run telephone wires. Your electrician will usually run phone wires at a lower cost than the phone company while he or she is doing some other task in your house. When you are renovating a house, consider putting phone jacks in many places. They are not expensive and, once in place, they save the trouble of adding them later and either fishing wire or exposing it on finished wall material. If you are renovating and not opening the walls, surface wiring is fine. The wire is thin and is hardly noticeable when mounted on top of baseboards and painted.

When adding phone jacks, place them near electrical receptacles. Both answering machines and computers now either require or use both telephone and electrical lines.

Low-Voltage Wiring

If you are working with low-voltage wiring, such as for stereos, televisions, and other electronic gear, remember that the routing requirements for low-voltage wires are nowhere near as stringent as those for 120-volt wires.

You can run low-voltage wiring in air ducts—if the wires are protected by heat-resistant insulation and rubber grommets where they enter and exit the ducts—between the edge of wall-to-wall carpeting and adjoining baseboard, behind baseboard without notching, under door thresholds, and outdoors without protection if the wiring has outdoor-rated insulation. Of course, you can also run low-voltage wiring on top of base molding and around door trim.

TABLE 10.1
Electrical Options for A New Circuit

THE PROJECT
Install a 20-amp separate circuit to a 2nd story, air-conditioner outlet. Include all tear-out patchwork and decorating.

Options	Cost/Circuit Contracted	Cost Including Patchwork Contracted	Cost/Circuit DIY	Cost Including Patchwork DIY	Difficulty Level DIY Advice	Comments and Recommendations
Conduit in Closet Install a PVC conduit in the rear corner of closet.	$75	$90	$40	$40	**2**	Good option if the closet is where you need the circuit.
Remove Trim Remove base molding and door casing and notch wall surface. Run metal-sheathed wire and reinstall trim.	$85	$145	$17	$22	**2**	Best used in homes with wide, 4″–6″ base and casing molding. Use BX cable.
Surface Mount Channel Install Wire-Mold™ raceway. No patching or tearout.	$165	$165 CC	$46	$46	**2** Easy for owner to install.	No patching, but looks tacky. A good interim option until a major rewire job is required.
Remove Floorboard Remove a 3″ strip of floorboard. Drill joists to run wire and renail flooring.	$145	$210	$17	$12	**3**	A good option for flat-roofed townhouses, tin ceilings, or beautifully wallpapered rooms. Minimal tear-out, so job is all but done when electrician leaves.
Conduit on Exterior Run exterior metal conduit on the rear wall.	$235	$235	$58	$58	**3**	A good choice for plaster on brick walls and rear or side elevations.
Frame False Wall Frame out a 2 × 3 wall and run electric lines. Hang and finish gypsum. Paint entire room.	$65	$340	$17	$85	**3**	Best used inside closets or next to fireplaces or flues where a natural jog in the wall occurs.

(Continued on next page)

TABLE 10.1 Continued

Options	Cost/Circuit Contracted	Cost Including Patchwork Contracted	Cost/Circuit DIY	Cost Including Patchwork DIY	Difficulty Level DIY Advice	Comments and Recommendations
Channel Out Wall Saw out an 8″-wide channel. Notch wire into studs. Patch with gypsum and repaint room.	$69	$364	$17	$66	3	Where 2 or 3 circuits are being added and the room is to be redecorated, this is a quick way to gain access. Keep the damage to the lower 3′ of wall and laminate gypsum or paneling for a wainscot.
Fish Wire Run wire across joists in basement. Drill and cut 6 holes in wall. Patch drywall and paint first floor room.	$82	$377	$17	$66	3	A good option where redecorating is planned. Experienced electricians can minimize and sometimes eliminate replastering.

Plumbing

Plumbing is often seen as one of the most expensive parts of a renovation project, but big savings can be realized in several areas.

Plan properly. Arrange the fixtures, appliances, and pipes so that you use the fewest possible pieces of pipe and the shortest possible pipe lengths. Use plumbing codes to the best advantage, save parts that can be saved, and apply permitted techniques that reduce the amount of labor or materials needed. Another way to save money is to use new, nontraditional and inexpensive materials, some of which are made expressly for amateurs. Finally, you can save money when purchasing and installing plumbing fixtures and water heaters.

PLANNING

If you have a major renovation under way and want to save on plumbing costs, the surest way is to locate the fixtures and appliances near one another. Long practiced by architects on both houses and skyscrapers, placing bathrooms back to back or baths and kitchens back to back reduces both the amount of pipe you need to purchase and the size required for supply and waste pipe (see Figure 11.1). Placing a laundry in or next to a bath or kitchen also leads to savings.

The same holds true for rooms on different floors. Placing one bath directly over another, or over a kitchen, reduces material and labor costs. So does placing a laundry directly over or under a kitchen or a bath, if it cannot actually be placed *in* either of these rooms.

Working Smart

Many older fixtures and some pipes are of much higher quality than those currently on the market. They can be reused with great success and little cost. In addition, you can remove ceramic tile from one location and then reuse it for a tub surround, floor, or wainscoting.

145

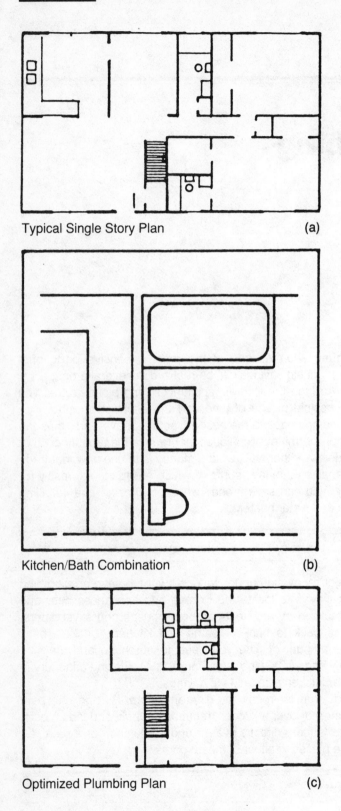

Typical Single Story Plan (a)

Kitchen/Bath Combination (b)

Optimized Plumbing Plan (c)

FIGURE 11.1 Illustration (a) shows an inefficient plumbing arrangement, the kitchens and baths being separated. Arrangement (b) is more cost-effective. Installing the kitchen and bath back to back (c) is the most cost-effective layout of both plumbing and electrical components.

If the porcelain on a tub or sink is chipped, you can repair it yourself for only about $20 to $30 using an epoxy touch-up kit. The epoxy will not last as long as real porcelain, but it can be reapplied easily. Meanwhile, keeping the old fixture saves you money, and you have a better tub or sink, even patched, than the average-priced new tubs and sinks available today.

Another aspect of working smarter is to think out the best approach to the work beforehand. When you have to expose old pipes or run new ones, be clever rather than resorting to demolition or other methods that require major cash outlays. For example, if you need to work on the pipes running beneath the floor of a bathroom, you probably will be far better off to remove portions of the ceiling below the bathroom rather than to work through the bathroom floor itself. The reason is that a ceiling is always less expensive to replace than a floor, which includes not only the finish material on top (say, ceramic or vinyl tile), but also two layers of decking.

Using the Rule Book to the Best Advantage

Whether you hire a plumber or do the work yourself, try to be savvy about the rules—which, despite the fact that plumbing is an ancient art, are still changing. When engineering studies reveal that more can be done with less, code officials respond by allowing narrower pipe diameters. In addition, manufacturers develop new materials that are more effective and easier to work with than older ones.

You should have some understanding of plumbing principles. Water is delivered to fixtures and appliances in *supply* pipes. Supply water is under pressure, between 30 and 50 lb/sq-in. The cold water comes from lines branching off the main supply line to the house. Cold water is forced under pressure into the water heater, which not only heats the water, but also retains its pressure so that the heated water is forced through a separate set of pipes when a fixture's or appliance's hot-water valve is turned on. Today, most supply pipes are ½-in.-diameter copper or plastic, except for the main supply line, which is usually ¾-in. copper and might extend as far as the water heater. Until the 1940s and 1950s, most supply pipes were galvanized iron.

Waste pipes carry water away from the fixtures and appliances. Water and waste move by force of gravity only, so waste pipes are always vertical or sloping slightly downward. Waste pipes contain a *trap,* a U-shaped bend in the pipe in which water always rests.

Traps are always close to the fixture or appliance. The water in the trap prevents sewer gas from rising through the pipe to the drain in the sink, tub, or whatever; the trap in a toilet is built into the toilet itself.

The waste system will not work properly if, when water and waste are trying to flow down, there is no vent behind them. The pull of gravity on the waste water could create a vacuum, and the waste water would drain in fits and starts, like a full soda bottle opened at the top and held upside down. Consequently, plenty of air must be available behind the water and waste so that no vacuum is formed.

This is the job of the *vent* system. Vent pipes connected to the waste pipes protrude through the roof or wall of a house and provide air, allowing atmospheric pressure to be present in the waste system at all times. The vent pipes also allow sewer gas to escape from the entire waste system to the outdoors.

Vent and waste pipes run to one (or more, in large houses) main vertical pipe called a *stack*. The stack runs downward to connect with the public sewer system or septic tank and upward to a hole in the roof or wall to vent gas out and allow outside air in.

Waste pipes can double as vent pipes, in two ways. First, a stack is a vent pipe down to the lowest "wet" connection to it. ("Wet" vents are pipes that carry both waste water and sewer gas for some portion of their length.) Second, even some smaller, horizontal wet pipes can double as vents, if certain requirements are met and the local plumbing code permits. Use of these wet pipes as vents has been increasingly permitted by codes and saves not only extra piping but also the labor of cutting holes through the roof. However, this doubling requires much more attention to design. We will discuss doubling in the section on Venting (page 148).

Modern Plumbing Codes

No uniform national plumbing code exists, although there are several model codes that are widely adopted. Jurisdictions can make any code they please, giving it the force of law, or they may adopt model codes and alter them or not to take account of local conditions. For example, where water is very *hard*—that is, contains a great deal of minerals—the local code may call for special pipe materials. In heavy snow and ice country, vents may have to be larger or protrude higher above the roof to prevent clogging in winter.

As a practical matter, homeowners do a lot of plumbing work without regard to codes or code inspections.

And if they follow a good do-it-yourself manual, the work usually suffices.

But knowing code provisions is important, not only because they have to be obeyed, but because they are a guide to well-designed, properly working, long-lasting, safe systems. And if you are working with contractors, being "code smart" will teach you many alternative methods of installing plumbing work that can save large amounts of money.

Most plumbing codes in use today were based on hydraulic formulas of the 1940s. But much has changed in 40 years. Families are smaller, houses have more baths, newer materials more efficiently supply water and remove waste, and fixtures use less water. The Council of American Building Officials (CABO) has revised its model plumbing code to reflect these changes and published a 1986 edition with major revisions to the waste, vent, and supply pipe requirements. This model code, or its most recent edition, may or may not have been adopted in your jurisdiction, but it is worth asking about—it may let you save money.

Applying Modern Plumbing Codes to Old Plumbing

A particularly important fact to know about plumbing codes (and, for that matter, all building-related codes) is that, for the most part, they allow older and archaic construction to stay in place. Usually, if the original work was built to the code of its day, it can stay.

Deciding when the new code requires changes in sound work built to an old code is a difficult task for an inspector, requiring judgment. Frankly, in our experience, there are some jurisdictions where the codes, particularly the plumbing and electrical ones, are administered with subtle conflicts of interest. For example, inspectors are themselves sometimes retired contractors and may demand unnecessarily expensive solutions, when more frugal alternatives may be just as effective. Unfortunately, unless you convince them that your method is sound, their judgment stands and carries the weight of law.

We know of one case in which the sole plumbing inspector (a retired contractor) in a small mid-Atlantic city reviewed the plans of several houses scheduled for major renovations. He demanded that all piping be new all the way back to the pipes in the street. The developer was willing to replace the interior lines, but had the underground lines tested and argued that they were satisfactory. The developer lost the argument and paid an extra $2,500 per house.

But most plumbing inspectors are more professional than this, more consumer-oriented, and less tainted by conflicts of interest. Still, knowing how they think may help you resolve some problems and save money.

Here are some issues that come up frequently when working on old plumbing, plus our thoughts on what to do about them.

Cross connections. A cross connection is a connection between hot- and cold-water pipes or, worse, between supply and waste pipes. Pollution of the cold-water supply is the concern, particularly if system pressure fails and a vacuum sucks waste water into the supply system. Even hot water is considered polluted, since there is sediment in the tank. Modern codes prohibit cross connections, the most common of which are some old-fashioned faucets. For example, a gooseneck faucet extending into an old tub with no overflow hole is considered a cross connection. Common sense says that gooseneck faucets are not a huge problem, and most inspectors will let them stay. But some inspectors will make you remove them.

Revents. Sometimes, when installing a new washer hookup or other fixture distant from other parts of your plumbing system, the inspector will want a revent, or long vent pipe back to the main stack. Using tips in this chapter will help you avoid the extra cost of doing this.

S-traps and drum-traps. These older traps, found under old sinks or attached to other old fixtures, are not permitted by most new codes, which call for *P-traps.* Most inspectors will not require you to tear out old-style traps unless the fixture is being replaced. However, we believe that archaic, functioning traps can be left in place if they do not gurgle too much. If they do, the water seal in the trap is being broken, allowing small amounts of sewer gas to escape to the drain opening of the fixture or appliance. In this case, P-traps should be installed.

Fixture shutoffs. Many modern codes require a hot- and cold-water shutoff valve in the pipes just below every sink, toilet, and other fixture. We believe that there is no health or safety reason for this requirement, and almost no code requires that existing buildings be upgraded in this fashion. Unless you want handy shut-off valves for your convenience when repairing faucets every 5 or 10 years, leave them out. When you want to make repairs, simply close the main shutoff valve where water from the street enters the house.

Clean-outs. These are capped-off openings in big waste pipes. Modern codes are specific about their number and placement and, unfortunately, old build-

ings often do not measure up. But having to break into your pipes to install clean-outs to meet modern codes is expensive. So if you have not suffered clogged pipes that are hard to clear, and if you are not replacing all the waste pipes in your house, we think that the extra convenience of having the number of clean-outs specified by modern codes is not worth the trouble.

Galvanized pipe. Some plumbers and code inspectors may advise replacing old iron pipes. They point out that some types of water cause corrosion of joints in iron pipes and mineral deposits, or both, which in turn lead to leaks and low water pressure. We recommend replacing iron pipe only when it causes headaches. Often, the trouble is confined to hot-water pipes, where mineral deposits have lowered the water pressure—in that case, replace all the hot-water pipes. But sometimes, iron "risers" concealed in the walls may be left and modern materials spliced to them.

Lead pipe. **CAUTION: Lead supply pipe contaminates drinking water. This poses a serious health hazard.** We recommend replacing all lead supply pipe, regardless of code requirements. Replacing lead waste pipe is less urgent, but the lead can leach into the soil or sewage system. Getting rid of such waste pipe helps the environment.

Whole-system replacement. When you are gutting a bathroom, kitchen, or whole house, an inspector may see the opportunity to require you to replace the whole supply and waste system. In very old houses with patched-together or deteriorated plumbing, this may be advisable. Work with your plumber and inspector to determine what can be saved.

Applying Modern Codes to Plumbing System Renovations

Knowledge of plumbing codes can also lead to savings when you install new fixtures, supply pipes, and waste systems. Here are some ways to use modern codes to your best advantage.

Venting

One good waste/vent configuration is called *wet venting.* In this system, a vent pipe doubles as a waste pipe (see Figure 11.2). In the wet-vent option shown in the illustration, tubs and a shower can use the slightly larger waste pipes (compared with those required by older codes) of the sinks and lavatories as their vents. The bigger pipe leaves room for water to travel one way and air to travel the other. Using this method

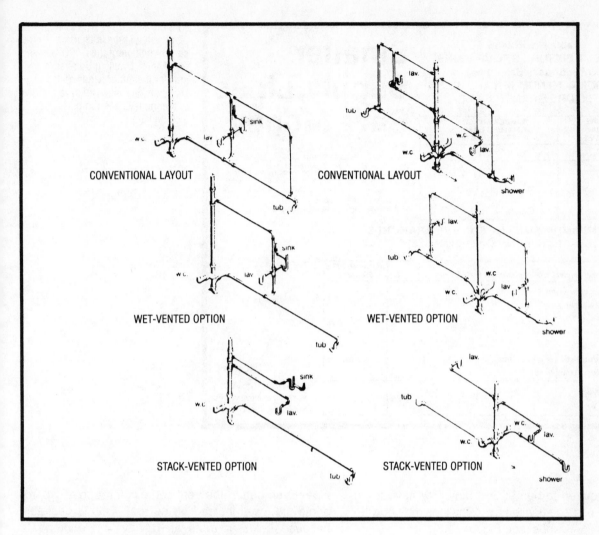

CONVENTIONAL LAYOUT

CONVENTIONAL LAYOUT

WET-VENTED OPTION

WET-VENTED OPTION

STACK-VENTED OPTION

STACK-VENTED OPTION

FIGURE 11.2   The top two drawings show conventional piping arrangements for the waste and vent lines to groups of plumbing fixtures. The middle drawings show how wet venting eliminates some of the vent pipes needed. The lower drawings show how stack venting eliminates even more vent piping.

eliminates runs of extra vent pipe to the stack or through the roof.

In fact, using wet venting in baths can eliminate at least one and often two vents or _revents;_ that is, pipes connected to the main stack. Wet venting in a three-fixture bathroom requires about 12 ft less of 1-½-in. vent pipe (compared to conventional venting) and saves tearing out and replacing about 48 sq ft of finished wall.

Stack venting is another technique that saves labor and materials. A waste pipe running to the stack also serves as the vent pipe. This method reduces labor, demolition, repair, and venting material costs even more than does the wet-venting technique. However, there are limits on the length of pipes serving double

duty in this way. Stack venting is permitted by code only when the fixtures are within a specified distance (usually, 10 ft) from the stack.

In renovation, the major advantage of stack venting is that you can tear out walls no higher than the fixture's waste line to replace pipe. Then the wall can be quickly repaired with a wainscoting technique (see Chapter 1, Walls).

Pipe Sizes

CABO's new code also allows some supply lines to be one size narrower than called for in its previous editions. For example, if the diameter of a main supply

Smaller Supply Lines Save Money

Table No. P-2406.5
SIZE OF FIXTURE GROUP MAINS
(Secondary Branches)
ACCORDING TO NUMBER AND SIZE OF FIXTURE BRANCH PIPES

FIXTURE GROUP MAIN SIZE	NUMBER AND SIZE OF FIXTURE BRANCH PIPES CONNECTED
³/₈"	Two ¹/₄"
¹/₂"	Three ³/₈" or Two ³/₈" plus two ¹/₄" or One ³/₈" plus four ¹/₄"

*Table applies to water-conserving fixtures and supply fittings having branches not greater than 10 feet in length. If length is greater than 10 feet, increase one pipe size. For special fixtures or fittings, size according to manufacturer's recommendation.
**Branch may be ¼ inch, provided length is not greater than 5 feet.

MINIMUM SIZES OF FIXTURE BRANCHES
(Fixture Water-supply Pipes)*

TYPE OF FIXTURE OR OUTLET	NOMINAL PIPE SIZE (IN.)
Bathtub (with/without shower head) Clothes-washer supply fitting Kitchen sink** Laundry tub (one or two compartment) Shower head Wall hydrant/sill cock/hose bibb Water closet (tank type)**	³/₈
Dishwasher Lavatory	¹/₄

FIGURE 11.3 The sizes of pipes listed in these charts from the current edition of the CABO One and Two Family Dwelling Code are smaller than in previous codes. Using smaller pipe can save not only in the money spent on pipes, but also on labor.

Charts reprinted from CABO One and Two Family Dwelling Code, 1986 Edition

line was required to be ¾ in., it may now have to be only ½ in. Fixtures supplied by ½-in. lines may now be supplied by ⅜-in. lines (see Figure 11.3).

These new regulations not only allow material cost savings, but also can lead to labor reductions. For example, it is far easier and less costly to fish a ⅜-in. supply pipe—which, by virtue of its smaller diameter, can be bought in a flexible material—through a wall than it is to demolish part of the wall, put in the traditional larger and rigid pipe, and then patch the wall.

Waste lines have also been resized to smaller dimensions. The new specifications are based on the reduced demand that modern water-saving fixtures place on a section of waste pipe. For example, the required diameter of trap arms—that is, the run of pipe from the fixture to the stack—has been decreased. Now, a 1-¼-in. line can drain a fixture up to 5 ft from the stack. Before, a 1-½-in. line was required.

In vent lines, similar changes have been permitted. Vent pipes have been oversized for so long that the change is more dramatic. A typical two-story home with two and a half baths and a kitchen used to require a 3-in. vent pipe. Now it can be serviced with a 1-½-in.

pipe. Even better, the vent can exit through an appropriate side wall instead of the roof. This is desirable because holes in roofs are always more prone to troublesome leaks than are ones in walls.

By using all these changes—provided they are permitted by the local code—you can save at least 15 percent of the total costs of labor and materials for a plumbing job.

PIPE MATERIALS AND METHODS

Manufacturers have evaluated the skill level of homeowners and responded with alternative materials or devices that accomplish a repair or new installation at a higher material cost, but a far lower labor cost (see Handy Items for Do-It-Yourself Plumbing on page 151). For example, a professional plumbing company that wants to connect ⅜-in. supply lines to a sink will use chrome-plated brass pipe *ferrules* (compressible metal washers), and compression nuts, all of which it buys in large quantities that give the company a per-connection cost of about 22 cents. You, however, can buy flexible plastic supply pipe and connectors in individual

Handy Items for Do-It-Yourself Plumbing

Item	Cost	Advantage
Water-Heater Installation Kits Allow you to connect corrugated, flexible copper supply lines on a new water heater with compression fittings.	$16	You don't have to learn to solder copper pipe; can bend pipe to fit.
Flexible Fixture Supply Tubes Made of flexible plastic or bendable copper.	$4	You don't need a tubing bender to hook up faucets and toilets.
Flexible P-Traps Made of corrugated polypropylene.	$6	Allows almost-aligned waste pipes to be connected.
Indoor Vent Valves These vacuum breaker air valves allow vent pipes to end in the attic and not have to go through the roof.	$22	Lifesaver for new bathrooms and washing machines in areas far from plumbing vent pipes. Also good for improving the venting system in older houses; for instance, a sink or tub that gurgles or has air locks preventing good drainage. Cutting holes in a roof for a new vent pipe can be avoided with this device.

packages that cost about $3 each. Buying this way and doing the job yourself is the most cost-effective method—you do not have to pay for expensive labor.

When copper prices increased in the mid-1970s, plastic piping systems quickly became popular. Although they first gained acceptance as waste and vent pipes, many kinds are now certified as supply pipes as well. Tables 11.1 and 11.2 (pages 157 and 158) show the costs of different pipe materials and their relative advantages.

Some of the new products, such as PVC waste and vent pipes, are even chosen by price-sensitive professional plumbers. Other new products, such as flexible water connectors, are really meant for amateurs and save them a great deal of trouble and the expense of a plumber's house calls.

Supply Pipe

If your plumbing job is contracted, using polybutylene (PB) for the supply pipe will end up costing you the least (see Table 11.1, page 157). PB pipes are also an amateur's dream. The pieces can be cut with a hacksaw and fitted securely together with glue or fittings (see Figure 11.4). This saves the trouble of soldering, which is the cheapest way to join copper pipe. In addition, if a run of pipe may freeze because of exposure to winter winds, PB is a good choice—if the water freezes the pipe will not burst.

PB pipe is flexible. It can be installed much more quickly and easily than other pipe materials, even though it costs about 15 percent more than CPVC (chlorinated polyvinyl chloride). PB's savings come from the speed of installation and, because of its flexibility, the reduced need for fittings. In the past, some PB fittings failed prematurely, but the design has been improved and the old kind is no longer made.

If you must run long lines with many sharp bends, copper or CPVC are probably better than PB. Both materials require accurate measurement and some shaped fittings. The difference between them is the skill level needed to join them. You can learn how to join CPVC in about ten minutes. You use a cleaner and then an adhesive such as model airplane glue.

Unfortunately, where local codes do not allow plastic as a supply pipe material, you must use copper. Cop-

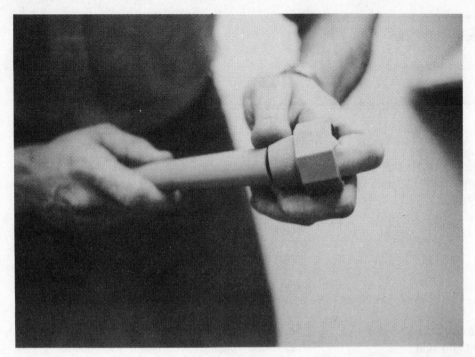

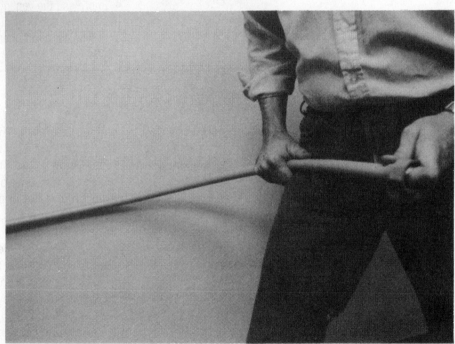

FIGURE 11.4　PB supply pipe is flexible and can be fished through walls like electrical cable. It comes in rolls of pipes up to 100 ft long. Fittings merely slip on the ends and are tightened with a wrench.

per is joined with solder and a propane torch, a process called *sweating*. Ninety percent of copper joints are easily made and you can learn to sweat these joints in less than an hour. The exceptions are (1) the lower portion of a 90-degree elbow, because the solder tends to run out of the joint; (2) the last fitting in a run if the pipe has any water left in it, because the water expands and tends to spoil the soldering; and (3) connections at valves, because the heat of the torch can damage the valve. **CAUTION: Never use lead-based solder on water pipe—it poisons the water.**

Still, even the skills needed to make these connections can be mastered in a day. Knowing how to sweat copper is a good skill to have. With it, you can save the $35/hour cost of a plumber; not only can you make new copper runs, but you can repair occasional leaks.

Two kinds of supply material can come in especially handy. One is flexible metal supply connectors and the other is general-purpose glue.

Flexible copper pipe that bends up to 180 degrees comes in lengths from 12 to 24 in. Such pieces do not need to be soldered to other lengths of pipe, but can be mechanically attached with ferrules and compression nuts. These come in ⅜-, ½-, and ¾-in. diameters and in two styles—corrugated and soft copper. Both kinds are cost-effective.

For supply lines to toilets (called *commodes* or *water closets* by plumbers) and sinks (if located in bathrooms, they are called *lavatories* in the trade), smooth, flexible copper pipe eliminates the need to make exacting measurements and sometimes agonizing turns in rigid copper pipe. An inexpensive bending tool allows you to use this type as easily as the more expensive corrugated type.

Corrugated pipe is often sold in installation kits for water heaters. It is cost-effective if you are not a whiz with rigid copper, because it makes the installation relatively quick and easy.

A general-purpose glue that can be used for both PVC and CPVC systems is a good buy. Manufacturers make special glue for each material, but if you are working with both materials, you might reach for one and grab the other. Using the wrong glue can cause leaks, because of the special characteristics of the glues and pipes. However, the general glue works fine for both pipe materials.

Another tip: Use a cleaner (also called pregluing solvent) that has a dye in it; doing this allows you to easily identify which pipes are primed and ready for glue.

Waste Pipe

Cast iron, copper, and brass were once the only materials used for waste and vent pipes. These are being quickly replaced by PVC, ABS (acrylonitrile-butadiene-styrene), and PE (polyethylene) (see Table 11.2, page 158).

When you are working on an existing house, you sometimes run into old, cast iron waste pipes. If they are doing their job, keep them—they usually have very long lives. But you can still splice into them with runs of plastic pipe because manufacturers make connectors for this purpose.

Even joining two pieces of cast iron pipe is not the hellish task it once was. Traditionally, iron pipe had a hub or flare at one end. The end of a connecting pipe was put into the hub and the joint was stuffed with *oakum,* which is a tar-impregnated strand of fiber. Then, molten lead was poured over the oakum to seal the joint. The process requires great skill and is still a perilous part of a plumber's license exam.

Joining cast iron today requires no hub. A fitting that consists of a neoprene-sleeve gasket and stainless-steel clamps does the job nicely. The no-hub connector will also join iron to plastic and steel to plastic.

Vents

Where codes allow, look into *automatic vents,* also called *pop vents.* These are devices that vent a fixture indoors. This means that a new vent does not have to be run up through the roof, a job to be avoided if possible.

The automatic vent provides a localized way to allow air into the waste-and-vent piping and prevent vacuums from forming. Located on the downstream side of a trap, the pop vent admits room air through a diaphragm each time the fixture is used and the pressure in the drain line falls below atmospheric pressure (see Figure 11.5). Pop vents are typically limited to fixtures with traps of 1-½-in. maximum diameter.

As of 1990, there are no national code standards regulating automatic vents. Each manufacturer's product gains approval through individual product application. The vents cost between $8 and $14, but often can save $200 over contractor-installed PVC vents that have to make runs to a stack, other vent pipe, the roof, or exterior wall. They are particularly good for a washing machine, an island sink, or another fixture far away from a vent connection. However, because they

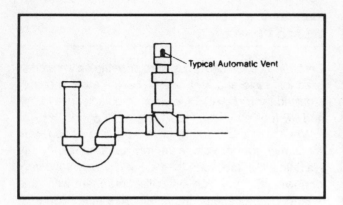

FIGURE 11.5 Automatic or "pop" vents can eliminate the need for costly wall demolition and repair by replacing pipe connections to existing vent pipes.

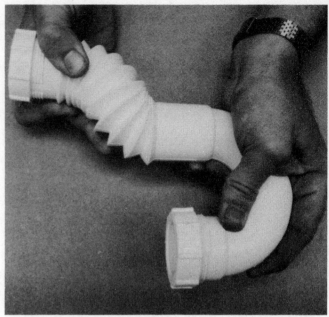

FIGURE 11.6 Flexible PVC tailpipes can make easy work out of connecting a sink or other fixture to a trap.

are mechanical devices that can fail by sticking open or shut, buy the highest quality ones you can.

Tail Pipes For Do-It-Yourselfers

Have you ever tried to wrestle a slightly out-of-line *tail piece* extending from a sink drain into a U-shaped trap that, in turn, must fit to connecting pipe coming out of a wall? If so, you will understand the advantages of a flexible tail pipe. Made of corrugated plastic, this extension will stretch, compress, and flex to meet the trap and then will hold its shape (see Figure 11.6). Another onerous plumbing task bites the dust.

PLUMBING FIXTURES

Equipment for bathrooms and kitchens comes in a variety of styles and prices. Vanities, faucets, bathtubs, and kitchen sinks are worth scrutiny and careful selection. Table 11.3 (page 159) lays out some of the choices and offers suggestions.

A washerless faucet is one that uses plastic balls or ceramic disks to control the water flow. A cartridge is the main mixing mechanism in a single-control faucet (double-control faucets can have cartridges, too).

If you want to save money, be wary of fashion. A well-made, all-metal, single-action faucet that will remain drip-free for 10 or 12 years without maintenance and that costs about $45 could cost $185 in a slightly altered and fancier guise. Moreover, fancy faucets from Europe may be alluring now, but in 10 years, when a part needs replacing, a substitute may be difficult to find.

One more tip about fixtures: The large laundry tubs

in basements of older homes were made of cement and held up well, but the modern fiberglass substitutes are fine. They are long-lived, are difficult to break, and cost only about $25.

Exposed Pipe and the Double System

When it is time to run pipe to the new fixtures, keep two money-saving techniques in mind. The first is to leave new piping exposed. In fact, this "techno look" is currently the rage in some very expensive housing around the world.

Concealing pipe is very costly. Rather than ripping open walls to insert pipes, run them up a corner of a room. Run vent pipes to a hole in an exterior wall and let them rise outdoors to the code-required height. Naturally, aesthetics will matter more in some rooms and along some outside walls than in or along others, so apply this idea selectively. If you ever tire of looking at the pipes, merely build a box, or *chase,* of studs and drywall around them.

If you do leave pipes exposed in a room, you may want to steady them with brackets. You also may want to insulate cold-water supply pipes so that moisture in the room air does not condense on them on humid days. Insulate hot-water supply pipes so that they won't scald someone who touches them. You also may want to insulate waste pipes to muffle the sound of water flowing through them.

The second money-saving technique is to use the *double system*. If you are replacing a lot of supply and waste pipe and are living in the house while this is going on, try to put in all your new pipes, valves, clean-outs, and so forth parallel to the old ones. Then, they can be spliced into the old system as you replace fixtures one at a time, and you will never have to suffer the inconvenience of going for a long time without water.

WATER HEATERS

The choice of a water heater depends mainly on whether natural gas is piped into the house. If a home has natural gas, the most cost-effective way to heat water is to use a conventional gas tank water heater (see Table 11.4, page 161). *On-demand* or *tankless* heaters use somewhat less energy, but their limited capacity and fluctuations from cold to hot to tepid have disappointed many consumers.

A water heater that uses electric-resistance heat is the standard choice where gas service is not available. Where oil is available and cheap, an oil-fired water heater, although expensive to buy, may be inexpensive to run.

In rural areas, a propane-fired water heater is often a good choice, but you should ask both the propane supplier and the electrical utility company for estimates of probable energy costs before you make your selection.

If you have a steam or hot-water central heating system, you probably have a hot-water heating attachment. These waste energy in the summer, requiring you to fire up the entire boiler just to heat potable water. A secondary, conventional water heater often pays for itself in 2 to 4 years.

A third possibility for heating water is to buy a heat-pump water heater, which is a combination of water heater and heat pump. In one variation, a small indoor heat pump connects to a water heater. In another, the heat pump is built into the top of the water heater (see Figure 11.7).

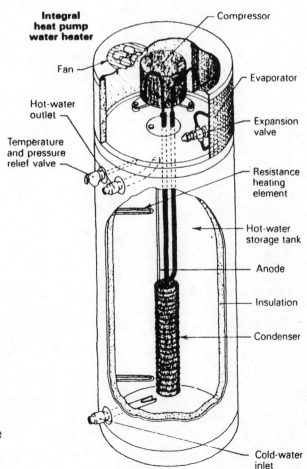

FIGURE 11.7 A heat-pump water heater with the heat pump over the tank. This water heater is a cost-effective replacement for an electric-resistance heater in warm climates because it also cools the air around it.

About the size of a small cabinet, the heat-pump portion absorbs heat (by means of a refrigerant) from the surrounding air and transfers it to the water in a standard-size tank. It uses only about a half or a third the electricity of an electric-resistance water heater. In addition, it cools and dehumidifies the surrounding air. Consequently, despite its high initial cost, a heat-pump water heater can be cost-effective in the deep South, where cooling the indoor air is desirable for much of the year.

Installing a tank water heater is easier than ever before. For about $16, you can buy an installation kit that has flexible pipes for both the gas and water connections. Since you can hook up the pipes with couplings, you don't need to know how to solder copper pipe. Nor do you need to cut the pipe to exact lengths.

Timers are a cost-effective add-on for electric water heaters. They are mounted near the water heater and control the times of day that the electricity to the tank is on. Instead of keeping the water hot all night, for example, the timer can turn off the water heater at bedtime and turn it back on just before dawn. But savings will result only if both the water heater and the hot-water pipes coming from it are adequately insulated. In addition, the greatest savings will accrue to owners with time-of-day electric rates.

TABLE 11.1
Options For Water Supply Lines

THE PROJECT
Replace the galvanized water supply lines to a 2nd-story, 3-piece bath. Supply lines sized to meet the requirements of the 1986 CABO code.

Options	Cost/lin ft Contracted	Cost/lin ft DIY	Project Cost Contracted	Project Cost DIY	Difficulty Level DIY Advice		Comments and Recommendations
Polybutylene (PB) Install ⅝″ flexible pipe and screw-on fittings.	$3.60	$0.97	$430 CC	$116	**1**	A DIYer's dream. Minimize fittings and remember to leave slack; this material expands and contracts.	Best exposed pipe due to ability to resist freezing. Screw-on fittings easy to use. This may become the supply pipe of choice.
Polypropylene (PP) Install ⅝″ flexible pipe and screw-on fittings.	$3.60	$0.95	$430	$114	**1**		
Polyvinylchoride (PVC) Slip on glued connectors to ½″ mains.	$3.80	$0.64	$440	$77 CC	**2**		Least expensive DIY option. Won't stand freezing.
Rigid Copper Install ½″ main with silver solder connections, type M.	$4.60	$0.83	$550 VB	$100 VB	**3**	Don't use old lead-based solder; you may poison your water.	Copper with sweat-type soldered fittings lasts as long as the house, is easy to modify, and is cheap to purchase if you learn to solder right. Use ¾″ pipe for main runs in a larger house (e.g., up to water heater) to improve pressure at fixtures.
Flexible Copper Install ½″ with silver solder connections.	$4.65	$1.65	$560	$200	**3**		Good choice for someone with weak soldering skills. Can be snaked through walls and requires fewer joints, since bends can replace elbow fittings.

TABLE 11.2
Options For Wastewater Lines

THE PROJECT
Replace the drain waste and vent to a 2nd story, 3-piece bathroom.

Options	Cost/lin ft Contracted	Cost/lin ft DIY	Project Cost Contracted	Project Cost DIY	Difficulty Level	DIY Advice	Comments and Recommendations
Acrylonitrile-Buladiene-Styrene (ABS) Install schedule-40* pipe for waste and vent with glued joints.	$8.00	$1.80	$400	$120	2		Recommended only for underground use due to flammability characteristics.
Polyvinyl chloride (PVC) Install schedule-40* pipe for waste and vent lines with glued joints.	$8.60	$2.25	$400 CC	$137 CC	2	Easy to cut and glue; put pieces together dry and then reassemble with glue.	Highly recommended, durable, easy to use. Should be the choice except where codes haven't gotten around to allowing it.
Cast Iron with Hub Install lead and oakum soldered joints in large main lines (use threaded pipe elsewhere).	$12.05	$5.50	$710 VB	$327	4		Quieter than PVC. Recommended only to replace part of an existing iron-hub system and/or where codes require it.
Cast Iron, Hubless Install neoprene sleeve with a stainless-steel coupling to connect large main lines (use threaded pipe elsewhere).	$12.20	$5.65	$715	$340 VB	3		Either PVC or pipes with hubs cost less except for breaking out or repairing a small section.
Copper Solder schedule-40* copper waste lines for waste and vent.	$22.50	$9.00	$1,355	$625	2	If you can solder pipe.	Not recommended. It doesn't last as long as cast iron in some situations.

*Schedule 40 refers to the weight and thickness of the pipe wall and thus is a gauge of its strength.

TABLE 11.3
Plumbing Fixtures

THE PROJECT
Replace a 24″ cast iron wall-hung sink, single-lever faucet with drain and shutoff valves included.

Bathroom Sink

Options	Cost Each Contracted	Cost Each DIY	Difficulty Level	Comments and Recommendations
Wall-Hung Sink Install a 20″ china sink with aluminum legs.	$330 CC	$152 CC	**3**	This is the least expensive option. The legs help to make sure it stays on the wall.
Vanity & Steel Sink Install a 24″ vanity with oak front, particleboard sides, no back, a postformed countertop, and separate enamel steel bowl.	$460	$225	**3**	Specifying postformed kitchen countertop offers hundreds of colors and leaves no seams to leak. A good choice for 2- and 3-bowl vanities (only one bowl is priced here). The bowl is very inexpensive.
Vanity & Polyester Marble Top Install a 24″ vanity with oak front, particleboard sides, no back, and a 1-piece synthetic marble top.	$510	$225	**3**	Not recommended. Synthetic marble tops burn, scratch, and break. The very expensive models begin to cost as much as a real marble top with a china sink.
Vanity & China Top Install a 24″ vanity with oak front, particleboard sides, no back, and a 1-piece china top.	$517 VB	$286 VB	**3**	China is the best choice for low maintenance, long life, and moderate cost. These 1-piece tops can't burn or scratch.

Faucets

Options	Cost Each Contracted	Cost Each DIY	Difficulty Level	Comments and Recommendations
Plastic, 2 Handles Install a chrome-plated plastic faucet with washerless valves, copper waterway, and a 1-year warranty.	$20	$130	**1**	Plastic doesn't hold up well, and in contracted jobs, the minor difference in price for plastic is eaten up by the labor costs.
Cast Metal, 2 Handles Install a chrome-plated, zinc and brass faucet with a copper waterway and a 5-year warranty.	$30 CC	$140 CC	**1**	Inexpensive. Most solid metal faucets balance low cost with long life.
Cast Brass, Single Control Install a chrome-plated brass faucet with plastic cartridge and a 10-year warranty.	$37 VB	$147 VB	**1**	The least expensive single lever with a 10-year drip-free warranty is usually the best buy.
Epoxy Finish, Single Control Install a faucet with epoxy colors on brass with plastic valve cartridge and a 10-year warranty.	$125	$235	**1**	Expensive option for kitchen color. European models may be impossible to repair in 6–9 years when you need the part.

(Continued on next page)

TABLE 11.3 Continued

Options	Cost Each Contracted	Cost Each DIY	Difficulty Level	Comments and Recommendations
Tub Replacement				
Fiberglass				
Install a molded fiberglass tub (about 5 choices of colors at this price).	$265 CC	$130 CC	**4**	The new guy on the block. Cigarettes mar surface. If used with fiberglass tub surround, this makes a leak-proof package. Requires special cleaners.
Steel Enameled				
Install a 16-gauge steel tub with white enameled finish.	$285 VB	$140	**4**	The standard. Chips relatively easily, but balance low cost, longevity, and performance.
Cast Iron				
Install a cast iron tub with white enameled finish.	$410	$210 VB	**4**	Very heavy. Uses more hot water, since the mass of metal acts as a heat sink. Chip-resistant.
Kitchen Sink				
Stainless Steel				
Single bowl	$62	$30	**3**	This material is a best buy. It can't chip, cleans well, and lasts as long as the kitchen.
Double bowl	$90 VB CC	$40 VB CC		
Steel Enameled				
Single bowl	$125	$75	**3**	Chips easily; not recommended.
Double bowl	$185	$110		
Cast Iron Enameled				
Single bowl	$200	$150	**3**	The highest quality if you want a colored sink. An expensive cosmetic touch.
Double bowl	$280	$180		

TABLE 11.4 Water Heater Options	**THE PROJECT** Replace the water heater in the utility area.

Options	Cost Each Contracted	Cost Each DIY	Difficulty Level DIY Advice		Comments and Recommendations
Electric Tank, Conventional Install a 52-gallon, 2-element, 3,500-watt with a 6-year warranty.	$505	$270	**3**	Make sure it's filled with water before the electricity is turned on.	Buy well-insulated tanks with dual heating elements.
Gas, Conventional Install a 40-gallon with a 10-year warranty.	$525	$320	**3**	Use flexible copper water supply lines if you can't solder copper pipe.	Buy with 10-year warranty. Least expensive way to heat water. Even if you have to add a flue ($100–$400), you'll usually save money switching over from electric-heated hot water.
Electric Tankless Install a 3,800-watt with a 6-year warranty.	$560	$400	**3**		Requires individual circuit breaker, and gives low gallon-per-minute output. Good only for low usage, like summer homes.
Gas Tankless Install a direct-vent 100,000-Btu.	$780	$530	**4**		Often promoted as major energy-saving item, since the "standby losses" (water in the heater cooling down) are almost nil. However, consumers have resisted the large temperature fluctuations and lower output when compared to tank models. Might be good in new additions with high water demand; e.g., hot tubs and large whirlpools.
Heat-Pump Water Heaters	$1,600	$975	**5**	DIY not recommended.	A cost-effective replacement option for electric homes in the deep South where waste cooling can be used most of the year.
Add-ons					
Insulation Jackets	$45	$22	**1**		Recommended anytime the factory insulation is less than R7 or the outside wall of the water heater feels warm. When your heater is in a very cold area (under 40°F), consider a jacket rated at R19.
Timers	$90	$38	**2**		Good option for electric tank heaters. Saves most where time-of-day electric rates are available.

12 | Heating and Cooling Systems

After the mortgage and taxes, heating and cooling bills are usually the biggest costs of owning a house, bigger than insurance and maintenance. Luckily, we can make improvements that reduce, sometimes greatly, the bills we must pay to keep warm in winter and cool in summer.

In this chapter, we look at three aspects of heating and cooling: (1) improving the efficiency of existing heating and cooling equipment; (2) adding heat, and possibly air conditioning, to a new addition or space in the house that was previously unheated or uncooled; and (3) replacing a heating or an air-conditioning system.

Some measures you can take to improve the efficiency of your existing equipment include tuning a furnace, changing the fan speed on a hot-air system, adding duct dampers to balance the heat from room to room, and installing flow-control valves to hot-water and steam systems. Adding heat or air conditioning usually requires either extending the ducts or pipes that serve the main portion of the house or installing space heaters. Replacing equipment requires you to carefully analyze the installation and operating costs of your various alternatives and to sort out truth from fiction in the manufacturers' sales pitches for their "high-efficiency" products (this book will help you do that).

The decisions you must make when trying to improve your heating and cooling systems, extend them, or replace them are complicated by various factors: the availability and price of fuels in your area; whether you want to mechanically cool your house as well as heat it; the length of time it takes to regain your investment in equipment and operating costs; and the different kinds of systems themselves—hot air, hot water, steam, electric resistance, and heat pump.

Solar heating, though beneficial, is beyond the scope of this book, except for some comments on passive solar heat-gain techniques. Determining which motor-assisted solar devices would be best for your house would require a book-size discussion of the technology and the many variables that could affect your decision.

HEATING VARIABLES

Fuels

Natural gas is generally the least expensive fuel—after free sunshine, obviously, and wood and coal in some regions. In rural areas without gas pipelines, *liquified petroleum* (LP) gas takes the place of natural gas. A new gas furnace, hot-water boiler, or space heater operated with either natural or LP gas are among the least expensive choices in heating equipment, because oil, coal, and wood require more costly fireboxes and chimneys (see Figure 12.1).

Oil is generally, but not always, more expensive than gas as a heating fuel, and an oil-fired furnace is the most expensive you can buy. Even so, in some places (usually at the end of a pipeline or near a port or refinery), oil is cheaper than gas, making an oil burner the wiser choice.

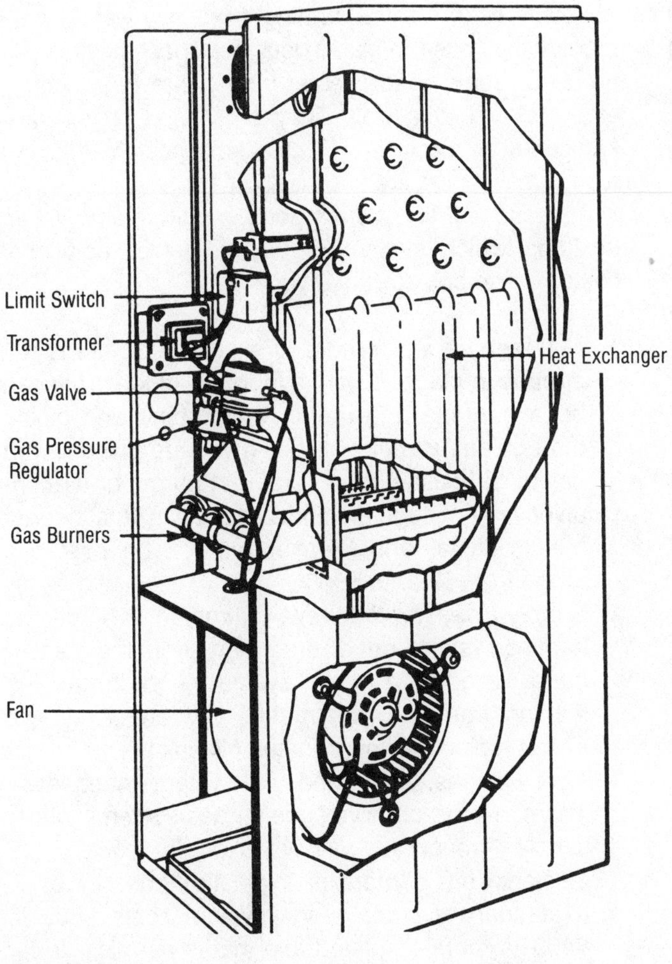

Electricity is used for heating in two different ways: resistance heat and heat pumps. A *resistance heat* system has baseboard heaters around the house with wires inside that warm and glow like those in a toaster. The heaters of a resistance heat system are generally much less expensive to buy than is equipment for other systems, but they consume large amounts of electricity and are expensive to operate. Consequently, a resistance heat system is not recommended unless (1) your house is near a hydroelectric plant, where the electric rates are low; (2) the system is used only in small spaces, such as bathrooms; or (3) the system supplements solar, wood, or coal heating.

Heat pumps use electricity to operate a compressor. A heat-pump compressor, like that of an air conditioner, compresses a refrigerant from a gas to a liquid. In the process of changing from a gas to a liquid, the refrigerant loses heat, which is released indoors to a ducting system that routes the warmed air to the rooms of the house. In summer, the process can be reversed, so that the heat is released outdoors; indoors, heat is absorbed from indoor air, making the heat pump an air conditioner (see Figure 12.2).

Using electricity to operate a compressor is two to three times more efficient than using it to heat wires. The efficiency drops when the outside temperature

Limit Switch

Transformer

Gas Valve

Gas Pressure Regulator

Gas Burners

Heat Exchanger

Fan

FIGURE 12.1   Hot-air gas furnaces are the least expensive in both initial cost and operating costs.

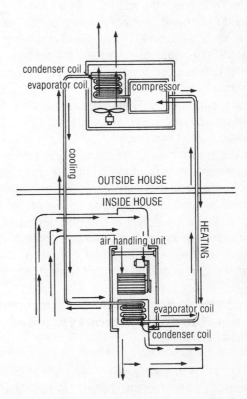

condenser coil

evaporator coil

compressor

cooling

OUTSIDE HOUSE

INSIDE HOUSE

HEATING

air handling unit

evaporator coil

condenser coil

FIGURE 12.2   Heat pumps are most effective in mild climates and where electric power is inexpensive.

dips close to freezing, however. For this reason, heat pumps are best used when year-round temperatures are not often outside the range of 40°F to 90°F. In places where the weather is consistently colder, it is possible to use a heat pump with a heat exchanger buried in the ground, but presently, these systems cost more than conventional ones. Still, the prices have been coming down, and if these newer types are available in your area, they are worth investigating.

Over the long run, heating with a heat pump costs about as much as heating with gas. This is true even considering the higher maintenance costs of operating a heat pump, which needs to be serviced annually and have its compressor rebuilt every 12 to 14 years.

Deciding on Air Conditioning

Decisions about heating systems are directly affected by your needs for air conditioning, because if you want central air conditioning, you will need ducts. If you already have or decide to install a hot-air system, you can use the same ducts, making the job of installing air conditioning considerably simpler.

A central air-conditioning system is not for everyone. In fact, if temperatures rarely exceed 85°F and the humidity is generally tolerable in your locale, you probably do not need central air conditioning or even window air conditioners. If you are in a warmer climate, you still may not want to spend the money, either for the equipment or for the monthly electrical bills in summer. Also, inexpensive measures may cool your house adequately. These include window and door screens, attic fans, whole-house fans, and evaporative coolers placed in windows.

On the other hand, air conditioning can be a good investment. In most of the country, the payback when the house is sold is excellent. Air conditioning, either central or window, helps to remove summer moisture from inside air, which puts a stop to the expansion and contraction of wood. In addition, air conditioning filters and cleans indoor air, an added benefit for city houses that are surrounded by polluted summer air.

Major Heating System Types and Installations

Hot air. A hot-air system uses sheet-metal, fiberglass, or plastic ducts to route air to habitable spaces. Heated air comes from a furnace or heat pump and is blown into the duct by a built-in fan. These systems are generally the least expensive to install, but the fan makes a whirring noise that can often be heard in the living spaces. In addition, air is blown around the rooms and stirs up dust, and the heat is not distributed as evenly as it is by hot-water radiators.

Hot water. A central boiler heats water that is pumped through ¾-in. pipes to radiators or baseboard heaters. These systems are by far the most expensive to install in most houses. The boiler itself is much more expensive than a furnace, although a system of baseboard heaters is sometimes a little less expensive to install than is duct work for a hot-air system—the amount of demolition and reconstruction for the ducts determines the relative cost. An average gas hot-water system costs almost twice as much installed as a hot-air system.

Steam. A steam system works like a hot-water system, but it runs steam rather than hot water in the pipes. Steam systems aren't seen much anymore and are rarely used to replace another heating system except in apartment buildings.

Space heat. Central heating need not warm every room of the house. Where it does not, space heaters can be used. Some space heater models are freestanding, others attach to a wall. They are fueled by oil, gas, kerosene, or electricity. Electric strip heaters that run along a baseboard are essentially space heaters.

Accessories. No system goes in quite alone. When deciding which system to buy, consider additional costs. These boil down to five:

1. *New service equipment.* If a source of fuel is not already in place, it will have to be added. This can be a gas line and meter, an oil tank and piping through an exterior wall, or—if you are going to add electrical resistance heat, a heat pump, or air conditioning—enough electrical capacity with attendant meter, cable, and breaker panel. The cost can range from $200 to $800.
2. *Supply lines to the new equipment.* All central heating systems need some wiring from the breaker panel. In addition, a gas system needs a gas line leading from the gas meter, and an oil system needs a pipe leading from the oil tank.
3. *Flue.* Oil, gas, wood, and coal systems need flues. There are inexpensive flues for gas systems: either simple through-the-wall types or, for some high-efficiency gas burners, plain plastic pipes. However, a standard flue for a gas system costs $200 to $400. A metal-insulated flue that is permissible for oil and wood burning carries a price tag of $400 to $800 for an average one-story installation. A ma-

sonry chimney that can be used for any combustion gases costs $1,000 to $2,000 (contractor built) for a 1- to 1-½-story house; the cost is less than half as much as if you do it yourself.

4. *Fireproofing.* Wood or coal stoves and oil heaters sometimes require floor and wall fireproofing. Some building codes require that a room housing a furnace or boiler have fire-rated walls and floors—this is mandatory when the heater is placed in a closet adjacent to a living area.

5. *Carpentry.* Central heating systems often require the demolition and repair of walls, floors, and roofs to run ducts, pipes, electrical cables, and flues. These costs must be considered.

Analyzing the Costs

We prescribe two rules for purchasing heating and cooling systems or upgrading the ones you have to more efficient systems: (1) try to balance the purchase price with the operating costs; and (2) any upgrade simply to save fuel costs should pay for itself in savings in no more than 7 to 10 years.

We pick the 7- to 10-year period for this reason. For home improvements, most people must borrow money at about 12 to 15 percent interest or else use cash that could be invested. A 7-year payback is about a 14 percent return on the money spent; a 10-year payback is a 10 percent return. If the payback period is longer, you would do better to put the money for the purchase or upgrade into a good savings program.

When you consider different systems, begin by writing down the purchase and operating costs of the least expensive system to purchase that you can live with and that you can buy in your area. Then compare the alternatives.

Here is an example of heating and cooling a 16 × 20-ft one-story addition.

	Initial Cost of Installation	7-year Operating Cost	Total
Option 1: *Least Expensive System to Purchase* Electric heat and window air conditioner	$900	$3,365	$4,265
Option 2: *A Better Choice* Small heat pump (for heating and air conditioning)	$2,200	$1,680	$3,880
Option 3: *The Best Choice* 17,500 Btuh gas wall heater plus a window air conditioner	$1,575	$1,800	$3,375

Decision: The 7-year cost, including purchase and use, of Option 3 is $885 less than that of Option 1 and $505 less than that of Option 2. Therefore, Option 3 is the best buy if you already have a gas line coming into the house. If you do not, Option 2 would be the best choice, because the cost of the gas hookup would outweigh the purchase and operating savings of Option 3 over Option 2.

IMPROVING THE EFFICIENCY OF WHAT YOU HAVE

When you heat a house, you want to get the greatest amount of comfortable heat from every fuel dollar you spend. Generally, that means making the heating system as highly efficient as it can be.

Before you rush to make improvements to the heating system, remember the goal: the most heat from every fuel dollar spent. Consider first all the inexpensive and fairly easy tasks around the house that improve heat retention. If the doors and windows leak air, close up the cracks with weatherstripping. If air penetrates around door and window trim, plug the gaps with caulk. Install insulation where you can justify the costs.

After you have done what you can to retain heat, then consider what you can do to make the heating system more efficient. Consult Table 12.1 (page 172). First, do the projects that cost the least and then work your way up to the more expensive. Even projects that cost $400 can pay for themselves in less than 2 years.

Some explanation may be helpful here.

By *fuel savings,* we mean the portion of the fuel bill that should be saved when the project is properly completed. By *payback period,* we mean the length of time it will take for the accumulated savings from the fuel bills to pay back the purchase price. An improvement that pays back 10 percent of its purchase price per year in fuel savings has a payback period of 10 years. By *cost-efficient,* we mean having a short payback period.

Here are ways to make your heating system more efficient.

Set back your thermostat. This practice should be followed in every home. You can do it manually before bed and after rising, or you can buy an automatic setback thermostat that does the work for you. An automatic setback thermostat will pay for itself almost immediately if you set it to drop the temperature by 5 to 8 percent for half the day.

Install an automatic flue damper. This is a disk set into a furnace's flue and connected to furnace controls. When fuel is burning, the damper is open and combustion gases can escape up the flue to the outdoors. After the flame shuts off, the damper closes to keep the gases—and their heat—in the furnace until the main flame of the furnace ignites again.

Insulate duct work. This improvement is especially important where the ducts run through unheated crawl spaces, basements, or attics, because the metal of the ducts is thin and—without insulation—heat moves through it rapidly. Manufacturers make insulation just for this purpose. We recommend insulating ducts to R4.

Replace filters in hot-air furnaces bi-monthly. Filters cost only about $1 each and are easy to slide out and in. Letting them get dirty by leaving them in for two to three months slows the delivery of air to the heat exchanger and, hence, to living spaces. Without a full air flow, all systems loses efficiency, and heat pumps can shut down completely.

Tune-up the furnace annually. Furnaces, boilers, and heat pumps, like automobile engines, need tune-ups to run at maximum efficiency. Oil-fired systems need tuning annually; gas-fired systems and heat pumps need tuning only about every 4 to 5 years. If the heating equipment is not tuned when needed, it will decline markedly in heat-producing efficiency. Professionals tune furnaces all the time, of course, but no law prevents you from getting some books and a little test equipment and doing some of the chores yourself.

Install an electronic ignition device. This is the newer form of gas-appliance ignition. It eliminates the need for a pilot light, thereby saving the cost of the gas needed to keep a pilot light running. In summer, a pilot light that has not been turned off burns for no purpose (assuming it is never cold enough to trip on the furnace's main burners) and uses up about $15 in natural gas. An electronic ignition device can be fitted to an older furnace, replacing the pilot light.

Replace the nozzle in your oil furnace with a smaller one. The nozzle that comes with a furnace is rated on the nameplate in gallons per hour. One gallon per hour is roughly equivalent to 100,000 Btu/hour of heat output. If your nozzle is oversized for your house (see Choosing the Correct Size, page 170), you can sometimes install a nozzle with a lower rating. If your house heats up very quickly on cold days, and the system

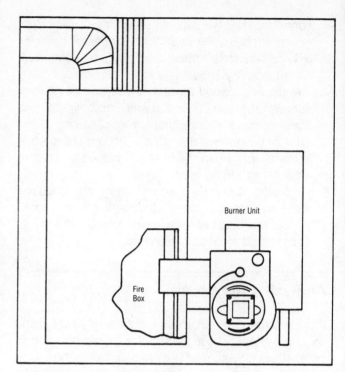

FIGURE 12.3 Oil boilers and furnaces over 15 to 20 years old can be made much more efficient by installing a modern flame retention burner unit.

turns on and off frequently, you probably have an oversized nozzle.

Install a flame retention burner. Older oil burners allowed the fire box to cool off quickly, wasting heat. Newer, flame retention models shut off the draft when they are not running. They pay back their cost in three to four years. (See Figure 12.3).

ADDING HEATING AND COOLING TO NEW SPACES

If, instead of improving your heating and cooling system, you want to add heating and cooling to, say, a new addition, an enclosed porch, or a basement or attic that has been made into living space, you have a new set of considerations (see Table 12.2, page 174). The most important are these:

1. Can the existing system be extended at all? The furnace, boiler, or central air-conditioning system may not have enough capacity to supply the heat or cooled air to the new space. Or the arrangement or location of the ducts or pipes may not allow for practical extension to the new space.

2. If you are extending heating to the new space, do you want to have air conditioning there, too?

3. Can you live with space heaters? These are more attractive than they were 15 years ago and fit better into a room, but, except for electric strip heaters and through-the-wall gas furnaces, they are still generally noticeable and take up some space.

4. What do the alternatives cost? We'll answer this question a little later on.

Expanding the Existing System

HOT-AIR SYSTEMS With hot-air systems, you must extend both supply and return ducts. You must cut holes in floors, and probably walls, for the registers that cover the ends of the ducts (see Figure 12.4).

In addition to extending ducts, you may need to boost the capacity of the system to deliver heated or cooled air to the new space. You may be able to replace the old furnace fan with a newer and larger one, or you may be able to set the old one to a higher speed. You also could add a smaller fan that fits into a duct—it boosts the air on its way to the new location.

FIGURE 12.4 Any register, be it wall or ceiling mounted, should contain a damper to help balance the air flow.

HOT-WATER SYSTEMS With hot-water systems, what you are extending is not so bulky as air ducts. The pipes needed are far smaller and are more easily routed and kept out of sight. Holes cut to accommodate them are smaller. But space must be made in the room for the radiators. These need not be large: Radiators not much larger than the baseboard are relatively unobtrusive and still heat sufficiently.

You can boost a hot-water system, too. You can add a supplemental pump along the supply route to help push the water along in its larger loop. In addition, you can install a larger nozzle on an oil furnace or larger burners on a gas furnace, if these are not already as large as permitted for the models they are in.

New Heating and Cooling Sources

If extending your present system to the new space is not practical, you will need a new source of heating and, if you want it, cooling. There are fewer options for new cooling sources than there are for new heat sources.

AIR CONDITIONING If less energy-consuming measures—such as screens, fans, or evaporators—will not do the job, your best option is to install a window air conditioner or two. Another alternative is to install a small heat pump outside the addition; it provides heat as well as cooling.

ELECTRIC STRIP HEATERS Although these heaters cost the least initially, the cost of electricity in most parts of the country makes them relatively expensive over the long term. We recommend that you use them only in small areas, like bathrooms, or as a supplemental heat source (see Figure 12.5).

GAS SPACE HEATERS Modern gas heaters are upright and narrow; they come in several different types.

A through-wall model fits against an exterior wall and covers its own exhaust hole. No flue is needed, because combustion gases go through a liner in the exhaust hole to an exhaust hood that fits against the hole on the exterior wall.

An in-wall model is set into a partition wall. It can heat two rooms at once, those on either side of the partition wall. However, it requires venting through the roof, which is usually more expensive than venting through a wall.

Freestanding models rest on the floor and vent their gases to an exterior wall.

Generally, gas space heaters draw air from relatively high above the floor, heat it with a gas flame, and blow it out to near the floor with a fan (see Figure 12.6). Gas piping must be extended to each heater, a job that costs about $200.

OIL SPACE HEATERS These heaters are similar to gas space heaters, but require a source of flammable oil or kerosene. We recommend properly vented oil space heaters that burn oil or kerosene piped from an outdoor or basement oil tank, not models set up to burn kerosene poured into a built-in reservoir.

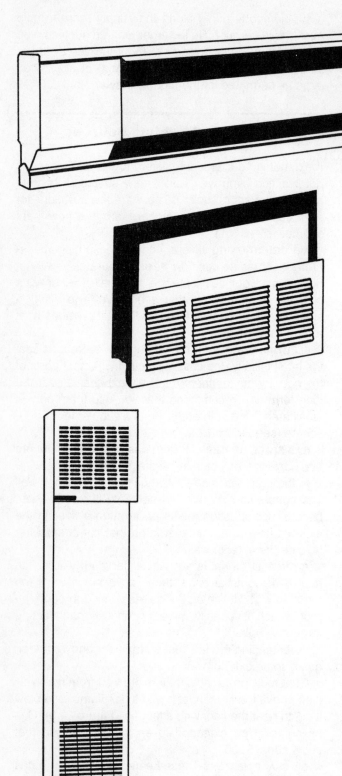

FIGURE 12.5 Electric space heaters can be an inexpensive way to add spot heat in the bath, on a cold exterior wall, or on a seasonal porch.

Oil heaters produce combustion gases that are hotter than the gases produced by gas heaters. This means that the vents must be of higher quality, which makes them more expensive. Installing an oil space heater is exceptionally expensive if you also must install an oil tank and piping. This improvement costs $500 to $800 contracted. If an oil tank is already in place, piping to the new space heater will cost about $100 contracted.

UNVENTED KEROSENE HEATERS We do not recommend kerosene heaters. They require the use of highly flammable kerosene in the living space, and they pollute the inside air more than do heaters that burn natural gas or oil. Catalytic heaters can release pollutants when poor grades of kerosene are used.

WOOD AND COAL STOVES We think that these stoves are acceptable, as long as you do not mind tending the fire and you do not have plumbing pipes that will freeze if the fire goes out. However, wood and coal stoves require very expensive flues, because their combustion gases are very hot. Prefabricated flues cost about $500, and masonry flues may cost as much as $2,000 or even more. The costs are even higher if complicated runs are needed to direct combustion gases from near the middle of a house to a flue that rises above roof level.

SMALL FURNACES AND HEAT PUMPS You can install small versions of your central heating system to heat an addition. You can also buy a small heat pump and place the condenser outside one of the addition walls. Heat pumps also provide air conditioning.

REPLACEMENT SYSTEMS

You may decide that you have to throw out the old heating system and install a new one. Before you do,

FIGURE 12.6 Wall furnaces like this direct vented-gas model are good choices for additions and for replacing unvented space heaters.

however, consider all the possible upgrades and repairs you could make to the old system (see Table 12.1, page 172, and previous sections of this chapter). Upgrades and repairs are generally less expensive and more cost-effective than tossing out the old and beginning from scratch.

But if a whole new system seems best (see Table 12.3, page 175), there are several factors that you should consider.

Air Conditioning

If you are installing a whole new heating system, think about air conditioning. You can get more cooling for the money you spend if the air conditioning can be coordinated with the heating.

The best buy in central air conditioning may be a heat pump. Depending on local prices of equipment and fuel, a heat pump may be less expensive than a gas furnace with air ducts also connected to an air-conditioning condenser.

If you want central air conditioning, installing a hot-water system plus the ducts for air conditioning is very expensive. You need two distribution systems—pipes and ducts—rather than just ducts for a combination hot-air and air-conditioning system.

If you decide to forego central air conditioning and buy window air conditioners, it does not matter what kind of heating system you decide on. When you buy window units, buy new, high-efficiency ones—never used ones over 3 to 5 years old. Older units are far less efficient and consume more electricity than they should. In addition, try to buy in the fall or winter, when the prices are lowest (see Figure 12.7).

Heating Plant Replacement

Before junking an old central furnace or boiler, make sure that it cannot be repaired. Oil furnaces sometimes need no more than a new burner costing $350 to $500. A gas furnace may need only a new fan bearing; a boiler may need only a tube or pump replaced. The determining factor is whether the firebox is beyond repair, and we recommend leaving this judgment to a professional. If you must replace your main heating source, the best values are a heat pump or a gas furnace. An oil furnace is the best choice where the cost of oil is lower than that of natural gas or where natural gas is not available.

If your present system is steam and the piping is sound, the best option is to replace the old boiler with a new one, while keeping the pipes and radiators. If the pipes are bad, you'll probably do better to buy a hot-air system. Hot-air ducts are expensive; however, if you conceal them, you'll need a carpenter as well as a heating contractor.

If you are renovating a house with a relatively open interior design, and you make it particularly tight and well-insulated, the most economical and efficient heating system is a noncentral one. An example of such a system is a wood stove supplemented by a gas through-the-wall heater that turns on when the wood fire goes out.

Taking Care with Efficiency Ratings

A furnace or boiler with a very-high-efficiency rating is not necessarily the best buy (see Figure 12.8). Very high ratings are the following:

- Gas burner: 96 AFUE
- Oil burner: 85 AFUE
- Heat pump: 3.8 COP

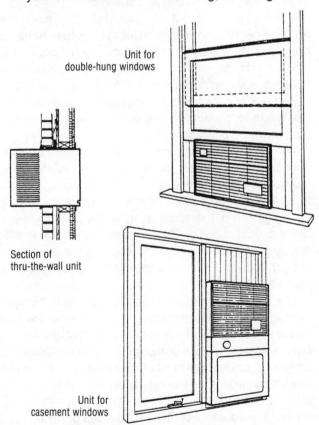

Unit for double-hung windows

Section of thru-the-wall unit

Unit for casement windows

F I G U R E 1 2 . 7 Window and through-the-wall air-conditioning units can be exceptionally cost-effective when cooling small houses or in milder northern climates.

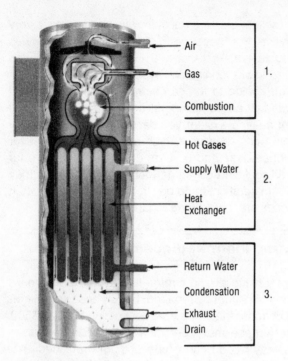

1.
- Air
- Gas
- Combustion

2.
- Hot Gases
- Supply Water
- Heat Exchanger

3.
- Return Water
- Condensation
- Exhaust
- Drain

FIGURE 12.8 Modern pulse and condensing boilers are up to 96 percent efficient. These are excellent replacement options for hot-water and steam systems, but are expensive compared to new forced-air systems.

AFUE means annual fuel utilization efficiency. It is a measure of how efficiently a fuel-burning appliance would operate over a hypothetical heating season. COP stands for coefficient of performance, the standard measure of heat-pump efficiency.

Very-high-efficiency heating systems do indeed deliver more heat for the fuel dollar, but they are more expensive to buy. In most cases, we believe that the marginal energy savings do not stand up to our 7-year payback test.

Buying a very-high-efficiency system probably is worth the extra cost only if (1) the technology used is 10 years old, and so found to be reliable; and (2) the payback period, which takes into account the cost of installation, is less than 7 years.

High-efficiency models, on the other hand, are always a good bargain. They have been tested, they are reliable, and they are less complicated than very-high-efficiency systems. High efficiency is defined as:

- Gas burner: 83 AFUE
- Oil burner: 80 AFUE
- Heat pump: 2.5 to 3.6 COP

Choosing the Correct Size

Choose the system that is the correct size for your house or addition. This is not an easy task, because every house is different not only in size, but in the number of windows, the amount of insulation, the foundation type, the air infiltration, the shading from trees, the prevailing winds, and so forth.

Even heating and cooling contractors must make educated guesses on the proper size of heating and cooling systems. When a heating contractor assesses what is needed to heat a house, he or she considers all or most of the variables in the preceding paragraph, then consults a formula to determine the correct size of the system for the house. The formula tells how many Btu's are needed to heat the house. (Btu, which stands for British thermal unit, is the standard measure of heat production. One Btu is equal to the amount of heat needed to raise one pound of water one degree F.)

In the past, contractors usually installed a furnace that was a size larger than needed, to "be on the safe side" or take care of the "worst winter in 100 years." But this practice is out of favor. Not only does the homeowner pay more up front for the oversize furnace, but the furnace itself burns inefficiently for the space that it heats. An oversize furnace turns on, heats the house quickly, and shuts off for a period. During that period of inactivity, warm combustion gases escape up the flue, and the ducts or pipes cool down, along with the air, water, or steam in them.

When a heating contractor tells you that your furnace is operating at 85 percent efficiency, the reference is only to the time its flame is on. If the furnace cycles on and off frequently, more of the energy in the fuel it burns goes up the stack than if the furnace were running continuously. This means that the real efficiency of the furnace over the whole cycle of turn-on, run, shut-down, and turn-on again is less than 85 percent.

The most efficient furnace or heat pump is the one that can produce just the amount of Btu's/hour that the house loses per hour on the coldest days of winter. Such a furnace or heat pump runs almost continuously on these coldest days, but provides an adequate stream of heat. On warmer days, the system is cycling—turning on and off—as little as possible, and minimum heat is lost up flues or in pipes or ducts.

These days, heating contractors—encouraged by conscientious colleagues, homeowners, energy-conservation activists, and consumer groups—are installing equipment much closer to the size required from their calculations, taking into account better insulated houses, and better control of air infiltration. We believe that if more care were given to calculating a well-insulated home's real heating needs, heating systems could be reduced by about 10 to 50 percent in capacity and 5 to 20 percent in cost. Buying the correct system saves money both on the purchase and for fuel each year thereafter.

You can learn something about how heating calculations are made by writing for a $10 manual called *Insulation Manual: Homes-Apartments* from the National Association of Home Builders National Research Center, 400 Prince George's Blvd., Upper Marlboro, MD 20772, (301) 249-4000.

If you determine that a system does not exactly match the requirements of your house, try to make your house more weatherproof and buy the smaller system.

What we have said about heating is true of cooling as well. Oversizing is inefficient, and undersizing is uncomfortable. It is best to buy the unit that most precisely fits your home's needs.

Sizing Your Air Conditioner

Air conditioners used to be rated for cooling power in tons. One ton of cooling capacity is equivalent to the cooling obtained by melting a ton of ice in 24 hours. Nowadays, window air conditioners are rated for cooling power by how much heat they can remove an hour, or Btu per hour, sometimes written Btuh. Window air conditioners are rated from 4,000 to over 15,000 Btuh, the equivalent of 0.3 to over 1.25 tons (one cooling ton equals 12,000 Btuh).

Central air-conditioning systems are still rated in tons. Home systems have capacities of about 2 to 5 tons.

Accessories

Two accessories can be added to hot-air central heating systems to make your home more comfortable: air cleaners and humidifiers. They need not be added when the equipment is installed or upgraded, but doing so is usually more efficient.

Air cleaners are expensive, about $350 for an ionized type that fits into an air duct near the furnace. But it does an excellent job of removing particles from the air, including dust and pollen that you may be allergic to. An ionized air cleaner also can remove many pollutants from city air, making the air in the house healthier to breathe.

Humidifiers also increase personal comfort and they too fit into a duct near the furnace. The evaporative kind is the less expensive, and its mechanics are simple—water, which is fed from a small pipe tapped to a cold-water line, is dripped down a grid through which the house air is blown. The atomized type uses less electricity, but it can cause rusting and mineral deposits inside the ducts.

Generally, humidifiers should be used only in drafty old houses. In a tight house, too much humidity is a more common problem than too little.

TABLE 12.1
Improving Furnace Efficiency

THE PROJECT
Improve a fuel-fired furnace to operate more efficiently. Paybacks assume a moderate climate. They will be longer in warmer climates, shorter in colder ones. *Payback period* is the approximate time it takes to recoup the investment through fuel savings.

Options	Project Cost Contracted	Project Cost DIY	Annual Fuel Savings	Payback Period Contracted Work	Comments and Recommendations
Change Filters	$10	$2	3%–5%	1–2 months	Best payback, but often overlooked.
Tune up Furnace	$65	DIY only with proper equipment	2%–10%	3 months to 2 years	On a very dirty, badly tuned furnace, you may even save 15%. For safety reasons, this should be done annually anyway.
Set Back Thermostat Install 1 thermostat and assume 4°F setback at night.	$115	$45	2%–4% of your fuel bill per year for every 4°F setback	3–5 years	Every house should have a programmable thermostat.
Modulating Aquastat	$265	not a DIY	4%–8%	4–7 years	For boilers; saves most in moderate climates with both spring and fall heating seasons.
Flue Damper Install on flue.	$315	$210	6% average	5–7 years	Saves about 8% in oil and 5% in gas furnaces. Closes the flue when the fire is off so heat doesn't escape up chimney.
Insulate Ductwork	$3/lin ft	$0.80/lin ft	2%–12%	2–10 years	The greatest savings result when ducts run through unheated crawl spaces or attics.

Options	Project Cost Contracted	Project Cost DIY	Annual Fuel Savings	Payback Period Contracted Work	Comments and Recommendations
Electronic Ignition Replace pilot light with electric ignition.	$410	not a DIY	3%–5%	10–15 years	
Flame-Retention Oil Burner	$580	not a DIY	8%–12%	4–8 years	15- to 20-year-old oil burners should be replaced and resized at the same time.

Important Note: Individual measures cannot be added up literally to calculate total savings. For example, when a heating plant is made more efficient, duct insulation has a longer payback. The estimated savings given here assume that you are doing three or four measures on a fairly efficient furnace (70%–75% before tune-up).

TABLE 12.2
Space-Heat Choices

THE PROJECT
Provide heat to a new 1-story, 20′ × 16′ addition containing a den and a ¾ bath. Assumes 25′ run to existing furnace or boiler in utility room.

Options	Cost/sq ft Contracted	Project Cost Contracted	Operating Cost	Comments and Recommendations
Electric Baseboard Install electric-resistance strips along outside wall.	$1.75	$560	High	A good option for the bathroom where additional spot heat will be appreciated. Expensive to operate for a den that's used all the time and/or in a cold climate. If chosen, beef up your wall insulation and don't install more running feet then you need.
Extend Your Furnace Add duct work to your hot-air furnace. Install drywall over ducts and paint.	$2.35	$760	Low	This is usually the least expensive, most efficient method to add heat, considering long-term fuel costs (unless your furnace is electric).
Gas Space Heater Install a 15,000-Btu direct-vent wall furnace. Run gas supply line to addition.	$3.06	$980	Low	Direct-vent furnaces are great for additions with gas service nearby where the furnace or boiler is too small for any additional load.
Extend Your Boiler Add pump and thermostat and baseboard radiator to create an additional zone in your system.	$4.60	$1,475	Low	If you have a boiler and don't need air conditioning, this is least expensive.
Through-the-Wall Heat Pump Install 25,000-Btu capacity heating and 2-ton capacity cooling.	$8.12	$2,600	Moderate	A good choice for a house that requires air conditioning and only minimal heat. Can be expensive to use in cold climates.

TABLE 12.3
New Heating System Options

THE PROJECT
Install a heating system in a 2,000-sq-ft, 2-story, 3-bedroom, 2-bath home undergoing substantial rehabilitation. This assumes that the cost of concealing the distribution system will be buried in the general work.

Options	Cost/sq ft Contracted	Project Cost Contracted	Comments and Recommendations
Electric Baseboard Install 1,500-watt per room with remote thermostat.	$1.60	$3,200	Consider only if (1) electricity is 4¢/KW or less; (2) your home will be insulated to R19 walls, R30 ceiling, double glazing, and solar orientation; (3) your heat load is small for other reasons; or (4) it's a backup system for wood or solar.
Gas Furnace Install a 75,000-Btu furnace (90% efficient).	$2.55	$5,100 CC	The least expensive both in initial cost and life-cycle cost for a heat-only option. This system, with window air conditioning, if needed, is your real cost saver.
Oil Furnace Install an 85,000-Btu forced-air furnace with an 86% efficiency rating.	$3.45	$6,900	A low-cost-operating option for homes without gas service or very cheap electricity.
Gas Furnace with Air Conditioner Install a 75,000-Btu furnace (90% efficient), with 3-ton electric air conditioner.	$4.11	$8,220 VB	Each component does what it does best, resulting in the best buy for a combined heating and cooling system.
Electric Heat Pump Install a model with 3-ton air-conditioning capacity and 130,000-Btu backup heat.	$4.15	$8,300	Good option for southern climates where electric heat is the other option. But if you can hook up to gas at competitive costs, do so. You'll have lower costs and less maintenance.
Gas Boiler Install an 85,000-Btu hot-water boiler with a single zone and copper baseboard radiators (86% efficient).	$4.66	$9,320	A dying form of heat, even in the far north where air conditioning isn't required, because the initial cost is so high. You pay a lot for heat that's slightly more even, quiet, and moist than forced air. Maintenance costs are higher than forced air.

(Continued on next page)

TABLE 12.3 Continued

Options	Cost/sq ft Contracted	Project Cost Contracted	Comments and Recommendations
Oil Furnace with Air Conditioner Install an 85,000-Btu forced-air furnace (86% efficient) with 3-ton electric air conditioner.	$4.96	$9,920	A reasonable alternative to a heat pump in climates requiring air conditioning but not serviced by gas.
Oil Boiler Install an 85,000-Btu hot-water boiler, with single zone and copper baseboard radiators (85% efficient).	$5.72	$11,420	See "Gas Boilers."

13 | Roofing

How long a roof lasts depends partly on its shape, its pitch, the weather to which it is exposed, the insulation below it, and the maintenance it receives. The most important factor, however, is what the roof surface is made of.

Most homeowners replace their roofs before the full life—as projected at installation—has expired. Sometimes, a roof is replaced because a renovation plan requires it, but often it is done because homeowners become frustrated with persistent leaks. Leaks are caused by poor maintenance, and timely repair can greatly extend a roof's life.

Small repairs to flashing, valleys, and worn areas can postpone the need to replace a roof for years. Exceptionally long-lasting roof materials—such as slate, clay tile, and metal—have lasted 100 years or more with yearly preventive maintenance and repairs. As a rule of thumb, you can afford to spend $40 to $80 in repairs for every year of extended roof life the repairs will permit; a good roofer can estimate how long the repairs will last.

The key to cost-effective roof repairs is periodic inspection to catch problems early, particularly when the roof covering is 15 to 20 years old or the age of the roof is uncertain. Become an expert on your roof, or have a professional look at it occasionally.

But even with the best of care, the roof material must be replaced eventually. Asphalt shingles are a common, sensible choice.

In this chapter, we will discuss ways to reroof both pitched and flat roofs. We'll also look into ways to save money when devising a plan for gutters and downspouts.

Remember, no matter what the new roof is made of, it should be leak-free; last at least 20 years; require very little maintenance; and stand up to abuse from snow, ice, and wind.

PITCHED ROOF MATERIAL CHOICES

Roofs that are not flat have *pitches,* or *slopes.* The standard way to describe the slope is by the number of feet the roof rises vertically (called the *rise*) for every 12 horizontal feet (called the *run*) (see Figure 13.1). If a roof has a 4-ft rise in a 12-ft run, it has a slope of 4 in 12.

Roofing materials come in various, and unequal, kinds. Some are suitable only for steep roofs (with slopes, say, of 7 in 12). Other materials can be used on lower slopes (say, 2 in 12). No matter what the roofing material, do not install a material on a roof with a slope lower than the minimum specified by the manufacturer.

The most common pitched roof material is asphalt shingles, which are suitable for roofs down to a slope of 4 in 12, or 2 in 12 using special procedures prescribed by the manufacturer. Older asphalt shingles are made by forming wood pulp and paper into a mat, saturating it with asphalt, and then covering the top with mineral granules. The granules add weight and body, prevent abrasions and, most importantly, keep sunlight from degrading the mat.

These wood-pulp-based shingles now have been all but replaced by shingles made with a fiberglass mat. These shingles are lighter and last longer. Because fiberglass deteriorates much more slowly than organic materials, fiberglass-based asphalt shingles should last 25 to 40 years, rather than the 15 to 30 years that the older, wood-based kind usually lasted. (Generally, both types of shingles last longer than their guaranteed life.) Fiberglass-based asphalt shingles are a bit more expensive than the old kind, but more than pay for themselves over their longer lives.

Of course, there are other suitable roofing materials that may be more appropriate than asphalt shingles in certain locations or on certain buildings. The following sections describe, in addition to asphalt shingles, other kinds of cost-effective roofing materials and their applications. Refer also to Table 13.1, page 190.

Asphalt Shingles

The workhorse of American roofing, asphalt shingles come not as single shingles, but in strips 3 ft long and 1 ft wide. On the most common type, two 5-in.-long slots, called *cutouts,* rise from the lower edge to half-

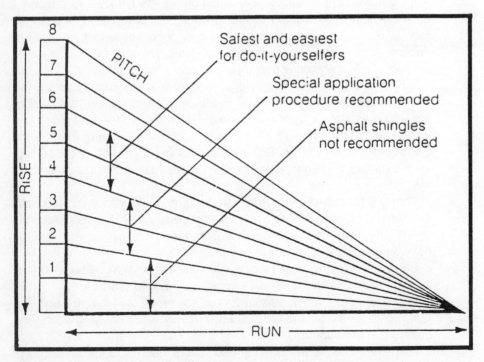

FIGURE 13.1 The slope or pitch of a roof is denoted by the number of vertical feet (called the *rise*) the roof rises in 12 horizontal feet (called the *run*).

way up the strip. When the upper half of one strip is covered by the lower half of another, the appearance is that of three separate 1-ft-wide shingles, called *tabs* (see Figure 13.2). Asphalt shingles cover the roof in two layers; asphalt cement placed just above the upper ends of the cutouts is used to bind two lapping strips together.

Shingles come either tabbed or tabless. With tabbed shingles, the area beneath a slot is exposed to the weather and wears away. Tabless shingles do not have the slots or the wear problem; they are a better buy because they last longer. Both tabbed and tabless shingles can be used on slopes as low as 2 in 12.

See the section on Cost-Effective Installation of Asphalt Shingles, page 183, for a discussion of installation methods.

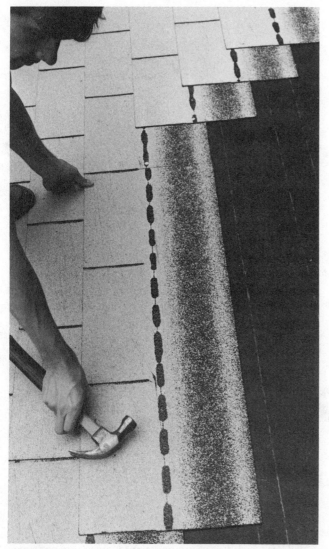

FIGURE 13.2   Fiberglass asphalt shingles are a best buy for both contractor and homeowner installations. (Photograph: Edward Allen)

Roll Roofing

The two types of roll roofing come in large, 36-in.-high rolls that are unrolled and cut to the length of the roof. One type is called *mineral surface,* or *MS;* it is installed as a single layer. The other type is called *selvage,* or sometimes *double-coverage* or *half-lap,* because half of each layer overlaps half of another one, creating a double layer across the whole roof.

Installation of roll roofing is relatively easy and, because the rolls are wide, large sections of roof can be covered quickly. However, roll roofing should be unrolled and laid in the sun on a moderately warm day before installation. If it is installed cold, it may expand and buckle later in the heat of the sun, even if it is nailed properly.

Most mineral surface and selvage roofing materials are now made with fiberglass, rather than wood pulp and paper. Fiberglass roofing lasts longer, is less sensitive to moisture, and is less susceptible to curling.

MINERAL SURFACE (MS) ROLL ROOFING MS roofing comes in 108-sq-ft rolls. (A common unit of roofing is the *square,* defined as enough material to cover 100 ft.) Mineral granules cover the whole upper surface. A higher course overlaps a lower one by about 2 to 4 in., covering nail heads (see Figure 13.3). The laps are sealed with asphalt cement.

MS is the least expensive roofing you can buy. Although it is sometimes applied to low-slope roofs when they begin to leak, this is a mistake. MS should not be used on a roof with a slope of less than 2 in 12. Even if MS is properly applied, the fact that it is laid in a single layer with virtually no overlap means that it does not last as long as shingles or selvage roofing.

SELVAGE ROLL ROOFING Selvage roofing comes with its upper half unprotected by mineral granules, because the upper half is completely lapped by the lower half of the course above it. The roof, therefore, receives a double layer of roofing material (see Figure 13.4). Hence, each 108-sq-ft roll provides only 50 sq ft of roofing, making selvage more expensive than MS.

On most roofs, the overlap is cemented and the sheets are nailed; on slopes of more than 4 in 12, the cement can be omitted. The resulting roof is at least as durable as one of asphalt shingles and costs only two-thirds as much. Installation is easy and, because the sheets are large, is quick.

When selvage is not just nailed but glued together with asphalt cement across the whole overlapping surface, it is one of the few coverings that can be used on a very low roof slope without leaking. When install-

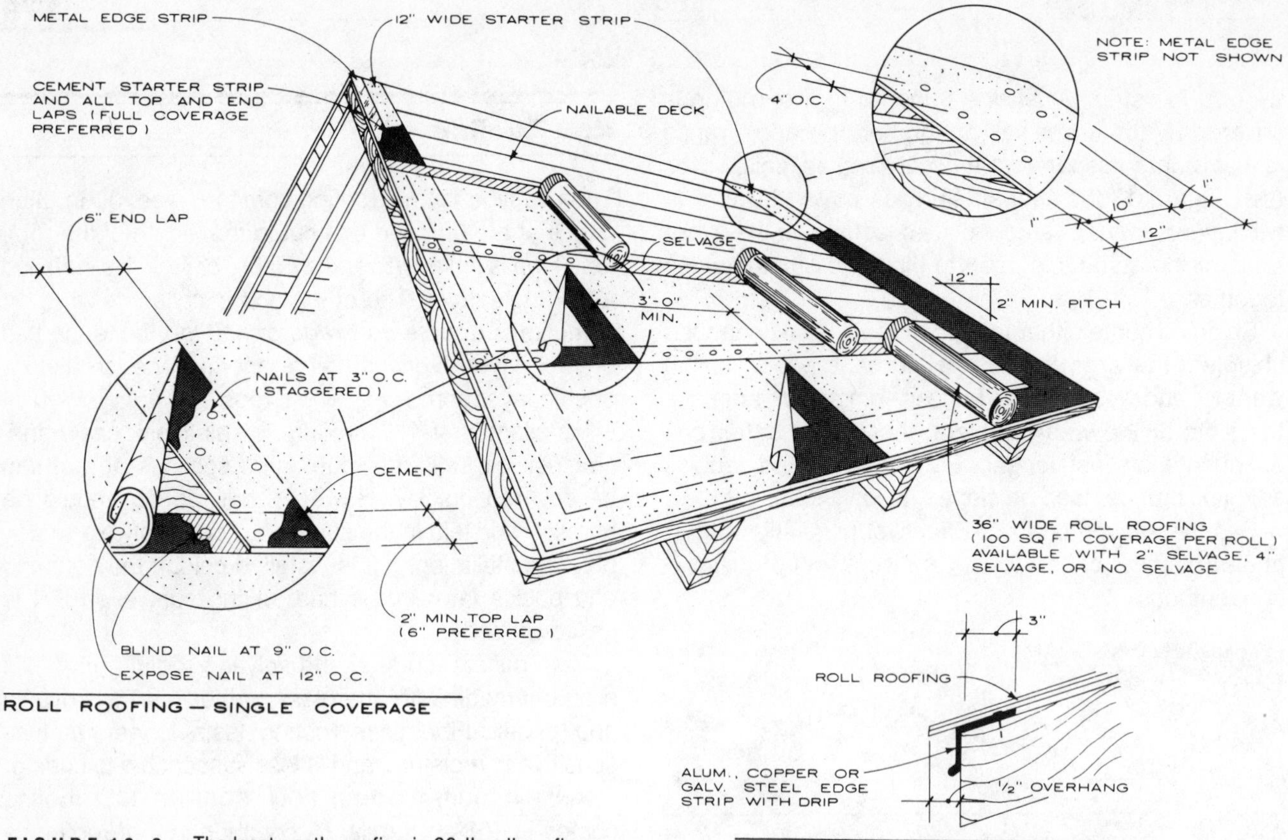
METAL EDGE STRIP
12" WIDE STARTER STRIP
CEMENT STARTER STRIP AND ALL TOP AND END LAPS (FULL COVERAGE PREFERRED)
NAILABLE DECK
4" O.C.
NOTE: METAL EDGE STRIP NOT SHOWN
1"
10"
1"
12"
6" END LAP
SELVAGE
3'-0" MIN.
12"
2" MIN. PITCH
NAILS AT 3" O.C. (STAGGERED)
CEMENT
36" WIDE ROLL ROOFING (100 SQ FT COVERAGE PER ROLL) AVAILABLE WITH 2" SELVAGE, 4" SELVAGE, OR NO SELVAGE
2" MIN. TOP LAP (6" PREFERRED)
BLIND NAIL AT 9" O.C.
EXPOSE NAIL AT 12" O.C.
ROLL ROOFING — SINGLE COVERAGE
3"
ROLL ROOFING
ALUM., COPPER OR GALV. STEEL EDGE STRIP WITH DRIP
1/2" OVERHANG
METAL EDGE STRIP DETAIL

FIGURE 13.3 The least costly roofing is 90-lb roll roofing.

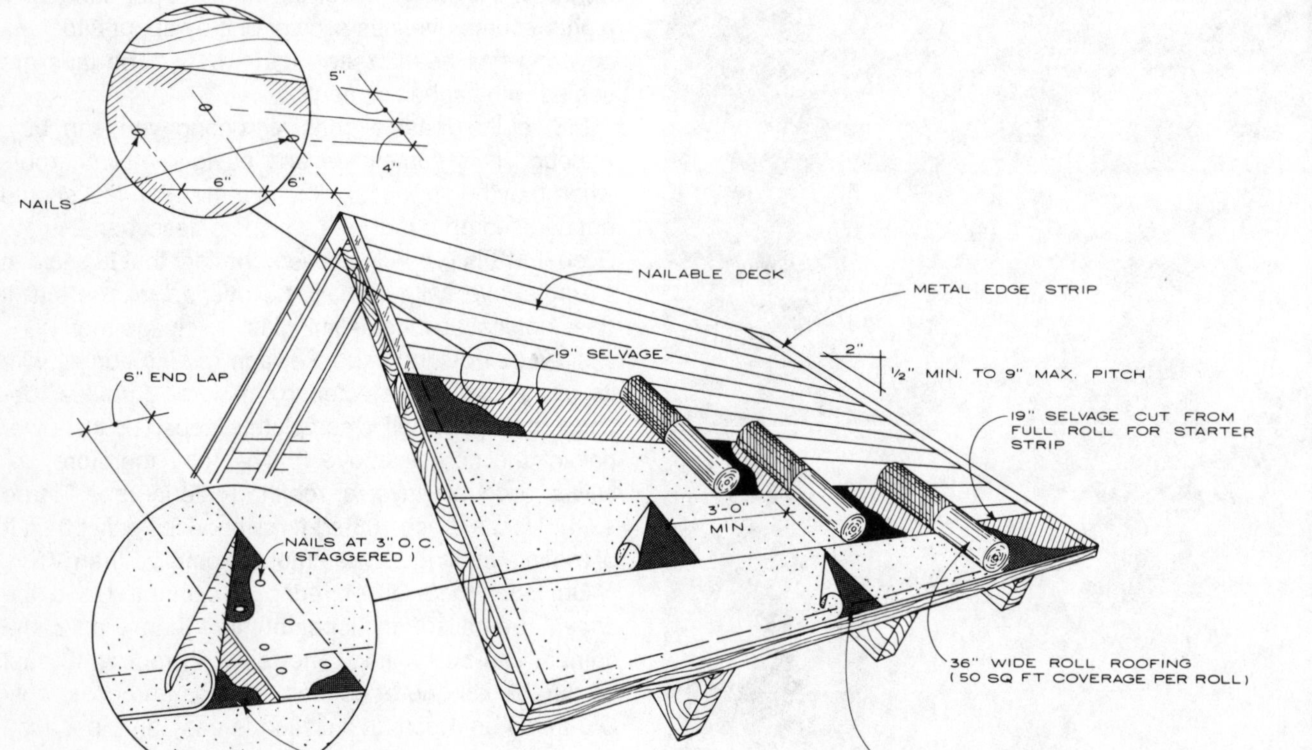
5"
4"
NAILS
6"
6"
NAILABLE DECK
METAL EDGE STRIP
19" SELVAGE
2"
1/2" MIN. TO 9" MAX. PITCH
6" END LAP
19" SELVAGE CUT FROM FULL ROLL FOR STARTER STRIP
3'-0" MIN.
NAILS AT 3" O.C. (STAGGERED)
36" WIDE ROLL ROOFING (50 SQ FT COVERAGE PER ROLL)
CEMENT
CEMENT ALL TOP AND END LAPS (MOP FULL WIDTH UNDER EACH LAYER)
ROLL ROOFING — DOUBLE COVERAGE CONCEALED NAILING

FIGURE 13.4 Selvage overlaps of 19″ provide a long-lasting, low-cost, easy-to-install roof that can be used on very low-slope decks.

ing selvage on a low-slope roof, however, follow the manufacturer's instructions exactly.

Sheet-Metal Roofing

Roofing with corrugated metal sheets was popular for elegant 1890s townhouses, as well as among farm families for homes and utility buildings. Corrugated sheeting is long lasting and inexpensive and requires less roof decking than most other materials. It comes in several corrugated styles and is suitable for slopes as low as 3 or 4 in 12. For more money, you can buy heavier gauges with long-lasting enamels in various colors.

Although twice as expensive as asphalt shingles, metal sheets last so long that the cost per year is low. In addition, they can be installed quickly if the roof design is simple, leading to labor-cost savings that more than compensate for the higher material cost. Where the roof design is complex, however, the labor charges are high.

Metal sheets work well where the decking is not made of plywood boards set edge-to-edge, but of wood strips laid across the rafters and spaced a couple of inches apart. Such *sheathing* was common for wood-shingle roofing. Where the old wood shingles have been taken up, the metal sheets can go directly down on the original sheathing with no additional work, saving a great deal of money and trouble.

Unpainted, galvanized, corrugated roofing begins to rust in 20 to 25 years. If coated periodically with a metal primer and exterior metal paint, it should last at least 60 years, if not indefinitely. Steel lasts somewhat longer than aluminum, and heavy-gauge steel lasts the longest of all, because wind, expansion, and contraction can tear weaker metals at the nail holes.

Metal Shingles

Tough metal shingles guaranteed for 50 years can be a good choice where desert heat shortens the life of other roofing materials. They are also good in snow country, because they conduct heat well and therefore shed ice dams faster than other materials do.

Metal shingles are made by Reinke. They are made of an aluminum alloy stamped into ½-in.-wide, ¼-in.-deep corrugations and are left in a natural aluminum finish or painted with a tough enamel.

Wood Shingles and Shakes

A shingle is cut regularly and has a relatively smooth surface; a shake is rougher and is cut in irregular sizes. Both look attractive on a house, and both can be applied over leaking asphalt shingles (see Figure 13.5). Shingles require no further preparation, but shakes do better when installed with interwoven layers of roofing felt (see Figure 13.6). Use shingles treated with fire retardant—doing so is prudent, and some codes require it. In fact, some codes do not allow wood-shingled roofs, treated or otherwise.

A modern alternative is a wood-fiber board that, when installed, gives the appearance of hand-split shakes yet costs less. The 1 × 4-ft boards are self-aligning and carry a 25-year warranty. The upper surface weathers from brown to gray.

Slate Shingles

Slate lasts 100 years or more, but it is five times more expensive than asphalt shingles in a complete roof

FIGURE 13.5 Wood shingles can be nailed directly over a single layer of asphalt shingles.

FIGURE 13.6   Shakes can also be laid over an existing roof, but because they are rougher and leave larger gaps between them, sheets of roofing felt—eventually completely concealed—are laid down with them.

replacement (see Figure 13.7). A slate roof is generally worth repairing, despite the cost of the shingles and the workmanship needed for the job, because it's so durable.

Roofing tiles in southern areas are similar in cost and durability to slate, and the same general comments apply.

COST-EFFECTIVE INSTALLATION OF ASPHALT SHINGLES

When working with asphalt shingles, there are a number of ways to save money. We'll discuss these in the following sections.

Metric Sizes

You can reduce roofing costs by about 10 percent by using shingles sized in the metric system, because they are slightly larger than inch-based ones. In inches, a metric shingle is 13-¼ × 39-⅜ in.; an inch-based one is only 12 × 36 in. Metric shingles are 20 percent larger, yet do not require more fasteners for each shingle.

Being larger, the metric shingles cover space more quickly and, over the span of the roof, fewer nails or staples are needed. The result is lower labor costs. Metric shingles can be difficult to find in some regions of the country, but it's worthwhile to ask.

Felt or No Felt

The usual way to install asphalt shingles is to begin by spreading 15-lb asphalt-impregnated roofing paper, called *felt,* onto the wooden roof sheathing. Allegedly, the felt underlayment provides waterproofing protection from wind-driven rain that can be forced up under the lower edges of the shingles.

A little-known fact is that roofing felt originally came into use as a buffer between new, resinous pine roof boards and new shingles that could be softened by pitch exuding from the pine in the hot sun. That problem no longer exists, at least with plywood and other manufactured sheathings, which do not exude pitch. Consequently, roofing felt generally is not needed. You can save the cost and trouble of applying the felt undercoat when (1) the roof pitch is 4 in 12 or steeper, or (2) the maximum wind velocity in your area is below 50 miles/hour. Your roof will not leak due to the absence of roofing felt, and the life expectancy of the shingles will not be affected. Eliminating the roofing felt saves you about 10 percent of roofing costs.

Figures 13.8, 13.9, and 13.10 show how tabbed asphalt shingles are laid down with roofing felt. The techniques are the same when no felt is used.

FIGURE 13.7 Making slate shingles is an old art, but the roof that results is exceptionally durable and expensive.

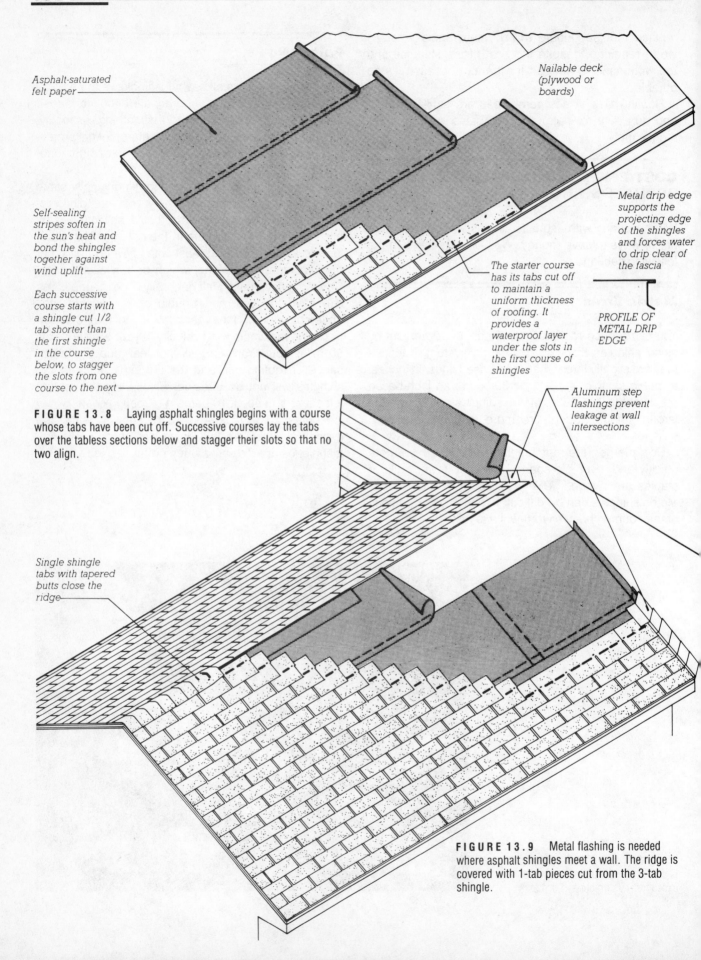

Asphalt-saturated felt paper

Nailable deck (plywood or boards)

Metal drip edge supports the projecting edge of the shingles and forces water to drip clear of the fascia

Self-sealing stripes soften in the sun's heat and bond the shingles together against wind uplift

Each successive course starts with a shingle cut 1/2 tab shorter than the first shingle in the course below, to stagger the slots from one course to the next

The starter course has its tabs cut off to maintain a uniform thickness of roofing. It provides a waterproof layer under the slots in the first course of shingles

PROFILE OF METAL DRIP EDGE

FIGURE 13.8 Laying asphalt shingles begins with a course whose tabs have been cut off. Successive courses lay the tabs over the tabless sections below and stagger their slots so that no two align.

Aluminum step flashings prevent leakage at wall intersections

Single shingle tabs with tapered butts close the ridge

FIGURE 13.9 Metal flashing is needed where asphalt shingles meet a wall. The ridge is covered with 1-tab pieces cut from the 3-tab shingle.

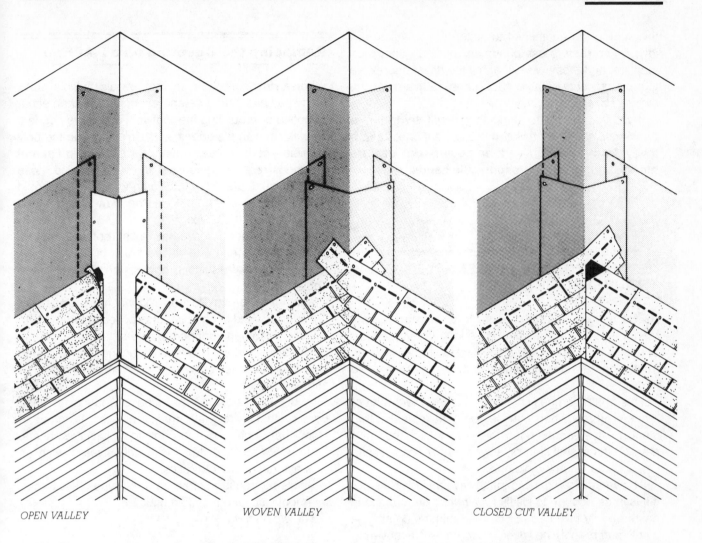

OPEN VALLEY   WOVEN VALLEY   CLOSED CUT VALLEY

FIGURE 13.10   In valleys, metal flashing fits beneath the shingles, or the shingles are interwoven or cut over 30-lb roofing felt.

Staples

Shingles are traditionally put down with hammer and nails. But using a pneumatic stapler can make the job go twice as fast (see Figure 13.11).

The life expectancy of a shingling job is not affected by using staples instead of nails, as long as two installation cautions are followed: Do not use staples on exceptionally hot days, when they can penetrate too far through the shingles, or on exceptionally cold days, when they can shatter the material.

Don't assume that two guys with a pickup truck will always be the lowest bidder on a roofing job. If they do not have a pneumatic stapler, they will have to spend longer on the work and charge accordingly. Get at least one competitive bid from a company that has

FIGURE 13.11   A pneumatic stapler fastens shingles more rapidly than hammer and nails. Do-it-yourselfers can rent a complete setup for $70–$90 a day.

invested in the equipment to fasten the shingles rapidly. Some roofers use pneumatic nailers rather than staplers, and these work fine, but the dollar figures we use on our chart (Table 13.1, page 190) are for the slightly cheaper stapler.

If you want to install shingles yourself, try to rent a pneumatic stapler or nailer. If you do rent one, **keep it away from children—either power tool can be highly dangerous in irresponsible hands.**

REPAIRS TO FLAT, LOW-SLOPED, AND TROUBLESOME ROOFS

As we've said, it is far cheaper to save your old roof than it is to tear off the old one and start over. Unfortunately, with flat or low-sloped roofs, repair is often frustrating because the sources of leaks are hard to find.

That frustration has cost many homeowners a lot of money. Homeowners whose roofs have leaks that elude their searches often throw up their hands and pay for the installation of a whole new roof despite plenty of life left in the old one.

Do everything within reason to save an older flat roof if it is large enough to justify repairs and the surface is neither badly blistered nor missing mineral coating. A small porch roof, however, may be worth covering without further fuss. If you cannot find a leak yourself, and the roof is large enough to justify some exploratory expense, hire a home inspector or other consultant not affiliated with a roofing company. He or she may have equipment such as humidity detectors and X-ray machines that can pinpoint leak sources. Often leaks stem from a single puncture or bad flashing.

The key to saving money is to make selective repairs and keep up with preventive maintenance. Whenever anyone recommends replacing a roof that looks basically sound, always get another professional's opinion before you go any further. In most cases, you can stretch the life of the roof by many years.

When a roof inspection reveals multiple leaks, one solution is to cover the whole roof with a new top layer of material. If the slope is low but not flat, the best choice is probably fiberglass-based, double-coverage selvage, which has an expected life of 20 years. For flat or nearly flat roofs, a flood coat of asphalt plus new gravel should suffice, even if it is applied only over small repairs. This treatment will last 7 to 10 years.

Replacing the Covering on a Flat Roof

When an inspection of a flat roof reveals multiple leaks, many patches, and a deteriorating surface, then either reroofing or rebuilding the roof with a slope is needed. Rebuilding with a slope is a feasible—maybe the only feasible—do-it-yourself option, because most flat roof coverings require equipment and skills beyond those of most amateurs. Still, rebuilding with a slope should be done only if the look of the new roof fits the architecture of the building.

When they need to overhaul a flat roof, most homeowners will choose one of two types of flat reroofing installed by professionals: built-up or single-ply (see Table 13.2, page 192).

BUILT-UP ROOFING Built-up roofing now consists of fiberglass-based asphalt sheets applied in three layers with hot bitumen mopped between them. It makes good sense to price this type of roofing first, and then look into the other options. It is often the most cost-effective choice.

SINGLE-PLY ROOFING This type of roofing is made from synthetic materials, mainly plastics. It comes in strips that adhere to one another or in huge sheets. The sheets are laid down with adhesives or with an overlayment of smooth rocks.

Single-ply roofing comes in three types: elastomer, thermoplastic, and modified bitumen.

The *elastomers* are

1. *EPDM* (ethylene-propylene-dienemonomer), which is usually installed in sheets; it remains flexible in cold weather and is popular, but is subject to deterioration from kitchen exhaust and contact with asphalt roofing materials
2. *Neoprene,* which is also laid in sheets; it is fireproof, and normally a dark color
3. *CSPE* (chlorosulfonated polyethylene), which is laid in sheets; it is fireproof, is more resistant to chemicals and ultraviolet light than is neoprene, and is available in more colors
4. *PIB* (polyisobutylene), which is laid in sheets; it stands up well to mechanical damage, but cannot be laid over coal-tar bitumen

Thermoplastics are made up mainly of PVC roofing materials. PVC has good tensile strength, fire resistance, and abrasion resistance, but does not weather as well as neoprene or EPDM. It cannot be laid over coal tar on asphalt, but it is easily repaired and reflashed.

Modified bitumen roofing is made of bitumen sheets, modifiers, and reinforcers. Self-adhering sheets are the easiest to install. They are laid down with each sheet overlapping another; they stick both to themselves and to the underlayment when moderate pressure is applied.

Your choice of roofing material depends on the complexity of the roof shape, the present layer of roofing, the stresses to which the roof will be subjected, the degree of installation difficulty, and finding the best purchase price. We suggest that you buy the cheapest roof that will last at least 20 years. If the guaranteed life is shorter, you should pay less. If it is more, judge whether paying a higher price is worthwhile to you. Always ask for the guaranteed life of a material and, for less common materials, demand proof.

Troublesome or Low-Slope Roofs

Sometimes, in previous renovations, when a chimney, small porch roof, or overhang was added to a house, little thought was given to the possibility that these additions would snare driven rain, snow, or ice. Unfortunately, they often do. When you are reroofing, one way to permanently fix the leaks caused by poorly

conceived improvements is to install new decking and, sometimes, minor framing, in a way that increases the slope of the roof in the problem area. Such a fix is particularly effective on a porch roof whose decking needs replacement anyway (see Figure 13.12).

DECIDING WHETHER TO TEAR OFF THE OLD ROOFING

All reroofing jobs require a decision about whether or not to rip up the old finish roofing down to the deck below. Doing this increases the cost of the job, but it needs to be done in the following circumstances.

When two or more old layers are already there. Most codes require you to take up roofing if two or more layers already cover the decking. The reasons are that the combined weight of the three layers may be too great for the decking and that you may not be able to fasten the new roofing securely through the previous layers. However, there are serviceable roofs of three layers, particularly if the third is metal. If you are in doubt about adding a third layer, consult a home inspector.

When any part of the roof deck is bad. A sagging or springy feeling when you walk on the roof indicates a

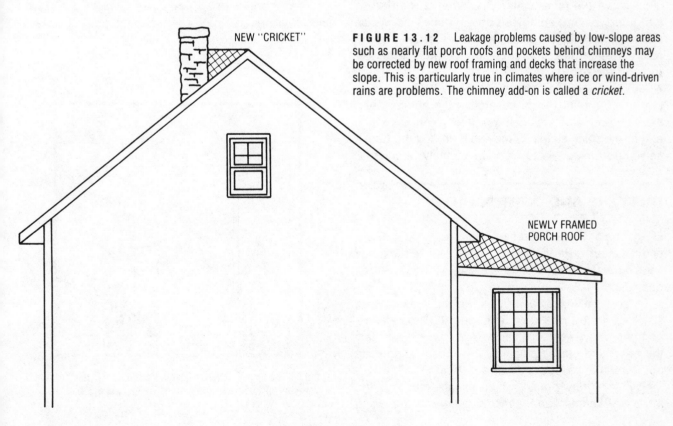

NEW "CRICKET"

NEWLY FRAMED PORCH ROOF

FIGURE 13.12 Leakage problems caused by low-slope areas such as nearly flat porch roofs and pockets behind chimneys may be corrected by new roof framing and decks that increase the slope. This is particularly true in climates where ice or wind-driven rains are problems. The chimney add-on is called a *cricket*.

decaying deck. When deterioration is detected, professionals usually tear off the finish roofing in at least that area so that they can properly inspect and repair the deck.

When a building inspector requires a whole new roof. Sometimes, but not usually, local code officials will require you to remove the old layers if you are planning to put down a new one. In fact, some building inspection departments are very fussy about old decks and even rafters being brought up to modern code standards. Sometimes they have good reason, and sometimes they are too cautious. There are 200-year-old rafters in New England, undersized by modern code standards, that have withstood exceptional snow loads and other tests of time. If your local department requires an upgrade, but you think your roof is solid, try to persuade the officials of that. Mainly, the codes do not apply retroactively to old construction, but they do rightly call for roofs that can stand up to the expected snow and wind loads.

Those are the three conditions for removing old finish roofing. Generally, if you have a single layer, you can cover it.

If you are removing old shingles, there is a technique that can make the work go faster: Use a long-handled, spade-type shovel. Its slight angle at the end makes it a good lever-action nail-puller, and it keeps your face high above the dust. **CAUTION: Wear a respirator. Many old roofing shingles contain asbestos. As an added precaution, wash your work clothes—separately from other clothing—immediately after removing the roofing.**

Another trick is to rent a small, open-top auto trailer that can be manually pulled around the house. Set it against the house wall below where you are working and throw shingles into it, moving it around the house as you go. Doing this saves hours of nasty cleanup.

GUTTERS AND DOWNSPOUTS

Many homes do not need complete gutter and downspout systems. Partial systems often can do the job of keeping water away from the siding, foundation, and doors.

To be sure, water usually is the most destructive force a building has to protect against. A foundation, no matter how well built, cannot hold back indefinitely the water that pools up against it; nor can siding keep out water that cascades down it in sheets.

Still, you may be able to eliminate much of the trouble of keeping and repairing gutters, or replacing

them, if your house meets a couple of requirements. If (1) the ground around your house is mostly unpaved, so that most of the water is absorbed into the ground, and (2) your house is no more than two stories high, you can be pretty sure that a complete system of gutters and downspouts is unnecessary.

The first requirement assumes that the grade of garden or lawn angles away from the house at no less a slope than 1 in. in 4 ft. If the slope is less, you will have water intrusion problems around the foundation with or without gutters. A truckload of soil brought in and placed around the house strategically can do more to save the foundation and keep the basement dry than can many more expensive repairs.

The second requirement is based on the fact that water falling from the height of a three-story roof can damage siding and window and door casings and should be channeled off in downspouts.

If your house does meet the two requirements, you can avoid much of the maintenance and cost of a full system of gutters and downspouts. One option is to install diverter flashing over doors that guides roof water to the sides (see Figure 13.13). If more water diversion is needed, you can put up a partial system. Such collections of shorter gutters and downspouts capture water where it concentrates and channels it away from the siding and foundations. For example, instead of full downspouts, you can put up *kickers,* short sections that run out from the gutter a couple of

FIGURE 13.13 Diverter flashing can be installed over a doorway as part of a low-cost alternative to a full gutter-and-downspout system.

FIGURE 13.14 A 2-ft *kicker* keeps rainwater away from the foundation, but is less expensive than running a full downspout from the roof to the ground.

feet into the air and let the rainwater fall away from the house (see Figure 13.14). Short sections of gutter can be installed along porches to eliminate sheets of water during a storm and persistent drips after.

Remember, gutters are particularly troublesome if you get lots of snow or leaves. Snow backs up, thawing and freezing, until downspouts are clogged, then forms ice dams that can pool water on the roof. The water finds its way under shingles or other roofing material and then into the walls and house. Leaves from over-

hanging trees also clog gutters, which can lead to water streaming down the siding and sometimes entering the walls.

If, however, your home does require a full system of gutters and downspouts, you have four kinds to choose from.

PVC. PVC is the newest gutter material on the market. PVC systems are glued together or fitted with rubber gaskets. PVC gutter and downspout systems are the most expensive, but they are fairly easy to install and make a good do-it-yourself project.

Seamless aluminum. This is the most common gutter and downspout material used today. Well-equipped contractors can form and cut the proper lengths right on their trucks as they are parked at your house, and they install the pieces quickly. Like gutters and downspouts made from high-quality PVC, aluminum ones should last 60 years if not damaged by ice dams, ladders, roofers, or falling branches.

Preformed aluminum. Made of the same gauge aluminum as the seamless kind that the professionals fabricate on site, these are pieces of standard lengths available in stores. Since you have to piece them together yourself, they are best for small jobs. For large jobs, even if you plan to do the work, get estimates from contractors of seamless gutters. Because they buy their aluminum in bulk and the labor of installing it is not great, they may be able to offer a complete job at a very reasonable price.

Galvanized steel. Once, galvanized steel was the only gutter and downspout material available other than wood, but it is no longer recommended. It will corrode and eventually rust; it needs more maintenance and has a shorter life than any of the other materials.

Wood. Molded wood gutters, usually of cedar, are suitable only when you are replacing a section of existing rotted wood gutter and you want the repair to match the original look. Wood gutters are expensive.

TABLE 13.1 Options for Reroofing a Pitched Roof	**THE PROJECT** Reroof a 2-story, gable-roofed home with 1,200 sq ft of roof surface and a $4/12$ pitch.

Options	Cost/sq ft Contracted	Cost/sq ft DIY	Project Cost Contracted	Project Cost DIY	Difficulty Level	Comments and Recommendations
Roll Roofing Install 90-lb fiberglass mat with 2″ overlap.	$0.60	$0.20	$720	$240	3	Good for emergency repairs that may end up lasting 10 years or more. If you're paying a contractor, put something better on.
Selvage Install 19″ selvage material with adhesive at lap.	$0.85	$0.32	$1,020 CC	$385 CC	3	This low-cost roof will last at least as long as fiberglass shingles at about half the cost.
Fiberglass Asphalt Shingles Install Class A, 240-lb-rated shingles with 25-year warranty.	$1.20	$0.55	$1,440 VB	$660 VB	3	These heavyweight fiberglass shingles are recommended for most applications where steel isn't acceptable. Do not use organic mat shingles. The slightly thicker 25-year material is a value buy.
Corrugated Metal Install 30-gauge galvanized metal sheets, 27″ wide.	$1.80	$0.77	$2,165	$925	3	Can last 100 years or more if maintained. Quick, inexpensive, should be used more. Sheets come in lengths of 4′ to 20′. Get an experienced person to help measure and start the job.
Cement Shingles Install 325-lb-rated, 14″ × 30″ shingles.	$2.10	$1.28	$2,525	$1,536	3	This roof is the best upgrade from fiberglass. For an extra $1,000, you buy 10 years of roof life.
Metal Shingles Install aluminum shingles with anodized finish (0.030″ thick).	$3.15	$1.65	$3,780	$2,000	3	Expensive, not fireproof, many colors available.

Options	Cost/sq ft Contracted	Cost/sq ft DIY	Project Cost Contracted	Project Cost DIY	Difficulty Level	Comments and Recommendations
Wood Shingles Install #1 cedar shingles with 5″ exposure, fire-retardant treated.	$3.80	$1.30	$4,560	$1,560	3	Like thatch and bark, a bygone product. High cost; high maintenance; average life. Buy only fire-retardant kind or you will turn your roof into a tinderbox.
Slate Shingles Install black or gray ¼″-thick shingles.	$8.20	$4.50	$9,800	$5,400	4	Expensive and doesn't match life-cycle cost of fiberglass or steel. Consider only repair of existing slate roofs unless you like the aesthetics.

TABLE 13.2
Options for Reroofing a Flat Roof

THE PROJECT
Reroof a 800-sq-ft, 1-story addition with a low-slope roof including tear-off work deck preparation required. All membrane roof options have thicknesses measured in mils—one thousandth of an inch.

Options	Roofing Cost/sq ft Contracted	Project Cost Contracted	Comments and Recommendations
Selvage Install 19″ selvage material with adhesive at lap.	$85	$680 CC	This low-cost roof will last at least as long as built-up fiberglass at about half the cost. Not for use on "dead" flat roofs.
Built-up Fiberglass Install 1 base sheet plus 3 plies of fiberglass felt paper, hot mopped.	$1.35	$3,175	Price this roof first, then compare the others. This should last 20 + years with minor maintenance. Use fiberglass felts.
Polyvinyl Chloride (PVC) Roofing Install 48-mil reinforced material, either loose laid or fully adhered.	$0.99–$1.60	$3,200	This and all following options are elastomers or membrane roofs. A fully ballasted PVC roof may be the least expensive if roof can accept 1 lb/sq ft of rock. Must be separated from all roofing "tars."
Ethylene Propylene Dienemonomer (EPDM) Roofing Install 55-mil material.	$1.04–$1.50	$3,600	Widely available.
Polyisobutylene (PIB) Roofing Install 100-mil material either loose laid or fully adhered.	$1.44–$1.85	$3,650	Requires separation from existing roofing with coal-tar contents.
Modified Bitumen Install 150-mil loosely laid with 4 lb/sq ft of ballast or fully adhered.	$1.07–$1.50	$3,680	Loosely laid types require only 40 lbs of rock per 100 sq ft for ballast. Can be applied over old roof. Self-stick products are available for DIY at about 65¢/sq ft.

Options	Roofing Cost/sq ft Contracted	Project Cost Contracted	Comments and Recommendations
CSPE (Hypalon) Roofing Install 35-mil material, fully adhered.	$1.95	$3,900	This white roof is gaining acceptance.
CSPE 40 Roofing Install 40-mil material, partially adhered.	$2.04	$4,000	Mechanically fastened. Very durable colors available.
Neoprene Roofing Install 60-mil material, partially adhered or fully adhered.	$2.43–$2.25	$4,700	Fireproof. Estimated life in excess of 30 years.

14 | Demolition

Cost-efficient demolition is an either-or proposition. Either you do as little as possible, or you gut the whole room or house to the structural frame.

Both methods have their efficiencies—middle courses do not. Minimal demolition is efficient because it saves replacement materials and work. Gutting a house is efficient because new systems are installed more quickly when finished walls are out of the way.

We recommend minimal demolition, because it usually is much more cost-effective than wholesale demolition. The more you work with the parts of the building you have already paid for, the more money you are likely to save. The more you reject those parts, the more you are likely to spend (see Figure 14.1). Wholesale demolition, called *gutting* in the trade, usually is justified only when the woodwork and plaster are in terrible shape or the present floor plan is poor.

Take this example of two contractors bidding to renovate a 1,000-sq-ft townhouse that will be vacant while the work goes on. One suggested gutting the whole building and starting over with the shell; the other wanted to demolish only what wouldn't work well or couldn't be saved. Their preliminary estimates and the carrying costs were as follows:

Complete Demolition

Demolition Costs	$4,000
Reconstruction Costs	$32,000
Carrying Costs for 8 Months*	$3,000
TOTAL	$39,000

Selective Demolition

Demolition Costs	$1,300
Repairs	$13,000–$20,000
Carrying Costs for 4 Months*	$500
TOTAL	$14,800–$21,800

*Carrying costs included the interest payments on the construction loan, taxes, insurance, and utilities incurred during construction (but not interest payments on the purchase cost).

FIGURE 14.1 With selective, not wholesale, demolition, you can add pipes and wires to a bathroom and still save the ceramic tile floor and wainscot.

As you can see, selective demolition could save you about $17,200 to $24,200 over the cost of complete demolition and reconstruction.

SELECTIVE DEMOLITION

Reducing the amount of demolition work requires a tolerant attitude and a keen eye for saving money. You may want to hire a professional to walk through the house with you and give you design ideas that incorporate existing materials and systems.

Selective demolition requires a thorough investigation of the house, first by room and then by system, such as plumbing or wall finishes. Each system must be studied before you can decide if it should be replaced or merely repaired. Here are some ideas that might affect your decisions.

You can sometimes save walls by totally removing ceilings. You can run wires, pipes, and ducts in an exposed ceiling, then nail up a new ceiling without much fuss. When you remove wall covering, however, you are also stuck with the job of taking down and then replacing baseboard, door and window trim, and electrical devices.

Kitchens and bathrooms often require the most demolition in order to run new pipes and wires. You might be able to confine wholesale demolition to these rooms, while leaving the others largely untouched.

KEEPING COSTS LOW

Main rule: If it isn't broken, don't fix it.

Corollary: Fix what is fixable; replace what is irreparable; and add only what is necessary to reduce costs for energy, maintenance, and operation.

The least expensive way to do demolition, of course, is to do the work yourself. Another advantage of the do-it-yourself approach is that you ensure the proper care of the pieces you want to save. Demolition crews are infamous for forgetting which pieces are to be saved or damaging them in their haste to get the work done as quickly as possible. The main disadvantage of doing your own demolition is that the work is hard, dirty, and dangerous—more on that later.

You can contract for demolition in two ways. You can have the work written as a labor task in an overall contract with a general contractor, in which case the general contractor oversees the demolition work, or you can write a smaller contract with a demolition contractor and oversee the work yourself.

When you deal with a general contractor, you give up a measure of control over who does the work, the methods used, and the care that is taken. But if you select a smaller, specialized contractor—and, better yet, make him or her responsible for reinstallation— the contractor and the contractor's workers are much more likely to demolish with care and precision. They will leave joints cleaner, trim less splintered, and light fixtures less battered.

You might try to get competitive bids from both demolition subcontractors and general contractors. Often, the subcontractors own older and smaller trucks and operate with small or temporary work crews. Because their overhead is lower, they often keep the job costs down (see Figure 14.2).

If you are planning major demolition, try to do it when neighborhood construction is slow. Labor is likely to be cheaper then. Also, during slow periods, rental rates for 40-cu-yd dumpsters may run half of what they usually do. When construction is brisk, these dumpsters sometimes cannot be had at any price (see Figure 14.3). When you rent a dumpster, pack it as you would a car for a cross-country trip, because you're paying for every cubic inch.

You do not have to throw everything away. Try to sell some of the materials that you remove. Kitchen cabinets are especially marketable. If you remove them carefully and clean them, you can probably receive several hundred dollars for them.

SAFETY FIRST

Demolition is dangerous. There is flying debris, dangerous dust, exposed nail ends, and unstable footing. Wear goggles, a hard hat, and gloves when any of the

FIGURE 14.2 Small contractors can be good for demolition jobs because they often have much lower overhead and can bid jobs lower.

FIGURE 14.3 A 40-cu-yd dumpster is suitable for most demolition. If it has to remain on the street, apply for a permit far enough in advance that it is in place when you want work to start.

above are present. Tough jeans and long-sleeve shirts can also protect you.

The biggest dangers are airborne and require a pesticide-level respirator. There may be asbestos, lead-based paint, rodent feces, fungus spores, plaster dust, and germs. All are dangerous; some can make you sick immediately, and some are thought to cause cancer years later. Accordingly, keep demolition pieces as large as possible, because the bigger the pieces, the less dust generated.

Asbestos

Asbestos is usually found as a white, crumbly material wrapped with cloth around pipes or boilers. If you suspect asbestos, do not remove it, but consult a professional. If more than minimal amounts are involved, you are required by federal law to have a qualified person remove it from the house; your health and the health of your neighbors depend on your compliance.

Lead-Based Paint

If you suspect lead-based paint, take extraordinary precautions, especially with paint dust—even low levels of lead in a child can cause permanent brain damage. Lead-based paint is now outlawed but is present in most homes built before 1977. **If you are renovating a house that contains lead-based paint, health officials warn that you should not do so while children or women of child-bearing age live there.** As an adult, you are less susceptible to lead poisoning than are children, but you should still wear a heavy-duty respirator.

Lead danger is most likely where old enamel paint on walls and trim has peeled and been ground into dust. **The dust is poisonous when inhaled or ingested,** as when a child crawls on the floor and then puts its fingers in its mouth. The danger can be reduced by carefully sweeping up, vacuuming, and properly disposing of the debris. (For disposal, call your public health bureau or public disposal facility.) **Never burn off paint that is suspected of containing lead,** and do not scrape it off indoors without extreme care in removing the debris.

Where lead-based paint dust is present, cleanup is essential. Unfortunately, even normal vacuuming is not wholly effective, because the most dangerous and absorbable lead particles are so small that they escape through the pores of a vacuum cleaner bag. Use a HEPA (high-efficiency particulate accumulator) vacuum cleaner. Vacuum twice, letting dust settle after the first cleaning. Then mop with a solution of trisodium phosphate every week for three to four weeks. (High-phosphate detergents collect lead particles most effectively.)

For more information on lead-based paint testing, removal, and protection, call your public health department.

Consideration for Others

The dust you raise in your home can harm people who are not even close to the work. For the protection of your neighbors—and to make the work go more efficiently as well—use a covered chute when tossing debris from second- and third-story windows.

Change your clothes and wash up before you rejoin your family so you don't expose them to toxic dusts and germs. **CAUTION: Babies, children, and older people are especially susceptible to airborne germs and dust particles**—try to keep them away from demolition areas. If you cannot, at least keep them away while dust is in the air and allow them in only after you have cleaned the area. **Pregnant women should also avoid demolition dust.**

DEMOLITION TECHNIQUES

To do an efficient demolition job, do it all at one time. Do not stagger the work floor by floor or room by room—major inefficiencies and costly slowdowns result when you have highly paid duct installers, electricians, and so forth slowed down by concurrent demolition activities. Accordingly, remove all the demolition debris from the house before mechanics begin their work.

For selective demolition work, use a paint spray-can to mark what you want removed. Then take measures to carefully protect anything you want saved. If you can, cover items you want preserved; mark them clearly to be saved if work crews might think they are to be removed. Better yet, label them, remove them, and store them before a demolition subcontractor comes onto the job site.

If you have asked your contractor to demolish selectively—especially for channels to accompany electrical cables, plumbing pipes, or air ducts—clearly mark the wall and ceiling areas to be cut with spray paint or magic markers, or ask the contractor to do so.

If part of a wall is being removed, do not let work crews beat on it with sledge hammers and crowbars—this will turn potentially useful portions of the wall into plaster rubble. Instead, cut the borders of unwanted sections with a carbide-tipped circular saw. Then pry out the area within. This method also leaves a clean joint for later patching. In addition, careful cutting minimizes dust, which is especially important if walls are suspected of being covered with lead-based paint.

When removing ceilings, use a hatchet to cut them away from the walls. Carefully drive the hatchet upward at the joint where the ceiling and walls meet. If you do not break this bond, you are likely to damage the top 3 in. of the walls.

If much of the plaster is taken off the wall, consider leaving the lath on. In some very old houses, the original builders shimmed the lath strips to compensate for roughly cut studs. Leaving the lath in place for ½-in. drywall makes a more even backing than the studs alone and probably will have the additional benefit of saving the trouble of resetting door and window jambs and trim.

Leaving the lath in place need not hinder efforts to add insulation to exterior walls. Stretch 6-mil plastic sheeting over the lath, stapling every 12 in. Then have cellulose or fiberglass insulation blown in through slits that can be patched with duct tape. The plastic also serves as an excellent vapor barrier. The drywall goes right over the top and is screwed or nailed through the sheeting and the lath to the studs.

15

Outside Work and Foundations

Although we say we have "bought a house," in fact we have bought land as well, a plot that extends beyond the house. Whether the extra land is a few square yards of patio space behind a city townhouse or the lawns, driveways, and walks of a suburban home, we soon discover that these areas not only intrigue us with improvement possibilities, but needle us with demands for repair.

Consider an average suburban yard. It serves a number of functions. Its driveway leads to parking for the car. Its walks, and the stairs at the end of them, lead to the house. Its appearance (one hopes) adds to the appeal of the whole property. Its trees shade the house from summer sun. Its open areas—patios, lawns, and decks—are used for recreation. Other vacant areas might hold storage or utility buildings.

While a yard might be paved in part with brick, flagstone, or asphalt—all discussed later—most outside improvements are made of concrete. Because concrete is such a common material for driveways and walks, we will discuss its purchase, installation, and repair in some detail. Concrete also is a common material for foundations, which we'll discuss at the end of this chapter.

Landscaping and lawn care do not fall within the scope of this book, except to say the following. Trees are an exceptionally effective and low-cost way to keep a house cool. Deciduous trees are even better, since they lose their leaves in fall and allow sunshine to warm the house in winter. Trees add value to the property when it is sold. And lawns are the cheapest recreational areas—cheaper to make and keep up than patios and decks.

BUYING, POURING, AND REPAIRING CONCRETE

Concrete is often called *"mud"* in the trade, but a slur is probably not intended. Concrete is a wonderful material. Think of it as liquid stone that can be molded to any shape. When it dries, you have something almost as hard as granite, and in the precise configuration you want.

Concrete is the most cost-effective material for patios. It is also the best long-term value for sidewalks. It is used effectively for driveways and is used almost universally for foundations.

Buying Concrete

Buying concrete is a kind of art, certainly a skill. You must know how to measure for the amount of concrete you need; and you must know how concrete companies make their product, how they deliver, and how they charge.

First, we'll show you how to calculate the amount of concrete you need. The calculations will be worthless, of course, if you measure incorrectly. So take care: Measure twice and order once.

To keep concrete costs down, order only what you need. Measure the form or excavation accurately. Then, to calculate how much *mixed* concrete is needed, in cubic yards, multiply the length in feet by the width in feet by the thickness in inches. Then divide the product by 342. The result is the number of cubic yards needed.

Example: For a formed area 10 ft long, 8 ft wide, and 4 in. deep, multiply 10 times 8 = 80; times 4 = 320; divide by 324 and come up with approximately one cubic yard of concrete to fill the excavation.

For a more complicated structure, such as a footing plus a wall, each component must be calculated separately.

Before you call a concrete delivery company, know how much to order. Once you know that, you also need to know how companies deliver and how they charge.

Concrete is sold by the cubic yard from mixer trucks. You are charged for each cubic yard you buy. In addition, concrete companies usually impose three kinds of surcharges: short load (meaning small load), overtime, and cleanup.

Short-load fees of $12 to $25 per cubic yard apply when you order less than a full truckload, which generally is about 9 cu yd. Some companies will waive short-load fees if you order at least 5 cu yd. Accordingly, try to schedule all your concrete jobs for the same day, so that the concrete can be poured during a single visit of the truck. Or, coordinate your work with that of a neighbor who needs concrete (making sure that you both measure very carefully).

Overtime fees are charged when you use more time than alloted to empty the truck of the cubic yards you have ordered. Companies have different ideas about what is free unloading time, from 4 to 10 minutes per

cubic yard. After that, they begin to charge from 50 cents to $2/minute.

A cleanup load fee is charged when you have underestimated the amount of concrete needed and a second delivery is required. The supplier will usually send a second truck, but because your order requires a nonscheduled trip on short notice and causes delays for other deliveries, you will be charged 50 to 100 percent more than for a standard delivery. Consequently, a cubic yard that normally costs about $50 can cost over $100 on a cleanup load fee, a costly mistake.

Ask the concrete company you are considering for its roster of charges, and work to avoid as many of them as possible.

Here is an example of a job correctly estimated and one that required overtime plus a cleanup load. The improperly estimated job costs about 70 percent more.

Correctly Estimated Job (No overtime fee, no reorder)

Base rate: 4 cu yd at $53/cu yd	**$212**
Short-load fee on 4 cu yd: $12 for each cu yd ordered that is less than 7 cu yd (7 cu yd minus 4 cu yd equals 3 cu yd) × $12	**$36**
TOTAL	**$248**

Overtime Job with 1-cu-yd Cleanup

Base rate: 3 cu yd at $53/cu yd	**$159**
Short-load fee on 3 cu yd	**$48**
Overtime fee for 45 minutes at $1/minute	**$45**
Cleanup load fee for 1 cu yd	**$113**
Trip surcharge for immediate response	**$60**
TOTAL	**$425**

Concrete can be ordered in two forms, plain and air-entrained. The latter is concrete into which air is blown as it is mixed. The air bubbles make the mixture more workable when the concrete is wet and serve as insulation in very cold weather. This helps to prevent cracking.

Air-entrained concrete is 2 to 4 percent more expensive than regular concrete, but some local codes require it for concrete poured outdoors. Even if it is not required, the added cost of air-entrained concrete is worth the extra winter protection and extended life.

If you have a choice, order concrete with "¾-inch stone"; larger stones make it more difficult to move the concrete within the forms. For most jobs, order standard (3,000-lb) strength, a measure of how much cement is put into the mix.

When the concrete arrives, the truck driver will often

ask you how much you want it "wetted up"—that is, how much water should be added. Start by saying "not too wet," and ask the driver to send small amounts down the chute. The concrete should not be so stiff that it stands up at a steep angle or is hard to move around or work with a trowel. Conversely, it should not be so wet that it is "self-leveling," as contractors jokingly call a mix that spreads out immediately and needs no pushing around.

Pouring Concrete

PROPER DESIGN If you want to save money on concrete work, it is important not to overbuild. Check your local codes. Don't exceed their standards unless you have a good reason to spend the extra time and money.

For example, wire mesh is not required as a reinforcement in sidewalks. If you need to reinforce the concrete in a limited area—say, over a pipe trench or in a poorly filled area—use reinforcing bars.

If you are working in a very cold climate, you may be tempted to increase the standard 4- to 5-inch thickness of concrete to prevent the cracking that results from freezing and thawing. However, concrete thickness has little to do with cracking, the usual cause of which is a poorly compacted or poorly drained soil or fill material under the concrete. You can save money by using less concrete and increasing the depth of a well-drained gravel base beneath it. Rent a compactor to firmly tamp any disturbed or new base material.

However, don't skimp on concrete thickness where heavy traffic is expected. If the concrete will have to support truck traffic, build those sections to what is called a *full highway* specification—that is, a 6-in. thickness with a higher strength mix plus reinforcing mesh.

POURING When the day to pour the concrete arrives, be prepared. Decide in advance where the truck is to stop. Usually, this is the street. The truck has a 10- or 12-ft chute, and you can ask in advance for a 12-ft extension.

Trying to route concrete more than 24 ft by chute is not practical. For greater distances, you will need a wheelbarrow. It is a good idea to place a piece of plywood under the wheelbarrow at the end of the chute to catch drippings that you would otherwise have to clean up. From the plywood, run planks of 2 × 8's or similar lumber to the place where the wheelbarrow is to be dumped, unless the ground is exceptionally hard. A wheelbarrow full of concrete is too heavy to push across a soft surface or lawn. Where huge quantities need to be moved or where a wheelbarrow will not work, hire a contractor with a concrete pump.

Having the truck back up across a lawn is risky. Its wheels could break a curb or leave deep ruts. In any case, a truck should never be allowed to drive over a septic tank or cesspool, which might cave in from the weight. If you really must have a truck cross a lawn, lay down 2-in.-thick planks along the wheels' path to distribute the truck's weight.

When the truck is ready to release concrete down its chute, have a crew of helpers ready. If you're using a wheelbarrow, one helper can use a shovel to pull concrete down the chute to the wheelbarrow, while another pushes the wheelbarrow back and forth from the truck to the excavation or forms that are to receive the concrete. A third helper can distribute the dumped concrete in the excavation or forms with a hoe. If you are not using a wheelbarrow, your helpers can concentrate on spreading the concrete. It is important to work quickly and efficiently so that you are not charged an overtime fee.

An alternative to hiring a concrete truck is to rent a power mixer, which plugs into an electric receptacle. You must shovel or pour in the gravel, cement, and water yourself, then turn the mixer on. It makes about 1 cu ft (⅛ cu yd) at a time, although larger trailer models with wheels can handle as much as 2 cu yd.

If you need more than a cubic yard or so, analyze the costs of mixing the concrete yourself against buying it premixed from a truck. Add up the costs of the mixer rental, cement, sand, and stone, and consider your own efforts at the hard labor of mixing. You may prefer premixed after all.

For really small jobs, you can buy bags of ready-mix concrete. All you have to do it is add water and mix with a hoe—a wheelbarrow makes a good mixing pan—then pour the batch where you need it.

FINISHING Once the concrete is poured and evenly distributed, it must be smoothed. The smoother you want the finish, the more work and the more cost. The roughest finish, which costs the least if a contractor is doing the work, is called *screeding*, necessary preparation for finer finishing. A straight 2 × 4, resting on opposite sides of the form, is pulled back and forth across the concrete surface, pushing a little ridge of concrete in front of it.

About twice as expensive as screeding, if you are having the work contracted, is finishing with a steel trowel. A steel-trowel finish takes far more skill and is required only when the concrete is going to be an interior finish floor or the subfloor for resilient flooring.

You can rent a power trowel—a rototiller-sized machine with four rotating paddles—but if you have never used one before, prepare yourself for a learning period.

In between these two finishes—in cost, labor, and skill level—are float finish and broom finish. A *float finish* uses a float, which is merely a piece of wood with a handle on top. You literally float it on top of the wet concrete and move it around to smooth the surface. For wider areas like driveways and patios, a longer—and rentable—*bull float* is used.

A *broom finish* is an additional step that follows a float finish. You add texture and a nonskid surface to the concrete by lightly drawing a broom over it. Unlike a steel-trowel finish, which requires a relatively high skill level, the float and broom finishes require no special skills and cost less.

Be sure to add some finishing touches to your concrete job. An *edging tool,* which makes a rounded edge on walks and driveways, is easy to use and costs only a few dollars. The rounded edge actually adds strength, because a right-angled edge is more breakable.

For driveways, walks, and large slabs, you'll need to pay attention to control joints and expansion joints. *Control joints* are grooves that are added to make suitable channels for hairline cracks, a result of the inevitable expansion, contraction, frost, and loads. Control joints are shaped into the concrete surface with a *grooving tool* about every 3 ft on walks and every 12 to 16 ft on driveways.

Expansion joints are advisable in very long concrete slabs such as driveways and sidewalks. They are made by laying strips of ½-in. asphalt-impregnated sheathing board into the concrete at intervals. These joints compensate for expansion and contraction, preventing the concrete from buckling or severely cracking.

For these tasks requiring special tools and skills, the novice do-it-yourself concrete installer has a very important potential friend, the masonry supply store. Tell counterpersons there the jobs you intend to do. They will give you advice and sell you the appropriate tools. They may even rent you a mixer and have the cement, sand, and stone delivered; or if they do not, they can tell you who can.

FORMS All good concrete jobs are poured into *forms,* although more than one driveway or walk has been attempted without them. For complicated forms, such as those for steps or walls, hire a contractor or plan to study form construction carefully. Here are some basic suggestions.

Driveways, walks, and slabs. The entire perimeter should be surrounded by 2 × 6 lumber held firmly with pointed 2 × 4 stakes driven into the ground about every 4 ft. A good form creates a straight, attractive, strong edge and gives you a level surface over which to run your screeding 2 × 4. Use an edging tool to dress the edges. Take care that the new surface drains properly: It should slope away from the middle or to one side.

Wider slabs. On wider expanses of concrete, some special preparations need to be made. Driveways or garage floors more than about 14 ft wide may require a center board of 1-in. lumber nailed to stakes. This board provides a place to rest the screed board in the middle—20-ft screed boards do not work very well. The center board is pulled out before the concrete hardens, and the depression is eliminated with a float.

Footings and walls. Building codes are quite specific about the requirements for footings and walls for new structures. Retaining walls, because of the pressure of the soil behind them, are particularly tricky. Retaining walls over a few feet high must be engineered. In fact, two of the most common mistakes of do-it-yourselfers are concrete forms and retaining walls that collapse from the extraordinary power of hydraulic pressure. Consult experts or manuals and code books before attempting any do-it-yourself concrete wall projects.

Repairing Concrete

Concrete is difficult to fix, but it is also difficult to break up and haul away. Whether you fix it or demolish it usually depends on the existing damage and the relative costs of the alternatives.

A new repair technique that has been developed recently is called *pump-lifting.* It can save old concrete where before it had to be broken and hauled away.

Take the case of a sidewalk that is sunken or tilted. The old remedy was to demolish, haul, regrade, and pour a new slab, all very labor-intensive and expensive. Pump-lifting can now raise or level the old walk. Operators drill through the existing hard concrete and then pump in new concrete, the force of which raises the old walk to level again. If you have a concrete floor, walk, or driveway that tilts in the wrong direction, consider having it pump-lifted—you could save considerably over tearing out and replacing.

Concrete steps, durable as they are, often need repair. If missing corners or small cracks are the problem, patching may be the most cost-effective remedy. If a corner is missing, reconstruct it in place with a latex-based ready-mix or sand-cement-epoxy mix, both available in stores, For cracks up to ⅛ in. wide, you can use a cement-based ready-mix cartridge set in a caulking gun. For larger cracks, use a mortar of 1 part portland cement, 3 parts sand, and just enough water to make a paste that holds its shape.

If the concrete is badly deteriorated or cracked, replacement is the best remedy. You have several options: new, poured-in-place concrete stairs, precast concrete stairs, or wooden replacement stairs either built in place or bought as a unit and fitted to the location (see Table 15.1, page 210).

The least expensive do-it-yourself replacement is to rebuild the stairs from lumber that you cut on site (see Figure 15.1). Buying and installing a wood stair kit is slightly more expensive. But the best long-term value is to do a good job yourself of pouring a concrete stair. Unfortunately, the work is fairly difficult. Easier, but

FIGURE 15.1 Both types of wood steps shown here are easy to construct and provide maximum support. Use of preservative-treated wood provides a 20-year life.

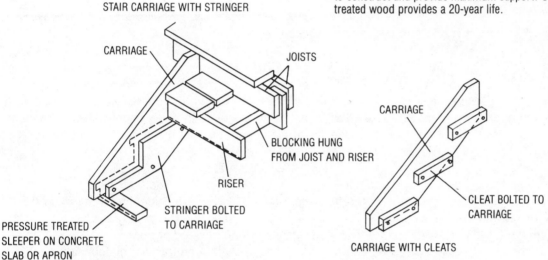

STAIR CARRIAGE WITH STRINGER

CARRIAGE

JOISTS

BLOCKING HUNG FROM JOIST AND RISER

CARRIAGE

CLEAT BOLTED TO CARRIAGE

RISER

STRINGER BOLTED TO CARRIAGE

PRESSURE TREATED SLEEPER ON CONCRETE SLAB OR APRON

CARRIAGE WITH CLEATS

FIGURE 15.2 Precast concrete steps fit many situations. They are inexpensive and can be installed quickly.

more expensive, is buying and setting in place a precast stair (see Figure 15.2). But you'll need help—these weigh at least 200 lbs.

NEW WALKS AND DRIVES

Walks and drives are meant to last for generations, and they can, with preventive maintenance. Concrete is a favored material for walks and drives because it is exceptionally durable, but it is by no means the only material you can use. In fact, you can do the job quite well for less money by using other materials. We'll take a look at driveway and sidewalk materials (see Tables 15.2 and 15.3, pages 211 and 212).

Concrete

Drives. Concrete is good for driveways, especially where heavy vehicles are expected. Put down as a solid slab, it is exceptionally durable, but is also the most expensive if contracted. Done yourself, it is less expensive relative to other materials, but requires a great deal of heavy labor.

Fortunately, you can make a very serviceable driveway with a 1950s flair by using two ribbons of concrete for the wheels of the car and leaving grass or gravel in between (see Figure 15.3). A driveway made of two concrete strips, in fact, is the least expensive option, either contracted or poured and finished as a do-it-yourself project.

Walks. Concrete also makes a good sidewalk material, as hundreds of thousands of miles of suburban walks testify. But concrete walks are not the cheapest option, and they require the labor of excavating and of building forms. If you decide to install a concrete walk,

buy air-entrained concrete—it holds up better in cold weather.

Asphalt

Drives. For driveways, asphalt is a top choice. It lasts about as long as concrete and costs less. But there is no way to lay asphalt yourself; you have to hire a crew.

Walks. Asphalt is a good sidewalk material. Considering its long life and relatively low cost contracted, it gives the best value. But it works best where freezing and thawing cycles are infrequent.

Gravel

Drives. The cheapest material for a driveway built by a contractor is gravel. As a do-it-yourself project, it comes close to the low cost of concrete ribbons. Its major drawback is in snow country—shoveling tends to scoop up some of the gravel and distribute it on nearby grass.

Walks. Gravel can also be used for a walk, although we have not listed it in Table 15.3 (page 212). Its low cost makes it worth considering. To diminish the annoyance of gravel spilling onto grass, you can build a retainer border of wood or brick.

A little-known, but attractive, material for both walks and drives is *crusher dust,* the fine rock particles that are the byproduct of a rock crusher. Any trucker who hauls crushed stone can deliver crusher dust. It levels nicely, packs down, and still allows water to drain through.

FIGURE 15.3 Concrete ribbons take a car's weight but do not cost as much as full slabs.

Soil Cement

A little-known, but cost-effective, alternative to concrete and asphalt is soil cement, sometimes called *soil stabilization*. It is prepared by mixing portland cement with soil, adding water, and compacting the result.

Driveways, walks, and even basement floors can be made by digging up about 6 in. of soil. A tiller is suitable, but a shovel will do. Then add about 1 part portland cement to 3 parts dirt, mix in an amount of water to dampen all the material lightly, and tamp into place—the formula varies with the sandiness of the soil. The resulting hard surface is not as strong as concrete or asphalt, but it is more durable than gravel.

The best soil for such work is sandy, with only moderate amounts of clay and silt, but a wide variety of soils can be used if you increase the amount of cement. In northern states, a special preparation of the subbase is required.

For more information on soil cement, write the Portland Cement Association, 5420 Old Orchard Rd., Skokie, IL 60077.

Soil cement is best for drives that don't need to support heavy trucks. Because drives come under more stress than walks, the preparation of the soil cement must meet or exceed the standards given by the Portland Cement Association. In northern climates, freeze-thaw cycles make soil cement a poor choice, because it is not as strong as concrete.

Pavers

Pavers are small masonry units placed together to make larger paved areas. Flagstone and brick are common pavers. So is concrete that is precast into rectangles, circles, and other shapes made for placing individually along the ground. Pavers can be made to interlock—that is, have zigzag edges that fit together—or can stand alone and separate—for example, 12-in. diameter concrete circles.

Drives. Pavers are not suitable for low-cost drives. Without a properly prepared subbase of concrete or asphalt to which the pavers are cemented, they will move under the weight of cars and trucks. Bricks make a beautiful driveway, but the costs of the subbase, cementing the brick, and the bricks themselves make a brick driveway an exceptionally expensive one.

Walks. On the other hand, pavers make excellent and inexpensive walks. Precast concrete pavers laid down one after another a footstep apart make a low-cost walk either contracted or done yourself. A flagstone walk is more expensive hired out than is a contracted poured concrete or asphalt walk, but as a do-it-yourself project, it compares with poured concrete. The cheapest walk is one made of flat stones, which are abundant and free in some rural areas.

Brick can be the most expensive walk material if you buy new bricks, but the price can be halved if you buy used bricks, which you can find for sale in a business phone directory. If you buy used brick for a walk—or for a patio or any outdoor work—be sure to buy bricks that were made for exterior use, because these are the only kind that will hold up to freeze-thaw cycles. Soft bricks made for interior use will permit moisture to enter and then will crack in freezing temperatures. Figures 15.4 and 15.5 show different patterns of pavers.

PATIOS

Patios are a good bargain for extra living space. Building an addition to the house to obtain another room of living space can cost about $65/sq ft, but you can contract out all the work for a fenced-in area with patio for only about $20/sq ft. Of course, you may be able to use the patio only part of the year, but the saving over added enclosed space makes it a highly attractive alternative.

A patio makes a good do-it-yourself project: The skill level needed is low, and if the job were to be contracted, about two-thirds of the contract price would go to labor (see Table 15.4, page 213).

Concrete. Patios made of concrete are the least expensive both to hire out and to do yourself. Laying down concrete pavers on a base of sand is the easiest way to build a patio and, if done by you, the cheapest. Making a poured concrete patio is troublesome because you must make forms and call a concrete truck for delivery (or mix the concrete yourself). But a poured concrete patio has the virtue of exceptional durability. A poured concrete patio has the additional advantage of being a potential subbase for a future covering of flagstone, brick, or any other paving material if you ever want to upgrade the patio's looks.

Pavers. Patios are often made of brick, flagstone, or other more expensive stones, and for good reason. All are durable and attractive. They can be arranged in pleasing patterns. They can be set on sand and then extra sand can be swept into the cracks between pieces.

Wood. A deck made of wood is more expensive than

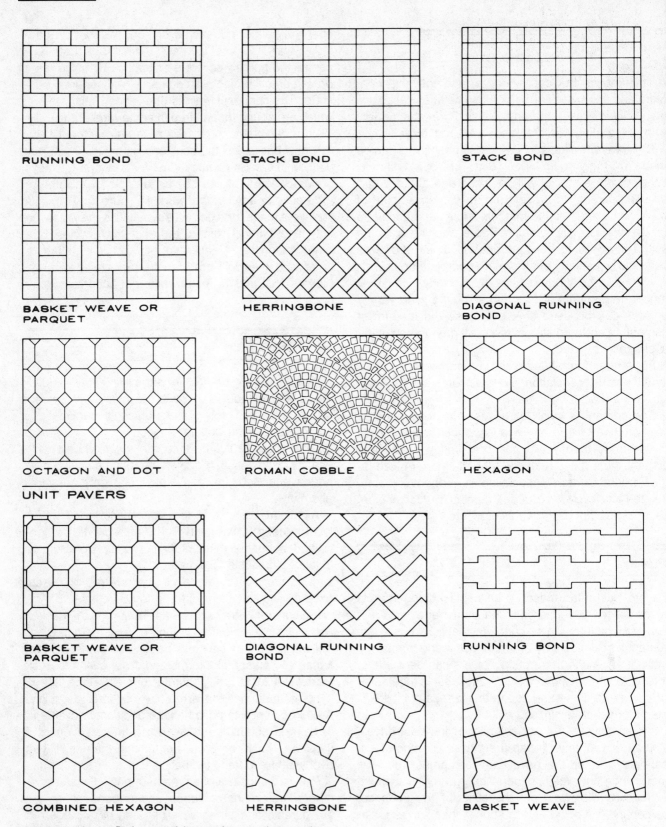

RUNNING BOND

STACK BOND

STACK BOND

BASKET WEAVE OR PARQUET

HERRINGBONE

DIAGONAL RUNNING BOND

OCTAGON AND DOT

ROMAN COBBLE

HEXAGON

UNIT PAVERS

BASKET WEAVE OR PARQUET

DIAGONAL RUNNING BOND

RUNNING BOND

COMBINED HEXAGON

HERRINGBONE

BASKET WEAVE

FIGURE 15.4   Paving materials come in many shapes and materials. Besides the more common precast concrete, brick, and flagstone, pavers of asphalt, marble, and granite are available. Interlocking varieties are available in concrete, brick, and asphalt.

FIGURE 15.5 These six pavements were all laid in sand beds; the two illustrations at bottom right show pavers of granite. (Photograph: Edward Allen)

a masonry patio, because the material is more expensive. Also, if the work is hired out, carpenters' wages can be higher than those of persons who work with concrete or pavers. Of course, if your kitchen or living room door is several or more feet above the ground, a wooden deck raised to that level has the virtue of eliminating the need for stairs.

FOUNDATIONS

If you want to build an addition to your home or erect a garage or utility building, you will need a working knowledge of foundations. A familiarity with foundations can also help you decide whether a concrete subbase would be appropriate for a new patio.

Foundation Types

Foundations come in different types, from slabs that "float" on the soil to full basements that extend below the frost line (see Table 15.5, page 214).

FULL BASEMENT This type requires major excavation. The walls extend below the local frost line to a wider base, called *footers* or *footings*. Enough headroom is made so that people can walk comfortably in the space created.

A full basement is the most expensive foundation to build. The costs of the excavation, soil removal, doors, forms for the high walls, stairs, and electrical service mount up. A full basement is typically twice as expensive as a shallower alternative called a *perimeter wall*.

PERIMETER WALL Sometimes called a *frost wall* in the North, a perimeter wall begins with footings below the frost line, but is only 2 to 5 ft high, extending about a foot above ground. Unlike a full basement, the space within perimeter walls does not have enough headroom to make it livable, but it can sometimes be used for storage. The walls themselves can be made of concrete building block, cinder block, or poured concrete. Building with block is sometimes cheaper than building with concrete, but the resulting foundation does not hold up as well in cold climates or where the soil is so clayey that it expands and contracts with ground water.

A perimeter wall for an addition might cost $2,500, while a full basement with stairs, door to the first floor, bulkhead door to the yard, and electrical service might cost $10,000 or more.

MONOLITHIC SLAB If local codes permit, *monolithic,*

also called *floating slab* can be an inexpensive poured-concrete foundation for an addition, garage, or utility building. It can also serve as the base for a patio.

The slab is made by grading the soil, excavating more deeply around the edges so that the concrete will take the form of an inverted shallow cup, and then pouring in the concrete. The slab moves with the soil because it is not anchored to subsoil below the frost line. Except in warm climates, a slab that serves as a foundation for heated space should be poured over 1-in.-thick rigid-foam insulation boards to protect it from exceptional cold. The only suitable product, because it does not absorb moisture, is expanded polystyrene (EPS).

In most cases, this is the least expensive foundation. Where a perimeter wall for an addition might cost $2,500 to $3,000, a slab will cost about $1,800 contracted. The upper surface can be left as is, if nicely finished, or can be covered with paint or vinyl flooring.

Where the local code requires the perimeter footing to penetrate to a depth below the frost line, the price goes up. In our opinion, making a slab's footings extend 4 to 5 ft in very cold climates is not necessary unless the soil is clayey or exceptionally water-bearing. If the soil is well drained and compacted, a slab that does not extend below the frost line will neither heave with frost nor settle much, if at all.

PIER FOUNDATIONS For clayey soils or soils that tend to settle because of nearby drilling and mining, a *pier foundation* is an inexpensive alternative to standard foundations and is more forgiving of a little soil movement. A proper pier foundation consists of regularly spaced concrete footings on which are erected pressure-treated wood posts or poured-concrete columns, formed with heavy cardboard tubes. Wood beams are laid on top of the posts or columns, and the wood floor joists are laid on top of these beams. Pier foundations of treated wood can also make very low-cost foundations for decks and porches.

FOOTER BLOCKS Recognizing that poured-concrete footings require skilled labor, can be expensive, and are troublesome at sites that concrete trucks would have trouble reaching, the National Concrete Masonry Association (NCMA) developed *footer blocks* (see Figure 15.6). These are interlocking concrete blocks that serve as poured-concrete footings. They are held together not only by their interlocking perimeters, but also by flat, truss-type steel reinforcements and a topping of mortar that also serves as the base for a concrete block or cinder block wall.

Footer blocks, where permitted, can be purchased from NCMA members and are acceptable footings for

FOOTING BLOCK SYSTEM

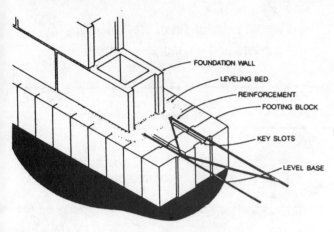

FOUNDATION WALL

LEVELING BED

REINFORCEMENT

FOOTING BLOCK

KEY SLOTS

LEVEL BASE

FIGURE 15.6 Easy-to-use footer blocks are placed vertically on a level surface. Their own shape and steel reinforcement bind them together.

one- and two-story houses. They can be laid by unskilled labor and in places that a concrete truck cannot reach.

For more information, write NCMA, P.O. Box 781, Herndon, VA 22070.

Foundation Design

Foundation design is a job for professionals or exceptionally well-educated do-it-yourselfers. Codes are very strict, generally for good reason. Improperly constructed foundations can diminish or ruin any investment placed on top of them.

Almost all building inspection departments in urban areas require a detailed, professional plan. In some places, the plan must include extensive provisions for drainage—plastic drainage lines must be placed at the footing level, covered with crushed stone, and led away in a trench to a place where they can drain.

In rural areas, with less rigorous codes and inspections, the owner is well advised to develop such a plan anyway and have it checked by a contractor, architect, or engineer. Many an expensive owner-built house or addition has been built on a poor foundation.

The least expensive foundation options described in this chapter are widely accepted, but not everywhere. Check with your local building inspection department before counting on anything other than a conventional foundation. The less conventional your choice of a foundation, the more you need professional advice.

TABLE 15.1
Exterior Steps Options

THE PROJECT
Replace an exterior set of steps 4′ wide with 5 risers and a handrail on one side.

Options	Project Cost Contracted	Project Cost DIY	Difficulty Level	Comments and Recommendations
Treated-Lumber Kit Install a kit with 3 precut stringers, a prefabricated wood railing, and 2″ × 12″ treads.	$265	$150	**1**	Easiest DIY. Quick. Can be adjusted somewhat to site measurement.
Treated Lumber, Field Cut Install three 2″ × 12″ stringers, a prefabricated wood railing, and 2″ × 12″ × 4′ treads.	$265 CC	$87 CC	**2**	Requires skilled worker.
Precast Concrete Install hollow precast concrete steps on precast footer slab and an economy metal railing.	$670 VB	$640	**1**	Requires truck-accessible location. Quick. Available only in stock sizes. Only possible DIY work is preparing site for slab and removing old steps. Embedded brick and stone veneers look nice, but sometimes peel off in severe climates (salt air or freezing).
Poured Concrete Build forms and pour concrete; install an economy metal railing.	$845	$265 VB	**3**	Heavy, expensive. Requires substantial footing. Long lasting.

TABLE 15.2 New Driveway Options					THE PROJECT Construct a driveway 10′ wide by 25′ long to meet an existing street apron.	
Options	Cost/sq ft Contracted	Cost/sq ft DIY	Project Cost Contracted	Project Cost DIY	Difficulty Level DIY Advice	Comments and Recommendations
Crushed Gravel Install 6″ of washed, crushed gravel in 2″ × 4″ treated pine edging.	$1.25	$0.71	$312	$177	**1** Easiest DIY.	Should be used more often. Quick, easy to maintain, low cost, with low environmental impact (doesn't contribute to storm runoff).
Ribbons of Concrete Install 24″-wide, 4″-thick concrete ribbons over 4″ gravel base with a broom finish.	$3.60	$1.42	$360 CC	$140 CC	**2**	Concrete ribbons balance the strength of poured concrete with the low cost of minimum coverage. Easy DIY job.
Soil Cement Install 6″ of clay base mixed with 8%–10% portland cement, compacted.	$1.90	$1.22	$475	$305	**1** A rototiller and a rented compactor can make this a weekend job.	Not recommended in northern climates.
Asphalt Install 2″ of binder, 1″ top coat over 4″ gravel base.	$2.50		$625 VB		DIY not recommended.	About the same life-cycle costs as concrete, but lower initial cost.
Poured Concrete Install 4″ slab over 4″ gravel base with a broom finish	$3.40	$1.42	$850	$355 VB	**3** Placing and finishing concrete is hard and demanding.	High cost, long life; use air-entrained concrete.

TABLE 15.3
New Sidewalk Options

THE PROJECT
Construct a 3'-wide × 80'-long sidewalk.

Options	Cost/sq ft Contracted	Cost/sq ft DIY	Project Cost Contracted	Project Cost DIY	Difficulty Level / DIY Advice		Comments and Recommendations
Precast Pavers Install 24″ × 32″ concrete stepping stones spaced 8″ apart over 4″ gravel base.	$1.95	$1.05	$495 VB CC	$265 VB CC	**1**		Quick; a good choice for slightly sloped areas where individual pavers can be cut into slope to make steps.
Asphalt Install 2″-thick asphalt over 4″ gravel base.	$2.10		$505		DIY not recommended.		Consider asphalt walks where freeze-thaw cycles are infrequent. Doesn't last as long as concrete.
Poured Concrete Install 4″-thick sidewalk, broom finished, over 4″ gravel base.	$3.90	$1.42	$935	$340	**3**	Always use air-entrained concrete.	Easier to finish than large slabs, but requires a lot of labor to place. Longest lasting.
Spaced Flagstone Install 1″-thick stepping stones.	$4.75	$1.40	$1,140	$336	**1**	Rototill and level the path first.	Quick, good looking; unskilled task that results in a handsome walk.
Brick in Sand Install common bricks in a 2″ sand bed with a brick-on-end border.	$7.00	$2.50	$1,680	$600	**2**		Bricks are expensive, but used brick can cut the DIY cost in half. Use hard brick. Old, soft brick can break up and flake due to frost action. Soft brick breaks easily with a hammer.

TABLE 15.4 Patio Options	**THE PROJECT** Construct a 12′ × 16′ patio.

Options	Cost/sq ft Contracted	Cost/sq ft DIY	Project Cost Contracted	Project Cost DIY	Difficulty Level	Comments and Recommendations
Poured Concrete Install 4″ slab over 4″ gravel base and broom finish.	$3.40	$1.42	$650 VB CC	$270 VB	**3**	Concrete lasts a long time and is inexpensive when compared to other patio options.
Precast Concrete Install 6″ × 8″ concrete pavers in interlocking pattern over 4″ gravel base.	$4.75	$1.25	$915	$240 CC	**1**	Easiest DIY method. Concrete pavers are uniform in size and thickness.
Flagstone in Sand Lay 1″–thick stones in 2″ sand bed.	$6.20	$1.68	$1,190	$320	**1**	Easy DIY method. Use a weed barrier under the sand.
Brick in Sand Lay bricks in interlocking pattern over 2″ sand bed.	$7.00	$2.50	$1,345	$480	**2**	Can be less expensive if used brick is available.
Wood Deck Install 2″ × 4″ treated pine deck with no railing.	$9.40	$2.70	$1,800	$518	**3**	Expensive. **CAUTION: Beware of most treated woods if you have little kids crawling around.** Toxins in the wood treatment can be absorbed through the skin; children who have touched treated wood are also likely to put their contaminated hands into their mouths.

TABLE 15.5
Foundation Options

THE PROJECT
Construct the footer, foundation, and floor deck for a 16′ × 20′ addition.

Options	Cost/sq ft Contracted	Cost/sq ft DIY	Project Cost Contracted	Project Cost DIY	Difficulty Level	Comments and Recommendations
Monolithic Slab Pour a 4″-thick slab with edges down-turned 24″ deep, 16″ wide. Install 2″ foam insulation in a 2″ bed of sand.	$5.70	$2.40	$1,800 CC	$750 CC	**3**	For level sites with good soil bearing capacity.
Perimeter Wall, Concrete Machine dig a 12″-wide trench 24″ deep. Form and pour a 6″-wide, concrete wall 18″ above grade. Frame 2″ × 10″ floor with ¾″ subfloor.	$8.65	$3.40	$2,770	$1,080	**3**	Least expensive floor joist system.
Perimeter Wall, Block Dig, form, and pour 8″ × 16″ footer. Construct wall 8″ thick, 2′ above grade. Frame 2″ × 10″ floor joists and ¾″ subfloor.	$9.85	$3.60	$3,150	$1,150	**5**	In some local markets where blocks are more commonly used, masons may offer block walls for less than poured concrete.
Pier and Beam Dig for 12″ round piers 3′ on center. Form and pour a 16″ × 12″ grade beam. Frame a 2″ × 10″ floor with ¾″ subfloor.	$14.30	$4.30	$4,580	$1,370	**3**	Recommended for poor soils where a basement isn't desired.
Full Basement, Concrete Excavate form and pour footers and 4″ floor slab. Form and pour an 8″ concrete wall. Frame a 2″ × 10″ floor with ¾″ subfloor 6′ below grade.	$28	$10	$8,930	$3,200 VB	**5**	Although more expensive, is a value buy where site slopes or the frost line is deep and the 320 sq ft of additional space is desirable.

PART TWO

Money-Saving Strategies

Planning and Design

In home improvements, it is easy to be penny wise and pound foolish. This book is meant to make you both penny wise and pound wise.

Being pound wise begins before the first hammer is lifted or the first telephone call is made to a contractor. It begins when you first think about what you want the finished product to look like.

You can pour a fortune into a house. This often happens because a desire for a "new" or "designer" or "perfect" appearance is carried too far. You can save a lot of money simply by cost avoidance and moderation. Sometimes, even frugal homeowners get swept away by popular misconceptions, because they don't know real costs and values. For example, although double-glazed windows are widely touted as energy savers, they are actually less efficient than weatherstripped older windows with storm windows over them.

In this chapter, we examine the motives for home improvements and discuss their payback. Then we look at how early and efficient planning of layout and room space can save money. Finally, we talk about specific planning ideas to hold down the budget of individual projects, such as kitchen and bathroom remodeling.

IMPROVEMENTS: REASONS AND RESULTS

Motivation

Before starting a big improvement project, it is important to look at what you are trying to accomplish. It is likely to be one or more of the following:

1. *Necessary repairs* for things that are broken or worn out; for example, old and ill-working plumbing
2. *Improvements to meet practical needs;* such as improvements for safety, security, energy efficiency, or more space
3. *Renovations for more comfort and enjoyment;* for example, a more convenient kitchen or a rec room for the children

4. *Makeovers;* remodeling with little or no practical purpose, for the sake of creating a different or a fashionable look

In categories 3 and 4, you are more likely to spend money needlessly. If you want to hang onto hard-earned money, try to remain in categories 1 and 2. A leaky faucet, a cranky toilet, and dingy bathroom walls do not call for a whole new bathroom.

But even if you are considering improvements that are not for functional or economic reasons, you can still save a great deal of money by carefully choosing methods and materials recommended in this book. No matter what you are doing, it always pays to look for ways to work with individual components (walls, fixtures, doors, trim, and so on) rather than to gut and redo whole rooms, or—even more expensive—rearrange the layout of rooms.

Remodeling contractors, architects, and interior designers naturally make the more drastic approach, because wholesale improvements lead to bigger and more profitable jobs. If you give them carte blanche to make over a room or your whole house, they will follow your wishes. But you needn't. You are the one who must make the basic design decisions that affect cost, and you can tell those you hire to hold the line at precise and limited improvements.

Making Improvements That Are Worth Their Cost

Annual surveys by *Practical Homeowner* magazine have dispelled a common myth: that home improvements are worth more than what they cost. The magazine's staff arranged for 20 home improvement projects to be completed on 20 different houses by contractors at prices that were about the national average and then asked professional house appraisers to reappraise their market value. Then the magazine calculated the increase in the value of the homes as a percentage of the cost of the improvements. Only two projects increased the value of the house more than their costs. They were an interior facelift (raising the value of the house 107 percent of its cost) and turning an attic into a living space (raising the value 104 percent of its cost). A third project, converting a basement to living space, raised the value of the house by 98 percent of its cost.

But no others came very close. A new fireplace added only 85 percent of its cost, a major kitchen overhaul only 74 percent, new siding only 61 percent, and a swimming pool only 46 percent.

We see three major ways to bring home improvement costs more into line with their investment value:

1. Cut labor costs by doing the work yourself.
2. Cut material costs.
3. Renovate selectively.

Cut labor costs—they make up 50 to 60 percent of a contractor's charges. Homeowners know this already: National studies have shown that do-it-yourselfers do twice as much home improvement work as contractors do. In fact, it is predicted that homeowners will do even more of the work themselves in the future.

Cut material costs by buying materials at discount prices. We tell you how in Chapter 19.

Renovate selectively—by component, fixture, or individual item rather than by room. Replace only those parts that are broken, are worn out, or waste energy.

BEGINNING CORRECTLY

Space Costs Money

In Europe, where housing is expensive and scarce, homeowners have been doing more with less for decades. There, you can typically find: small rooms; rooms that have dual functions—such as living and dining, or living and study; floors without carpeting; few electrical outlets; no fancy electrical fixtures; few, if any, built-in cabinets; few or no closets; and few bathrooms, some with a shower but not a tub. Design strategies such as these save money in Europe and would save money here.

Indeed, trends toward European design in the United States are becoming more prevalent because of present economic realities. For many years, the costs of land, mortgage money, and construction have risen faster than incomes. This makes the space we live in, whether calculated by the house or by the room, increasingly expensive. National agencies and organizations like the National Association of Home Builders, The Enterprise Foundation, Habitat for Humanity, and the U.S. Department of Housing and Urban Development have responded by encouraging lower cost housing. This book contains many recommendations based on the research and demonstration projects of these groups.

Conserve Space, Conserve Money

In both new construction and renovation, one of the main factors in cost is space. Larger rooms require more work and cost more. It is a direct relationship; so direct, in fact, that the costs of new construction and renovation are often calculated in cost per square foot. A figure is determined and is then multiplied by the number of square feet to be worked on.

Therefore, from a cost standpoint, it is important to consider a standard for the "proper" size of various interior components of a house. The bare-minimum standards suggested by The Enterprise Foundation follow. They exceed almost all national standards for health and safety, but they also assume careful placement of furniture and some built-ins to save space. Some of these dimensions may be too small for your taste, but they may help you begin to think about your own space needs.

- Living room: 160 sq ft, at least 11 ft on one side
- Kitchen: 50 sq ft, at least 6-½ ft on a side, with a 3-ft passage, 40 sq ft of shelving, 15 sq ft of countertop, and 10 sq ft of drawer space
- Combined living/dining area: 150 sq ft, at least 7-½ ft on a side
- Separate dining area: 100 sq ft, at least 8-⅓ ft on a side
- Master bedroom: 100 sq ft, at least 9-⅓ ft on a side
- Secondary bedrooms: 80 sq ft, at least 8 ft on a side
- Bathroom: Enough area to accommodate a tub, toilet, and sink; 35 sq ft, at least 5 ft on a side
- Laundry: 5 ft minimum for a washer and dryer side by side
- Bedroom closets: 4 ft long, 1 ft 11 in. deep
- General storage: 200 cu ft, plus 60 cu ft in bedrooms; accessible attic or crawl space
- Stairs: 2 ft 8 in. wide with 6 ft 6 in. of headroom; a maximum rise of 8 in. and a minimum run of 9 in.; a landing of 2 ft 6 in.
- Hall: A width of at least 2 ft 8 in.
- Doors: Minimum heights, 6 ft 6 in.; widths: for a primary entrance, 3 ft; for closets, 2 ft 8 in.; for bathrooms, 2 ft; for interior rooms, 2 ft 6 in.
- Ceilings: For habitable areas, 7 ft 6 in.; for bathrooms and utility areas, 7 ft; for a basement, 6 ft 8 in.; for halls, 7 ft

Cost-Cutting Design Principles

When you begin to think about how a renovation, or even a small job, should be carried out, you can make decisions in the very early stages of conceptualization that will lead to saving money. Here are some ideas that have proved cost-effective over the years.

Change floor plans as little as possible. Your cost rises in direct proportion to each running foot of wall you remove or install.

Get rid of unneeded space. A porch may look nice, but if you never use it and it is a headache to maintain, remove it. Likewise, tacked-on additions, sometimes built as servant rooms or storage sheds in older buildings, can be costly to maintain. If an addition is dilapidated and disrupts the overall look of the house, tear it down (but check codes first—zoning rules may have changed, preventing you from rebuilding the structure you demolish). If part of the house is not being used, such as an upper story, close it off and weatherstrip the door.

Expand into secondary space only as the budget allows. Finish the basement later. Use an upper floor for storage until you can afford to finish it the way you want. Do not renovate much beyond your immediate needs—an investment deferred is money saved.

Add new rooms within the house's "footprint." Renovating an attic, basement, or garage to enlarge a room or create a new one is not cheap, but it is far less expensive than adding new construction onto the house. Within your existing shell, you have a foundation, exterior walls, a roof, and all the connections you need for water, heating, and electricity close by.

To illustrate, making a room in an unfinished attic or basement can run from $10/sq ft to $30/sq ft. But having a contractor make the same space by constructing an addition can run from $40/sq ft to $80/sq ft, depending on local costs and the materials chosen.

Put new plumbing near old plumbing. When moving a kitchen or adding a bath, make the new location as close as possible to existing supply, waste, and vent lines. Or if you are just moving plumbing fixtures, keep them within code-required distances of existing waste lines (that is, for sinks and tubs, 10 ft; for a toilet, 3 ft). If you do not, you may be required to run a new vent pipe through the roof to make the fixture drain properly.

LOW-COST PLANNING IDEAS

Individual Rooms

You can save greatly if you incorporate cost-effective designs. Ideas for individual rooms follow.

KITCHENS The kitchen is the most expensive room in the house. The least expensive design is the one that sets most of the appliances and counters along a single straight wall. The most expensive design is a U-shape with a countertop island in the middle.

Closets in corners are the least expensive way to store food. Good ones are 3 ft wide and have louvered doors.

An 18-in. space between the refrigerator and the wall makes a handy broom and mop storage area. In addition, you can save the cost of a cabinet over the refrigerator, because the refrigerator top itself is a free storage area.

The least expensive countertop to buy and maintain is one that is postformed. This kind eliminates the backsplash joint by molding the backsplash to the countertop as a single piece.

For kitchen flooring, vinyl-composition tile has the best combination of lowest initial cost and good durability. It won't be damaged when you move the refrigerator or stove.

Along the wall over the countertop backsplash, install tile, aluminum sheet, or plastic laminate that is both decorative and easy to clean. (Note: Use an oil-based primer on kitchen walls; it will serve as a vapor barrier and keep moisture from penetrating to insulation and wood framing on exterior walls.)

Consider a freestanding stove; it is less expensive than the combined cost of a cabinet and built-in stove. In addition, a freestanding stove will not add to your property taxes in most states, but a built-in one may.

LIVING/DINING AREAS In small houses, consider combining the living and dining rooms into a single room. This strategy is particularly practical when the wall separating the dining and living rooms needs repair. It is often less expensive to remove a partition wall than it is to repair it, and it is certainly less expensive than it is to remove it first and then replace it. Making two small rooms into one larger, multipurpose room means less wall space to keep clean and painted, more flexibility with furniture, and a greater feeling of spaciousness (see Figure 16.1).

BEDROOMS Before you go too far in thinking about adding a bedroom, make sure that you cannot live with the ones you already have. If you feel cramped, look to the beds, which take up more floor space than anything else in the room. Rather than let them hog so much space, elevate them. This is the idea behind bunk beds. If only one bed is needed in a room, you can still use the space below for storage or a desk (see Figure 16.2).

In a small room, you can use the space between the end of the bed and the wall as a closet or as open storage space. The technique works even in a master bedroom (see Figure 16.3).

BATHROOMS Calculating by the square foot, bathrooms are more expensive even than kitchens, but

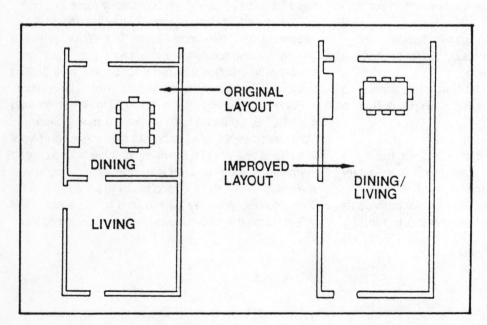

FIGURE 16.1 Remove nonbearing walls where you can increase the living space at a minimum cost.

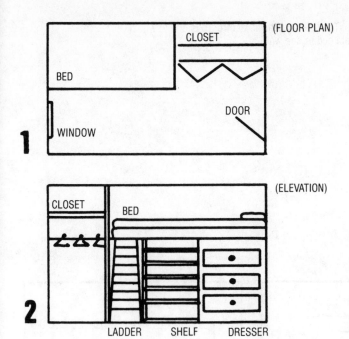

FIGURE 16.2 A bed raised off the floor can make room for storage space or a desk.

efficient design can hold down costs. The most cost-effective arrangement of fixtures is to line them all up against one wall so that the supply, waste, and vent pipes can run together (see Figure 16.4). In addition, one partly divided bathroom is less expensive than two separate and complete bathrooms (see Figure 16.5). You can divide the bathroom with a partition and door, then place a sink or two on one side and the toilet and tub on the other. If you are hooking up a clothes washer and dryer for the first time, consider putting them in an alcove in the bathroom rather than in the basement. You save steps—by not having to trudge to the basement—and money—by not having to run long lengths of supply, waste, and vent pipes.

In renovation, remember that it costs less to retain what is workable than it does to replace it. But when replacement is necessary, you save—sometimes greatly—by installing standard, not custom, equipment. The cost difference between a serviceable water-saver toilet and a designer model can be over $300.

Remodeling

STORAGE The rule of thumb is to include about 5 sq ft of storage space for every 100 sq ft of living space. For ideas on how to make the most storage for the least money and effort, see Chapter 7, Cabinets and Storage.

In addition to those ideas for interior storage, also consider outdoor or unheated storage. Garages and storage sheds cost less than a third of what heated storage space costs and add nothing to your heating bills. Storage sheds come in kits available from mail order catalogs, larger building materials stores, and some suburban department stores (see Figure 16.6). Similarly, unfinished basement storage costs half as much as finished first-floor space, so use your basement to your best advantage before adding closets.

SERVICE EQUIPMENT If, when remodeling, you are relocating or installing service equipment, locate it suitably. A water heater set as close as possible to the kitchen, bath, and laundry reduces the piping needed to reach those rooms and also reduces the heat loss of hot water resting idle in pipes.

Similarly, if a new electrical service entrance is

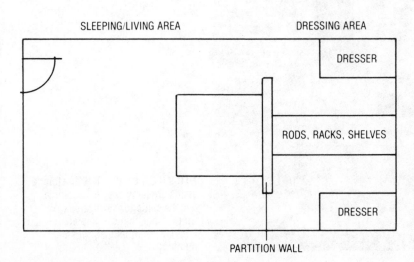

FIGURE 16.3 This master bedroom makes a suitable sleeping and living area and also creates ample space for dressing and storage by moving the bed against one side of a partition wall. On the other side are rods, racks, and dressers. No extensive framing for closets is needed, nor are closet doors.

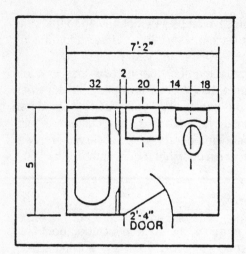

FIGURE 16.4 The least expensive bathroom is one in which all plumbing is contained in one wall.

FIGURE 16.5 Single divided bathrooms are less expensive than two separate ones.

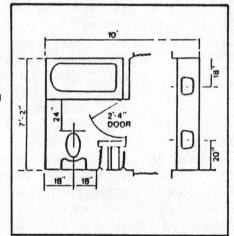

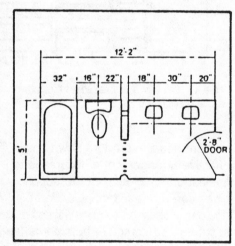

FIGURE 16.6 Outside storage sheds are fairly easy to assemble and save interior storage space. Store things that can tolerate fluctuations of temperature and humidity.

needed, locate it centrally but as close as possible to heavy appliances like ranges and dryers. Since such appliances require more expensive cables, the shorter they are, the better. Moreover, with short runs of cable to these appliances, slightly less electrical energy is lost (in the form of heat) along the way.

The principle of strategic positioning of major components applies as well to heating and cooling systems.

Additions

SEASONAL ADDITIONS If you want additional living space, you are not confined to expanding the house. You may do just as well to enclose a porch. Even a patio, deck, or fenced-in area must meet your needs, and the savings are substantial.

Refer to Table 16.1 (page 224). A modest 12 × 16-ft addition costs about $12,000 contracted. But an enclosed porch including a new foundation costs a third less. Unenclosed spaces cost far less still and yet make enjoyable family areas.

BUILT-ON ADDITIONS If you do choose a formal addition, consider a two-story one, which give you the same living space as a one-story addition that takes up twice the land. For a two-story addition, you are purchasing only half as much roof, foundation, and roof insulation and only a third the heating and plumbing runs. In addition, such a two-story arrangement is roughly 15 percent more energy-efficient than an equivalent one-story layout.

DECORATING ON A BUDGET

There is no need to stop thinking ahead when the room layouts and other major work are complete. Even when your planning and design work has moved to the decorating stage, there are schemes for saving money.

Use low-cost stand-ins. For example, install $29

PVC paneling as a tub surround until you can afford $9/sq ft ceramic tiles. Install wiring and a switch, but put up a $15 fixture until your budget allows the $100 fixture you really want.

Buy good-quality paint in colors that will enliven your rooms. Decorate rooms with colors that cost little or nothing extra. For example, you pay nothing extra for the color you want in a rug and only a little extra for the standard colors on kitchen appliances. And you pay nothing extra for the standard colors in paint. But you pay dearly for bath and kitchen fixtures that are not white. And you'll pay four times more for brass than for chrome fixtures in a bathroom. For color, paint rather than stain interior wooden trim. You can buy lower grade wood and cover its blemishes with paint, rather than higher grade unblemished wood, the surface of which shows through stain.

Go modern. A modern architectural style is often very cost-efficient in a completely renovated area. If kept simple, a modern style is the least encumbered with fancy detail work and most effectively conveys an aesthetic of minimalism, exposing the skeleton and arteries of a house. The modern style uses little or no trim, plain doors, exposed brick, exposed structural beams, and even exposed and painted pipes and duct work.

PUTTING IT ALL TOGETHER

Some of the ideas in this chapter—and throughout the book—save a little money, and some save a lot. When you put them all together, however, they can save thousands of dollars.

In Tables 16.2 and 16.3 (pages 225 and 227), we have accumulated money-saving ideas for application in a renovation and in the construction of a new addition. You can compare what each job would cost if done conventionally and if done with an eye for combining short- and long-term value.

TABLE 16.1
Cost Comparison of New Indoor or Outdoor Activity Area

THE PROJECT
Construct a 12′ × 16′, 192-sq-ft space for family activity next to a rear door.

Options	Cost/sq ft Contracted	Cost/sq ft DIY	Project Cost Contracted	Project Cost DIY	Difficulty Level	Comments and Recommendations
Fenced Area Install 40′ of preservative-treated basketweave fence 60″ high to create private space.	$5.40	$2.50	$1,050 CC	$480	**2**	This least cost option is a good place to start.
Stone Patio and Fence Lay flagstone in sand with 24′ of fencing at side.	$21.00	$6.20	$2,250	$800	**3**	A quick way to make some usable, private outside space.
Wood Deck Build pressure-treated pine deck with 2″ × 4″ rails, 2″ × 2″ ballasters and steps.	$9.60	$2.90	$2,275 VB	$745 CC	**3**	An inexpensive way to civilize outdoor space.
Enclosed Porch Pour a concrete deck, cover with vinyl tile. Construct a shed roof with insulated glass sliding doors to enclose porch.	$44.00	$18.75	$8,400	$3,600 VB	**5**	Add a little heat and/or air conditioning and 1 or 2 outlets, and you've got a room at ⅔ the cost of the addition. Not advisable in very hot or very cold climates except for occasional use.
Addition Build a 12′ × 16′ 1-story den with pitched roof. Install vinyl siding, insulation, paneling, carpet, heat, and electricity to minimum CABO code.	$64.00	$28.00	$12,300	$5,400	**5**	A DIY installation will add good resale value.

TABLE 16.2
Whole House Savings—Renovation

THE PROJECT
Renovate a 1,200-sq-ft, 3-bedroom, 1½-bath home including kitchen and bath upgrading, window improvements, wall and floor repairs, and energy-saving measures.

Conventional	Cost	Value Buy	Cost
Kitchen Cabinets, 12 lin ft Remove cabinets and countertop. Install oak base and hanging cabinets and a postformed countertop.	$2,220	Remove countertop and all cabinet doors. Install oak doors and drawer fronts. Veneer all exposed stiles with oak. Install a postformed countertop.	$1,020
Sink and Faucet Install an enameled steel double-bowl sink and a white epoxy single-control faucet.	$420	Install stainless-steel double-bowl sink with a chrome-plated brass, single-control faucet.	$237
Bath 7′ × 6′ Install a 5′ cast iron tub with white enamel finish.	$410	Install a 5′ molded fiberglass tub in white.	$265
Install a floor of 1″ × 1″ ceramic tile in adhesive.	$390	Lay vinyl sheet goods floor over ⅜″ plywood underlayment.	$135
Install a 24″ oak-front vanity with 1-piece synthetic marble top.	$510	Install a 24″ oak-front vanity with 1-piece china top.	$517
Windows, 16 Fiberglass Replacement Remove existing sash and install fiberglass double-glazed windows.	$6,150	**Windows, 16 Vinyl Replacement** Remove existing sash and install vinyl double-glazed windows.	$3,520
Patio Construct a 12′ × 16′ brick patio over a 2″ sand bed. Use interlocking pattern and provide brick on-edge border.	$1,345	Construct a 12′ × 16′ patio of 4″ concrete over 4″ of gravel.	$650
Floors Belt-sand and refinish 3 rooms with 2 coats of polyurethane.	$704	Circular-sand and refinish 3 rooms with 3 coats of polyurethane.	$480
Walls Replace ceiling with ½″ gypsum to repair leak damage under bath.	$285	Laminate ceiling with ⅜″ gypsum to repair leak damage under bath.	$147
Closets Construct a 4′-wide, 30″-deep closet of 2 × 4′s and ½″ gypsum.	$820	Install PVC-coated wire shelf and double-pole kit in 2 closets.	$180

(Continued on next page)

TABLE 16.2 Continued

Conventional	Cost	Value Buy	Cost
Energy Use For 20% savings: —Add 6″ of insulation to the 6″ in attic. —Caulk exterior cracks at windows, doors, sill plate. —Install pilotless ignition on gas furnace.	$1,135	For 20% savings: —Install setback thermostat. —Change filters every month if you have a dusty house; every 3 to 6 months otherwise. —Install flue damper. —Caulk interior cracks.	$565
TOTAL	$14,389		$7,716
SAVINGS			**$6,673**

TABLE 16.3	THE PROJECT
Whole House Savings—New Addition	Construct a 2-story, 640-sq-ft addition with 1 bathroom and a bedroom over a 16′ × 20′ den/entertainment room.

Conventional	Cost	Value Buy	Cost
Foundation Install 8″ × 16″ footer, 8″ concrete block wall to create crawl space.	$3,150	Install monolithic slab; pour footer and slab on grade.	$1,800
Floor Framing On 1st and 2nd floor, install 2″ × 10″–16″ on-center with 3/4″ plywood sheathing.	$3,330	On 2nd floor only, install preengineered 2″ × 4″ trusses 24″ on-center with 24/32″ plywood sheathing glue-nailed.	$1,800
Roof Framing Install 2″ × 12″ rafters 16″ on-center with 1/2″ plywood sheathing.	$1,600	Install 2″ × 4″ trusses, 24″ on-center with 7/16″ oriented-strand board deck.	$1,550
Roof Install #1 cedar shingles nailed in place.	$1,216	Install 240-lb, metric-sized shingles stapled to deck.	$385
Windows Install 6 double-glazed, double-hung, vinyl-clad wood windows.	$2,190	Install 4 double-glazed, single-hung, solid vinyl windows. Install 2 double-glazed, fixed-pane windows.	$1,410
Exterior Framing Install 2″ × 4″, 16″ on-center.	$885	Install 2″ × 6″, 24″ on-center.	$895
Exterior Siding Install T1-11 plywood, 5/8″ thick, stained 2 coats.	$1,975	Install vinyl siding over insulation board.	$2,600
Interior Walls Install 1/2″ gypsum, paper-taped and 3-coat finish, finish all rooms, 2 coats of paint.	$3,696	Install 1/2″ gypsum, hung, mesh fiberglass-taped, and 2-coat finish. Tape and spray finish all ceilings. Panel first-floor den with 1/4″ veneered plywood paneling.	$3,300
Floor Finish Install in all rooms except bath, prefinished 5/16″ oak parquet wood tiles.	$2,520	Install in all rooms except bath, FHA approved 25-oz nylon carpet over 1/2″ urethane foam.	$1,120
Linen Closet Construct a 24″ × 30″ linen closet with a 2′ door and 6 shelves.	$440	Hang 6 vinyl-coated wire shelves in the bath space created between the tub foot wall and the exterior wall.	$85

(Continued on next page)

TABLE 16.3 Continued

Conventional	Cost	Value Buy	Cost
Plumbing Install a 3-piece bath, with ¾″ copper supply and a 4″ iron waste stack.	$3,190	Install a 3-piece bath with ½″ copper supply and 3″ PVC stack and waste lines.	$2,990
Electric Wire addition to NEC using metal work boxes, overhead light fixtures.	$1,900	Wire addition to NEC using PVC work boxes and switched outlets as lighting.	$1,450
Heating System (5-year cost) Install electric baseboard heat in all rooms.	$4,720	Extend duct from existing gas forced-air furnace. Caulk main house to minimize infiltration leaks.	$3,320
TOTAL	$30,786		$22,705
SAVINGS			**$7,781**

Energy-Saving Ideas

All sorts of energy-saving home improvements have been touted since the Arab oil embargo of the early 1970s. Many are very worthwhile, some are less worthwhile, and others do not save you the cost of implementation for many years. Some improvements never do pay back their costs, because they must be redone before their costs are recovered.

How can a homeowner decide what really is a sensible energy improvement? The most common method is to determine the *payback* of the possible improvement, from adding storm windows to upgrading a furnace.

After addressing payback, we discuss the two basic types of energy-saving measures. The first type includes improvements that are done along the house's *envelope;* that is, the walls, floors, roof, windows, and doors. The second type includes measures that are carried out on the interior machinery and fixtures that use energy. Next, we take up the subject of how to buy energy-efficient appliances. Finally, we include a brief discussion of solar energy.

PAYBACK

Simple Payback

Payback is a relatively simple concept. If a caulking job costs you $100 and saves you $100/year in fuel costs, it has a 1-year payback. If an insulation job costs you $1,000 and saves you $200/year in fuel costs, it has a 5-year payback. Think of the cost of the improvement as money deposited in a savings account that you can withdraw (maybe) only if you sell the house. The caulking earned you a 100 percent return in a year, the insulation 20 percent. We bet these pay better than most of your formal investments in, say, mutual funds.

Complications

The theory may be simple, but applying it gets complicated, for these reasons:

The cost of an improvement is not really known until you do it. This book has some good cost estimates, but your local costs may be higher or lower, enough to seriously affect the payback. Doing an improvement—say, wall insulation—may be much cheaper for your neighbor, who is putting on new siding anyway, than for you, because you will have to paint over the holes made in your siding to blow in the insulation and he or she will not.

Climate is a factor. The savings for the same improvement can vary greatly from region to region and from city to city (or even from desert to mountains that are within two miles of each other), because energy improvements save more where it is very hot or very cold.

The quality of installation is a factor. Poorly installed weatherstripping may be worthless. Wall insulation blown in at the wrong pressure may settle. An ill-fitting insulated door may let out more warm air than it saves because of its insulating qualities.

Some "energy-savers" do not last long enough to pay back their installation cost. Storm doors, for example, often sag within a year or two, creating air cracks that negate their whole purpose. Many last only 7 to 10 years. For these reasons, they are usually a bad buy.

Some "energy-savers" simply do not save at all. The most notorious example is double-glazed windows that replace sound older windows with good storm sashes over them. In this case, the replacements may have a negative payback—they actually hold in less heat than the old windows.

Some improvements partly cancel each other out. Making a furnace more efficient, for example, actually reduces the payback of an insulation job. If you improve the furnace and do not insulate, less expensive heat is escaping through your walls.

Energy costs vary by fuel and over time. Insulation saves more in an electric-heated house than in one heated by gas, because it reduces your purchase of a more expensive fuel. And if oil prices fall, as they once did dramatically, all improvements in oil-heated houses start paying back less.

There are other variables too numerous to mention. These include your own habits (opening windows in winter for fresh air; taking long, hot showers; and so forth), solar exposure, and even the temperature of your water supply.

Energy Audits

One of the major purposes of this book is to give you information about materials, installation methods, and relative costs so that you can separate fact from fiction and good from poor improvements.

Many utility companies and government energy offices offer pamphlets, workshops, and telephone advice on the paybacks of various improvements. But beware: Their advice is based on average cases that cancel out all or most of the variables we've discussed. This is why these same agencies advise an individual energy audit—a survey by a trained inspector—to recommend individualized measures and to better predict their payback time.

But even such audits tend to rely on averages and are not very accurate. Unless you hire an engineer, you are unlikely to receive an audit that considers the actual average temperature at your house, the solar exposure, the water temperature, and so on.

Still, any audit is usually good enough to make payback predictions within a certain range of reliability. Generally, you can be sure that improvements predicted by an audit to have a 4-year payback are worth investing in. The 5- to 10-year payback predictions deserve close scrutiny.

In this book, we generally recommend that you aim for a maximum payback period of 7 to 10 years. The reason is that a 7-year payback gives about a 14 percent return on your investment; a 10-year payback, a 10-percent return. If you consider that most energy improvements wear out sometime or deteriorate and need repair (like windows), your return is actually a little less.

The actual return you aim for is up to you. It may include the satisfaction of knowing you are not unnecessarily using up natural resources or polluting the environment. These are intangibles. What we present is a simple arithmetical way to determine which energy improvements pay for themselves within a reasonable period of time, assuming that fuel prices are stable over the next 10 years.

Other Factors Affecting Energy-Saving Decisions

The cost of borrowed funds, the cost of doing the work yourself, and the future prices of fuel all affect energy-saving decisions.

BORROWING MONEY Simple payback becomes complicated if you borrow money to make the improvement. The rate of interest you pay for the improvement should never exceed—or even equal—the percentage of yearly payback, which is calculated by dividing the estimated fuel savings per year by the total cost.

Let's say you are thinking of insulating a brick wall, and the cost of having the plaster removed, a stud wall placed in front of the brick, the insulation set between the studs, and a new wall finish applied would be $1,900. And say that you think this effort will save $190 in fuel each year. But let's also say that you are borrowing the $1,900 from a bank and have to pay 10 percent interest on it.

The saving for each of 10 years is only 10 percent, but you are paying 10 percent a year on the loan you took out to have the work done. The improvement is not worthwhile under these conditions—it only just pays the interest on the loan. You'd be better off not to have the work done or to find a less expensive way to do it.

USING FREE LABOR There is another important factor to keep in mind when deciding on energy improvements. Improvements will have a longer payback if you hire contractors to do the work for you, simply because you are paying for their coordination work, labor, and profit margin. However, if you do the work yourself (and do not put a dollar value on your time), the cost can be far lower and the payback consequently shorter.

ANTICIPATING RISES IN FUEL COSTS If you believe that fuel costs will rise more quickly in the next 10 years or so, you may want to consider jobs with 10- to 15-year paybacks. The cheapest way to protect against higher fuel bills is to do a little more of what you are already doing. For example, if you are insulating an attic, a few more inches of insulation will not cost much more. Or if a somewhat more efficient replacement window or furnace costs only a few additional dollars, by all means put it in.

Of course, if prices do rise, you can also make improvements at that time. Keep in mind, however, that wall insulation and solar exposure are exceptionally expensive to alter once any major renovation is done.

DOING THE QUICKEST PAYBACKS FIRST No matter how various factors affect your energy-saving decisions, this general rule should apply: First make the improvements that pay for themselves quickly and then do the others as time and money permit (see Table 17.1, page 239). Naturally, everyone should make the improvements that cost nothing at all (which, of course, pay for themselves immediately). Once those are done, complete those that have the next shortest pay-

back periods and the lowest costs. Then do the ones with the longer payback periods and the higher costs.

ENVELOPE IMPROVEMENTS

The perimeter of your house is a major battle line in the effort to save energy dollars. Whatever heated air in winter or cooled air in summer you have already paid for, you want to keep in the house; conversely, you want to keep out the outside air.

Plugging Air Leaks

The best leak-plugging techniques are caulking, weatherstripping, and closing vents.

Caulking is at least as effective from the inside as from the outside, and it is far less trouble. Therefore, caulk cracks around window and door trim from the inside. For electrical outlets on exterior walls, use gaskets. Pay special attention to cracks overhead, because heat rises. Look for gaps around ceiling light fixtures, chimneys, ill-fitting attic doors, and the corners where ceilings meet walls.

Check all windows and doors for weatherstripping. In colder climates, a new, exterior, insulated metal door with magnetic weatherstripping is usually cost-effective. Always use high-quality weatherstripping.

Finally, make certain that openings to the outdoors are closed off. Such openings are not always obvious. Check chimney dampers, mail slots, kitchen and bath vents, and window air conditioners to make certain they are closed tightly when not in use.

Insulation

Insulation's job is to slow the transfer of heat out of a house in winter and into it in summer. All parts of the exterior shell share in this work—windows, doors, walls, roof, and floor.

WINDOWS Two layers of glass are always a good investment, either as double-glazed windows or as storm windows put up over single glazing. If existing single-glazed windows are in good condition, we strongly recommend the lower cost alternative of storm windows. A single-glazed window has an R-value of 0.9, but two layers of glass are rated R1.7 to R2.2, twice that of a single-glazed window.

Windows let in the sun's warmth, a welcome or unwelcome trait depending on whether you are trying to heat or cool your house. In the North, let as much of the window as possible be exposed to the sun. In the

South, cut the amount of sunlight that reaches the window's glass by fastening awnings over the windows, affixing sunshade film to the glass, or hanging up sunblocking screens.

DOORS Most exterior doors have an R-value of only 1 or 2. And unfortunately, storm doors do not help much. Unless a $150 to $200 storm door is also going to be used as a screen door for summer cooling, it is not cost-effective to buy and install. Most storm doors fit so poorly that they fail to stop air infiltration, which is their main purpose. In addition, they usually wear out before they pay for themselves in fuel savings, unless they are of high quality and make a tight seal.

Consequently, consider an insulated exterior door. When it's time to replace your old door, a good buy is a metal or fiberglass-insulated door with a rating of R7.

Do not overlook doors and hatches to unheated attics. Rapid heat loss through them is typical, but you can install insulation on their attic sides to raise their R-values.

ENVELOPE INSULATION *Ceilings* are particularly important. We recomend R24 to R30 insulation there.

For uninsulated *frame walls,* cellulose is usually cost-effective if it can be blown in with some quality assurance. Fiberglass and rock wool are almost as good as cellulose. If plaster or drywall must be removed for some reason, exposing the studs of the framing, we recommend that you install at least fiberglass batt insulation. Some people believe that mineral wool is more durable; in cold climates, you may want a layer of foam board over the studs as well.

Whether you insulate or not, vapor barriers in cold climates are mandatory in humid rooms such as bathrooms and are desirable elsewhere. At minimum, caulk all visible interior cracks and use a vapor barrier paint.

When dealing with a *masonry wall,* check the condition of the plaster. If it is good and does not otherwise have to be removed, insulating the wall is usually not cost-effective. Except in very cold climates, the heat saving does not justify the cost of demolition, studs, insulation, vapor barrier, new drywall, and new trim. If the wall is to be gutted, or already is bare brick that needs drywall, insulation is cost-effective in cold climates.

Not nearly as much heat is lost through *floors* as is lost through roofs and walls. Since hot air rises, it doesn't tend to escape through floors. In addition, carpeting and composition tiles over cold floors are a form of insulation. And, if hired out, insulating a floor is expensive when workers have to work on their backs in crawl spaces.

Consequently, insulating a floor generally is not cost-

effective unless access beneath it is easy, your home is in an exceptionally cold climate, or you live in the deep South where you run air conditioning more than you run heating.

Foundations are sometimes insulated on the exterior with expanded polystyrene (EPS) board covered with a stucco-type cement. Since the boards need to extend a foot or two below ground, some digging is required. Adding exterior board insulation can have a 5- to 7-year payback in very cold climates. The exact payback depends on the installation costs, which increase if extensive flashing is needed below the siding.

Insulation of a bare foundation on the inside is usually prohibitively expensive unless you are making living space there anyway. Fire codes wisely prohibit exposed foam insulation boards—they either are very flammable or give off highly toxic smoke. Hanging exposed fiberglass can work in an unused crawl space or basement; otherwise, studs and some wall covering are needed.

Ventilation

House envelopes can be improved in other ways. One is to make certain that the vapor barrier on the side of the insulation facing the interior is sound. If the barrier permits water moisture to penetrate or work its way around it, the moisture will condense inside the insulation and rob it of some of its insulating capacity. Just as bad, the condensed water may penetrate to wood and cause rotting.

The other method is to make an opening at the top of the house so that, in summer, warm air rises and escapes through it, pulling in its wake cooler air near the ground. Taking advantage of such *thermosiphoning* can be as easy as opening a top-floor window or mounting a vent on the roof ridge.

In addition, heat should be allowed to escape from attics in warm climates. The simplest means of doing so is to add ridge vents (sometimes called roof vents) and soffit vents. Air enters the latter at the eaves, rises through the attic and escapes through vents at the ridge, keeping the house cooler in summer (see Figure 17.1).

EQUIPMENT OPERATION AND IMPROVEMENT

You can make immediate savings simply by running some of your equipment more prudently. We list here the most important suggestions by equipment category.

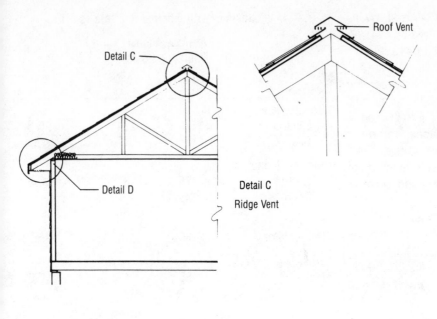

Detail C

Detail D

— Detail D

Typical House Section

Roof Vent

Detail C
Ridge Vent

Air Passage

Softfit Vent

Detail D

Softfit Vent louvers should face towards fascia

FIGURE 17.1 Ridge and soffit vents have no moving parts and ventilate attic areas very efficiently.

Heating:
- Set back the thermostat every night and when you are not at home. Or, for about $40 to $60, install a programmable setback thermostat that turns down the heat for you every night—you set it manually for a vacation (see Figure 17.2).
- Close all drapes and shades at night to slow heat loss. This is highly effective in northern areas and is essential in passive solar-heated houses, where heat gained in the day will otherwise radiate back out through the windows at night.
- Remove window screens and store them away in the winter to gain 15 percent more sunlight—and solar heat—coming through the windows.
- Bleed radiators of air.
- Turn off a pilot light on the furnace in summer.

Heating and cooling:
- Close off the heating and cooling registers to little-used rooms.
- Keep closet doors closed.
- Cover cooking pots in summer.

Hot Water:
- Lower the hot-water temperature.
- Take showers, not baths.
- Use cold water for the laundry.
- Drain sediment from the hot-water heater.

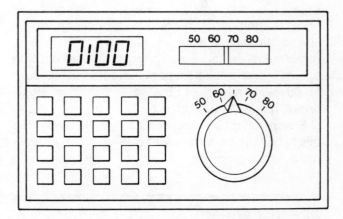

FIGURE 17.2 Programmable setback thermostats always "remember" to turn up the heat in the morning and turn it down when everyone's out. Setting your heat at 68°F saves up to 8% over a 70°F setting.

Electrical appliances:
- Clean refrigerator condenser plates.
- Use a microwave rather than an electric oven when possible.
- Run dishwashers with full loads only.
- Use one high-wattage bulb instead of two medium-wattage ones.
- If you have off-peak electric rates, do the laundry and dishwashing during off-peak hours.

- Dry large and bulky items like blankets and towels on a line instead of using an electric dryer.
- Change the furnace and heat-pump filters regularly.

In addition, you can use more of the heat coming from radiators if you place ½-in. foil-faced panels behind them—the foil radiates heat back into the room.

A good way to keep fireplaces, furnaces, and other heaters from drawing warmed room air up their flues with combustion gases is to route outside air through a pipe or other conduit to a place near the point of combustion.

Finally, you can save water by installing flow restrictors on showerheads to cut down on the gallons per minute used, placing "water dams" in toilet tanks to limit the number of gallons used in a flush, and fixing leaky faucets promptly. Any hot-water saving translates into energy savings.

BUYING EQUIPMENT

To save money on an appliance, you must consider both its purchase price and its operating cost, which is a function of its energy efficiency. To save money initially, you might favor a model with a low purchase price. But this model might use more energy than it should and have a short life. Alongside it might be a larger model that is more expensive, but less costly to operate—energy-efficient appliances do, indeed, save on operating costs (see "Savings with Efficient Appliances," page 234). Which is best?

Energy ratings can help you through quandaries like this to find the model that best suits your budget, your house, and your needs.

Energy Ratings

Most appliances are now prominently labeled with a displayed yellow "Energy Guide" (see Figure 17.3). The label gives the estimated annual operating cost of the appliance, assuming that the purchaser is a member of a family of four or five. The label also gives operating-cost estimates based on different energy costs. Like the miles-per-gallon ratings of new automobiles, these estimates do not guarantee operating costs once the appliance is running in the house, but they are good for comparisons with other similar appliances.

Hot-water heaters are rated differently, by their energy factor (EF), which is a coefficient of performance

Savings with Efficient Appliances

Average Annual
Operating Costs

Appliance	Energy Efficient	Existing	Annual Savings
Water Heater			
Electric	$170	$345	$175
Gas	135	170	35
Air Conditioner			
Central	175	370	195
Room	45	70	25
Frost-Free Refrigerator	80	135	55
Frost-Free Freezer	85	155	70
Clothes Dryer			
Gas	30	35	5
Electric	60	80	20
Stove			
Gas	30	35	5
Electric	60	75	15
Color TV	30	75	45

Sources: American Council for an Energy-Efficient Economy. Assumed energy costs are 8.6¢/kilowatt-hour and a gas price of 65¢/therm.

based on the cost of providing 64.3 gallons of hot water per day. The higher the EF number, the better the efficiency of the water heater.

Unfortunately, it is difficult to compare gas, electric, and heat-pump water heaters. An EF of 0.64 for a gas hot-water heater is good, but an electric water heater should have an EF of about 0.95 or 0.97. This is because you always lose some heat of the combusted natural gas up the flue, while all the heat of the electric coils is transferred to the water (and water-heater walls). A good EF for a heat-pump water heater is 3.0.

But despite the fact that a gas water heater has the lowest EF, it might well be the best purchase in most areas of the country, because a unit of heat from gas is less expensive than a unit of heat from electricity.

A heat pump is rated by a heating seasonal performance factor (HSPF) for heating and a seasonal energy efficiency ratio (SEER) for cooling. Both ratings are relationships between output and energy consumption.

SEER is also a measure of central air-conditioner efficiency. Room air conditioners are rated by the

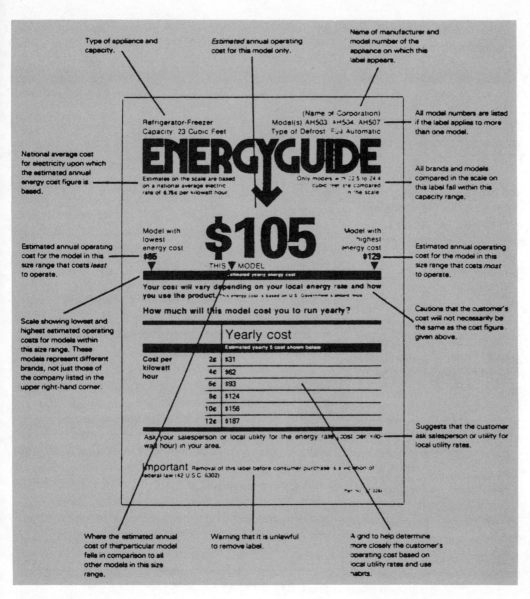

Type of appliance and capacity.

Estimated annual operating cost for this model only.

Name of manufacturer and model number of the appliance on which this label appears.

National average cost for electricity upon which the estimated annual energy cost figure is based.

Estimated annual operating cost for the model in this size range that costs *least* to operate.

Scale showing lowest and highest estimated operating costs for models within this size range. These models represent different brands, not just those of the company listed in the upper right-hand corner.

Where the estimated annual cost of this particular model falls in comparison to all other models in this size range.

Warning that it is unlawful to remove label.

A grid to help determine more closely the customer's operating cost based on local utility rates and use habits.

All model numbers are listed if the label applies to more than one model.

All brands and models compared in the scale on this label fall within this capacity range.

Estimated annual operating cost for the model in this size range that costs *most* to operate.

Cautions that the customer's cost will not necessarily be the same as the cost figure given above.

Suggests that the customer ask salesperson or utility for local utility rates.

FIGURE 17.3 The energy guide label is your clearest comparison of the operating costs of major equipment and appliances. The label shown here is from a refrigerator.

energy efficiency ratio (EER), which is similar to the SEER.

Heating Equipment

For tips on buying heating equipment, see Chapter 12, especially the section called Replacement Systems (page 168). Generally, you need to carefully analyze your home's heating requirements and find the furnace or boiler that is the correct size for the job. Buying very-high-efficiency equipment is generally not worth the added expense. The best buy is a furnace or boiler that carries a high efficiency rating. Consider both the purchase price and the operating cost of the equipment based on the efficiency of the equipment and the cost of the fuel it will use.

Water Heaters

Your water heater consumes more energy than any other home appliance except the heating system and the air conditioner, if you have one. Because water heaters consume so many energy dollars, they should be selected carefully.

A 40-gallon unit is usually adequate for a family of four or five unless the heat source is electricity, in which case many plumbers recommend 80-gallon tanks to compensate for the slower recovery time of electric heaters. Smaller heaters can be installed if you are not heaing water for major appliances such as a washing machine or a dishwasher, and if water-saving fixtures are used.

A good way to get the most out of any water heater is to buy a timer to shut the heater down at night and turn it on again a half hour before you rise in the morning. You also save dollars if you turn the water heater down or off when you leave on vacation; some models have thermostat settings labeled "Vacation."

Another way to save hot water is to buy foam insulation that fits onto hot-water pipes coming out of the water heater. This insulation is available in hardware stores and is designed to slip onto ½-in. and ¾-in. supply pipes. Insulating the pipes keeps the water in them hot—even in cool basements—at least for a time, so that you do not have to hold your fingers under hot-water tap until, gallons later, the water turns from cool to warm and finally hot.

In the deep South, heat-pump water heaters are a very sensible alternative to electric-resistance water heaters, even though they are three to four times more expensive. They use less electricity and they cool the air of the room around them as they work. Farther north, they become less practical, because the cool air they produce as a by-product of heating the water is not needed for much of the year.

Refrigerators

The size of a refrigerator has little to do with its energy consumption. A 16-cu-ft model uses only slightly less electricity than a 19-cu-ft one. In 1985, the best-rated operating cost of a 16-cu-ft refrigerator was $72; of a 19.9-cu-ft one, $78. So for an 11 percent increase in operating cost, you get 26 percent more space.

Consequently, if you consider the convenience of not having to drive to the grocery store as often and the possible savings in gasoline and in being able to buy food in bulk, then the larger refrigerator may be the best bargain over the long term.

On average, refrigerators use 33 percent less electricity than refrigerators did 10 years ago. Design plays a part—top freezers, fairly standard now, are more efficient than the interior freezers that used to be common.

To save money, avoid extras such as automatic defrost and ice makers; they add to the purchase price and operating cost.

In the deep South, it is best to buy very efficient models with lots of insulation, because the waste heat that is produced (refrigerators remove heat from their interiors and release it to the surrounding room) when the motor is running warms your house and has to be removed by running your air conditioner. In the North,

refrigerator insulation is not so important; the waste heat produced is welcome more of the year, and efficiency can take second place to purchase price.

Ranges

In gas ranges, select models with electronic ignition instead of pilot lights. These save several dollars a month in operating costs over models that have to continuously burn pilot lights.

A stove with lots of insulation makes sense if you can get it at a good price. The trouble is that heavily insulated ovens are usually also self-cleaning, and sell for a higher price. The higher price plus the higher operating costs of the self-cleaning feature (if you use it) offset the advantage of the extra insulation.

Window Air Conditioners

Old window air conditioners are energy hogs compared with new models (check their wattage against ones in stores), so do not bother to buy used ones that are more than 3 to 5 years old. When you buy new window air conditioners, select ones with an EER of at least 8.0.

To get the most out of window air conditioners, use them only in bedrooms. Set a small fan on the floor near the doorway to draw the cool air that they produce into other parts of the house.

SOLAR STRATEGIES

Active systems use a fan or pump to circulate heated air or water; passive systems rely solely on sunshine and natural convection currents. A simple passive energy technique (if you live in a cold climate) is to cut down an evergreen tree to allow more sun to reach your house.

With subsidies and tax credits, if available, you may be able to do better, but our experience is that active solar collectors are generally not cost-effective for producing either hot water or space heating. Unless you get a real bargain on a solar hot-water system and do some of the work yourself, it will not come close to paying back 10 percent of its installation costs per year. Include the maintenance costs and the limited life spans of many active solar units, and you have an improvement that is admirable from an environmental standpoint, but will not make good sense for the budget unless fuel prices go up dramatically.

On the other hand, passive solar improvements sometimes pay for themselves quickly and require less disruptive construction. The true savings, though, cannot be predicted without a detailed analysis.

There are two solar-collecting techniques—both of the passive type—we can heartily recommend: colors and landscaping.

Colors. In warm climates that require lots of cooling, paint the exterior of your house white or light yellow to reflect solar energy. Roofs can be white if shingled and can be covered with aluminized coatings if flat. Conversely, in cold climates, use dark colors such as brown, black, or dark green to maximize the solar energy gain.

Landscaping. Deciduous trees are very effective solar screens in summer, yet let sunlight through in winter (see Figure 17.4). Planting them is an exceptionally cost-effective energy-saving measure. As mentioned, removing sun-blocking evergreens can save heating costs.

SOLAR HEATING AND COOLING APPURTENANCES

Passive solar hardware can be built or bought. The most effective types fall into the categories below.

Trombe Wall

A simple passive solar collector, called a *Trombe Wall* after its inventor, can be a smart investment on a south-facing wall. Built of little more than glass or plastic and plywood painted black, plus ducts and flapper valves that help route air to the inside, it can have a quick payback period. Consult a solar construction manual.

Windows

East-, south-, and west-facing windows absorb heat; north-facing windows lose heat. Depending on your climate, you'll want more or less of one kind or the other.

If you live in a cold climate and are doing major work, consider eliminating a north-facing window; it can siphon off as much as $20/year in fuel costs.

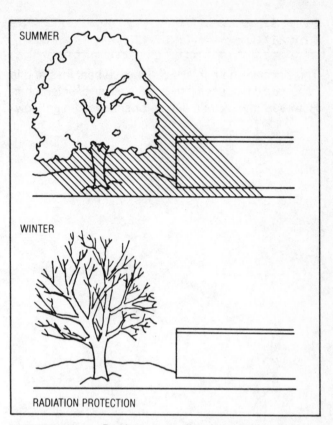

SUMMER

WINTER

RADIATION PROTECTION

FIGURE 17.4 Deciduous trees offer a low-cost, long-lasting way to reduce winter heating bills and summer cooling costs. Well-placed trees also add resale value and clean the air.

Sun Blockers

Some products that block the sun from windows or prevent its rays from coming through may be worth their cost. Solar films are thin plastic sheets applied to glass that prevent 35 to 70 percent of the sun's radiant energy from penetrating into the room; they cost about 50 cents/sq ft.

Window awnings can cut the sun's rays to a window by 70 to 80 percent. Similarly, drawing draperies when the sun is shining brightly through a window can reduce a room's temperature.

Specially made solar screens can cut sun exposure by 50 to 60 percent. These screens also keep insects out, like ordinary window screens. They are woven, vinyl-covered fiberglass designed to block the sun's radiant heat, and we recommend them on all new windows and storm windows in the South and West.

Simply removing your old screens to put solar screens in their place is not cost-effective. But if you are removing the old screens for another reason, and you live in a warm region, it makes sense to put in the sun screens.

Low-E Glass

This special kind of glass can reduce heat loss and is important in houses relying on passive solar heat. However, if you close drapes or shades at night, low-E glass is effective only on north-facing windows and others with little solar gain. Low-E glass actually cuts down the gain slightly through windows that get more sun. That is desirable in warm climates, but not in cold ones. For more on low-E glass, see Chapter 5, Windows.

TABLE 17.1

Energy Savings: No-Cost and Low-Cost Ideas

Before you specify wall insulation and a new heating system for your home, make all the no-cost or low-cost improvements. Savings assume a moderate climate and an annual heating bill of $800 before the improvements.

Direct Energy Cost-Savings

	Annual Fuel Savings	Approximate Cost/ Household	Payback Period
Lower water-heater temperature from 140°F to 120°F.	$45	$0	Immediate
Set back thermostat manually by 4°F/day, 12°F/night.	$195	$0	Immediate
Set back thermostat manually by 0°F/day, 12°F/night.	$170	$0	Immediate
Maintain proper heating distribution by adjusting registers, duct dampers, and/or zone values.	$0–$100	$0–$45	Varies
Reduce window infiltration with temporary storm windows or rope caulk.	$50–$330	$20–$35	1–6 months
Install flow restrictors on faucets and shower heads. Saves 5%–10% of water-heating bill.	$60	$20	3 months
Insulate water heater to R-4.	$45	$25	5 months
Insulate heating ducts in unheated spaces.	$40	$40	1 year
Close windows tightly and latch.	1% in heat	$0	Immediate
Change filters on schedule.	3%–5% in heat	$2	1 month
Turn off standing gas pilot lights at end of heating season.	$2–$5/month.	$0	Immediate

Working with Design Professionals and Contractors

There are two extremes to approaching home improvement work. One is to do all the work yourself, including the design, the securing of permits, and the physical work. The other is to do no more than hire an architect or a design-build remodeler, tell him or her what you want, and then write the checks. The first approach will always cost the least (if all goes as planned), but also definitely requires a lot more knowledge and effort. The second approach will cost the most, but will be less stressful (if all goes as planned).

Many people with fairly big jobs in mind choose a middle course. They hire an architect, a home inspector, or a designer to help with the design; they hire a general contractor or subcontractors; and they do some of the work themselves.

Big jobs always involve what the professionals call construction management. This is really managing people—the designer, the bidders, the successful contractor or contractors, the building inspectors, and possibly a bank inspector—to get the best product at the lowest possible price.

THE STEPS OF A CONSTRUCTION JOB

In planning the approach that is best for you, it is helpful to understand how construction professionals map out the stages of a construction job. These are the stages through which they proceed.

1. *Design Stage.* Come up with blueprints and/or written specifications. If a remodeler is doing the design, it may simply be called the *estimate.*

2. *Bidding Stage.* Put the plans or specifications out to bid to general contractors or various trade specialists (plumbers, electricians, carpenters, siding contractors, and so on). Compare costs and qualifications and choose the contractor or contractors.

3. *Construction Stage.* This stage includes more than just doing the work. The remodeler or general contractor, any subcontractors, and possibly you, the owner, must manage different phases of the work. The work must be scheduled. It must be checked for quality and conformance

to the plans. Contractors and suppliers must be paid. The budget must be tracked. Change orders may have to be negotiated. Building code inspectors and possibly bank inspectors must be satisfied.

All these steps are nearly invisible if you hire a design-build contractor. Your simplest course is merely to hire a remodeler to come up with a design and an estimate, then get several other competitive bids. But if you manage the work yourself and know what you are doing, there can be a number of opportunities for saving. If you do not know the steps and have few management skills, you are in danger of falling into the infamous "black hole."

Probably the biggest savings can be gained by using this book as a guide and designing some or all of the work yourself. The second biggest savings can come from subcontracting the work—you save money by doing the coordination yourself.

On a large job, design costs are usually at least 5 percent of the total cost. Design costs are sometimes hidden in a contractor's bid, but they are there. Sitting with you for several nights, taking down ideas, and going back to the office to draw up plans are not considered a public charity by contractors. They build it into the price of the work.

You can save money by designing a job yourself—at least, choosing the basic methods and materials, if not producing the actual blueprints. Architects and builders do not make the most money by proposing least cost methods. Moving walls around, tearing things out, and putting in custom-designed work result in a bigger contract. This is fine if you want it and can afford it, but this book shows how other alternatives can save you a lot.

Remodeling general contractors build in a 10 to 30 percent margin for managing subcontractors. They are usually good at it and often earn every penny. You can save a good part of that surcharge if you do this hard work yourself. Sometimes, general contractors simply won't do the kind of work you want. In that case, you may be better off to hire a repair person and separate contractors for the electrical work, siding, plumbing, and so on. But in a very conventional remodeling job, a general contractor's management ability and contacts with good subcontractors may be hard to match.

DESIGNING THE WORK

You need remodeling plans for a number of reasons. First, they formalize what you have in mind. Second, the building department may need plans to issue you

a permit—plans definitely will be needed for structural work, plumbing, electrical work, and heating/cooling work. And third, contractors who are bidding on the work need plans so that they can see the scope of the job, calculate labor and materials costs, and instruct their workers accurately once the work begins.

The design can be done by one or more of the following people:

- You
- A design-build remodeler
- A subcontractor who can produce written plans or blueprints
- An architect
- An engineer (for major foundation, structural, or mechanical problems)
- A professional home inspector (some of whom are licensed engineers)
- A professional from a publicly funded housing-rehab program (these programs usually concentrate on houses in an older neighborhood)
- An energy auditor (often provided free by local utility companies)

Before deciding to pay for design work, see what design—and even financing—help is available. Many cities and rural areas have public or nonprofit agencies that offer grants and low-interest loans to income-qualified families for renovation and weatherization work. They generally help draw up the plans at little or no cost.

Even if you are paying for design work, you have many options. Certified home inspectors are often better qualified than architects to assess heating plants, energy improvements, and needs for simple repairs. Their rates are often lower than architects' and most of them can produce biddable specifications.

On the other hand, architects may be better qualified to design an attractive addition or changes in floor plans. Design-build remodelers often have excellent designers on staff for major improvements that are hard for you to design. Many state laws require that a licensed architect or engineer design new structural work such as an addition, garage, or high retaining wall; but some states permit builders or owner-occupants to do this work regardless of their engineering qualifications.

Most cities with populations over 30,000 to 50,000 have plumbing, heating, and electrical supply houses with engineers on their staffs. If you can set up an account and are going to spend a few thousand dollars on materials, their engineers may come to your house and draw up plans and a materials list, including prices. The cost of their visit and work is usually built into the materials prices. Often, they will make this effort only for licensed contractors, but it is worth asking about.

An intermediate step is to ask your plumber and heating contractor to request this supply-house design service. But no matter who does the inspection and system design, be there to ask why and where things are being specified, and ask about the quality of what is specified. You will learn a lot and the engineer will learn more about your needs. Remember, it is your money being spent every time the engineer writes something down.

If a licensed professional such as an architect designs the work, it is not mandatory that he or she supervise that work. Most architects calculate one part of their fee for design and another for bidding and supervision. If you do the bidding and supervision, you may cut this fee in half.

Having a good design in hand should put you at an advantage when approaching a remodeler for an estimate, as long as you do not keep changing it. Remind the remodeler's salesperson that you have saved some of the company's cost of doing the job. If the builder is going to work with an architect, make sure that they are comfortable working together. They should meet and talk over the plans. Ask them both, continually: "Is there a better way to do this to save money?" Amazingly, many owners are embarrassed to ask this question.

Table 18.1 (page 247) lists different ways to design and write the specifications for a home improvement project. For a mere $10 in materials, you can make measurements and draw floor plans. This is particularly easy to do without help if you are not moving any walls and just want to indicate what is going where. Many do-it-yourself books describe how to produce these plans and put symbols on them. Good measurements help contractors to better estimate and order materials.

An architect will charge you $400 to $1,500 just to do the measuring and floor plans. The charge will increase to $800 to $3,000 if the architect also writes the specifications—that is, a precise list of what is to be used, their sizes, model numbers, and so forth—and drafts the plans for mechanical, electrical, and plumbing work. But a home inspector could do a reasonably good job for less.

Plumbing, electrical, heating, and kitchen cabinet subcontractors can usually draw up their own plans. Subcontractors specializing in kitchen and bathroom remodeling usually have designers on staff who can plan the whole project.

GETTING READY TO BID THE WORK

If you want to save money when you go to get bids, have good plans that are not subject to change. This will speed up the contractors' estimating process and make it easier for them to price the job accurately. If you live with other people (children included) or are a co-owner, make sure that everyone either is satisfied with the plans or at least has been consulted. Family disputes after the work begins are a major source of expensive change orders.

However, you may change the plans based on bidding. When you see real prices, it may make sense to go for a cheaper option. Contractors also may suggest alternatives that require less labor or materials that they can get at especially low prices. If you are using an architect, talk these things over; if you do decide to make changes, make them in the plans, too.

It is important to distinguish among the various kinds of bids.

An *estimate* is just an estimated price for the work, one that the contractor hopes to achieve. We do not recommend accepting a proposal with the word *estimate* at the top, a description of the work, and a price at the bottom. Such a proposal may not be legally binding and can result in serious disputes.

A *time-and-materials* proposal specifies the hourly rates of various employees who will work on the job and includes an estimate of total labor and material costs. This type gives you a little more control, if you can keep track of workers' time on the job. It is not recommended except for plumbers, electricians, and similar workers who are putting in a limited number of materials that have known costs. These proposals are better if they list all the materials with a price next to them.

A *not-to-exceed* proposal gives an estimate and states a maximum price for the work. We recommend these for contracts over a few thousand dollars and for work where all the materials are hard to itemize. Honest contractors will sometimes deliver the final product for less than the not-to-exceed figure. They figure their actual labor and material costs and add a reasonable margin for supervision and profit. If it is less than the proposal price, you will benefit. If it is more, they have legally agreed to take the loss, or less profit.

A *fixed-price* proposal specifies work to be delivered for a certain price. You may pay a little, or even a lot, more for this assurance, but on a big job by a general contractor that you are not watching daily, it is probably worth it. In rural areas and some small towns where, thankfully, a "person's word is his bond," a request for a fixed price may be met with stony silence, while the contractor is thinking, "Of course it's a fixed price—I'm going to charge you exactly so much an hour for my time and exactly what the materials cost." You may have to agree to such an arrangement, but if you do, get lots of references.

A *contingency allowance* can be built into a not-to-exceed or fixed-price contract. This is advisable when there are big unknowns, such as what is inside a wall or a floor that is going to be torn out. Suggesting an allowance of 5 to 10 percent of the job should give you leverage for lower bids when unknowns exist. If everything goes well, you save the contingency. If it does not, you approve a change order for unexpected time and materials. However, some small contractors are unfamiliar with this technique.

Many how-to books are available that include contract procedures, model contracts, and change-order forms such as the ones used by architects and contractors. These are highly recommended reading for do-it-yourself construction managers. They advise you how to check contractors' qualifications and insurances and handle the payments. But again, outside urban areas and off the beaten path, such methods may scare off bidders. If so, you will have to improvise.

Remember that design work is also contracted. Make sure that you have clear and acceptable terms and prices for this work. The same basic techniques and types of contracts as described above apply to architects and other design professionals.

Also bear in mind that all these legal agreements are for naught in two instances:

1. The plans and specifications are so vague that you could never prove what you were supposed to be buying.
2. You change your mind so often that the plans are useless.

DO YOU NEED A GENERAL CONTRACTOR?

Unless you are doing all the labor on a large project yourself, there are only two ways to get the job done from a management standpoint: Hire a general contractor or hire a group of specialized subcontractors.

If you have a good contract, a general contractor is completely responsible for delivering all the work. The firm usually employs its own crews for general carpentry, but often hires subcontractors for specialized trades, such as electrical, siding, roofing, foundation work, and so on. A general contractor is responsible for specifying work to subcontractors (if you have good plans), ensuring the quality of their work, and paying them.

You may choose to do this management work yourself. Or you may hire a so-called general contractor who asks you to pay subcontractors separately, even though his or her firm may coordinate the work. In the industry, such a person is called a *lead subcontractor* and is not a real general contractor.

If you manage the job yourself or use a lead subcontractor, no one is specifically liable for getting all the work done and coordinating it. Subcontractors are responsible only for what they put in their proposals. If one subcontractor performs poorly, spoils the schedule of another subcontractor, or leaves a mess for others to fix, you may face cost overruns. No amount of contract language will fix this—it takes people management. You must be assertive about your expectations for timeliness and quality and be willing to "penalize" a subcontractor who is performing poorly. Sometimes you have to nag and scold, and learn the phone number of the coffee shop where your subcontractor has breakfast. On the other hand, you must listen to real problems and be flexible.

There is an alternative to managing a group of subcontractors all by yourself. Architects, professional construction managers, and some inspection professionals may manage the job for you. They will bid the work, help qualified contractors oversee and coordinate the work, and approve payments—for a fee of 7 to 10 percent of the job's costs. They are usually interested only in bigger construction jobs—those costing $5,000 to $10,000 or more. If you go this route, make sure you have a clear contract (as you should with everyone else you are paying).

All jobs require scrutiny by building code inspectors. If you have a construction loan, your job may require a bank inspector as well. Home inspectors can also evaluate work for you, as can architects. A list of fees is given in Table 18.2 (page 249).

FINDING A CONTRACTOR

Working with contractors can be a pain or a pleasure. Usually it falls in between.

If you want to save money on home improvements, you first must do homework on who to work with. Choosing a contractor or contractors who are going to be good for both your budget and your house is important, and often difficult.

The best way to begin is to ask people you trust, starting with friends. Other people who are familiar with contractors, their work, and their reputations are bankers who make construction loans, real estate agents, lumberyard owners, local building inspectors, agents who sell construction bonds to contractors, public and private housing rehabilitation agencies, and local fire insurance agents.

Another way to find out about contractors is to visit the local bureau that licenses them. Anyone with a license at least is registered with an office where complaints can be filed and, in some areas, has passed a competency test and posted a bond against bankruptcy or other default. You can also look through building permits on file at the building department for the names of contractors who have done jobs like the one you have in mind.

The above advice applies to subcontractors, too, and much of it also applies to architects—who, according to tradition, are not supposed to publicize themselves too much.

To check on a contractor's work, ask for references and for the names of former clients. Call them up and ask how well the contractor worked for them; you might even ask to see the work. You can check the Better Business Bureau or your state consumer protection agency to see if there have been any complaints against the person you are thinking of hiring.

The rule of thumb is to narrow your list of contractors to three and ask each to submit bids. Be as precise as possible in your specifications. Write down the model numbers of such things as dishwashers, the thickness and color of tile, the model and finish on light fixtures, the exact number of pieces of plywood needed to repair the roof, and the number of coats of paint in the bathroom.

Doing this saves twice. First, contractors have a better idea of what is required and are less likely to feel the need for large contingency factors that will cover unforeseeable troubles. They still need some contingencies, of course, because they will be at risk if they get the job, but you can reduce these contingencies.

Second, it protects you. For example, say you really wanted three coats of paint in the bathroom. The contract said "paint the bathroom," and you got only one coat. Legally, you will have to pay the contractor more to come back two more times to apply the extra coats. Being specific prevents disputes: If you specified the tile brand and color, there should be no question that you got a cheaper tile instead.

In addition to being specific about what you want, ask contractors to suggest changes that would save money without sacrificing quality. They may be able to suggest different equipment, materials, or methods that are less costly.

Another way to reduce costs is to ask for more than the traditional three bids. The more bids you ask for, the more likely it is that the price of the lowest bid will drop. Taking the lowest bid, even one that you think is very low, is not necessarily a gamble. You may get a very low bid for several reasons: A contractor may be out of work at the moment and willing to take a job at a reduced rate; a contractor may not want to lay off workers during a slow period; or a contractor who is just starting out in business may be eager not only to get work, but also to please the customer (you). However, double-check references and make sure the bidder has gone over all the specifications. Some very inexperienced contractors do bid low and then are not able to complete the job.

WORKING WITH THE CONTRACTOR

You need not, of course, accept the lowest bid. The character of the contractor and how well you think you are going to get along with him or her count for something.

Leave as little to chance as possible. Spell out as much as you can in the contract, including all the specifications in the bid document. Put in the date that the work is to begin and the date it is to end. Try to write in a clause that would penalize the contractor for every day after the specified completion date that the work is not finished.

Include a payment schedule. Include a clause about who is responsible for cleanup at the end of the day and the end of the job. The contract should state that the contractor releases you from liability to any subcontractors, should the contractor go bankrupt. Require that the contractor have sufficient workmen's compensation and liability insurance to pay for on-the-job injuries to workers.

When the work is under way, new ideas will inevitably crop up. If you and the contractor decide on a change, put it in writing, initial the paper, and attach it to the contract.

Most changes are expensive, especially those that involve tearing out work already done, such as moving a pipe chase to accommodate new plans for a bookshelf. Work that has been done once costs money to take apart and money to redo; plus, you pay for your new idea, the bookcase.

Sometimes, changes reduce your cost. If you decide that you really do not need a window beside the stairway, you need an amendment to the contract that allows you a credit for work not done and materials not bought.

When the time comes for final payment, make certain that all the work is finished to your satisfaction. Check the final bill for any additional charges and make sure they're proper. Check to be sure you've received proper credits.

CONTRACTORS AND NEIGHBORS

Unless you live on an estate, your neighbors will be affected by major renovation work. It is best to warn them in advance; tell them what is being done and how long it is meant to last. Do this whether or not the work is going to come close to a property line. Neighbors can be justifiably irritated with noise and dust; worse, but not uncommon, are ceiling cracks, water runoff, and mice, rats, or insects that are driven from the work area through common walls or across property lines.

Be respectful of a neighbor's rights and wishes, and remedy any messes you make if you are doing the work yourself. If a contractor does the work, be sure the contract states that he or she must repair any damage to others' property; otherwise, the responsibility falls on you. If you live in a building with common areas, check with the condominium association or superintendent about the contractors' use of stairs, elevators, and halls. If the work will affect a common wall with another property owner, check the prevailing regulations about common walls. If the work will come close to a property line, check zoning regulations on setback; you may not be able to build within a certain distance of that line, or of a sidewalk or a street.

MOBILIZATION COSTS

The "Mobilization Costs" below are useful for understanding how contractors figure their costs. It lists the prices that different subcontractors usually charge for a house call; that is, coming to the job site for even the most minor work. In the trades, these are called _mobilization costs;_ they are what subcontractors charge to drive through traffic with all their tools and haul equipment into your house for work. A contractor may be at your house an hour, but the job might require three hours to get to you and then return to other work—hours that could be spent working profitably somewhere else.

Use the table when you're thinking about telephoning one of these skilled people. You may want to tackle the small jobs yourself or at least try to group jobs so that the contractor could do several in one visit. Otherwise, small jobs and one-time repairs can cost ten times more than usual.

Mobilization Costs

Floor Sander	$60
Vinyl Floor Mechanic	$70
Hardwood Floor Layer	$135
Carpet Installer	$90
Ceramic Tile Layer	$100
Plasterer and Mixer	$265
Drywall Mechanic	$135
Paper Hanger	$125
Painter	$65
Carpenter	$75
Plumber	$60
Electrician	$70
Roofer	$80

SHAVING CONTRACT COST

No matter what system you use to contract the work, there are many ways to shave the costs of the actual work.

Table 18.3 (page 250) shows different ways to lower the cost of a hypothetical home improvement project. One way is to provide the labor, or portions of it, yourself. In Table 18.4 (page 251) we look at the same project and list the cost of each component completed either by professionals or by you.

Another way to lower costs (summarized in Table 18.4) is to tell your contractors that you will supply the materials, and then hunt around for bargains that they might pass by. Such bargains could take the form of used or salvaged items, materials from mail order catalogs, and so forth. If you are thinking of supplying materials yourself, however, bring it up early in your discussions with the contractors. They make some of their overhead and profit by marking up materials. By supplying materials yourself, you are saving them some trouble, but you're also depriving them of justly deserved profit.

Another cost-reducing measure you can take is to act as one or more subcontractors yourself. You can do some carpentry, tiling, painting, or whatever other job suits your skills and take its expense out of the overall contract. In all such cases of shaving the bid,

carefully spell out in the contract or proposal the work you are doing yourself, to avoid disputes later.

In Table 18.5 (page 253), we look at the costs of a single $27,000 home improvement and show what each management option adds to the total subcontract costs. Being your own general contractor incurs only the costs for permits, travel, and plans—about 1 to 3 percent to the total subcontract cost. Using a lead contractor adds about 3 to 10 percent, and using a general contractor can add 25 to 40 percent.

With these aids, you should be able to understand the construction job from conception to completion, work sympathetically but firmly with contractors, and take advantage of money-saving opportunities along the way.

TABLE 18.1
Options for Plans and Specifications

THE PROJECT
Draft plans and specifications sufficient to receive building permits on a renovation job involving a new heating and cooling system, bath and kitchen remodeling, and extensive maintenance jobs throughout the house with a subcontract cost of $27,000 requiring 90 days.

Options	Project Cost Contracted	Difficulty Level DIY Advice	Comments and Recommendations
Owner-Prepared Measurements and Floor Plans Draw owner-prepared floor plans on graph paper using template, building code book, and budget.	$25	**2** Buy a drafting template and measure twice.	Everybody should do this themselves. It helps the entire process when the owners know sizes of spaces, their minimum needs, and their maximum budget.
Use Subcontractors Request proposals from at least 2 subcontractors in each required field. Require each subcontractor to prepare outline specifications and all code-required submissions.	$400	**3**	This is especially appropriate if you aren't using a general contractor, because you can promise the contract to the subcontractor. Plumbers, heating equipment, electric, and kitchen cabinet suppliers can quickly design their trade area if provided basic direction and a budget.
Use a Rehab Specialist Contract with a professional rehab specialist to prepare specifications and a minimal floor plan.	$600	**1**	Jobs with minimal new space, normal construction requirements, and average finishes can be easily specified by rehab specialists. Many work for governments or nonprofit organizations and may design from 3 to 100 jobs a year using specification as the major design document.
Use a Student Architect Contract with a senior architectual student referred by a local university to draft full plans and supporting specifications.	$600	**2**	Architectual and engineering students have good drafting skills, are usually creative and willing to please. Their weakness may show up in mechanical requirements and local code compliance, so make sure the plans are reviewed by the plumbing and heating subcontractors, as well as the code inspector, prior to final payment.

(Continued on next page)

TABLE 18.1 Continued

Options	Project Cost Contracted	Difficulty Level DIY Advice	Comments and Recommendations
Use a Design-Build Contractor Hire a general contractor with turnkey design services in-house.	$1,400	**1**	For certain specialty areas like baths and kitchens, many specialty contractors will include the design in the price of normal overhead. For larger and more diverse jobs, some renovation contractors have in-house designers available at discount rates. *Note:* If the contractor is getting someone else to do the design work, it may actually cost you more than if you bought it yourself.
Use a Full-Service Architect Contract with an architectural firm to provide measured drawings, plans, and specifications.	$2,000	**1**	Best used for jobs with unusual design requirements, additions, and reconfigurations of floor plans.

TABLE 18.2
Inspection Options

THE PROJECT
Inspect and approve payments for a renovation job involving a new heating and cooling system, bath and kitchen remodeling, and extensive maintenance jobs throughout the house costing $27,000 and requiring 90 days.

	Cost/ Inspection Contracted	Project Cost Contracted	Comments and Recommendations
Code Inspections Rely on building code inspectors (electrical, mechanical building inspections).	$0	$0	Plan on missing some work to be present when the building inspector is at the site. Quality of service varies dramatically jurisdiction by jurisdiction. Least cost and least protection.
Bank Inspections Rely on three bank inspections.	$0–$200	$375	Many construction lenders will require these inspections to release money and will share the results and corrective suggestions.
Home Inspection Firm Contract with professional rehab specialist or home inspector for 2 inspections and reports per month.	$35–$200	$600	Although this service varies with the specialist's experience, the better inspectors are a best buy in supervision cost.
Architect Inspections Contract with an architectural firm to perform inspections twice a month.	$75–$300	$900	Most architects want to inspect the work they designed, so the additional cost may be discounted or included in the base fee, if the architect prepared the plans.

TABLE 18.3
Strategies for Reducing Construction Costs

THE PROJECT
Complete a renovation job in a 1,200-sq-ft home involving a new heating and cooling system, 1½ baths, 12′ kitchen, 200-amp rewire, extensive floor-plan modifications, costing $61,250 if contracted out.

Options	Project Savings DIY	Project Cost After Savings	Difficulty Level	Comments and Recommendations
Provide All Labor Owner's family pays only for materials.	$25,250	$36,000	**5**	Work at the most expensive rate your skill level allows.
Be a Subcontractor Hire a general contractor, but retain 25% of the work for the owner's family as formal subcontracts to general contractor.	$11,025	$50,225	**1-5**	Time coordination can get to be a problem. Many finish details are good choices because they happen at the end of the process. Vinyl flooring, ceramic tile, and painting are easy areas to consider. Other areas are demolition, furniture packing, prime painting, landscaping, and any owner skill.
Get More Bids Solicit and receive 5 bids.	$6,125	$55,125	**2**	Although the lowest bid isn't necessarily the best, getting at least 5 bids can result in a 10%–20% reduction in final job costs.
Provide Materials Contract for labor only to individual subcontractors. Owner pays for all materials delivered to site.	$3,680	$57,580	**1**	Make sure you get an appropriate reduction in the general contractor's mark-up or you will be providing materials and still paying the profit on them. Search time is expensive. Focus on hard-to-find, mail order items, appliances, and owner selections.
Normal Costs Hire a general contractor to provide all labor, materials, overhead, and supervision.	$0	$61,250	**1**	

TABLE 18.4
DIY Savings on a Large Renovation Project

THE PROJECT
A $68,000 rehabilitation of a 3-bedroom, 1½-bath, 1,200-sq-ft home completed by professionals or the owners.

Component	Contractor Completed	Cost	Owner Completed	Cost
Demolition	Gut to studs and floors, leave stairs. Clean up during job.	$2,050	Buy protective equipment and 30-cu-yd dumpster with two pickups and disposals.	$925
Masonry	Install a prefabricated metal fireplace and flue.	$2,400	Install a prefabricated metal fireplace and flue (materials only).	$1,045
Carpentry Framing Doors	Restud to plan. Install 2 new exterior and 6 new interior doors.	$6,400 $1,900	Restud to plan (materials only). Install 2 exterior and 6 interior prehung doors.	$3,600 $970
Windows	Repair and retrim 11 windows.	$900	Repair and retrim 11 windows (materials and tool rental).	$490
Plumbing	Install a 3-piece bath, a powder room, and a kitchen with dishwasher, sink, and disposal. All new supply and waste.	$4,100	Purchase and install a 3-piece bath, a powder room, and a kitchen with a dishwasher, sink, and disposal. Install a PVC waste and polybutylene supply.	$2,600
Heating and Air Conditioning	Install gas central furnace and electric air conditioner.	$5,100	Purchase equipment, set in place. Install prefabricated duct work. Subcontract furnace, air conditioner, and control hook-up.	$4,300
Electric	Install 200-amp service and rewire home to NEC.	$2,300	Pull all wire to junction boxes. Install all switches, devices, and fixtures. Subcontract for service increase and breaker panel wiring.	$1,400
Finishes Walls and Ceilings	Install ½″ gypsum, painted.	$6,800	Hang, finish and paint ½″ gypsum throughout (materials and tool purchase).	$2,200
Floors	Install vinyl sheet goods in kitchen and baths; sand and refinish wood elsewhere.	$2,400	Install vinyl sheet goods in kitchen and baths; circular sand and refinish wood elsewhere (materials and tool rental).	$700
Exterior	Paint all Exterior trim.	$2,200	Paint all exterior trim (materials, equipment purchase, and rental).	$450
Kitchen	Install 15′ of cabinets, countertop, range, and refrigerator.	$3,950	Install 15′ of cabinets, countertop, range, and refrigerator.	$2,900

(Continued on next page)

TABLE 18.4 Continued

Component	Contractor Completed	Cost	Owner Completed	Cost
Mark-up Costs	General contractor (overhead at 22%, profit at 16%, contingency at 12%)	$20,750	12% contingency	$4,860
TOTAL JOB COST		$61,250		$26,440
Design and Supervision				
Inspection	Existing condition with measurements.	$450	Measure house (materials and equipment purchase).	$45
Design and Specification	Full architectual plans and specifications.	$4,600	Select materials from local suppliers, develop specifications from national code book.	$20
Job Supervision	By architectual firm.	$1,700	Use DIY books and code inspectors' guide to proper installation.	$50
TOTAL COST TO OWNER		$68,000		$26,555
SAVINGS				**$41,445**

TABLE 18.5
Construction Management Options

THE PROJECT
Coordinate all subcontractors and material purchases for a renovation job involving a new heating and cooling system, bath and kitchen remodeling, and extensive maintenance jobs throughout the house, with a subcontract cost of $27,000 requiring 90 days.

	Construction Management Cost Percentage	Construction Management Cost	Difficulty Level	Comments and Recommendations
Owner General Contractor Owner to coordinate all subcontractors and purchase all materials.	1–3	$540	3	Not for the fainthearted. In most cases, you are trading time, inconvenience, and budget liability for the savings.
Use a Lead Subcontractor Usually, a carpentry sub to help the owner to select and direct other subcontractors.	3–10	$1,800	2	Explain how much help you're requesting early in the contract negotiations, and this can be a very cost-effective way to ensure experienced oversight of the job.
Use a Construction Manager To bid, supervise, and coordinate subcontractors on behalf of owner.	10–16	$3,780	1	A construction manager acts as your agent and shares any savings, but you absorb cost overruns. They are as good as their list of subcontractors and their coordination skills.
Use a General Contractor To perform all supervision and coordination tasks as part of a construction contract.	25–40	$8,910	1	General contractors not only do all the work, they offer a not-to-exceed price for the entire job.

19 | Saving Money on Tools and Materials

Unless you are going to hire out all the work and do nothing but make approvals and sign checks, you will need some tools and materials, even if just a paintbrush and paint. So you might as well be a smart shopper—smart enough to save hundreds, even thousands, of dollars over the course of a home improvement project. With a little effort, you can avoid paying retail price for tools and materials.

TOOLS

Tools can be expensive. In many cases, however, a more expensive tool will allow you to do a job better and more quickly than a cheaper one will. So, which tools do you buy, which do you rent, and which do you leave to others to use?

To help you answer this question, we recommend that you first decide on the projects you think you would like to do, then look at the bid price for that segment of the work. Then estimate the cost if you were to do the work yourself, either alone or with a helper or two. Add in the cost of buying the tools—or renting expensive ones—your best guess of the cost of materials, and what you would have to pay helpers, if any.

Subtract this cost from the bid price to get the potential savings of doing the work yourself. With these potential savings in mind, reevaluate your willingness to undertake the work. If the savings are sufficient, make a list of the tools you will need.

You should buy tools if

- They are inexpensive
- They will be useful later for other projects and maintenance
- The purchase price is only a little more than the rental price

You should rent tools if

- They are expensive

- They are so specialized that you would probably use them only once
- They are difficult to store

We can add one more reason to rent: If you are considering buying a used tool, but want to test its reliability first, rent it for a day or two so you can evaluate its quality.

Table 19.1 (page 258) lists rentable tools, their retail and rental prices, and their uses, plus comments about each. We have divided the tools into three groups: *necessary tools,* those that are most commonly used by amateurs for general home improvement projects; *teammate tools,* those that serve well in place of a helper; and *skill enhancer/time-saver tools,* those that help you do a job either better or faster. **CAUTION: Some of these tools are exceptionally dangerous. Be sure you receive operating and safety instructions from the rental agency before you rent them. Use them only with the proper safety equipment and clothing.**

You can, of course, walk into a store, take a tool from the shelf, and pay the list price. But with a little planning, you needn't. The "Bargain Hunter's Calendar" at the right lists both tools and materials and the times of the year they normally go on sale. Father's Day, for example, is a time of discounts on power tools, and Labor Day features sales on insulation and storm windows. In addition to the holiday sales, merchants often offer unusually good prices in the spring, at the beginnings of seasons when they want to attract business, and at the ends of seasons when they have to clear their shelves for new inventory.

Another way to buy tools at a discount is to buy them used. Garage sales and newspaper classified ads are good places to look. Many tools, if treated properly, last a lifetime. This is especially true of hand tools, but less so of power tools, whose bearings and motors can wear under the strain of construction work. Always test used power tools before you buy—if they run without unusual noise or vibration, they will last at least through a project or two, and maybe far longer.

Tool rental rates vary widely, so do not jump at the tools offered by the nearest tool-rental store. Shop by phone for the best rate among the stores within easy driving distance. If you know contractors or tradespeople, call them; they may be willing to rent you tools they know they will not be needing for a while.

Don't overlook borrowing. For short periods, you might be able to borrow the tool you need from a relative, a friend, or a friendly subcontractor.

A Bargain Hunter's Calendar

Month	Type of Merchandise	Event
JANUARY–FEBRUARY	Power Tools Carpet Appliances Contract Inside Work	After Christmas Presidents Day Sales Slack Time for contractors
MARCH–APRIL	Air Conditioners Paint Building Materials Exterior Tools	Preseason Sales
MAY	Small Appliances	Mother's Day Sales
JUNE	Power Tools	Father's Day Sales
JULY–AUGUST	Hardware Paint Large Appliances Building Materials Treated Lumber Outdoor Furniture	Summer Sales Circular Sales
SEPTEMBER	Insulation Storm Windows Exterior Doors Contract for a Deck	Preseason Sales Deck Builders Running Out of Work
OCTOBER	Stoves	Best Selection
NOVEMBER	Air Conditioning	Postseason Prices
DECEMBER	Power Tools Hand Tools Contract Inside Work	Christmas Sales Slack Time for Contractors

Besides the usual hammers, screwdrivers, and other everyday hand tools, we recommend that you own the following tools for home improvement work:

- A pesticide-level respirator
- A 2-horsepower circular saw
- Safety goggles
- A carbide-tipped circular saw blade (it cuts through old nails)
- A carbide-tipped hand saw
- A ⅜-in. variable-speed reversing power drill
- A large pry bar (pulls two pieces of nailed wood apart
- Nippers and a "cat's paw" (they pull nails out of wood)
- A 24-in. level
- A tool apron
- Heavy gloves

MATERIALS

Discounts

Never buy materials retail—unless you have a $35/hour plumber or similar worker taking a breather while awaiting your return.

Materials supply stores usually offer credit accounts to contractors, plus a discount on everything they buy. The discount ranges from 10 percent on general building materials to 60 percent on specialized items at specialized supply houses. Most suppliers will offer you some discount for orders of $200 or more, even though they know you will not be buying nearly as much as a professional. They are happy to have your business, because they know you could be going to the next supplier down the road.

Anyway, it never hurts to ask for a credit account and contractor's discount. After a credit check, they will probably give you both. Even if you do not get a credit account, ask for the contractor's discount—with it, you could pay 10 percent less at the counter. If you do get a credit account, and the terms offer a 2 percent discount for paying the monthly bill within 10 days, take advantage of the discount by paying promptly.

When you are in a supplier's store, be on the lookout for volume discounts. For example, you may want to buy three dozen screws. If you buy by the piece or the dozen, you might pay more than you would for a single 1-lb box that contains 100 or more screws. Buy the whole box, because you will always use more than you think. At the end of the job, if you have more left over than you care to store, sell the excess or give it away.

Finally, if your contract with a subcontractor calls for *allowance items*—decorative or discretionary items

like light fixtures that are written into the contract as something like "three $25 fixtures"—buy them yourself with the subcontractor's discount at his or her supply store, and you may be able to walk away with $45 fixtures for $25 each.

The Best Places to Buy

MANUFACTURERS You can save 20 to 60 percent on materials when you can buy directly from a manufacturer. Check the Yellow Pages and make some calls before you visit any retail supplier. If you are buying rugs for a room or two, you may be able to get them from a manufacturer's distribution center. The same applies to specialized millwork—before buying items such as custom-sized windows, stairs, and fancy trim through a retail lumberyard, go directly to the manufacturers of such pieces and see if you can buy them there, at a savings rather than paying the lumberyard's markup. But note: some lumberyards have their own shops and can make custom pieces for you.

WHOLESALE HOUSES Similarly, electric, plumbing, heating, and other wholesale supply houses can save you lots of money if they will give you a decent discount off the retail price. Otherwise, beware—you may do better at a discount building supply store.

DISCOUNT BUILDING SUPPLY STORES Certain materials are almost always better to buy from building supply discount stores. They often beat the specialized wholesalers and lumberyards on the price of drywall, electrical wire, copper pipe, faucets, locks, standard-sized windows and doors, paint, and other high-volume, nonlumber items. But always be sure to buy good-quality merchandise made by reputable companies.

Discount retailers are also good places to buy generic models of plumbing and lighting fixtures. By contrast, specialized showroom supply houses must charge a premium to cover the costs of carrying a large inventory of trendy styles and paying the salespeople who spend hours helping customers make their selections.

LUMBERYARDS On the other hand, our experience has been better with real, old-fashioned lumberyards in obtaining wood products, odd-size windows and doors, and specialized fasteners. (We call a *real* lumberyard one that is crowded with contractors at 8:00 A.M.) The quality and selection of lumber and plywood are better, even if the price is a little higher. When you want specific sizes and grades of framing lumber, finish lumber, moldings, or sheathing, good lumberyards save a lot of running around. Often their sheathing materials, particularly plywood, are of a higher grade than those carried by the discount stores. Real lumberyards are also good places to try to wrangle a discount, because they are used to giving them to contractors.

NATIVE LUMBER MILLS Some urban areas have small sawmills surprisingly close by that offer lumber bargains. What they have depends on the area—in the Midwest, hardwoods for trim, flooring, and fence boards; in New England, framing lumber, pine finish wood, and white cedar shingles; in the Pacific Northwest, redwood or cedar shingles and shakes; in the South, some hardwoods and various kinds of pine lumber.

But at these mills, most of the goods are green or air-dried, so you must dry them further or allow for the inevitable shrinkage. One way to do that is to buy *V-groove* pine boards rather than square-edged boards—the V-shaped tongue-and-groove joint hides future shrinkage. In addition, make sure that your building code permits air-dried lumber before framing with it. And read up on techniques for working with not-quite-dry wood.

FARM SUPPLY STORES Large farm supply stores in the distant suburbs are great places for bargains on certain things that farmers buy in volume; for example, metal roofing, fencing, culverts, underground drainage lines, and plastic pipe.

CEMENT FABRICATORS AND BRICKYARDS Most big cities have one or more factories that make concrete building and patio blocks, and these are the best places by far to buy those materials. A factory or brickyard is also the best place to buy precast concrete steps and bricks. Buying these heavy materials through a middleman adds greatly to your cost.

Damaged, Discontinued, and One-of-a-Kind Goods

Inquiries can often lead to astonishing bargains. Ask suppliers if they are trying to unload any merchandise that is slightly damaged, out of package, or otherwise difficult to sell retail.

Appliances. When shopping for a heavy appliance such as a stove or refrigerator, ask outlets if they have slightly damaged models in the back of the store. You may find exactly the kind you want with dents in the side or rear that will never show. Floor models are often deeply discounted. So, too, are appliances taken out of their packaging and returned for some reason. Some may have been repaired by the dealer, but still come with a warranty. All these appliances are usually in perfectly good operating condition, but are far less expensive than perfect and packaged models.

Wallpaper. Ask wallpaper suppliers which styles they are trying to move in a hurry. Usually, there will be many styles that are selling for 25 to 95 percent off their original prices.

Ceramic Tile. Ask ceramic tile dealers if they have small lots in their warehouses. Usually, there are many styles available in quantities of less than 50 sq ft that can be had for 20 to 80 percent off.

Paint. Ask paint suppliers if they have mistinted paint. Even if such paint is not exactly the color you want, you can use it as an undercoat, saving 25 to 50 percent.

Other Construction Items. Never stop asking. We have heard of people buying huge, $200 double-glazed glass panels for $50—someone had ordered them in the wrong size, the buyer refused to accept them, and the dealer wanted them off his hands. We have heard of people buying slightly damaged but repairable $350 fiberglass bathtubs for $50. Others have bought display models of $500 prehung, insulated, metal exterior doors for $75.

Secondhand Materials

One way to snare good kitchen cabinets at a bargain is to call the upscale kitchen remodelers. They are usually in the business of installing fabulous kitchens for expensive houses. In the process, they remove the cabinets that are there. These are often lovely and of high quality themselves, just boring to the people who have lived with them. You can buy them from the remodeler for a fire-sale price.

Apartments that are being converted to condominiums also yield kitchen cabinets. They also may offer up footed cast-iron bathtubs, intricate wood molding, lighting fixtures, chandeliers, ceramic sinks, marble steps, and the like.

Some people have gone into the business of salvaging building materials that are discarded from renovation jobs. They stock dozens of used doors, sinks, tubs, locks, pillars, stained glass, fireplace mantles, medicine cabinets, and the like. What one person calls "used," another calls "antique." Their prices are generally excellent, even if some stripping, cleaning, and fitting are required. Keep in mind that some fixtures are just as good old as new. Cast-iron radiators are a good example. New, one might cost $200; from a salvage dealer, $45—and the old one will work as well as the new one after its inside is flushed.

TABLE 19.1
Tools: Renting Versus Buying

Tool	Cost to Buy	Cost to Rent/Day	Best Uses	Comments and Recommendations
Necessary Tools				
Floor sander and edger	$1,600–$2,400	$55–$70	Sanding new hardwood floors	Takes a while to learn to control.
Floor buffer and orbital sander with sanding mesh	$950–$1,500	$26–$32	Sanding older floors or pine floors	Takes longer, but is easier to control.
40′ ladder	$110–$380	$15	Exterior painting, carpentry	Weekly or monthly rates are a bargain if the job will take a while.
Carpet stretcher, lever operated	$110–$160	$12–$16	Laying wall-to-wall carpet	The knee kickers leave you unable to walk after a day of banging the carpet.
High-Efficiency Particle Accumulator vacuum cleaner	$1,200–$1,800	$40–$60	Cleaning up lead paint dust	A must for preventing lead poisoning.
Electric snake	$280–$1,400	$24–$32	Clearing drains	Half the cost of hiring a pro.
Ceramic tile cutter and nipper	$85–$100	$11–$13	Cutting ceramic tile	Snapping tile is easy once you get the feel of it.
Teammate Tools (Tools that make 2-person jobs into 1-person jobs)				
Drywall lift	$600–$1,000	$12–$17	Installing drywall on ceilings	This wheeled table allows a single person to load a full 4′ × 8′ sheet of drywall at waist height and then crank it up tight to the ceilings.
Cement mixer, 1½ cu ft	$250–$400	$16–$20	Mixing cement	For pouring small areas.
Electric brad shooter	$35–$50	$4–$6	Installing trim	Because this tool fastens with one hand, you can position perfectly and shoot without help.
Trailer-mounted post-hole digger	$600–$800	$60–$85	Fencing	Easily digs a 6″- or 8″-diameter hole 3′ deep every 10 minutes, all day long if the soil isn't too stoney.
Appliance dolly	$200–$260	$12–$16	Moving appliances	By yourself, you can move the stove, refrigerator, and freezer out of the kitchen.

Tool	Cost to Buy	Cost to Rent/Day	Best Uses	Comments and Recommendations
Skill Enhancers and Time-Savers				
Electric plane	$55–$135	$8–$14	Resizing doors to fit	Beats even the sharpest hand plane on cross-cut jobs. Remove nails first.
Screw gun	$85–$120	$8–$12	Hanging drywall	Cordless models are great for ceilings.
Reciprocating saw	$95–$165	$8–$12	Difficult cuts	A renovator's dream. Cuts where no other saw can. Can turn a ½-day chiseling session into a 3-minute job.
Electric miter box	$110–$300	$10–$14	Installing trim	Quick and accurate; a real time-saver.
Flooring nailer	$65–$90	$11–$14	Tongue-and-groove flooring	Positions the wood and nails at the precise angle, every time, without hitting the adjoining piece of flooring.
Airless spray setup	$1,000–$2,500	$50–$75	High-volume painting	Minimizes overspray. Paint a vacant house in a day, or a fence in 3 hours. Restain the exterior in 6 hours.
Power washer (3,000 lb/sq in.)	$1,000–$2,600	$50–$70	Exterior cleaning of brick aluminum siding; painting prep	Clean graffiti, remove deteriorated mortar, or wash siding. Ten times faster than a scraper when preparing for paint.
Wallpaper stripper	$200–$260	$14–$18	Stripping layers of wallpaper	Twice as fast as a hand scraper with half as many wall gouges.
Roofing stapler and compresser	$800–$2,000	$35–$60	Shingle roofs	Speeds up a tedious job.
Magnetic sweeper	$50–$300	$6–$10	Pick up nails in yard	In half an hour, you'll remove hazards to feet and tires.
Hammer drill	$65–$150	$6–$12	Drills holes in masonry	Four times faster than a good drill in concrete.
Mini-backhoe	$5,000 +	$165–$200	Footings, landscaping	Controls are like an arcade game. Digs faster than 5 shovels.
Trenching machine	$5,000 +	$125–$300	Ditch digging for pipes, wires	Install sprinkler and yard lighting systems in a day with 6"-wide trenches.

(Continued on next page)

TABLE 19.1 Continued

Tool	Cost to Buy	Cost to Rent/Day	Best Uses	Comments and Recommendations
Rototiller	$500–$1,600	$45–$70	Preparing ground for patio blocks	With 2 or 3 passes with the rear-tine tiller, you've got a workable bed for patios or a pile of easy-to-dig dirt.
Electric jackhammer	$900–$1,400	$65–$80	Breaking up concrete	Still hard work, but a lot better than a sledge hammer.
Chipper	$300–$600	$40–$60	Shredding limbs and debris	Makes quick work and a small pile out of a huge tree.

Illustration and Photo Credits

The authors make grateful acknowledgment to the following for permission to reproduce photographs and drawings in this book:

Figures 2.5, 3.2, 4.9, 4.10, 5.1, 5.3, 6.3, 6.4, 6.10, 9.1, 9.3, 9.4, 9.6, 9.7, 10.8, 13.2, 13.5, 13.6, 13.7, 13.8, 13.9, 13.10, 15.5 were reprinted with permission from Allen, Edward, *Fundamentals of Building Construction: Materials and Methods,* Second Edition, copyright © 1990 by John Wiley & Sons, Inc.

Figures 9.3, 9.4, 9.6 were reprinted courtesy of the American Plywood Association.

Figures 8.3, 8.4 were reprinted courtesy of the Brick Institute of America.

Figure 13.7 was reprinted courtesy of Buckingham-Virginia Slate Corporation.

Figures 13.5, 13.6 were reprinted courtesy of the Cedar Shake & Shingle Bureau.

Figures 1.1, 1.2, 1.3, 1.5, 1.6, 1.7, 1.8, 1.9, 1.10, 2.1, 4.1, 4.2, 5.4, 5.5, 6.1, 6.7, 6.11, 6.12, 7.1, 7.2, 7.6, 7.7, 7.8, 8.1, 8.2, 8.6, 10.1, 10.4, 10.5, 10.6, 10.7, 10.9, 10.10, 11.1, 11.2, 11.3, 11.4, 11.5, 11.6, 11.7, 13.1, 13.13, 13.14, 14.1, 14.2, 14.3, 15.2, 15.3, 15.6, 16.1, 16.2, 16.4, 16.5, 16.6, 17.3 were reprinted from *The Cost Cuts Manual,* courtesy of The Enterprise Foundation.

Figures 4.3, 4.5, 4.6 were reprinted from *The Cost Cuts Newsletter,* Volume 3, #3, courtesy of The Enterprise Foundation.

Figure 12.8 was reprinted courtesy of HydroTherm, Inc.

Figures 12.2, 12.7 were reprinted with permission from Illinois Small Homes Council-Building Research Council, *Cooling Systems for the Home,* copyright © 1971 by the University of Illinois, Champaign, Illinois.

Figures 4.4, 4.7 were reprinted courtesy of Owens-Corning Fiberglas Corporation.

Figures 2.2, 2.3, 2.4, 2.7, 2.8, 3.1, 3.3, 3.4, 4.8, 4.11, 5.3, 6.6, 6.10, 9.5, 9.8, 9.9, 10.2, 10.3, 10.8, 13.3, 13.4, 15.4 were reprinted with permission from Ramsey, Charles G. and Sleeper, Harold R. *Architectural Graphic Standards,* Eighth Edition, Prepared by the American Institute of Architects, John R. Hoke, Jr., A.I.A., Editor; copyright © 1988 by John Wiley & Sons, Inc.

Figure 12.1 was reprinted with permission from Sarviel, E., *Construction Estimating Reference Data,* Craftsman Book Company, Carlsbad, California.

Figures 13.6, 13.11 were reprinted courtesy of Senco Products, Inc., Cincinnati, Ohio.

Figures 1.4, 1.11 were reprinted courtesy of United States Gypsum Company.

Figure 9.2 was reprinted with permission from Wakita, Osamu A. and Linde, Richard M., *The Professional Practice of Architectural Working Drawings,* copyright © 1984 by John Wiley & Sons, Inc.

Figure 2.6 was reprinted courtesy of the makers of Armstrong vinyl flooring.

Index

To receive your $2.00 Cash Rebate, complete the rebate certificate by hand-printing your name and complete address. Mail your rebate certificate together with a receipt of purchase with book price circled to:

Consumer's Guide to Home Improvement,
Renovation & Repair
Rebate Offer
P.O. Box 1107
Grand Rapids, MN 55745-1107

Print Name_____

Address_____

City_____ State_____ ZIP_____

Signature_____

This certificate must accompany your request. No duplicate accepted. Offer good in the United States and Canada. Offer limited one to a family, group, or organization. Void where prohibited, taxed or restricted. Allow 4-6 weeks for mailing of your rebate. Offer expires **January 31, 1992.**